Myth and Magic

Art according to the Inklings

edited by
Eduardo Segura & Thomas Honegger

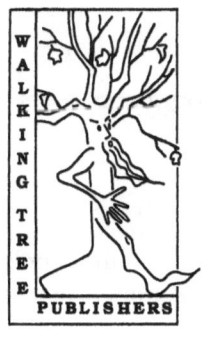

2007

Cormarë Series

No 14
Series Editors
Peter Buchs • Thomas Honegger • Andrew Moglestue

Library of Congress Cataloging-in-Publication Data

Segura, Eduardo and Thomas Honegger (editors)
Myth and Magic: Art according to the Inklings
ISBN 978-3-905703-08-5

Subject headings:

Tolkien, J. R. R. (John Ronald Reuel), 1892-1973 – Criticism and interpretation

Tolkien, J. R. R. (John Ronald Reuel), 1892-1973

Lewis, C.S. (Clive Staples), 1898-1963

Barfield, Owen, 1898-1997

Rowling, Joanne K., 1965-

Inklings

Fantasy fiction, English – History and criticism

Middle-earth (Imaginary place)

Literature, Comparative.

All rights reserved. No portion of this book may be reproduced, by any process or technique, without the express written consent of the publisher.

To my wife, Ana, and to our children, Ignacio,
Guillermo and Martin, visible image of the invisible Gift
(E.S.)

To LLD – in the spirit of friendship
(T.H.)

Table of Contents

Eduardo Segura & Thomas Honegger
Preface   i

Martin Simonson
Recovering the 'Utterly Alien Land':
Tolkien and Transcendentalism   1

Tom Shippey
New Learning and New Ignorance:
Magia, Goeteia, and the Inklings   21

Dieter Bachmann
Words for Magic: *goetia*, *gûl* and *lúth*   47

Verlyn Flieger
When is a Fairy Story a Faërie Story?
Smith of Wootton Major   57

Colin Duriez
Myth, Fact and Incarnation   71

Patrick Curry
Iron Crown, Iron Cage:
Tolkien and Weber on Modernity and Enchantment   99

Thomas Honegger
A Mythology for England?
Looking a Gift Horse in the Mouth   109

Devin Brown
Lewis's View of Myth as a Conveyer of Deepest Truth   131

Miryam Librán-Moreno
'A Kind of Orpheus-Legend in Reverse':
Two Classical Myths in the Story of Beren and Lúthien   143

Eugenio M. Olivares-Merino
A Monster that Matters: Tolkien's Grendel Revisited   187

Margarita Carretero-González
A Tale as Old as Time, Freshly Told Anew:
Love and Sacrifice in Tolkien, Lewis and Rowling   241

Fernando J. Soto and
Marta García de la Puerta
The Hidden Meanings of the Name 'Ransom':
Strange Philology and 'Contradictions' in
C.S. Lewis's Cosmic Trilogy   267

John Garth
'As Under a Green Sea':
Visions of War in the Dead Marshes   285

Eduardo Segura
Leaf by Niggle and the Aesthetics of Gift:
Towards a Definition of J.R.R. Tolkien's Notion of Art   315

Preface

The idea of a volume on the Inklings' notions of Art, Literature, and Language – and the dire necessity of such a book – came to me as the result of the cold, distant evaluation my doctoral dissertation received by the staff of the 'Academia' who judged it, back in 2001. It was sad seeing how those professors – all of them holding PhDs in Philology – seemed to be unable to understand a word of the core of my argument, where I tried to explain the relationship between linguistic creation, and sub-creation, within the framework of Aesthetics. I honestly think it was not my fault. Their rationale, as well as the intellectual pitfall that Tolkien himself tried to avoid with his proposal of an Oxford English School, has been perfectly depicted by Tom Shippey in 'Lit. and Lang.', the first chapter of his *The Road to Middle-earth*, and also in his paper 'Fighting the Long Defeat: Philology in Tolkien's Life and Fiction', republished recently in his book *Roots and Branches*, which is also available in the Cormarë Series (no. 11).

The only exception to that hostile approach to Tolkien was Professor Andrew Breeze, a good friend of Tom Shippey's, and one of the last representatives of the 'old school' of Philology – that of Tolkien. He alone hailed some of my contributions with relief, appreciation, and respect. After that sad experience, Professor Breeze and I became good friends, too. I can still remember his deeply moving farewell before I went back to my hometown, when he read for me (Tolkien would have been delighted) Elrond's words to the Fellowship at the hour of their departure from Rivendell into the shadows – but also into hope.

Over the last six years I have frequently been revisited by that feeling of perplexity: Why that animosity against Tolkien? My doctoral dissertation was just an attempt to show the process of the literary genesis of *The Lord of the Rings*, its deep co-relation with *The Book of Lost Tales*, *lato sensu*, and how an analysis of Frodo's quest within a narratological framework is able to shed a brilliant light on the question of how Philology, the invention of languages, and Literature were interlaced in Tolkien's vision of literary creation, *i.e.*, sub-creation. This was the key to the understanding of the whole: What was sub-creation to Tolkien? Was it just a means to invent *another* Neverland called Middle-earth, some kind of a Faërie of his own? I didn't think so. I thought then, and I am sure of it now, that Tolkien was deeply aware the connection between words and possible worlds, between what Aristotle called *mímesis práxeos*, and Art; that his creation was deeper, richer, than a simple attempt to 'escape' by means of invented or imagined, alternative worlds. He knew sub-creation was the natural consequence of the human condition: that of being a creature prone to create, to imitate God, and mainly to serve others.

Inspired by this conviction, I began, in 2005, to gather as many contributions as I could in order to prepare a book that would be of some help towards a profounder understanding of what the Inklings considered the key of literary creation, and of Art. The selection of the scholars was made not only according to their evident merits, but also – and I write this with pleasure, humility, and pride (and without prejudice) – according to the friendship that we share. Their expertise was self-evident, and so I had only to ask them for an effort to focus their attention on the topic from a general perspective. It was then that Professor Thomas Honegger, who had been one of the original contributors, came to me as a kind of Gandalf – in the sense of an *angélos*, as Tolkien explained the role of the character –, to save me from circumstances beyond my control which had made it impossible for me to prepare the book for publication as planned. The volume found a new home, so to speak, in the Cormarë Series of Walking Tree Publishers. So, the book you have in your hands is the result of many efforts, care, and watchfulness, like Niggle's Tree.

I was furthermore deeply concerned about the fact that English has, without doubt, become the *koiné* in Tolkien studies – some sort of Middle-earth Common Speech. Therefore, I also wanted to offer the few Spanish Tolkien scholars a welcome opportunity to present their work to a wider audience, so that the range of *Tolkieniana* could be enriched beyond nationalities, or language in this volume. The same is true for the inclusion of the Swiss contributions (though they, traditionally, are a multilingual people anyway). Again, a decision Tolkien would have approved – and never mind that this is pure 'literary criticism', or 'books on books'.

The chapters have been distributed in no special order, so that they can be read as independent parts of a whole. We have tried to look at the central elements of our reflection – Myth, Art, Magic – from multiple perspectives, so that the reader may reach his or her own conclusions. An in-depth study of Charles Williams' works is still to be made and I wish that, in the not too distant future, we may publish a volume on the allegorical novels of this almost unknown Inkling.

The aim of this volume is to become a first stepping-stone in the process of reconstructing those conversations in which the Inklings discussed, argued, and thoughtfully debated on Myth and Language. Unfortunately, we can no longer attend their meetings, and Tollers and Jack never really made headway with their planned book on the origins of language. The echo of Barfield's ideas is, no doubt, a privileged path to a deeper, richer understanding of what Tolkien, Lewis and their fellow Inklings achieved.

Eduardo Segura & Thomas Honegger
Granada & Jena, Fall 2007

Recovering the "Utterly Alien Land": Tolkien and Transcendentalism

MARTIN SIMONSON

Abstract

The notion of Recovery, as J.R.R Tolkien explains it in his well-known essay 'On Fairy-stories', seems to have eclipsed previous expressions of the same concept, but facts are that the idea was far from being a newcomer on the scene of literary theory and philosophy. It had been previously discussed over many centuries, most notably in Neoplatonic philosophy, Romantic theory and Transcendentalist thinking. However, Tolkien launched the idea from theory to practice in a much more immediate way than that of his predecessors. In the following paper, I will explain Tolkien's approach to the notion of Recovery both with reference to some of the preceding theoretical and literary expressions of the same urge, and to his particular creativity and storytelling strategies.

When discussing the art of J.R.R. Tolkien, the logical point of departure is usually found in the essay 'On Fairy-Stories', in which Tolkien outlines the principles that govern fairy-stories, as he understands the term. Of the three basic principles – Recovery, Escape and Consolation – much has been written, and the attempts to trace Tolkien's ideas to previous literary theory have revealed some important connections to Romantic thought.[1] However, comparatively little attention has been paid to the relationship between Tolkien's ideas and American transcendentalism. In this essay I wish to dig deeper into the soil that gave birth to Tolkien's concept of Recovery, compare his efforts at achieving it with the writings of Ralph Waldo Emerson and Henry David Thoreau, discuss how they differ and try to disclose why this is so.

---

[1] See, for example, Seeman (1996).

Though the following passage has been quoted so often over the years that many Tolkien fans and scholars probably know the words by heart, it seems fair to start with Tolkien's (OFS 77) views on the concept in 'On Fairy-Stories':

> [...] we need recovery. We should look at green again, and be startled anew (but not blinded) by blue and yellow and red. We should meet the centaur and the dragon, and then perhaps suddenly behold, like the ancient shepherds, sheep, and dogs, and horses – and wolves. This recovery fairy-stories help us to make. In that sense only a taste for them may make us, or keep us, childish.
> Recovery (which includes return and renewal of health) is a re-gaining – regaining of a clear view [...] We need, in any case, to clean our windows; so that the things seen clearly may be freed from the drab blur of triteness or familiarity – from possessiveness.

For our present purpose, it is interesting to notice that Tolkien, when he laid out these ideas, partly echoed a long tradition of pagan and Christian Neoplatonic philosophy that addressed the question of how fallen man might be able to recover contact with Nature.

Plotinus, in his *Enneads*, conceived the problem as the overflowing of a spring that, when the flow reaches the material world, has come so far from its divine source that Evil occurs. Neoplatonized Christianity in general regarded the fall of man as a falling away from Oneness, as represented by God, into a fragmented state of multiplicity. Hence, redemption was seen as a process of reintegration. For Plotinus, the solution lay in looking inward, toward the essence of things, while Neoplatonized Christianity postulated the existence of a powerful current of love sent out by God to transport us back to Him.

The idea that multiplicity leads to Evil was also present in much of German idealism. As Abrams (1973:170-171) says, from the 1780s on, a number of the keenest and most sensitive minds found radically inadequate, both to immediate human experience and to basic human needs, the intellectual ambiance of the Enlightenment, with (as they saw it) its mechanistic world-view, its analytic divisiveness (which undertook to explain all physical and mental phenomena by breaking them down into irreducible parts, and regarded all wholes as a collocation of such elementary parts), and its conception of the human mind as totally diverse and alien from its nonmental environment.

Transcendental idealism, as expressed by Schelling and others, held that imagination was the key that enabled us to conceive of, and reconcile, contradictions, thus leading us back towards a unity with Nature. The Romantic stance was a variation upon the theme of original Oneness as equated to Goodness, while multiplicity implied a fall into evil and suffering that Man must overcome. In the Romantic mindframe, the "return to unity is not a return to undifferentiated unity of its origin, but a unity which is higher, because it incorporates the intervening differentiations" (Abrams 1973:183-184). For the Romantics, imagination was a tool that could be used to help us move in this direction – an enhanced awareness of reality.

In Coleridge's opinion, taken from *Biographia Literaria* (1817), custom is what prevents us from seeing clearly, and the trademark of poetic genius is to be able to describe "familiar objects as to awaken in the mind of others a kindred feeling concerning them and that freshness of sensation which is the constant accompaniment of mental, no less than of bodily, convalescence" (Coleridge 1965:60). A similar view is found in Carlyle's *Sartor Resartus* (1830-31), in which he expresses the idea that custom blinds us to the miracles of the everyday by "persuading us that the Miraculous, by simple repetition, ceases to be Miraculous" (Trilling and Bloom 1973:34). Carlyle asks himself: "Am I to view the stupendous with stupid indifference, because I have seen it twice, or two-hundred, or two-million times?" (Trilling and Bloom 1973:35)

The American philosopher Ralph Waldo Emerson made Carlyle's work known in the United States, and incorporated much of his thinking, largely derived from the Romantics, in what became known as the transcendentalist movement, of which he was one of the founders. As Emerson wrote in 'The Transcendentalist' (1841-42), transcendentalism was really idealism, one of the two main outlooks upon life, the other being materialism. The difference, according to Emerson (2000:81), is that "the materialist insists on facts, on history, on the force of circumstances and the animal wants of man; the idealist on on the power of Thought and Will, on inspiration, on miracle, on individual culture."

One of the most influential essays written by Emerson is "Nature" (1836), which came to be considered the manifesto of the transcendentalist movement. Early on, Emerson states what he perceives as one of the fundamental problems of Man:

> To speak truly, few adult persons can see nature. Most persons do not see the sun. At least they have a very superficial seeing. The sun illuminates only the eye of the man, but shines into the eye and the heart of the child. The lover of nature is he whose inward and outward senses are still truly adjusted to each other; who has retained the spirit of infancy even into the era of manhood. (Emerson 2000:6)

Emerson, too, believes that man has fallen away from the original oneness, and that only as children are we able to perceive the world as it is, as unity. To adjust the inward and outward senses is to see oneself as part of the original unity. Evidence of man's fall would be our present estrangement from Nature: "We are as much strangers in nature as we are aliens from God. We do not understand the note of birds. The fox and the deer run away from us; the bear and tiger rend us." (Emerson 2000:33) Like Coleridge and Carlyle, he identifies custom as one of the main obstacles for perceiving the miraculous in the everyday, and claims that the duty of the writer is to "fasten words again to visible things; so that picturesque language is at once a commanding certificate that he who employs it is a man in alliance with truth and God" (Emerson 2000:16).

In Emerson's view, language itself has become an obstacle that hinders our perception of God in nature, and the task of the writer is to find the words to penetrate the veil of familiarity and enable us see our original relation to God and the world that surrounds us as Oneness. This act, according to Emerson (2000:16), is the will of God, because "good writing and brilliant discourse are perpetual allegories. This imagery is spontaneous. It is the blending of experience with the present action of the mind. It is proper creation. It is the working of the original Cause through the instruments he has already made."

These ideas not only recall Tolkien's belief that we must return to a childlike perception of reality to be able to grasp the miracle of everyday phenomena (the writing and reading of fairy-stories is Tolkien's particular way of "adjusting the inward and outward senses"), but also that good story-telling partly aims to recover an original relationship with the natural world,[2] and that "sub-creation" is an act of allegiance with God.[3] Emerson further implies that the intuitive and spontaneous use of the right words for the natural objects they represent is a speech-act in the sense that it creates the world it describes, making it visible to the reader. A similar strain can be found in Tolkien's art, though the process is significantly modified, as we shall see.

---

[2] When discussing the desire to talk to beasts that can be found in many fairy-stories, Tolkien (OFS 84) uses an analogy not much different from Emerson's, claiming that such a desire is not due to "an alleged 'absence of the sense of separation of ourselves to the beasts'," but rather the contrary: "A vivid sense of that separation is very ancient; but also a sense that it was a severance: a strange fate and a guilt lies on us. Other creatures are like other realms with which Man has broken off relations, and sees now only from the outside at a distance, being at war with them, or on the terms of an uneasy armistice."

[3] In 'Mythopoeia', Tolkien justifies the fantastical elements of fairy-stories by asserting that sub-creation is a God-given right: "Though all the crannies of the world we filled/With Elves and Goblins, though we dared to built/Gods and their houses out of dark and light,/and sowed the seed of dragons – 'twas our right/(used or misused). That right has not decayed:/we make still by the law in which we're made." Quoted in Flieger (2002:42-43).

However, before discussing Tolkien's particular approach to story-telling we will remain overseas yet for a while, because Henry David Thoreau, one of Emerson's disciples, was also very much intrigued by the possibility of world-making – so much, in fact, that it became one of his major intellectual preoccupations – and it is in his writings that we find one of the most compelling nineteenth-century antecedents to Tolkien's later expression of the same urge.

Thoreau probably came across Emerson's 'Nature' as a student at Harvard, and after a short, disappointing career as a school-teacher in Concord, he began working for the philosopher as a gardener, with full access to his library. This rather unusual arrangement combined the naturalist's passionate efforts at understanding the mysteries and intricacies of the natural world, with the student's insatiable thirst for knowledge, and helped setting the course for Thoreau's life-long obsession, namely to write a natural history, reaching out simultaneously to ancient myth, of Concord and its whereabouts. Emerson encouraged the young writer to put down his observations and discoveries in a journal, and Thoreau followed his advice. His most famous book is *Walden*, based on the journal he kept during a two-year long reclusion in a cabin he built for himself on Emerson's land by Walden Pond, but he also wrote many other essays.[4] In our discussion of the pre-Tolkienian concept of "Recovery through literature", we will focus on two of these, *A Week on the Concord and Merrimack Rivers*, and *Walking*.

A Week is, on the surface, the account of a boat trip undertaken by Thoreau and his brother John in the late 1830s. The way this trip is described, however, reveals a deeper concern – primarily, it is about seeing the world with new eyes, acknowledging that the past is not necessarily so much different from the present, since the same old, universal laws still govern our lives. The book represents an attempt at putting words to a world-vision in which

---

[4] The most widespread and influential of which being, perhaps, *Civil Disobedience*, that outlines what Thoreau conceived of as an intellectual's proper response to slavery and oppression.

the familiar becomes strange (and strangely appealing, revealing our original unity with the world) and in this way to recreate it for the reader. In order to do so, Thoreau tries to recover the original use of words. He begins the essay with a reference to the original name of the river (presently named Concord only by convention), explaining that its Indian name is 'Musketaquid', which means 'grass-ground river'. According to Oelschlaeger (1991:143), with this reference "Thoreau attempts to disclose a presence concealed by conventional designation, a presocial, primal, and therefore genuine meaning," the reason for which being that "[a]ncient and dead languages now held a fascination for Thoreau, particularly when they recognized living nature; that element bonded him with archaic sensibilities and thus with a time before the enfolding of meaning within the merely present."

English literature, Thoreau felt, was comparatively tame, being only a repetition of the Greek and Latin works that expressed the original relationship to the Universe. Complaining about the present apathy in literature, Thoreau (1982:221) says that

> [t]he bard has in great measure lost the dignity and sacredness of his office. Formerly he was called a seer, but now it is thought that one man sees as much as another. He has no longer the bardic rage, and only conceives of the deed, which he formerly stood ready to perform.

The deed Thoreau refers to is world-making, the envisioning of a world through words, making the act of speaking equivalent to the act of creating. In order to recover the old 'bardic rage', he wants to use a completely 'natural' language that puts us back in direct contact with the original meaning, now lost: "We have to be told that the Greeks called the world [...] Beauty, or Order, but we do not see clearly why they did so, and we esteem it at best only a curious philological fact," he says in *Walking* (Thoreau 1982:625). Thoreau began to conceive of a system of natural energies as a language of its own – a mythical language – putting forth the challenge in the following terms: "Where is the literature which gives expression to Nature? He would be a poet who could impress the winds and streams into his service, to speak for him; who nailed words to their primitive senses" (Thoreau 1982:616).

According to Thoreau, wildness is what may save modern, fallen Man, because in wildness is the original expression of God. Language, to do justice to wildness, must be equally wild, and for Thoreau, ancient myth was what best expressed it. However, to write ancient myth anew did not seem very feasible, and Thoreau began experimenting with other ways to portray modern experience of timeless nature and the wild (Richardson 1986:232); that is, a new myth of wildness for the contemporary reader. In spite of his efforts, Thoreau (1982:625) feels that he can only get flickering pictures of this other, higher, and original vision of reality, which is simultaneous with our conventional way of perceiving the world: "I feel that with regard to nature I live a sort of border life, on the confines of a world into which I make occasional and transient forays only." These transient forays are usually set off by unprejudiced observation of Nature as a recipient of the divine. One instance of this is his contemplation of a familiar place in his neighbourhood:

> I took a walk on Spaulding's farm the other afternoon. I saw the setting sun lighting up the opposite side of a stately pine wood. Its golden rays straggled into the aisles of the wood as into some noble hall. I was impressed as if some ancient and altogether admirable and shining family had settled there in that part of the land called Concord, unknown to me – to whom the sun was servant – who had not gone into society in the village – who had not been called on. I saw their park, their pleasure-ground, beyond through the wood, in Spaulding's cranberry-meadow [...] The farmer's cart-path, which leads directly through their hall, does not in the least put them out, as the muddy bottom of a pool is sometimes seen through the reflected skies.
> (Thoreau 1982:625-626)

Reading Thoreau, be it his *Journal*, *Walden*, or *Walking*, one gets the impression that the author is continually struggling with a conventional frame of awareness to get glimpses of the eternal, and that, once he breaks through, the English words he must use to convey his experience do not quite attain that degree of mythical, original meaning as to express the sense of raw wildness to which he aspires, especially as he insists on metaphors easily interpreted in terms of a modern, anthropocentric awareness, such as 'park' or 'pleasure-ground'.

What Thoreau does achieve is to present a suggestive, simultaneous *mélange* of modernity and eternity, civilization and wildness at the same time, and to make something new out of the combination. His philosophy of words is clearly indebted to the Neoplatonic thinkers, by way of German idealism, British romanticism and Emersonian transcendentalism, but his literary essays reveal a further step toward the usefulness of a combination of the untamed elements in nature with the imprints of modern civilization, that the former were not quite ready to acknowledge.

A Week at the Concord and Merrimack Rivers, together with *Walking*, and, to a lesser extent, *Walden*, represent early attempts at finding a mythic language of the wild to express a modern perception of the eternal and to recover a fresh perception of the world, seeing words as the ultimate tools that man must use to bridge the two realities and make the other world visible.

Thoreau, living in America, was sad at seeing how fast the land, with all its natural wonders, open spaces and possibilities for redemption, had turned into commodity, and felt a pressing need to redirect the course toward a more subtle understanding of the natural element. The East coast was becoming increasingly civilized, and many Romantic painters, such as Thomas Cole and Albert Bierstadt, and literary naturalists like John Muir, who had turned to the unspoilt American landscape in order to experience and express a Recovery of the pristine beauty of the natural world, now headed West.

Tolkien, writing in a time and a place in which the natural environment had been long-since desacralized, turned into a commodity or contemplated as mere space on a map that must be conquered by technology and modern warfare, would mainly look to the Northwest of the past for inspiration, but his vision was also rooted in Neoplatonic, Romantic, and transcendentalist thinking. The notion of Recovery and the inhibiting effects of custom clearly repeat, indeed almost paraphrase, Coleridge, Carlyle and Emerson, and the idea of the writer as a subcreator was explicit in Emerson's thinking, as we have seen. Likewise, Owen Barfield's conception of words and their semantic unity with the natural and supernatural world, which had a profound influence on Tolkien,[5] was preceded by Thoreau's elaboration on the same theme and partly inherited by Neoplatonized Christianity and Romantic thought, as we can appreciate in Flieger's (2002:37-38) summary of Barfield's theory:

> Language in its beginnings made no distinction between the literal and the metaphoric meaning of a word, as it does today [...] Humankind in its begin nings had a sense of the cosmos as a whole and of itself as a part of that whole [...] We now perceive the cosmos as particularized, fragmented, and entirely separate from ourselves. Our consciousness and the language with which we express that consciousness have changed and splintered[.]

For Barfield and Tolkien, as for Emerson and Thoreau, words were the tools we must use to bridge the gap and recover unity. As Flieger (2002:47-48) points out,

> *Poetic Diction* makes it clear that it is in and by words that we feel and express a sense of separation and that it will be through the creative power of words that we can return. The poet, through the use of metaphor, is a maker of meaning and a recreator of perception. Poetry – poetic diction – reinvests the world with meaning and rebuilds our relationships with it.

---

[5] For a full account of this influence, see Flieger's (2002) seminal study *Splintered Light*.

Indeed, transcendentalist philosophy in general – and Thoreau's in particular – seems to have been a forerunner to Tolkien in many senses. Of *A Week*, Robinson (2004:53) says: "The book's probing of the relationship between Christianity and mythology, its critique of the narrowness of conventional society, its passionate concern with the dynamics of conversation and friendship, and its keen awareness of the natural world all reflect important strands of Transcendentalism." The same words could have been used to describe *The Lord of the Rings* (though it is true that many facets of the work would have been left out by such a reductionist approach to its thematic scope).

Is Tolkien, then, merely a twentieth-century echo of the Romantic and transcendentalist attempts at achieving Recovery through literature? The answer takes some pondering. Tolkien is clearly very much concerned with reinvesting words with original meaning, and, like the Romantics, he was not after a return to undifferentiated unity, but rather a "unity which is higher because it incorporates the intervening differentiations" (Abrams 1973:183-184), as the words at the end of 'On Fairy-Stories' imply: "So great is the bounty with which [the Christian] has been treated [...] that in Fantasy he may actually assist in the effoliation and multiple enrichment of creation." This kind of higher unity is what Thoreau hints at when he portrays a reality that puts the literal and the metaphoric – that is, the timeless/mythic, and the modern/everyday – on a simultaneous level, as in his particular vision of Spaulding's farm quoted above.

Tolkien similarly creates a world which is both familiar and strange at the same time, updating older words, traditions and world-visions by putting them in constant dialogue with more modern conceptions of reality, mainly represented by the hobbits. However, both Tolkien's point of departure and the refined process that leads up to the textual outcome is radically different from Thoreau's. While Tolkien, like Thoreau, made use of old words to convey ancient realities, his words and languages were often invented, or semi-invented,[6] and they triggered the creation of invented contexts to make them credible, albeit with clear links to "real" historical, cultural and literary contexts of our own world.

In a letter to his editor, Tolkien (*Letters* 219) explains that "The invention of languages is the foundation. The 'stories' were made rather to provide a world for the languages than the reverse. To me a name comes first and the story follows." One example of this is what happened to the pre-existing world of Middle-earth when the word "hobbit" appeared in his mind. In a note to the letter quoted above, Tolkien (*Letters* 219) added: "I once scribbled 'hobbit' on a blank page of some boring school exam. paper in the early 1930s. It was some time before I discovered what it referred to!"

Discovery of context by means of inventing linguistically credible etymologies was, for Tolkien, a crucial part of his particular creative labours.[7] In the case of the discovery of context for the word 'hobbit', the entry on this word in *The Ring of Words* explains that Tolkien came up with the non-existant but "well-formed Old English compound *holbytla*" (modern English holebuilder), later used by the Rohirrim to describe hobbits, as a result of 'reverse engineering': "Tolkien is playfully suggesting that if there had been an Old English word *holbytla* [...] it might well have come down into modern English as *hobbit*" (Gilliver et al. 2006:144-145).

Shippey's account of the word features an ample discussion of possible sources, mentioning the bourgeois Babbitt of Sinclair Lewis's eponymous novel as one possibility (acknowledged by Tolkien himself) – the story being, however vaguely, reminiscent of Bilbo's – and the word 'rabbit'. Both these sources and the reversed etymological engineering contribute to the fact that "'hobbit' as word and concept threw out its anchors into Old and modern English at once" (Shippey 2003:70).

---

[6] Gilliver et al. (2006) in *The Ring of Words* show how Tolkien's work on the *OED* actually gave rise to many of his "invented" words.

[7] Garbowski (2004:80) also highlights this feature as fundamental to Tolkien's process of creating a sense of recovery in his fiction: "If the artist were simply 'inventing' the world, then it would in part be the magic of control and domination he criticized."

The outcome of the process of creating a context for 'hobbit' is the Shire as portrayed in *The Lord of the Rings*; that is, a region that resembles modern England (or at least nineteenth-century rural England), but with roots that reach back to earlier stages in Northern European history and culture, much like England's own.[8] However, the Shire is only one part of a much larger world, in which these earlier stages are still very much present and actively operating, such as Rohan (the context of *holbytlan*). Tolkien, in *The Lord of the Rings*, actually communicates a process of exploration and discovery of these ancient contexts by means of a ficticious chronicle known as *The Red Book of Westmarch*, written by hobbits, who, by interpreting these older and more 'foreign' realities, make them accessible to the modern reader. The labouriously (though at the same time intuitively) wrought "inter-traditional dialogue" that permeates all levels of the text (Simonson, forthcoming) elucidates the relationship between the old and the new and conveys, at the same time, the underlying parallels to our own, present-day reality.

From what we have seen so far, Thoreau's process of finding a mythic language to reveal and express a deeper dimension closely linked to the natural world, with room for both the mythic and the commonplace on a simultaneous level, is thus inverted by Tolkien. In the latter's vision, it is the word that comes first, and with it the invented context and the stories. However, the process of taking the hobbits on a trip of discovery to increasingly archaic and unfamiliar settings involves not only reversed etymological engineering. For one thing, between the word and the world come the maps. Though the same impulse was to be found in *The Hobbit* – see Tolkien's (*Letters* 215) claim that after having discovered the word 'hobbit', "I did nothing about it, for a long time, and for some years I got no further than the production of Thror's map" –, the map that appears in the earlier narrative was, as Shippey (2003:100) points out, merely decorative. It was when Tolkien began working on *The Lord of the Rings* that he fully came to realize the importance of

---

[8] Shippey (2003:102) provides an outline of these correspondences.

exact – albeit invented – maps for the creation of credible contexts (cf. *Letters* 177).

In spite of the exactness of the maps, the story not only filled the frames of the preceding geographical representations, but sometimes it ended up interrogating their accuracy and relevance. This is the case of Tom Bombadil's house in the Old Forest. Christopher Tolkien tells us (*Return* 114, 327-328) that his father did not seem to be very sure of the exact location of Tom's house – at least, the different drafts offer contradictory descriptions, the cabin being situated sometimes on the south side of the Withywindle, sometimes on the north. However, it turned out that all these ponderings actually became quite redundant, because the final outcome shows a very blurred and vague sense of the geography surrounding the cabin, perhaps due to the mythic quality of the setting in the final version.[9] From the word, in this case the name Tom Bombadil, contexts arise and are geographically laid out by maps.

---

[9] In the final textual version, the narrator tells us that Tom's cabin is situated "up, down, under hill" – that is, in no particular place but in all places at the same time, a kind of primordial reality. Elements related to mythic paradigms in this episode include Frodo's strange sensation bordering on religious revelation, which makes him recite verses previously unknown to him. Furthermore, Tom Bombadil's discourse covers all imaginable topics, good things as well as evil, as he sums up the history of the universe for the hobbits, taking them to "strange regions beyond their memory and beyond their waking thought" (*LotR* 146). Tom's language is, perhaps, a conscious attempt on behalf of Tolkien to make this character embody Barfield's ideas about the old semantic unity (see Shippey 2003:105-106). Tom Bombadil further claims that he was the first being on Earth and plays with the Ring as if he were beyond good and evil. Frodo loses his sense of time at Tom Bombadil's house, and he feels strangely compelled to confess his fears to him. Similarly, at the Barrow-downs Tom Bombadil, who appears instantly when called for (like the gods in the Classical epic tradition), is presented as a force of light and order waging battle against destructive darkness. Merry's dream, the sharing out of the magic swords, and the visions that Tom evokes in the hobbits' minds, speaking of the remote past in which the swords were forged and showing a man with a star on his brow, also add to the transcendence of the experience. For a full discussion of the presence of mythic narrative paradigms in this episode, see Simonson (forthcoming). We may add that Tolkien, in one of his letters, claims that "[w]e are not in 'fairy-land', but in real river-lands in autumn," though it should be noted that the next sentence continues: "Goldberry *represents* the actual seasonal changes in such lands" (Tolkien *Letters* 272, my italics). The insistence that the land is 'real' may of course also be due to the fact that Tolkien, in this letter, was criticising Forrest J. Ackerman's script for a projected screenplay based on *The Lord of the Rings*, in which he perceives a linguistic treatment leaning too far toward a childish fairy tale, and therefore feels the need to emphasise the 'reality' of Middle-earth.

The maps are filled by stories that sometimes transcend the map-reality and take the shape of myth, which in turn affects the portrayal of space.

The digression of the Old Forest and the Barrow-downs is thus highly revealing of Tolkien's creative process, but it may also tell us something important about the author's general aims with the tale. According to novelistic standards of economy in plot-making, the adventure is actually quite superfluous, not adding anything of substance to the furthering of the story. One explanation for this may be that in Tolkien's narrative, the construction of a tight plot is not of *prime* importance. I have elsewhere argued (Simonson, forthcoming) that this may be due to the fact that, apart from the novel, the narrative is heavily indebted to other narrative paradigms, such as romance and myth, in which plot is not always central. Shippey (2003:109), for his part, claims that in *The Lord of the Rings*, "landscape and the beings attached to it are in a way the heroes," and that the digressive episodes in the story exist due to Tolkien's wish to connect the imagined world with our own, because

> they suggest very strongly a world which is more than imagined, whose supernatural qualities are close to entirely natural ones, one which has moreover been 'worn down', like ours, by time and by the process of lands and languages and people all growing up together over millenia.[10]

Rosebury (2003:32) takes the argument one step further and contends that in the Tom Bombadil-episode, "what looks like excess from the point of view of a plot-based structure is wholly necessary for a different kind of structure," alluding to the author's desire to create a feeling of intense sympathy for Middle-earth and its peoples (by extensive and careful portrayal) in order to make the reader care sufficiently about their potential destruction.

---

[10] This description, while fitting for the portrayal of Ithilien, for instance, is not really valid for the Old Forest, which has not been deteriorated by time, languages and people – in fact, like Lórien, it is a place which, to some extent, exists *outside* time.

While I agree with Rosebury on this, I believe that the interpretation may be invested with further significance if we connect Tolkien's strategy with his particular creative impulse. If we believe Tolkien when he says that his story-telling creativity is based on discovering feasible contexts for his invented languages, the narrative as such necessarily becomes an exploration of Middle-earth itself, as if the writer were filling empty spaces on a rudimentary map as the writing progressed (which is basically the procedure outlined by the four volumes of *The History of The Lord of the Rings*). In short, if the exploration of context – that is, physical, cultural, and historical space – *as such* is a central part of *The Lord of the Rings*, the development of the plot is, if not secondary, then at least only of equal importance to the presentation of the discoveries. The fact that the Tom Bombadil-episode survived the subsequent revisions, in spite of its apparent redundancy within the framework of the larger narrative, indicates that for Tolkien the discovery and revelation of the world had become just as important as the advancement of the plot.

We may venture to conclude that the idea of Recovery is at the heart of such an approach to story-telling, mainly because of the fact that the process engenders a simultaneous portrayal of different worlds. When the hobbits enter the Old Forest and arrive at Tom Bombadil's house and the Barrow-downs they break through to the world of myth, and when we return to the familiar world of Bree, we know that it only exists on a simultaneous level. Which is more real, Bree or the Barrow-downs? No answer is given, because the text provides us with three different realities of equal importance. The invented (though coherent) map-reality of Middle-earth and the mythic, 'super-supernatural' realm (which transcends the map-reality) in which Tom Bombadil and the Barrow-wights dwell, simultaneously co-exist and convey a sense of Recovery by revealing ancient elements (which used to be hidden by a routine perception) in the reader's contemporary reality, in turn alluded to by the literary, cultural, religious and historical correspondences between the phenomena of Middle-earth and those of our own world.

As the hobbits move on, Tolkien keeps putting the reader in contact with societies defined by the languages they speak, different from our own but at the same time similar, that transmit an elusive scent of our own past and cultural heritage. To be able to grasp the essence of these societies, we must necessarily contemplate the reality designated by their words with different eyes (in other words, we must recover an earlier vision of our place in the world), but this does not imply that we need to lose contact with the present. In *The Lord of the Rings*, the word, and the secondary world that takes shape around it, is the key to the myth-making and to a deeper understanding of our place in the modern world. Tolkien thus updates Thoreau's comparatively lame attempts at expressing a vision of timeless nature with a mythic grammar for the contemporary reader, partly as a result of his linguistic learning and skills in creating 'asterisk words',[11] partly because of an innate desire to create 'asterisk *realities*', to borrow Shippey's expression, for the words and languages he invented, and to invest it all with spatial and temporal coherence.

Words may be evidence of man's fall, Tolkien implies, but at the same time they present us with the unique possibility to make use of the subcreative gift which, if efficiently expressed, may open up paths towards a new unity with both the natural and the supernatural worlds. Tolkien shared this conviction with the Romantics and the Transcendentalists. However, by using a fourfold process, from word-making to myth-making by way of map-making and a very special kind of plot-making, largely aimed at presenting his discoveries, Tolkien takes the previous ideas of Recovery and sub-creation one step further. Hence, while the expression may be rooted in the same concerns, the spontaneous and intuitive use of language hailed by Emerson as the proper

---

[11] Asterisk words are reconstructed words from ancient languages, such as Proto-Germanic, of which there is no written record but that would obey the general rules of linguistic evolution. Gillver et al. (2006:52) explain the process in the following terms: "Trying to make sense of an enigmatic word-form requires the exercise of linguistic skills, but this very activity leads the researcher into a wider realm of history or of legend (imagined history): it calls upon the interplay of the imagination with the known facts. The reconstruction of word-forms goes hand in hand with the imaginative recreation of the lost world in which they are supposed to have been used."

means to put us back in touch with Oneness is somewhat differently handled by Tolkien. For Tolkien, Art is a gift – in this context a capacity to explore and reveal what "the drab blur of triteness and familiarity" has hidden from us, by means of creating imaginary though plausible contexts for the half-familiar words he invented. This gift, at once linguistic and imaginative, is what defines the particularity of Tolkien's approach to Recovery within the framework of Neoplatonic, Romantic and Transcendentalist thinking.

Biographical Note

Martin Simonson studied English philology and translation at the University of the Basque Country in Vitoria, Spain, and holds a Ph.D. from the same university, with a dissertation on the narrative dynamics of *The Lord of the Rings*. He has contributed with several essays on Tolkien's work for previous WTP publications and *Tolkien Studies*, and will soon publish a full-length study on the interaction of narrative genre in *The Lord of the Rings*. Martin's current research is focused on American nature writing and literary myth-making in the context of the Great War. He is currently teaching Swedish language and literature at the University of the Basque Country.

Bibliography

Abbreviations

OFS: 'On Fairy-stories' in Tolkien (1966:3-84).
Letters: see Carpenter 2000.
LotR: see Tolkien 1993.
Return: see Tolkien 2000.

Abrams, Meyer Howard, 1973, *Natural Supernaturalism: Tradition and Revolution in Romantic Literature*, New York and London: Norton.
Carpenter, Humphrey (ed., with the assistance of Christopher Tolkien), 2000, *The Letters of J.R.R. Tolkien*, first edition 1981, Boston: Houghton Mifflin.
Coleridge, Samuel Taylor, 1965, *Biographia Literaria*, (first published 1817), Oxford: Oxford University Press.
Emerson, Ralph Waldo, 2000, *The Essential Writings of Ralph Waldo Emerson*, (edited by Brooks Atkinson), New York: Modern Library.
Flieger, Verlyn, 2002, *Splintered Light: Logos and Language in Tolkien's World*, (revised edition, first edition 1983), Kent, OH, and London: The Kent State University Press.
Garbowski, Christopher, 2004, *Recovery and Transcendence for the Contemporary Mythmaker: The Spiritual Dimension in the Works of J.R.R. Tolkien*, Zurich and Berne: Walking Tree Publishers.
Gilliver, Peter et al., 2006, *The Ring of Words: Tolkien and the Oxford English Dictionary*, Oxford and New York: Oxford University Press.
Oelschlaeger, Max, 1991, *The Idea of Wilderness*, New Haven and London: Yale University Press.
Richardson, Robert D., 1986, *Henry Thoreau: A Life of the Mind*, Berkeley, Los Angeles and London: University of California Press.
Robinson, D.M., 2004, *Natural Life: Thoreau's Worldly Transcendentalism*, Ithaca and London: Cornell University Press.
Rosebury, Brian, 2003, *Tolkien: A Cultural Phenomenon*, (revised and expanded edition, first edition 1992: *Tolkien: A Critical Assessment*), Houndmills: Palgrave.
Seeman, Chris, 'Tolkien's Revision of the Romantic Tradition', in Patricia Reynolds and Glen H. GoodKnight (eds.), 1996, *J.R.R. Tolkien Centenary Conference 1992*, Milton Keynes: The Tolkien Society, pp. 73-83.
Shippey, Tom, 2003, *The Road to Middle-earth*, (revised and expanded edition, first edition 1982), Boston and New York: Houghton Mifflin.
Simonson, Martin, forthcoming, *The Lord of the Rings and the Western Narrative Tradition*, Zurich and Berne: Walking Tree Publishers.
Thoreau, Henry David, 1982, *The Portable Thoreau*, (edited by Carl Bode), New York: Penguin.
Tolkien, John Ronald Reuel, 1966, *The Tolkien Reader*, New York: Ballantine Books.
---, 1993, *The Lord of the Rings*, (first edition 1954-1955), London: HarperCollins.

---, 2000, *The Return of the Shadow: The History of The Lord of the Rings*, (vol. 1, edited by Christopher Tolkien, first edition 1988), Boston and New York: Houghton Mifflin.

Trilling, Lionel, and Harold Bloom (eds.), 1973, *Victorian Prose and Poetry* (The Oxford Anthology of English Literature), New York, London, and Toronto: Oxford University Press.

New Learning and New Ignorance: Magia, Goeteia, and the Inklings

TOM SHIPPEY

Abstract

Lewis's most far-reaching academic work, *English Literature in the Sixteenth Century, Excluding Drama*, opens by arguing that teachers and students often anachronistically introduce modern oppositions into their view of the Renaissance, especially that between magic and science. In this article Lewis's arguments are considered, and are compared with the images of magic he presented in his fiction, and with those which he shared with his fellow-Inklings, Tolkien and Williams. One thing common to all three is the distinction (variously expressed) between 'magia' and 'goeteia'. It is argued that Lewis in effect attempted to replace James Frazer's triangle of magic, religion and science, familiar from *The Golden Bough*, by a more complex opposition between, on the one hand, scientism and goeteia, and on the other, religion and magia. .

It is one of the ironies of academic life that the work to which C.S. Lewis probably devoted the most time and the most effort is now among his least-read. This is the Oxford History of English Literature volume, *English Literature in the Sixteenth Century, Excluding Drama* (OUP, 1954). It is not without its admirers. Very recently a reviewer of a similar modern reference work contrasted it with Lewis's, and commented on the latter's "idiosyncratic brilliance" and "maverick excellence" (Rawson 2006:3). Nevertheless it has certainly not found a mass market. The reasons are obvious. The title itself is a dull one; and the period being surveyed is arguably the dullest of any period of English literature of which we have extensive knowledge. On page one Lewis himself described the first half of it (in poetry) as "a drab age," and remarked that in both prose and poetry "All the authors write like elderly men." One of the exciting elements in that early period may well have been the continuation of "medieval drama" and the change-over to the new style of Kyd, Marlowe, Shakespeare: but that topic was expressly excluded by Lewis's title. Finally, and whatever the work's other merits, it makes for very hard reading, as Lewis no doubt knew. The first few pages refer casually to Pico della Mirandola (1463-94), Marsilio Ficino (1433-99), Paracelsus [Aureolus Bombastus von Hohenheim] (1493-1541), [Heinrich Cornelius] Agrippa [von Nettesheim] (1486-1535), names barely known (if at all) to most students of English literature. A little later Lewis switches casually from the *De Rerum Natura* of [Bernardinus] Telesius (1509-88) to the *De Rerum Sensu et Magia* of [Tommaso] Campanella (1568-1639), giving no introduction to either name. Six pages later he mentions that "pleasing little tract *De Nymphis*"; from what Lewis says I would be interested to read it, but he gives no reference.[1] Lewis must have known what effect such casual assumptions of a generally non-existent background knowledge would produce. Why did he do it?

I would suggest that in this as in so many other cases, Lewis was deliberately 'counterpunching'. One of his targets was the belief, common in university departments of English, that by Shakespeare's time, anyway, 'the triumph of English' had taken place. By contrast, Lewis silently asserted, in the sixteenth century writing in English remained a sub-culture: serious work was done in Latin. Along with the 'triumph of English' theory was another one current if unexpressed in the English departments of both Oxford and Cambridge in the 1950s and 1960s, which might be stated, with deliberate crudity, something like this:

> The Middle Ages were a regrettable waste of time. Fortunately, in the sixteenth century, the Renaissance took place. Gunpowder was invented. America was discovered, as was printing. Humanism broke the mould of the Middle Ages, as did the 'new astronomy' mentioned by Donne. The way was open for the rise of the middle classes, the

---

[1] It must be the *Liber de Nymphis, sylphis, pygmaeis et salamandris et de caeteris spiritibus* of Paracelsus.

> Reformation, the 'triumph of English' aforesaid, and the arrival of Shakespeare. And, again, John Donne.

I have put this in deliberately stupid form – for one thing, most of the dates are wrong – but attitudes like it were certainly part of the students' intellectual furniture, and were not on the whole corrected by the faculty. Lewis refers to such notions with satirical economy in his novel *That Hideous Strength* (1945). Wishing to make the point that Jane Studdock, for all her inherited powers as a seer, is "not perhaps a very original thinker," he has only to mention the topic of her PhD thesis, which is "Donne's triumphant vindication of the body" (10). Donne, triumph, and the physical as opposed to the intellectual, or even less likely, the spiritual: to Lewis these are already the stuff of cliché. Lewis's combative intention is signaled further by the title of his first chapter, "New Learning and New Ignorance." The cliché-ed view had much to say about "new learning," but it forgot the "new ignorance."

The first topic Lewis chose to deal with in his survey – it is, one has to say, a most unexpected and unpredictable opening – was magic. Was this not a medieval survival, rapidly got rid of by the new astronomy, the new science, even new and rational forms of religion, as suggested for instance by the title of Sir Keith Thomas's famous work (it covers a rather later period) *Religion and the Decline of Magic* (1971)? What point did Lewis want to make by directing his readers to that? And – here I approach the main topic of this essay – what relation did the topic have to Lewis's fiction, and indeed the fiction of his fellow-Inklings?

Lewis's argument, in pages 1-14 of *Sixteenth Century*, is by no means easy to follow, but I make an attempt to paraphrase it here.

- In the first place, he asks what created the sudden efflorescence of English literature in the later sixteenth century. Some have suggested that it was "humanism"; Lewis sees no connection. Others have opted for the "new astronomy," creating a Darwinian or Freudian change of world-view; Lewis again sees no sign of this.

- In fact, and conversely, what he does see is a kind of deadening, the beginnings of a substitution of "a mechanical for a genial or animistic view of the universe" (3). But how could this be felt as liberating? The change was in any case not foreseen.

- Still "counterpunching," Lewis suggests that the modern triumph of a scientific world-view tends to read itself back into the past, and to assign sixteenth-century thinkers to one of two groups, "the conservatively superstitious" versus "the progressive or enlightened." But this was not the case. Those who attacked astrology (and therefore might be scored as "enlightened"), might also be firm believers in magic.

- A more important distinction, in the period, was magician versus astrologer – both superstitions, to our way of thinking, but quite different ones: the astrologer stern, deterministic, the magician optimistic, empirical, a rejector of Aristotle and the schoolmen of the Middle Ages – indeed very similar in his high hopes to Francis Bacon and the early scientists.

At this point in his argument Lewis pauses for a couple of asides, which perhaps have contemporary point: Lewis knew as well as anyone that there was a great deal of "new ignorance" not only in the sixteenth century, but also in the twentieth. By "magic," he says, he does not mean "mere witchcraft," as practiced by "the poor, the ignorant, or the perverted" (7). For all the hysteria of the *Malleus Maleficarum* (1497), and of course the interest in the subject shown by James VI and I, King of Scotland and then of England, Lewis was inclined to doubt that very much witchcraft was going on in the sixteenth century.

Evidence collected under torture counts for nothing. He asks his readers accordingly to dismiss from their minds "Gilles de Retz, Black Mass, Hieronymus Bosch, and Mr. Crowley" (7).[2] He might have added, and no doubt thought, "and Margaret Murray, Wicca, and other inventions of the 1920s."

Returning to his slowly-developing theme, Lewis argues that there was in this area a *real* difference between the Middle Ages and the Renaissance: their ideas of magic were different. "Only an obstinate prejudice about this period," he declares – one sees that he is by now definitely and openly "counterpunching" –

> could blind us to a certain change which comes over the merely literary texts as we pass from the Middle Ages to the sixteenth century. In medieval story there is, in one sense, plenty of "magic". Merlin does this or that "by his subtilty", Bercilak [in *Sir Gawain and the Green Knight*] resumes his severed head. But all these passages have unmistakably the note of "faerie" about them. (8)

They are, in a word, not scientific.

> But in Spenser, Marlowe, Chapman, and Shakespeare the subject is treated quite differently. "He to his studie goes"; books are opened, terrible words pronounced, souls imperilled. The medieval author seems to write for a public to whom magic, like knight-errantry, is part of the furniture of romance: the Elizabethan, for a public who feel that it might be going on in the next street.

---

[2] Aleister Crowley (1872-1947) is the odd one out here. A self-dramatizing occultist and Satanist, he was flattered by his tabloid title of "the wickedest man in the world" – evidently absurd, if one thinks of other twentieth-century contenders. He may have served as a model for Charles Williams's character Sir Giles Tumulty, discussed below: Crowley and Williams were both members of the occult Order of the Golden Dawn. But Lewis here intends to make the subject of witchcraft faintly ridiculous.

"Neglect of this point," Lewis declares, "has produced strange readings of *The Tempest*, which is in reality [...] Shakespeare's play on *magia* as *Macbeth* is his play on *goeteia*" (8). This last, it should be noted, is a rare word at any period, and is brought in by Lewis without explanation or support.

Turning back from what Renaissance magic was not to what it was, Lewis argues further:

- authors like Agrippa treat the Middle Ages and such authors as Roger Bacon as merely deluded.

- Agrippa is convinced that the universe is full of intermediate spirits, neither angelic nor diabolic, who may be controlled by humans.

- and when a sixteenth-century Englishman thought of 'Platonism', he thought principally of "the doctrine that the region between earth and moon is crowded with airy creatures who are capable of fertile unions with our own species" (10), copulation which is not in the slightest degree 'Platonic', in the modern sense, but which is very much part of "a spiritual cosmology" (11) markedly opposed to the mechanical and deterministic one also coming into being. Prospero's Ariel is just the kind of creature they are thinking of.

- and what this does is to create "the possibility of an innocent traffic with the unseen" (12), i.e., the possibility of 'high magic' or *magia*.

This possibility was not really innocent, Lewis concludes. It was yet another of those "dreams of power which then haunted the European mind" (13), just like the Baconian dream of science. Both *scientia* and *magia* promised new visions of unlimited human development and control – visions quite alien to the Middle Ages.

Such is Lewis's argument, one which he thought important enough to take the leading place in his most ambitious academic work. Arguing with someone of his erudition may seem a bold enterprise, but in the first place there was nothing Lewis liked better than stout contradiction; and in the second place the vigour with which he puts a particular case – "Only an obstinate prejudice" etc. – is sometimes an indicator of its challengeability. Is medieval magic so clearly of faerie, so certainly unstudious that only "an obstinate prejudice" can deny it? Lewis himself notes Merlin's "subtilty"; Bercilak's magic seems to depend on Morgan le Fay, whose name proves her fairy ancestry, but Bercilak also calls her himself "that conable clerk," which pays tribute to her learning; in Lewis's third main example, Chaucer's "Franklin's Tale," the magician is very definitely a learned clerk from the university. Meanwhile the Renaissance witches in *Macbeth* show no sign of book-learning; and as for Ariel, while he may well be one of Agrippa's *aereos daemones*, morally neutral spirits figure in medieval works as well, such as the *South English Legendary*. What Lewis says about his collection of Latin Renaissance writers may, indeed, be true, and give a true picture of the age. But it could also be argued that in making such a severe disjuncture between the medieval and the newly modern, as also between *magia* and *goeteia*, Lewis was actually giving academic justification to a theme which he had already broached in his fiction: a theme furthermore of great interest not only to himself but also to the Inklings as a group.

Much of the argument about magic in *Sixteenth Century* had previously appeared in the third novel of Lewis's "space fiction" trilogy, *That Hideous Strength*. The turning point in the struggle between good and evil in this work is the bringing back of Merlin, not from the dead, but from suspended animation. He is brought back as a representative of what Lewis calls "medieval magic," and the difference between him and the new twentieth-century breed of scientist-magicians is made very clear by Dr. Dimble, the university don who in this work clearly acts as a spokesman for Lewis's own ideas. Dimble explains at one point:

> [Merlin is] the last vestige of an old order in which matter and spirit were, from our modern point of view, confused. For him every operation on Nature

> is a kind of personal contact, like coaxing a child or stroking one's horse. After him came the modern man to whom Nature is something dead – a machine to be worked, and taken to bits if it won't work the way he pleases. Finally come the Belbury people, who take over that view from the modern man unaltered and simply want to increase their power by tacking on to it the aid of spirits. [...] Of course they hoped to have it both ways. They thought the old *magia* of Merlin, which worked in with the spiritual qualities of Nature, loving and reverencing them and knowing them from within, could be combined with the new *goeteia* – the brutal surgery from without. (352)

One should note that here *goeteia* is not linked with the illiterate witches of *Macbeth*, but with NICE, the National Institute for Co-Ordinated Experiments: both are evil, but that is the only similarity. Merlin's medievalism, though vital for the plot – he has been allowed to be revived, Ransom the Pendragon explains to him, just because as a medieval person he may without sin do what would be definitely sinful in a modern – moreover seems to have elements of the sixteenth century about it. When he offers to waken the powers of Nature against the Pendragon's enemies (355-356), he is surely doing exactly what Campanella thought might be possible with the elements, as Lewis says in *Sixteenth Century* (6), "to awake their sleeping sense (*sopitus sensus*) by *magia divina*." Either Merlin is not as medieval, or Campanella is not as distinctively Renaissance, as Lewis wanted to make out.

Perhaps what Lewis really wanted, and was prepared to juggle his arguments to provide, was an image of an innocent magician. He was fairly sure that no such person could exist nowadays, but conceivably in the past the rules were different. Dr. Dimble once again is made to put the point about Ariel and his colleagues, the 'airy daemons', the elementals whom Merlin can command:

> while it may be true at the end of the world to describe every eldil either as an angel or a devil, and

> may even be true now, it was much less true in Merlin's time. There used to be things on this earth pursuing their own business, so to speak. They weren't ministering angels sent to help fallen humanity, but neither were they enemies preying upon us. Even in St. Paul one gets glimpses of a population that won't exactly fit into our two columns of angels and devils. And if you go back further. [...] all the gods, elves, dwarfs, water-people, *fata, longaevi* [...]
>
> I think there was room for them then, but the universe has come more to a point. [...] At any rate, that is the sort of situation in which one got a man like Merlin. (351)

The awakening of Nature, one may say, is a shared Inkling theme. According to Tolkien's Treebeard, it is what the elves used to do, "waking trees up and teaching them to speak and learning their tree-talk" (*LotR* 457, III/4).[3] Perhaps that is how the Ents themselves arose. In the second "Narnia" volume, *Prince Caspian*, we also find Aslan waking the nymphs and dryads, and the trees, and the river-god from his slumber, to break the bridge of Beruna and defeat the usurper Miraz. Tolkien's Tom Bombadil, surely, whatever else he may be, is also an "elemental," drawing his power from Nature, impossible to separate from the land of which he is the presiding *genius*. All these scenes and characters betray a certain wish-fulfillment, as humans and hobbits find themselves able to talk to animals, trees, plants, rivers, to join a universe "tingling with anthropomorphic life" (*Sixteenth Century*, 4); though one might note that in Lewis's poem 'The Magician and the Dryad,' the dryad expresses dismay at being woken, finds anthropomorphic life far less satisfying than vegetative, and dies when released.[4]

---

[3] Page numbers for *The Lord of the Rings* are given from the corrected one-volume edition, with 'Note on the Text' by Douglas A. Anderson (London: HarperCollins, 2001). However, since page numbers are of limited utility for works so often reprinted, I also give references to that work by book and chapter, and to Lewis's 'Narnia' novels and Williams's novels by chapter.

[4] See Lewis (1965b), *Poems*.

But is such a thing licit, for Christians? Is it not – like Bacchus and Silenus in *Prince Caspian* – a relic of the pagan?[5] In *That Hideous Strength* both Ransom and Dimble note the risk. "It was never *very* lawful, even in your day," says Ransom to Merlin (356). While dealing with nature-spirits may have been licit for Merlin in earlier centuries, Dimble reflects – as polygamy was licit for Abraham, under the Old Law – neither magic nor polygamy may have been entirely good for their practitioners at any time. There is something "withered" about Merlin, says Dimble (352). The old English word for "withered" is "sere," and Lewis's Merlin is something of a "sere-man": not yet a Saruman, and indeed the deadly enemy of the modern versions of Saruman, but sharing something with them just the same. It is the suggestion, by Mrs. Dimble, that using Merlin is rather like fighting NICE with its own weapons, which provokes the explanation/apologia by her husband cited above.

What I am suggesting is that there is a discrepancy between Lewis's argument about magic in *Sixteenth Century* and his fictionalization of magic in *That Hideous Strength* nine years before. In the former he argues that there are three categories: (1) the medieval magic which comes from faerie; (2) the illiterate Renaissance *goeteia* of the witch-cult, as portrayed in *Macbeth*; and (3) the learned Renaissance neo-Platonic *magia* of scholars like Campanella, which depends on control of neutral spirits. In the novel, however, Merlin's medieval magic looks very much like Campanella's, without the bookishness – though Merlin is in his way a learned man, who talks Latin fluently, and knows Greek and Hebrew as well, not to mention the language of (Lewis's mistaken spelling) Numinor. Meanwhile *goeteia*, though still opposed to *magia*, has also become learned, in the hands of the scientists of NICE. The simplest way of resolving the discrepancy is to say that Lewis needed a morally neutral, pre-

---

[5] The point is noted in *Prince Caspian*, when Susan says to Lucy, "I wouldn't have felt safe with Bacchus and all his wild girls if we had met them without Aslan." "I should think not," says Lucy (138, end ch. 11, 'The Lion Roars.') In ch. 5 of the same work Dr Cornelius only teaches Caspian the theory of magic, practical magic not being a proper study for princes. The 'Narnia' novels are cited here from the uniform seven-volume boxed set issued by Puffin Books in 1965.

separation style of magic for the purposes of his fiction. Alternatively, one might argue that the consistent element is the distinction between 'white' and 'black' magic, in the twentieth century as in the sixteenth – Merlin once again functioning in a 'grey' area.

The Inklings must surely have discussed this problem among themselves, and one conclusion they perhaps all assented to is that 'magic' is too inclusive a term. Tolkien has a scene in *The Lord of the Rings* which seems designed to make just this point. In the chapter 'The Mirror of Galadriel' (II/7) Sam Gamgee says, "I've often wanted to see a bit of magic like what it tells of in old tales," and Lothlórien, he reckons, is the place to see it. Galadriel decides to grant his wish and show him her Mirror, though she says that she cannot control it. "[The Mirror] shows things that were, and things that are, and things that may yet be" (353). Later, after Sam has seen a vision of disaster in the Shire, and says he wants to abandon the quest and go home, she tells him also:

> the Mirror shows many things, and not all have yet come to pass. Some never come to be, unless those that behold the vision turn aside from their path to prevent them. The Mirror is dangerous as a guide of deeds. (*LotR* 354)

It is, in fact, very like the visions which the witches show Macbeth; and Macbeth's attempt to avert the visionary future by killing Macduff and his family both fails, and is responsible for his own death. Maybe neither would have happened if Macbeth had not "turned aside from his path to prevent them." Sam concludes, "I don't want to see no more magic" (354). But maybe it was not 'magic'. Galadriel also says to him:

> this is what your folk would call magic, I believe; though I do not understand clearly what they mean; and they seem to use the same word of the deceits of the Enemy. But this, if you will, is the magic of Galadriel. (*LotR* 353)

Galadriel, then, is uncertain about the word 'magic',[6] and furthermore thinks that two words are really needed, one for her 'magic', and one for "the deceits of the Enemy." Tolkien drew attention to the point in a very long letter of 1951 to the publisher Milton Waldman, in which he distinguishes elvish from human conceptions of magic, but further, and very much in agreement with Lewis, argues that the modern urge to power, which Tolkien calls "the Machine," is "more closely related to Magic than is usually recognised" (*Letters* 146).

Behind the Inklings' discussions, however, one may sense also a long discussion between scholars in the nineteenth and twentieth centuries, well summarized by Ronald Hutton in the chapter 'The New Old Paganism' in his book *Witches, Druids and King Arthur* (Hutton 2003:98-106). Summarizing Hutton still further, the basic argument seems to have been over the relationship between magic and religion: clearly some commentators felt that the two were actually very similar concepts, but that to many 'magic' (false, deceitful) was what other cultures did, while 'religion' (true, benevolent) was the prerogative of one's own faith and culture. It was in fact an argument about 'multiculturalism'. With this neither Tolkien nor Lewis, nor Williams, would have had much sympathy, and indeed the scholarly debate appears to have been unproductive, and mostly circular. Nevertheless a point I have made twice elsewhere about both Tolkien and Lewis is that sometimes their fictional constructions seem to have been energized not so much by old mythology, about which they both knew a great deal, as by *theories* about old mythology.[7] Tolkien perhaps developed his concept of the elves from the nineteenth-century debate about the interpretation of (in particular) Snorri Sturluson's *Prose Edda*; while Lewis, even more clearly, framed much of the action of his last novel, *Till We Have Faces*, on different and competing nineteenth- and twentieth-century notions about the nature of myth. Both authors, meanwhile, rejected earlier theories in favour of more complex notions of their own.

---

[6] See also Bachmann in this volume.

[7] For Tolkien, see Shippey (2004); for Lewis, see Shippey (2007).

As regards magic, I would suggest that behind both Lewis's and Tolkien's views there lies the famous argument of J.G. Frazer, in *The Golden Bough*, which is, that there are not two but three conceptions. I have taken the liberty of summarizing his view, for brevity, in the diagram below. It will be noted that in this triangle, any two of the points will be in agreement against the third:

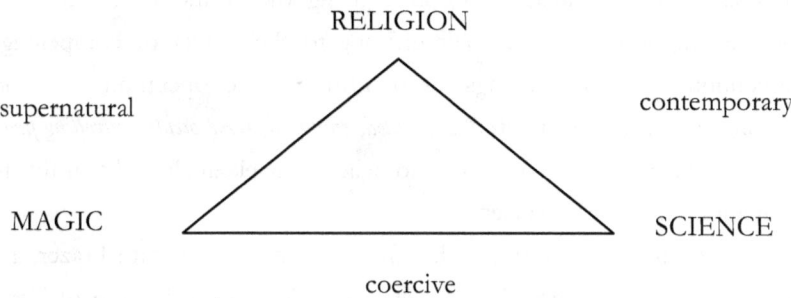

Thus, magic and science are fundamentally coercive: the practitioners of both are trying to get a result in the real world. Frazer indeed says of magic, "its fundamental conception is identical with that of modern science," and he goes further in arguing that it even has 'Laws' like those of Isaac Newton, expressed by Frazer as "the Law of Similarity" and "the Law of Contagion."[8] The idea was taken up eagerly by several science fiction writers, who imagined worlds in which these laws had become as well-understood and as productive as those of modern physics (see Shippey 1977). Both concepts are, however, in Frazer's view, different from that of 'religion', which is essentially supplicatory: God, or the gods, are not to be manipulated by human beings, who can only request help or favour, not control it.[9] 'Magic' and 'religion' are meanwhile similar in

---

[8] I quote here from Frazer (1935, I:220). Frazer's phrasing kept altering from the first edition, but the idea of the Laws of Similarity and Contagion is there from the start.

[9] This distinction was a harder one to make, and Frazer postulated a growing separation of the two. Nevertheless he insisted that the one (religion) assumed "conscious and personal" ruler(s) of the universe, as opposed to the "unconscious and impersonal" forces called on by the magician/scientist (Frazer 1935, I:224). Lewis's goetic magicians, of course, *are* calling on conscious beings, though they are not divine.

that they rely on forces which in one way or another – this distinction created much of the rather sterile debate summarized by Hutton – are not seen as regularly operative in the real world, which 'science' definitely is. Finally, 'religion' and 'science' are both forces which are actively accepted in the contemporary world, though held by some to be in opposition, by others to be capable of resolution: 'magic', by contrast, is defined in the *Oxford English Dictionary* as, "the pretended art of influencing the course of events [...] by processes supposed to owe their efficacy to the power of compelling the intervention of spiritual beings, or of bringing into operation some occult controlling principle of nature." *Pretended, supposed, some occult controlling principle*: it is clear that the lexicographer has no belief in magic at all, and that this is the dominant opinion of his society.

Lewis, to put matters very briefly, in essence agrees with Frazer, as one can see from several scenes in *The Chronicles of Narnia*. At the start of *The Silver Chair* Jill and Eustace are desperate to escape from the bullies of Experiment House. Eustace tells Jill about Narnia, which he has visited once already, and they both wish they could get there. "How?" asks Jill, and Eustace replies, "The only way you can – by Magic." But could they "do something to make it happen?" asks Jill. Eustace nods, and she goes on:

> "You mean we might draw a circle on the ground – and write things in queer letters in it – and stand inside it – and recite charms and spells?"
>
> "Well," said Eustace after he had thought hard for a bit, "I believe that was the sort of thing I was thinking about, though I never did it. But now that it comes to the point, I've an idea that all those circles and things are rather rot. I don't think he'd like them. It would look as if we thought we could make him do things. But really, we can only ask him."
> (15)

Aslan, then, cannot be coerced, and Jill's childish notion of magic is incompatible with him and unwelcome to him. Narnian 'magic', it seems, is different, like Galadriel's, and perhaps needs another name. There is a more coercive, and in several ways more 'scientific' notion of magic in *The Magician's Nephew*, where Uncle Andrew is a magician of sorts. He carries out experiments; he even uses guinea-pigs, both real and metaphorical (Digory and Polly); and he creates rings to travel between the worlds. There is something unscientific, though, in the hints he gives in chapter 2 about how he has learned magic:

> I had to get to know some – well, some devilish queer people, and go through some very disagreeable experiences. That was what turned my head grey. One doesn't become a magician for nothing. My health broke down in the end. (25)

As with Merlin, the practice of magic is bad for the practitioner. Perhaps, indeed, what he has been doing should be called *goeteia*, 'witchcraft', for when the children bring the Queen Jadis back to England with them in chapter 6, she looks at him and recognizes a kind of similarity to herself, "I see [...] you are a Magician – of a sort [...] a little, peddling Magician who works by rules and books. There is no real Magic in your blood and heart" (69-70). Jadis, however, released into Narnia, will become the White Witch of *The Lion, the Witch and the Wardrobe*. She will feel in Narnia "a Magic different from hers and stronger" (95, ch. 8). Narnian magic, then, is different from Jill's conception in being beyond human control; different also from Uncle Andrew's rule-bound quasi-science; and different again from the witchcraft of Jadis. In *The Lion, the Witch and the Wardrobe* the White Witch calls for the sacrifice of Edmund by appealing to "the Deep Magic" of "the Emperor-over-Sea" (128, ch. 13). But there is "a deeper magic still which she did not know [...] when a willing victim who had committed no treachery was killed in a traitor's stead, the Table would crack and Death itself would start working backwards" (148, ch. 15). It is this which brings about the resurrection of Aslan, clearly parallel to the Resurrection of Christ. This 'deeper magic', Narnian magic, is in essence religion. Lewis preserves what is in effect the Frazerian triangle, though (like Tolkien's hobbits) he allows the same word to be used of what we might call 'white' and 'black' magic – he avoids these terms – or alternatively *magia* and *goeteia*.

Goeteia is a rare and unusual word: so unusual, indeed, that as late as 1989 the *Oxford English Dictionary* still had no listing in that form, offering only 'goety', which is given as "Obs[olete] exc[ept] arch[aic]," and defining the word as "Witchcraft or magic performed by the invocation and employment of evil spirits, necromancy." There is furthermore no trace in the citations of Lewis's opposition of *goeteia* and *magia*. According to J. Sanford's 1569 translation of Agrippa, "The partes of ceremoniall Magicke be Goecie, and Theurgie," a distinction repeated several times between 1652 and 1834. One writer in 1681 indeed accepts that there are thought to be two types of magic, distinguished "so as to condemn indeed the grosser, which they called Magic, or Goety."[10] One may wonder why Lewis used such a rare word, and imposed a new definition on it.

Possibly the answer is, that he learned word and concept from Charles Williams, whose influence on the other Inklings may in this area have been underestimated. The story of Williams and Lewis's first acquaintance is well-known. Lewis read Williams's novel *The Place of the Lion* at almost the same moment in 1936 as Williams was reading the proofs of Lewis's first major academic book *The Allegory of Love*, as part of his duties with Oxford University Press. Each man was deeply impressed, and Williams wrote Lewis a 'fan letter', which arrived while Williams was still very much on Lewis's mind.[11] The coincidence was the start of a friendship which lasted till Williams's death nine years later. It is also not too much to say that Williams 'kick-started' Lewis's career as a novelist. John Rateliff (2000) has pointed out how unpromising the situation must have seemed for both Lewis and Tolkien early in 1936, both men rather under-published academically for their age and seniority, and neither having made anything of their intended careers as poets. At this point

---

[10] *OED*, op. cit., VI: 648.

[11] See Wilson (1990:148-50).

Williams perhaps showed Lewis two things. He showed that it was possible to write a novel with an underpinning of learned neo-Platonism *in the form of popular fiction*, indeed as a 'thriller'. And he showed that it might be possible to revive what Lewis would later call "the Discarded Image," i.e. the late Classical / early medieval view of the universe, even in competition with the "new (scientific) learning" of the twentieth century, and indeed to put it in the form of science fiction. It is this which we see happening in chapter 5 of Lewis's first novel, *Out of the Silent Planet* (1938) – the start of which is strikingly similar to the start of *The Place of the Lion* – when Ransom, in the spaceship into which he has been 'shanghaied', finds himself not in the cold dead dark "outer space" of his and the modern imagination, but in the radiant, vibrant, living cosmos of the medieval imagination. Furthermore, if coincidentally, Williams's example fitted unexpectedly well with what Lewis and Tolkien had already agreed between themselves, namely that each should write a work which would demonstrate "the reality of myth."

It is tempting to say, especially in view of Lewis's second novel *Perelandra* and his second major academic work *A Preface to Paradise Lost*, both published in 1942, that what both Tolkien and Lewis were in effect doing was repeating the *finesse* of Milton in *Paradise Lost* (book 10:669 ff.), where Milton, describing the consequences of the Fall, carefully offers two alternative explanations of the phenomena of the changing seasons, one based on the old geocentric astronomy, the other on the new heliocentric astronomy:

> Some say He bid His angels turn askance
> The poles of earth twice ten degrees and more
> From the sun's axle [...]

In very much the same way Tolkien was to offer a mythical geography in his repeated attempts to tell the story of "the Lost Straight Road," while conceding that in real geography this no longer existed. His argument that the Road was no longer straight but 'bent', *wraithas* in Tolkien's reconstructed Early

Germanic phrase,[12] contributed both the idea of the 'wraiths' to Middle-earth and almost certainly the idea of the 'bent' eldil to Lewis.

Lewis was to use the word "wraith" as well, very strikingly in *That Hideous Strength*, but it is a Williams word too. He uses it at the end of chapter 6 of *War in Heaven* (1930), "The wraith of the child drifted into the midst of the dance" (Williams 1963:76), and again in a similar context near the end of chapter 17 (Williams 1963:244). *All Hallows' Eve* (1945) has it at the end of chapter 2, "He felt [...] more like a wraith than a man" (Williams 2003:48). In this area it is not at all clear which of the Inklings had an idea first, or how ideas were shared and jointly developed, as they evidently were, but Williams's 1930 usages predate all the others. It may also have been Williams who contributed both the word and the idea of *goeteia*. He actually uses the word – as said above, an extremely rare one – in chapter 9 of *All Hallows' Eve* once more, where the dead girl Evelyn tries to direct the course of the deformed body in which her spirit has been imprisoned: "It went as if against a high wind, for it was going with the sun and against all the customs of Goetia. Had it been a living witch of that low kind, it would have resisted more strongly [...]" (Williams 2003:221). Goeteia furthermore, however one spells it or defines it, forms the core of Williams's entire sequence of seven "occult thrillers," *War in Heaven* (1930), *Many Dimensions* (1931), *The Place of the Lion* (1931), *Shadows of Ecstasy* (1931), *The Greater Trumps* (1932), *Descent into Hell* (1937), and *All Hallows' Eve* (1945). Recurrent features in this sequence are:

- the idea of a sacred object being used, or wanted to be used, for magic: the Stone of Suleiman in *Many Dimensions*, the Holy Grail in *War in Heaven*, the ancient tarot cards in *The Greater Trumps*

---

[12] See *Lost Road* 43. Christopher Tolkien (*Lost Road* 8-9) shows that 'The Lost Road' itself seems to have arisen out of discussions with Lewis no earlier than 1936. Tolkien's concept of a hidden world no longer normally accessible dates back a further twenty years or more, but the word *wraithas*, 'bent', is new to 'The Lost Road'. Possibly the Williams/Tolkien uses are coincidental, though not the Tolkien/Lewis ones: but the Inklings might well have remarked and discussed the coincidence.

- the modern scholar-anthropologist who uses his learning to become a black magician: Sir Giles Tumulty in both the two first above
- the goetic operation described in detail: the creation of a succubus in *Descent into Hell*, the creation of the dwarf-shape in which two wandering souls are imprisoned in *All Hallows' Eve*
- the figure of a powerful magus, searching for the secret of eternal youth: Considine in *Shadows of Ecstasy*, Simon the Clerk in *All Hallows' Eve* again.

Consistent in the Williams meta-plot is the figure of the magician, or would-be magician, searching only for personal power, and opposed not by other magicians but by a coalition of ordinary people strengthened by religious devotion, and backed at decisive moments by the intervention of Providential figures like Prester John, "John the Priest," in *War in Heaven*. A crucial weakness for the magicians is their conviction that there is *only* magic; there is no such thing as religion; religion is indeed just another word for magic (as argued by some of the figures in the twentieth-century scholarly debate). Simon the Clerk, in *All Hallows' Eve* is thus well aware of the Christian myth, of the Incarnation, Passion, and Resurrection, but sees them all as only the account of a failed experiment, which he means to repeat successfully:

> Once, as he had learned the tale, the attempt at domination had been made and failed. The sorcerer who attempted it had also been a Jew, a descendant of the house of David, who clothed in angelic brilliance had compelled a woman of the same house to utter the name, and something more than mortal had been born. But in the end the operation had failed. Of the end of the sorcerer himself there were no records; Joseph ben David had vanished. The living thing that had been born of his feminine counterpart had perished miserably. It had been two thousand years before anyone had dared to risk the attempt again. (end of chapter 3)

As Simon has "learned the tale," Christianity is just a garbled and mistaken response to *magia*, or *goeteia*.[13] Frazer's triangle of forces is reduced to a polarity, science and magic, both coercive, both in human hands alone.

Neither Lewis nor Williams, of course, endorsed this view in any way at all, and the whole point of Williams's novels is to prove it an error. But what it expressed was, perhaps, an Inkling fear: very briefly, that as in the modern world religion might be downgraded to magic, so magic might be fused with science – or rather, to repeat a distinction Lewis himself made more than once, with 'scientism', science's popularized and degraded offshoot.[14] That is what is happening in *That Hideous Strength*. NICE, the new and threatening power which aims to take over first England and then the world, presents itself as entirely modern and scientific, exploiting just the kind of rhetoric which we have been accustomed to hearing from politicians, and which was even commoner in the immediate post-War years than it is now. The Director of the Institute, figurehead though he is, is clearly a comic caricature of the later H.G. Wells, spokesman for progress and atheism, vulgar, pompous, ill-educated, but irredeemably confident that his tiny outfit of opinions and half-digested misinformation is adequate for the greatest purposes. Behind Jukes/Wells, however, stand the figures of the Deputy Director Wither – a 'wraith' himself, and another 'sere'-man or Saruman – and his colleague with the symbolic name Frost; with behind them in their turn the real 'Head', the

---

[13] In chapters 8 and 9 of *All Hallows' Eve* we hear more of Simon's views of the Resurrection and the Ascension. Williams also mentions early legends of Merlin, perhaps in this case drawing on Lewis's specialised knowledge: in chapter 8 again, "as in some tales Merlin had by the same Rite [baptism] issued from the womb in which he had been mysteriously conceived, so this child of magic [Betty] had been after birth saved from magic by a mystery beyond magic." For these citations, see Williams (2003:177, 208).

[14] See Lewis 1967, in particular pages 76-78. Lewis makes the very fair points that he had purposely included a scientist of real standing in *That Hideous Strength*, who is one of the first victims of NICE; while the dupes and villains, Wither and Studdock included, are philosophers or 'soft scientists'. He adds that he had previously made his position quite clear in the last few pages of *The Abolition of Man* (1944). See note 15 for the Haldane – Lewis dialogue more generally.

guillotined head of the murderer Alcazan, kept alive by science, but acting as a conduit for diabolic powers called down by magic.

To Lewis, that was the threat in the twentieth century, as in the sixteenth: both eras very obviously marked by 'new learning', and both, in Lewis's view, similarly threatened by 'new ignorance'. What connected them was a dream of power. In the minds of Pico, or Ficino, or Agrippa, Lewis says in *Sixteenth Century*, the dream was one of re-creating human nature, re-establishing the connection of the human soul with the angels themselves, "the highest orders of created beings," and in this way recovering the soul's "original dominion over the whole created universe." In fact, they thought – and here Lewis is in a way paraphrasing the belief of Simon the Clerk quoted above – "such recoveries have occurred. Pythagoras and Apollonius of Tyana are cited as examples" in Ficino's *Theologia Platonica* XIII. iv (13). Lewis calls such beliefs at once "megalomania" and "anthropolatry" (12), but as said above notes that "the new *magia*" "falls into its place among the other dreams of power which then haunted the European mind," most obviously, "beside the thought of [Francis] Bacon." Magic and Baconian experimental science are very much contrasted in the minds of twentieth-century thinkers, but that is because, says Lewis, "we know that science succeeded and magic failed. That event was then still uncertain" (13). Lewis concludes his account of sixteenth-century magic by saying that what the magicians and the scientists shared was "something negative. Both have abandoned an earlier doctrine of Man," which offered humanity both a guarantee, and a limit (14). The new limitlessness offered human beings the prospect of unlimited power over the natural world, but at the same time the threat of meaninglessness, insignificance in a universe not centred on humans and not built to their scale.

That, surely, is the threat which Lewis saw arising once again in the twentieth century. This time the threat came only from science, or rather, to repeat the distinction made above, from 'scientism'. He saw the terrible threat of limitless ambition in J.B.S. Haldane's essay 'Last Judgement', paraphrased and parodied in Weston's speech to the eldil of Malacandra in *Out of the Silent*

Planet, chapter 20.[15] He repeats the threat in Filostrato's strange ambition, expressed in *That Hideous Strength* (chapter 8/III), to destroy Nature entirely and shave the planet bald, so that there shall be nothing on it but the works of humanity. And one may add that another element in the 'scientism' of Haldane and of Filostrato is the conviction – openly Marxist in Haldane's case – that 'scientism' must not only be scientific, but also be centrally planned by institutions of the state: in the twenty-first century we can be quite sure that that will not work. Connected with the 'scientist' ambition, though, is the haunting fear that nothing makes sense, that human life is merely a vanishingly thin skin over a vast eternal chaos into which all of us must fall. Weston again expresses this – unless it is the Un-man speaking – near the end of *Perelandra*, in chapter 13, as he begs his enemy Ransom not to leave him.

Both the ambition and the fear stem from the new Godless universe imagined by astronomers, biologists, geologists, physicists. In their fiction the Inklings saw new science fused with or taken over by old *goeteia*, in NICE, in Simon the Clerk, in a more metaphorical way in Saruman: two of Frazer's three forces joining together to defeat and eradicate the third. In *Sixteenth Century* Lewis put forward his argument that both forces had originated at the same time and with similar motives. Everyone was aware of the 'New Learning', for they could see its effects in the world around them. He thought they needed to be just as aware of the 'New Ignorance', for its effects, psychological rather than physical, were just as present in the contemporary world.

A final and positive image of magic appears in the figure of Coriakin the magician in chapters 9 to 11 of *The Voyage of the Dawn Treader* (1952). He is even one step beyond the planetary eldils of the 'space fiction' trilogy, for we learn in chapter 14 that he is a dethroned star. Nevertheless he is always called "the magician," and he has one of the traditional features of that role, the great

---

[15] 'Last Judgement' is printed in Haldane's collection *Possible Worlds and Other Essays* (1927). Haldane responded to Lewis's trilogy of novels with an equally derisive review, 'Auld Hornie, FRS' (Haldane 1946). This was replied to in its turn by Lewis in 'A Reply to Professor Haldane' (Lewis 1967) cited above.

Book of spells from which Lucy reads. He is also a servant of Aslan, and on familiar terms with him. Aslan indeed asks him, speaking of the "Dufflepuds," the extraordinarily stupid monopod dwarfs entrusted to his care, "Do you grow weary [...] of ruling such foolish subjects as I have given you here?" Coriakin says (with here a deliberate echo of Shakespeare's Prospero, see *Tempest* V.i.50) he is not weary but "a little impatient, waiting for the day when they can be governed by wisdom instead of this rough magic" (chapter 11, 138). Even benevolent Narnian *magia* is here presented as only a stage, something short of direct access to wisdom, to Aslan, and implicitly to religion. One might then sum up Lewis's attitude to magic with another diagram, a square rather than the Frazerian triangle offered above. This would go:

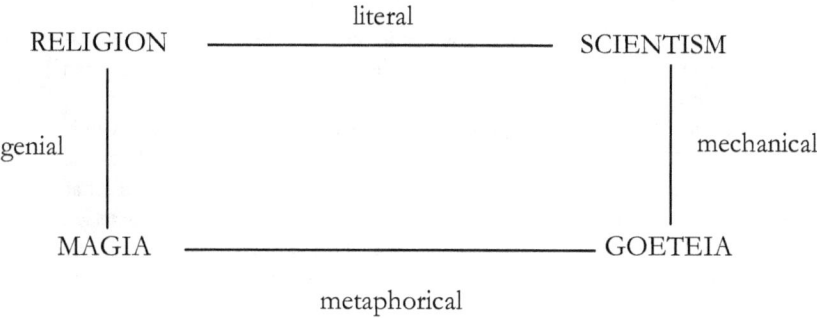

The diagram does not make a perfect fit with everything Lewis wrote, but as I have suggested above there is not a perfect fit between Lewis's fictional and his academic writings. I am inclined to think that he overstressed the difference between medieval magic and magic as described by Campanella or Paracelsus in order to make a tactical point about the real nature of the Renaissance: his fictional Merlin, at any rate, is a Campanellan. Nevertheless, the diagram does, I believe, indicate three things, which are: (1) the shared Inkling fear of a Godless science falling into the hands of men obsessed with power (which is exactly what was happening in their lifetimes, with the dictators

Hitler and Stalin); (2) the idea of magic, both good and bad, as a metaphor, in the form of narrative romance, for real-life experience; (3) and most of all, Lewis's strong and consistent preference for 'the discarded image', the cosmology of late antiquity and the Middle Ages, the universe "tingling with anthropomorphic life," crowded with spirits good, bad and neutral, animating the trees and the rivers and the beasts and the many species of *longaevi*. He may or may not have been able to *believe* in this as sober reality, but he regretted its replacement – and could, after all, claim that while it had been abandoned, it had not necessarily been disproved.

Biographical Note

As an undergraduate, Tom Shippey attended C.S. Lewis's last lectures at Cambridge. Since then he has taught at six British and American universities, and currently holds the Walter J. Ong Chair at Saint Louis University. He has published widely on Old and Middle English and related languages, edited several volumes of fantasy, science fiction, and SF criticism, and has written three books on Tolkien, most recently *Roots and Branches: Selected Papers on Tolkien* (Walking Tree Publishers, 2007). His continuing interest in Tolkien's professional predecessors appears most recently in his edited collection *The Shadow-walkers: Jacob Grimm's mythology of the monstrous* (MRTS, 2005).

Bibliography

Abbreviations:

Letters: see Carpenter 1981
Lost Road: see Tolkien 1987
LotR: see Tolkien 2001

Carpenter, Humphrey (ed., with the assistance of Christopher Tolkien), 1981, *The Letters of J.R.R. Tolkien*, London: George Allen & Unwin.
Frazer, James George, 1935, *The Magic Art and the Evolution of Kings*, (vols. 1-2 of *The Golden Bough: A Study in Magic and Religion*, 3rd edition, 12 vols.), New York: Macmillan.
Haldane, John, 1927, *Possible Worlds and Other Essays*, London: Chatto & Windus.
---, 1946, 'Auld Hornie, FRS', *Modern Quarterly* 1:32-40.
Hutton, Ronald, 2003, *Witches, Druids and King Arthur*, London and New York: Hambledon and London.
Lewis, Clive Staples, 1945, *That Hideous Strength*, London: Bodley Head.
---, 1954, *English Literature in the Sixteenth Century, Excluding Drama*, Oxford: Oxford University Press.
---, 1965a, *The Chronicles of Narnia*, (uniform seven-volume boxed set), Harmondsworth: Puffin Books.
---, 1965b, *Poems*, New York: Harcourt Brace & World.
---, 1967, 'A Reply to Professor Haldane', (first printed in *Of Other Worlds: Essays and Stories*, edited by Walter Hooper), New York: Harcourt Brace and World, pp. 74-85.
OED, 1989, (2nd edition, edited by J.A. Simpson and E.S.C. Weiner), Oxford: Clarendon Press.
Rateliff, John D., 'The Lost Road, The Dark Tower, and The Notion Club Papers: Tolkien and Lewis's Time Travel Triad', in Verlyn Flieger and Carl F. Hostetter (eds.), 2000, *Tolkien's Legendarium: Essays on The History of Middle-earth*, Westport, Conn. and London: Greenwood Press, pp. 199-218.
Rawson, Claude, 2006, Review of *The Cambridge History of English Literature, 1660-1780* (edited by John Richetti, Cambridge: Cambridge Universit Press, 2006), *TLS* for March 10th 2006, pp. 3-4.
Shippey, Tom, 1977, 'The Golden Bough and the Incorporation of Magic', *Foundation* 12:119-34.
---, 2004, 'Light-elves, Dark-elves, and Others: Tolkien's Elvish Problem', *Tolkien Studies* 1:1-15.
---, 2007, 'Imagined Cathedrals: Retelling Myth in the Twentieth Century', in Stephen Glosecki (ed.), 2007, *Myth in North-West Europe*, Tempe, AZ: MRTS, pp. 307-332.
Tolkien, John Ronald Reuel, 1987, *The Lost Road and Other Writings: Language and Legend before The Lord of the Rings*, (edited by Christopher Tolkien), Unwin Hyman: London.

---, 2001, *The Lord of the Rings*, (corrected one-volume edition, with 'Note on the Text' by Douglas A. Anderson; first edition 1954-55) London: HarperCollins.

William, Charles, 1963, *War in Heaven*, (reprint; first edition 1930), London: Faber and Faber.

---, 2003, *All Hallows' Eve*, (reprint; first edition 1945), Vancouver, BC: Regent College Publications.

Wilson, Andrew N., *C.S. Lewis: A Biography*, New York and London: W.W. Norton.

Words for Magic: *goetia, gûl* and *lúth*

Dieter Bachmann

Abstract

The question of 'magic' in *The Lord of the Rings* is, in Tolkien's words, "very large, and difficult." If we are to believe Galadriel, this is merely due to a terminological confusion in mortal tongues. But to Tolkien the philologist, there is no 'mere' terminology.

Finding himself conversing with the queen of the Elves at the heart of her realm, Sam is closer to elven magic than he ever dared to desire, but he is also told that he may not have had a very clear notion of the thing he desired:

> For this is what your folk would call magic, I believe; though I do not understand clearly what they mean; and they seem also to use the same word of the deceits of the Enemy. (FotR 2.7, *LotR* 381)

Here, I would like to argue, somebody – either Galadriel or Tolkien, or perhaps both – is not quite honest with the audience. It may well be Galadriel; it is hard to believe that she, with her High-Elven intelligence and linguistic competence, should "not understand clearly" the semantics of Westron. Her admission may be simply a rhetorical device[1] for the benefit of Sam, nudging him towards the realization of where his confusion lies. But perhaps Sam is not confused; after all, it becomes clear on the following pages that Galadriel is not entirely in control of the conversation, and her 'failure to understand' the association of her own arts with those of the Enemy sound hollow as soon

---

[1] Observe Tolkien's use of the same in *Letters* (428, no. 349), saying "I do not understand why you should wish to associate my name with TOLK" to express that the proposed etymology is simply without merit.

as she is forced to concede that she would be unable to prevent her transformation into a similarly terrifying despot if she were given the One Ring.

Tolkien did comment on this passage, in his draft of a letter to Naomi Mitchison in 1954 (*Letters* 199, no. 155):

> I am afraid I have been far too casual about 'magic' and especially the use of the word; though Galadriel and others show by the criticism of the 'mortal' use of the word, that the thought about it is not altogether casual.

We see that Tolkien here endorses Galadriel's position, giving his auctorial seal of approval to her implication that the problem lies really in the confusion of 'mortal' languages, while any Elf would, of course, see through this tangle effortlessly. How, then, would the question be phrased in Elvish? Turning to the 'Etymologies', we find the root ÑGOL- "wise, wisdom, be wise", yielding Quenya *nole* "lore, knowledge", but which in Sindarin, as *gûl,* "was only used for evil or perverted knowledge, necromancy, sorcery" (*Lost Road* 377; *Morgoth* 350): far from being a merely 'mortal' problem, the semantic shift dismissed by Galadriel as the confusion of mortals has taken place in Elvish itself! At best, from a 'chauvinist' Quenya point of view, it might be argued that it is an effect due to mortal *lands*, or more specifically to the evil infused into these by Melkor. Also, it must be granted that there is the root LUK- "magic, enchantment", which gives us *Lúthien* "enchantress", and which does not seem to be affected by the ambiguity of ÑGOL-: in Sindarin, Sam would have to permit the question whether he is he talking about *gûl,* or about *lúth*. Still, we cannot at this point dismiss the vexing ambiguity in the notion of 'magic' as merely due to hobbitish rusticity. Lady Galadriel, or perhaps Professor Tolkien, owes us an explanation.

Tolkien does embark on such an explanation in the draft of the letter mentioned above, involving a distinction between *magia* and *goeteia*. With so much semantic confusion in both English and Elvish, it may be useful to review the history of these two words. It is true that *magic* is derived from the

Old Persian *maguš*, the name of the Zoroastrian astrologer-priests of the Medes. Ultimately from an ethnonym Μάγος it may well be from the same root as English *might*, with an original meaning of 'powerful'. But the notability of the word is due to its further history in the Greek language: μαγικῆς τέχνης 'magical arts' became the generic term for the occult practices so *en vogue* in Hellenism and throughout the Roman period, and via Latin *ars magica* entered the European vernaculars as a matter of course. On the other hand, the less familiar γοητεία, a native Greek word, has a much more modest literary pedigree, its habitat being 'indigenous' Greek sorcery,[2] which in the Hellenistic occultist 'New Age boom' came to be seen as rather less exciting than the exotic μαγεία of Persia or Egypt. The word passes into obscurity, and re-surfaces in Renaissance magic, is taken up by the Baroque grimoire *Clavicula Salomonis*, and from there by Aleister Crowley (in 1904) in the sense of "invocation of [evil] spirits", and so came to the (partly ironic) attention of the Inklings. That this latter must have been the case is evident from the near-simultaneous appearance of this rare word in C.S. Lewis's *English Literature of the Sixteenth Century* (published in 1954) and in Tolkien's abandoned draft of a letter of September 1954.

The great Renaissance occultist Heinrich Cornelius Agrippa classifies *goetia* as 'ceremonial magic', that is, the invocation of spirits (the action of the magician's mind on other minds), while 'natural Magic' or *magia* proper is the action of the mind on matter (the 'primary world').[3] Tolkien's use is faithful to that definition, while Lewis proves the less conscientious philologist in that he borrows the *goetia* vs. *magia* dichotomy, but, as Tom Shippey points out in this volume,[4] uses it in a different sense, essentially to express 'black' vs. 'white' magic. This identification of *goetia* with the 'black arts' is a little confusing, but

---

[2] The pre-Socratic philosopher Pherecydes of Syros reportedly divided the Dactyli, the Greek 'Dwarves', into γόητες 'sorcerers' (who inflict curses) and ἀναλύοντες 'healers' (who revoke curses).

[3] *De incertitudine et vanitate scientiarum* (1526), English by James Sanford in 1569.

[4] See also Drout (2006, s.v. 'Lewis, C.S.').

it does reflect historical Renaissance opinion: 'black magic' or *nigromancy* is of course the practice of *necromancy* or communication with the spirits of the dead, which falls clearly under 'ceremonial magic'. And in Renaissance magic, this came to be rejected as blasphemous, while 'natural magic' remained well respected, and in fact in due time evolved into our natural sciences. This state of affairs is taken for granted by Tolkien.[5] He insists, however, that in his sub-creation, "both sides use both," and that the moral distinction lies in the magician's motive or purpose, not in the technical question of whether he is acting on matter or on a spirit. Neither Lewis nor Tolkien make use of *theurgia*, Agrippa's term reserved for the invocation of good spirits, the possibility of which was hotly disputed among Renaissance occultists.[6]

At this point it is important to note that Tolkien's only recorded use of the word *goetia* is in an unsent draft. He did not include the passage in the letter sent because, as he was writing it, he realized that the point he was making was not tenable: noting alongside the final paragraph as he abandoned it "but the Númenóreans used 'spells' in making swords?" he called into question his assertion that in *The Lord of the Rings*, "the use of 'magic' cannot be come by by 'lore' or spells." This is incidentally the very line of argument of those wishing to find that there is not, in fact, any magic in the *The Lord of the Rings* at all, since the 'wizards' are really angels.[7] That this does not work is immediately clear, already from the existence of magical artefacts, such as rings or daggers, which are imbued with powers independent of the person wielding them (and

---

[5] "*magia* could be, was, held good (per se), and *goeteia* bad" (*Letters* 199).

[6] For the purpose of Middle-earth the term is rendered unusable by its strong association in Neoplatonism with the One (Eru). If anyone in Arda is capable of theurgy in this sense, it is probably Mandos alone.

[7] So Wala (2007), who claims that "Magic, as we conceive of it, simply does not appear in *The Lord of the Rings*"; and even that "magical language doe not exist." A similar argument was made by Hageböck (2003), who has been answered by Kegler, Fornet-Ponse, and Kegler (2004). Both Wala and Hageböck commit the fallacy of setting up a simplistic or even idiosyncratic definition of magic, falling far behind Tolkien's 'not altogether casual' thoughts on the word, and proceed to show that their definition does not answer to 'magic' as found in *The Lord of the Rings*.

of magical doors that will be moved by nothing, not even by angelic wizards, save 'the spell of command'), and by the veritable Renaissance magic practiced in Gondor, where "withered men compounded strong elixirs, or in high cold towers asked questions of the stars," not to mention the 'Black Númenóreans' who became "enamoured of evil knowledge" (TTT 4.5, *LotR* 704). Anyone wishing to cite letter number 155 in support of an argument surrounding the nature of magic in Tolkien's work would do well to keep in mind that it does not contain an opinion voiced by Tolkien, but one he decided not to voice. With his draft, it appears, Tolkien for his purposes also rejects the terminology of *goetia* vs. *magia*, even though his conception of magic did make the distinction between manipulation of matter and the communication with other minds: it simply would not do to apply a term as sinister as *goetia* to the 'elvish' art of subcreation or enchantment so dear to him. Both Tolkien and Lewis want to make a distinction based on intention, not practice, the difference between Renaissance witchcraft or modernist technology, on the one hand, and medieval or Romanticist *faerie* or 'elf-magic' on the other.[8]

The 'Ósanwe-kenta', written a few years after the publication of *The Lord of the Rings*,[9] although not directly addressing the question of 'magic', sheds some light on Tolkien's further thoughts on these matters. Here we find the Quenya term for *goetia* or 'ceremonial magic', *ósanwe*: the direct communication between two minds or monads (*sámar*) without the aid of any material means (in effect, the 'telepathic' ability exhibited by both Galadriel and Sauron and enhanced by the *Palantíri*). The prefix *ó-* expresses mutuality, making implicit the important theological point that such communication cannot be enforced by the 'sender' but always requires the active participation of the 'receiver', and that all *sámar*, although they may be of greater or lesser power, are ultimately of

---

[8] Or between will and wonder, as Patrick Curry (Drout 2006, s.v. 'Enchantment') writes: "if the hallmark of magic is will, that of enchantment is wonder."

[9] In 1959 or 1960. The text was edited by C.F. Hostetter and published in *Vinyar Tengwar* in 1998.

the same essence. The counterpart, 'natural magic' remains unaddressed in this text, but we may assume that it would be derived from the root KUR, perhaps *kunwe* "craft".

Based on these findings, we can derive a fourfold division of different kinds of 'magic', distinguishing the artistic from the technocratic motive, and the pure communication of thought from the magic that affects the material 'primary world':

'magic'	'ceremonial magic', *goeteia* in L 155, *ósanwe*	'natural magic' *magia* in L 155, *kunwe*
will to power, utility, Lewis' *goeteia*	Agrippa's *goeteia*, "the deceits of the Enemy", Renaissance witchcraft or spiritist incantations, *gúl*	industrialisation, 'bulldozing', *magia* as "the vulgar devices of the laborious, scientific, magician"
wonder, aesthetic pleasure, 'elf-magic', Lewis' *magia*	enchantment, subcreation, *Faerie*, *lúth* (Agrippa's or Neoplatonist *theurgia*?)	artefacts like Fëanor's *Silmarilli*, Gandalf's fireworks etc.

It becomes clear that if Tolkien did not want to re-arrange the meaning of the term, as Lewis did, he would have had to subsume under the sinsister term *goeteia* the concept of enchantment or Faerie that was so central to him and his mythopoeia, and which here ostensibly figures "at the furthest pole from the vulgar devices of the laborious, scientific, magician" (OFS 114).

We also see that the domain of *lúth* in its English terminology is literally the domain of *Romance*, that is, of words derived from medieval French. Thus, Latin *incantatio* conveys the practices of Hellenistic pagan occultism, and of its Renaissance re-enactment. It is enough to give the word its French guise of *enchantement* to arrive at the term chosen by Tolkien as suitable for *lúth* or 'elf-magic'. Similarly, *Faerie* itself (retained in its Spenserian spelling to protect it from too ready association with the unrelated *fair*, which produced the Victorian *fairies*),[10] properly *fay-ery*,[11] has hardly longer any connection with the stern Roman *fates*. But taking Latin *[ars] magica* to form French *magique* and from there English *magic* gives a more ambiguous result. We do end up with a powerful term of Romance, indispensible in tales of elvish enchantment, but at the same time it is not sufficiently removed from its Latin original to be dissociated from its 'vulgar' or occultist applications, and so acts, as it were, as a witness of the transition from late classical paganism to medieval Romance, presenting difficulties or even dilemmas directly relevant to Tolkien's project of mythopoeia.

In the 'Lay of Leithan', *magic* occurs more than 40 times, hanging from boughs and lurking in gulf and glen. Compare to this a mere 18 instances in all of the *The Lord of the Rings*, none of which occurs in poetry. They are rather restricted to the discussion of 'magic rings' and Sam's notions of elf-magic, so that seven out of 18 instances are to be found in his discussion of 'magic' with Galadriel.[12] Clearly, Tolkien's use of the word in *The Lord of the Rings* is very conscious and disciplined. 'The Mirror of Galadriel' is both at the spiritual heart of the tale and the very keystone of the narrative arc. We can assume with certainty that every word in this chapter has been pondered over for years. Tolkien has not been "too casual about 'magic'," he is deliberately talking *about* being casual with the word and its dual flavour of enchantment and 'power' (the etymological meaning of Old Persian *maguš*), "an ominous and sinister word in all these tales" (*Letters* 152, no. 131). The problem is thus not simply an *homonymie fâcheuse*, as Galadriel would have us believe somewhat

---

[10] These unloved diminutive creatures are perhaps not so much due to the association with 'fair', which is often used to happy effect by Tolkien himself (e.g. in the compound 'elven-fair'), but rather by the leftover '-y' which lends itself to be taken for the diminutive suffix.

[11] See Flieger in Drout (2006, s.v. 'Faerie').

[12] Galadriel is singularly given the epithet of 'Mistress of Magic' by Faramir (5.5), who thus shows his deeper understanding of the question than Éomer, for whom she is a 'Sorceress'.

disingeniously, but one with deep roots in both language and substance. Tolkien does not pretend to solve it, as he well might have, by the introduction of elvish terminology along the lines sketched above, but rather embeds the dilemma in his tale as it is, even discussing it explicitly in Galadriel's voice, in this central scene – perhaps in this single instance even forgoing his principle that a good story must not be burdened by pedagogical asides directed at the reader.

Biographical Note

Dieter Bachmann holds a dual degree in physics and Indo-European linguistics, and is currently working on his dissertation project at the University of Zurich.

Bibliography

Abbreviations

Letters: see Carpenter 1981
Lost Road: see Tolkien 1992b.
LotR: see Tolkien 1992a.
Morgoth: see Tolkien 1994.
OFS: see Tolkien 1997.

Carpenter, Humphrey, (ed., with the assistance of Christopher Tolkien), 1981, *The Letters of J.R.R. Tolkien*, London: Unwin Hyman.
Drout, Michael C. (ed.), 2006, *J.R.R. Tolkien Encyclopedia*, New York: Routledge.
Hageböck, Michael K., 2003, 'Kunst und Technik. Anmerkungen zu Tolkiens 'Magie'-Begriff', *Inklings-Jahrbuch* 21:37-85.
Kegler, Karl R., Thomas Fornet-Ponse, and Adelheid Kegler, 2004, 'Was besagt die Untersuchung von Magie für Tolkiens Welt? Eine Entgegnung auf Michael K. Hageböck', *Inklings-Jahrbuch* 22:212-241.
Tolkien, John Ronald Reuel, 1992a, *The Lord of the Rings*, London: Grafton.
---, 1992b, *The Lost Road and Other Writings*, edited by Christopher Tolkien, first published 1987, London: HarperCollins.
---, 1994, *Morgoth's Ring*, edited by Christopher Tolkien, first published 1993, London: HarperCollins
---, 1997, 'On Fairy-Stories', in J.R.R. Tolkien, 1997, *The Monsters and the Critics and Other Essays*, edited by Christopher Tolkien, London: HarperCollins, 109-161.
---, 'Ósanwe-kenta', edited with introduction, glossary, and additional notes by Carl F. Hostetter., *Vinyar Tengwar* 39:21-34.
Wala, Marcin, 2007, 'Tolkien's Ea: A Magic-less Universe', in Justyna Deszcz-Tryhubczak and Marek Oziewicz (eds.), 2007, *Considering Fantasy. Ethical, Didactic and Therapeutic Aspects of Fantasy in Literature and Film*, Wrocław: ATUT, 191-196.

When is a Fairy Story a Faërie Story?
Smith of Wootton Major

Verlyn Flieger

Abstract

Fairy-stories, Tolkien maintained, are not about fairies, but about Faërie, "the realm or state in which fairies have their being." In his essay 'On Fairy-Stories' he maintained that "Most good 'fairy-stories' are about the *aventures* of men in the Perilous Realm." His last short story, *Smith of Wootton Major*, exemplifies what in the essay Tolkien meant by *Faërie*, the essay by explaining, the story by depicting, so that that the story becomes the practical application of the criteria in the essay – the appropriate subject matter, the proper quality, and the threefold face that fairy-stories show their readers. *Smith of Wootton Major* is thus a Faërie story in Tolkien's purest sense of that word.

It is a safe bet that when in 1939 J.R.R. Tolkien gave his Andrew Lang lecture 'On Fairy-Stories', with its extended discussion of what does (and does not) constitute a fairy story, he did not have *Smith of Wootton Major* in mind, since that story was not conceived until the mid-1960s. The reverse of that bet, however, seems equally safe, that when he wrote *Smith of Wootton Major* he very probably *did* have 'On Fairy-Stories' in his mind. For the two work together. Both *Smith of Wootton Major* and 'On Fairy-Stories', each in its own way, exemplify what Tolkien meant by the word *Faërie*, the essay by explaining it, the story by depicting it, with the result that the story becomes the practical application of the criteria set up in the essay. Among these criteria are the appropriate subject matter for fairy-stories, their proper quality, and the threefold attitude or "face" that fairy-stories show their readers. We will come back to these criteria in greater detail at a later point in the discussion.

But first, a word or two about the story. Of all Tolkien's works large and small, *Smith of Wootton Major* has perhaps received the least critical attention from both scholars and the public at large. In part, this is the story's – or Tolkien's – own fault. On its surface, the tale is misleadingly slight, causing many readers and reviewers either to dismiss it as trivial without examining it closely, or to take it at face value as a fairy tale – again, without examining it closely. Those who do look for deeper import have tended to allegorize its simplicities, to look for a message rather than a meaning in this story of a mortal man's visits to fairyland and what he finds there. While such visits and their opposite expression, the visits of fairies to the mortal world, are the standard stuff of fairy tales, *Smith* is more than just a fairy tale in the popular sense of that term. It is a *faërie* tale, that is, in Tolkien's own words, "a tale about *Faërie*: the Perilous Realm itself, and the air that blows in that country" (OFS 114).

The poetic vagueness of a phrase like "the air that blows in that country" is the first clue to Tolkien's purpose in writing the story, for this was less to create a conventional narrative than to capture, like a butterfly in a net, the atmosphere, the essential nature of the Perilous Realm more traditionally known as Fairyland. Hence the story's lack of plot, and the absence of a "happy ending" in the accepted fairy-story sense. The hero Smith climbs no beanstalk, fights no giant, slays no dragon. He does not bring home a golden goose or magic harp. He finds no hapless maiden to rescue from the clutches of a witch, nor any sleeping maiden to awaken with a kiss. He does not marry the princess. This deliberate omission of the usual fairy tale motifs is one of *Smith of Wootton Major*'s distinguishing characteristics.

Without such standard fairy tale machinery, the story's action is simple – its detractors would say simplistic. The background situation sets up the story. Looking for trinkets to bake as party favors into the cake at a children's feast, the Master Cook of the village of Wootton Major finds a tarnished silver star in the bottom of the spice box. He is told by his apprentice Alf (in reality the King of Faery) that the star is "fay."[1] Though the unimaginative Cook has no notion what that means, he nevertheless puts the star into the cake batter along with all the other small prizes. A young boy at the party swallows the star without noticing, and it lies hidden, "tucked away in some place where it could not be felt," until his tenth birthday, when it reappears to be put on his forehead. Few in the village can see the star, but all notice the sudden beauty of his voice and the unexpected grace and style of the utilitarian things he makes, for the boy becomes a blacksmith like his father before him.

With the fay-star as his entrée, Smith begins his journeys into Faery. This is the heart and purpose of the story, a highly compressed account (fifteen pages out of a total of fifty-five) of his wanderings in fairyland, the wonders he experiences there, the dangers he encounters and the mysteries he witnesses but does not fully understand. His last visit includes a summons from the Queen of Faery, who gives him a message for the King, "*The time has come. Let him choose*" (*SWM* 38). The "time" is the time for Smith to relinquish the star, but with the special permission that he may choose to whom it should go next. He does so choose, and then, in bereavement and acceptance of his loss, returns to his family and ordinary life, "back to hammer and tongs" (*SWM* 52).

But where exactly has he been? The simple answer is Faery, of course, but what that word means, both to Smith and to Tolkien, takes some probing, for the narrative's gossamer surface at once conceals and reveals one of the most important words and concepts in Tolkien's lexicon – that is, Faërie, the Otherworld of fairy tales and fantasy. The glancing and allusive description

---

[1] Tolkien's choice of the word *fay*, rather than *magic*, to characterize the star is deliberate. The word is derived from Old French *faie*, "one with magical powers," itself derived from Latin *fàtà*, plural *of fàtum*, "fate." Although early in the essay he states that, "Faërie itself may perhaps be most nearly translated by Magic," he goes on to say that this is "magic of a peculiar mood and power, at the furthest pole from the vulgar devices of the laborious, scientific magician" (OFS 114). His spelling of *Faërie* shows through its etymology that Tolkien intended the word to carry a far older and darker meaning than that conventionally carried by the word *magic*, with its connotations of spells and cabalistic signs on the one hand, and sleight-of-hand and illusion on the other.

cited above, that Faërie is a "Perilous Realm," a country with a special "air" or atmosphere, shows only the tip of a particularly Tolkienian iceberg. Throughout his writing life (and that was a long one) *Faërie* was for Tolkien a word and an idea that embraced many meanings. It was at once a literary construct, an imaginal exercise, a make believe world, a place to go to, and an altered state of being – a series of ideas easier to picture than to explain, very like his spelling of the word.[2]

His precedent was medieval. The word appears in Gower's *Confessio Amantis* (c. 1450), Chaucer's 'Wyfe of Bath's Tale' (late 14th century), *Sir Orfeo* (c. 1350), and *Sir Gawain and the Green Knight* (c. 1400), the latter two of which Tolkien edited and translated. In these, the word is used to refer variously to fairyland, and to an atmosphere of magic or enchantment: "the air that blows in that country." When the Wife of Bath asserts that in the days of King Arthur "Al was this land fulfild of fayerye" (ll. 857-60) she means the land was filled full of magic and enchantment, both as practice and as atmosphere. When Gower, in an example later cited by Tolkien, describes a young man "as he were of Faierie," he means as if he came from or belonged to Faierie, a specific place, if only an imaginary one.

A note in Tolkien's edition of *Sir Gawain and the Green Knight* calls the Green Chapel "nothing else than a fairy mound" (*SGGK* 86). It seems clear that Tolkien carried these interlinked meanings – the practice of magic, the place where magic is practiced, and the quality of magic that imbues that place – into his own discussion of the term in 'On Fairy-Stories'. Some twenty-five years later, with the essay as his standard, he deployed all these meanings in *Smith of Wootton Major*.

---

[2] To the continuing confusion of readers and critics alike, Tolkien's orthographic practice, while remaining fundamentally true to sound and sense, varied perceptibly, going from *Faërie* (in the essay) to *Fayery* or *Fayerye* (in the story's rough drafts) to *Faery* (in the final published version). It is worth noting, however, that he seldom, other than a few special or conventional instances, used the spelling *Fairy* except in a derogatory sense. I will stick to Tolkien's practice by following whatever spelling is used in the work referred to, thus *Faërie* when referring to the essay, and *Faery* when referring to the story.

The story began as Tolkien's effort to correct what he saw as a serious misapprehension of the word *fairy* on the part of George MacDonald, for whose story *The Golden Key* he had been asked to write an introduction. Finding MacDonald's story not to his taste, Tolkien attempted to correct the sugary Victorian idea of fairies and fairyland as "little" and "pretty." Searching for a way to explain (once again) the difference between the popular or Disney concept of fairies as gossamer winged creatures living in daffodils, and his own much older, sterner notion of Faërie, he gave as negative example a cook who "thought of making a cake for a children's party. His chief notion was that it must be very sweet [...]" (*SWM* 75).

And with the cake, now containing the fay-star, we are back to the conjunction of practice and theory, the intersection of *Smith of Wootton Major* with 'On Fairy-Stories'. To show how patently the story is the essay's exemplar, let us look at the criteria Tolkien established in the essay. First there is subject matter. Fairy-stories, Tolkien maintained, are not about fairies, but about Faërie, "the realm or state in which fairies have their being." This realm, he insisted, contains many things besides the supernatural creatures that are the usual trappings of fairy tales, the giants, dragons, fays and dwarfs. It also holds the visible, "real" world as we know it: "the seas, the sun, the moon, the sky; and the earth, and all things that are in it: tree and bird, water and stone, wine and bread, and ourselves, mortal men, when we are enchanted" (OFS 113).

The significant terms here are *Faërie* and *enchanted*, characterizing both the quality of the magical otherworld and the change it effects in the humans who interact with it. For it is the last-mentioned item in Tolkien's list, "ourselves, mortal men, when we are enchanted" who comprise the center of any good fairy tale, who supply the one essential human ingredient. "Most good 'fairy-stories'" declares Tolkien, "are about the *aventures* of men in the Perilous Realm." This is explicitly the case with *Smith of Wootton Major*. The story's central character, the Smith whose craft is also his name, is the enchanted mortal man, the reader's guide into the Perilous Realm. Smith himself, however, has no guide, nor indeed any stated reason for going. He has no goal, no quest, no pot of gold or giant's daughter to win. Unlike the hero of a typical *echtra*, a Celtic Otherworld journey, he follows no beckoning supernatural figure; nor like some does he stumble into Faërie by accident. He goes there with intent but no purpose, content simply to wander and experience and marvel. He can and does go where he will, his passport the fay-star that came to him in his slice of cake.

The function of the star is limited, however. It will conduct, but not explain. Smith can explore, but is never given any clue to the marvels and mysteries he encounters. He is a tourist without a guidebook. True for the hero of the story, this is equally true for the reader, who wandering through Faery with Smith, experiences but has no way to understand the wonders there seen. The story depicts, but does not elucidate. In accord with its Faery setting, the tale enacts mysteries but declines to solve them. In this regard, *Smith of Wootton Major* stands as Tolkien's severest, most uncompromising, least accessible piece of fiction, stubbornly refusing like his Faery itself to give the reader any key with which to unlock its secrets. And that is precisely the point. The land of Faery is what it is, no more and no less. It is entire and other and self-sufficient, and has no need to explain itself to any outsider. In the essay (his second on the subject) that Tolkien wrote to accompany his story, he noted that "Faery is a vast world in its own right, that does not depend for its existence upon Men, and which is not primarily nor indeed principally concerned with Men" (*SWM* 93).

How does this fit with the second criterion, the necessary quality of the story? Tolkien is explicit that fairy-stories must create a Secondary World inside of which all that occurs must have both "a quality of strangeness and wonder," and "the inner consistency of reality" such that however marvelous the sights or events, they can command "Secondary Belief," and the reader can accept them as credible (OFS 139, 138). Yet Tolkien has gone to some lengths to create a world whose chief quality seems to be its incomprehensibility to outsiders. "Anyone," Tolkien declares, "can say *the green sun*" but "to make a Secondary World inside which the green sun will be credible, commanding

Secondary Belief, will [...] demand a special skill, a kind of elvish craft" (OFS 140). The story's uncompromising refusal to explain its wonders seems in direct opposition to this, for without a credible explanation for those wonders, just what is their "inner consistency"? How can we as readers believe them? Why should we? Just how skilled was Tolkien at the "kind of elvish craft"? What is his green sun?

I suggest that the green sun in *Smith of Wootton Major* is the fay-star which conveys Smith, and with him the reader, on the journeys into the story's Faery. If readers accept the star, they will accept as well the rules governing the Perilous Realm to which it gives access. The mystery of the star is validated first by the word of the Apprentice, a mysterious figure who knows something about the star that the Master Cook does not know, and second by the patronizing skepticism of the Master Cook, who is clearly incapable of understanding anything beyond the ordinary and precious little even of that. Readerly sympathy is aroused for the one, and contemptuous dislike for the other. When the star reappears on Smith's forehead, it is perceived by only a few, chiefly Smith's own family, but also by the reader, who is thereby enlisted as one of the perceptive few and one of the chosen.

Having a star as the magic talisman was a wise choice. It was also Tolkien's second choice, as the various drafts of the story make clear. His first candidate for the magic trinket was a ring which the boy would then wear on his finger. It did not take long for Tolkien to realize that this particular image carried too much baggage. It would inevitably be associated with the Ruling Ring of his great work *The Lord of the Rings* and thereby carry all that token's negative associations of evil and power and dominance. The switch from ring to star was not, however, a mere substitution; it changed subtly the direction and quality of the magic, for the very word *star* carries connotations of *unearthly, inhuman, unattainable*, all of which carry over from the star itself to the Faery world it represents.

Last of all Tolkien's criteria, and most complex in execution, is the attitude of the story, first internally toward the events and characters within it, and second externally toward the reader for whom it must "command Secondary Belief." For just as the reader looks at, enters into the story, so the story looks at, and both challenges and engages the reader. Fairy-stories, Tolkien wrote, have three faces: "the Mystical towards the Supernatural; the Magical towards Nature; and the Mirror of scorn and pity towards Man" (OFS 125). Has *Smith of Wootton Major* these three faces? Where and how are they manifest?

Undoubtedly the story has a mystical face towards the supernatural, and the fay star conveys its expression. If we accept the dictionary definition of *mystical* as "suggesting the existence of realities beyond intellectual apprehension" it is certainly possible to see exactly this in Tolkien's depiction of the supernatural elements in his story. Although we have seen how Tolkien persuades his readers to accept the presence and power of the star, the reality that lies behind it, and the reason for its existence are nowhere explained.

Having swallowed it at the party, the boy Smith does not notice what has become of it, waiting patiently inside him until its day will come. On his tenth birthday the boy wakes early and hears the dawn-song of birds beginning far away, coming towards him, rushing over him and passing on "like a wave of music into the West." He begins to sing "high and clear, in strange words that he seemed to know by heart" (*SWM* 20), and in that moment the star falls out of his mouth. Catching it, he claps his hand to his forehead, and there the star stays "for many years." The light of the star passes into his eyes, and his voice, "which had begun to grow beautiful as the star came to him, became ever more beautiful as he grew up" (*SWM* 20).

Possession of the star admits Smith to Faery, but we are not told how; nor are we shown the passage from one reality to the other, contiguous though they seem. The star also protects him, though again we are not told how, and only obliquely from what. "The Lesser Evils avoided the star, and from the Greater Evils he was guarded" (*SWM* 24). The capital letters underscore but do not explain the dangers inherent in Tolkien's Perilous

Realm, and suggest a complex and unfathomable range of powers against which the star is Smith's defense.

Of the Magical face toward nature, there are a number of examples, perhaps the most awe-inspiring being Tolkien's description of the Sea of Windless Storm with its silent waves rolling endlessly out of Unlight. Surely the most benign is the flower placed in Smith's hair by the elven maiden (actually the Queen of Faery), who dances with him. "The flower did not wither or grow dim," says the story, and Smith makes a casket in which to keep it and it is handed down in his family, a magical Living Flower, for many generations. Most impressive is the King's Tree, springing up out of a hill of shadow "tower upon tower" into the sky with a light in it like the sun at noon, with leaves and flowers and fruit growing simultaneously on its boughs. The Tree has at once a magical nature and a natural magic that derives from its very being as a tree, albeit a superlative one.

And finally and perhaps most importantly, there is the Mirror of scorn and pity toward Man. This face has a more complex expression than the other two, for scorn and pity, while at first glance they seem to be separate emotions, are not always that easy to distinguish from one another. Certainly the story displays scorn toward Nokes the Master Cook, whose own patronizing (not quite pitying) scorn for his Apprentice Alf ("elf") betokens his inability to see beyond the mundane. The original of Nokes is, of course, the cook in Tolkien's introduction to *The Golden Key*, whose notion of a very sweet cake as most suitable for children is the measure of his ignorance of the deeper implications of Faery. Nokes unwittingly disobeys one of the strictest rules in Tolkien's essay, thereby invoking it against himself. "There is one proviso: if there is any satire present in the tale, one thing must not be made fun of, the magic itself. That must in that story be taken seriously, neither laughed at nor explained away" (OFS 114). Nokes is Tolkien's negative example. He makes fun of the star and belittles its magic, thus turning the satire against himself and inadvertently making him the butt of his own joke.

Moreover, on two separate occasions, in the village scenes that bracket Smith's journeys into Faery, Alf himself shows both scorn and pity for Nokes. There is scorn in his speakingly silent response to Noke's smirks and heavy-handed jokes on the subject of *fairy* at the party, and at the end of the story he is first over-polite in listening patiently to Noke's musings on what became of the star, and then scathing in his rebuke: "You are a vain old fraud, fat, idle and sly" (*SWM* 59). Alf's final revelation of himself as the King of Faery leaves Nokes cowed and cringing. There is pity in his final gift to the old man, who has joked that if one of Alf's "fairy friends [...] waves his little wand and makes me thin again, I'll think better of him" (*SWM* 58). The gift is even then one that Nokes cannot understand and so talks himself out of accepting it with gratitude, reasoning that, "[i]f you stop eating you grow thinner. That's natural. Stands to reason. There ain't no magic in it" (*SWM* 60).

But there is a darker, bleaker face shining in the mirror of scorn and pity, this time on Smith himself. The most complex and perplexing episode in *Smith of Wootton Major* – Smith's venture onto the Lake of Tears,[3] its consequences, and the subsequent conversation between Smith and the birch tree – reveals as nothing else in the story Smith's ignorance of the deeper implications of the perilous realm of Faery, what Tolkien's essay calls its "pitfalls for the unwary and dungeons for the overbold." And both unwary and overbold Smith certainly is when he sets his foot on the lake and is unexpectedly and violently attacked for his trespass. He is "filled with wonder" at the shapes of flame and the fiery creatures he sees in the lake's "immeasurable depth," and tries the water with his foot, only to find that it is "harder than stone and sleeker than glass" (*SWM* 29).

Emboldened – overboldened – Smith steps onto the surface and promptly falls, and with a sound like winter ice cracking with cold the lake itself gives a ringing boom that wakes the Wild Wind. Swept ashore and driven up the slopes by the Wind, Smith clings to a birch tree that, bent double by the

---

[3] So named only in the drafts of the story, but not in the published text, where it is called simply "a lake."

force of the Wind, encloses him in its branches. When the Wind passes on, Smith sees that the birch is naked to the elements, its boughs having been stripped of their leaves by the blast. The birch weeps, its tears falling "like rain" from its branches. Both grateful for his rescue and contrite at the tree's sacrifice, Smith commends the birch. The scene and its attendant dialogue, among the least sentimental in the entire Tolkien corpus, reveal – as much to the reader as to Smith – ignorance of and unimportance to the larger operations of Faery that is the lot of "ourselves, mortal men, when we are enchanted."

> He set his hand upon its white bark, saying: 'Blessed be the birch! What can I do to make amends or give thanks?' He felt the answer of the tree pass up from his hand: 'Nothing', it said. 'Go away! The Wind is hunting you. You do not belong here. Go away and never return!' (*SWM* 30)

Speaking, it seems clear, for Tolkien, the tree does not explain to Smith what he has done wrong, only tells him the bitter truth – that he does not belong in Faery. He has been a visitor and is now a trespasser. The scorn and pity directed at Smith in this episode are those of Faery itself, which needs no visitors and encourages no trespassers. Though Smith disobeys the birch tree's injunction against returning, and does in fact visit Faery again, it is with the knowledge that he is there on sufferance, and that his passport may be revoked. This, of course is exactly what happens, and makes the story's and Tolkien's final and major point.

Much critical speculation has been expended on the possible autobiographical elements in the story, for the temptation, if one knows anything at all about Tolkien's life and work, is to see the author in the protagonist. If Tolkien's earlier short story *Leaf by Niggle* chronicles the struggles of the artistic temperament with the demands of daily life, *Smith of Wootton Major* can be read as dramatizing the relationship of the artist with the world of imagination, the ongoing engagement of the creator with the act of creation. In this regard, the story has been called Tolkien's farewell to his art, his Prospero speech. He himself called it "an old man's story, filled with the presage of bereavement," and it is not difficult to identify the bereavement that Smith feels on giving up the star with what may have been Tolkien's heartache toward the end of his life that his best years were spent, his best work was behind him. Humphrey Carpenter suggests that the "appalling depths of gloom" into which Tolkien sank from time to time toward the end of his life, coupled with his "growing grief at the approach of old age," led him to write *Smith of Wootton Major* (*Biography* 242).

This is an easy and obvious connection to make, and without doubt a valid one. I do not challenge it. Nevertheless, an equally significant autobiographical element may reside in Tolkien's first-hand account of what it is like to wander in Faery (read 'the realm of imagination') and his deliberate refusal to unlock for Smith or the reader the mysteries of the Perilous Realm. Describing himself in 'On Fairy-Stories' as "hardly more than a wandering explorer (or trespasser) in the land, full of wonder but not of information," he had gone on to say that although,

> [i]n that realm a man may, perhaps, count himself fortunate to have wandered, but its very richness and strangeness tie the tongue of a traveler who would report them. And while he is there it is dangerous for him to ask too many questions, lest the gates be shut and the keys be lost.
> (OFS 109)

Wandering explorer. Trespasser. Shut gates. Lost keys. These words and phrases capture as much for Tolkien as for Smith the Faery of *Smith of Wootton Major*. The figure of the Smith as maker, as craftsman, wandering in the enchanted world of Faery, apprehending marvels but not comprehending them, most certainly embodies for himself as well as his author the tongue-tied traveler who would report them, as Tolkien had tried to do. Smith exemplifies for his creator the instinct without understanding that is the lot of the artist, who can use imagination and even to some degree direct it, but who cannot analyze it or explain its workings. For, as Tolkien said of *Beowulf*, "myth is alive at once and in all its parts, and dies before it can be dissected" (MC 15). Like Smith, Tolkien knew well enough that his art was a gift and not a purchase, that it could be polished by skill but never replaced by it. He knew that like the fay-star it came in its own time, unsought and unforced, and that it could not be bought or traded or commanded, but only accepted with gratitude for its presence and used with reverence for its power.

Smith of Wootton Major is thus a Faërie story in Tolkien's purest sense of that word. It is "a tale about *Faërie*, the Perilous Realm itself, and the air that blows in that country."

Biographical Note

Verlyn Flieger is a professor in the Department of English at the University of Maryland, where she teaches courses in Comparative Mythology and the works of J.R.R. Tolkien. Her books on Tolkien include *Splintered Light: Logos and Language in Tolkien's World*, re-published in 2002 in a revised and expanded edition, *A Question of Time: Tolkien's Road to Faërie*, given the 1998 Mythopoeic Award for Inklings Scholarship, and *Interrupted Music: Tolkien and the Making of a Mythology*. With Carl Hostetter she is editor of the critical anthology, *Tolkien's Legendarum: Essays on The History of Middle-earth*, which won the 2000 Mythopoeic Award for Inklings Scholarship. Her fantasy novel. *Pig Tale*, was published by Hyperion in 2002. Visit her web sites at http://www.mythus.com/.

Bibliography

Abbreviations:

Biography: see Carpenter 1977
MC: '*Beowulf*: The Monsters and the Critics' in Tolkien (1983:5-48)
OFS: 'On Fairy-Stories' in Tolkien (1983:109-161)
SGGK: see Tolkien and Gordon 1925
SWM: see Tolkien 2005

Carpenter, Humphrey, 1977, *J.R.R. Tolkien: A Biography*. London: George Allen & Unwin.
Chaucer, Geoffrey, 1987, *The Canterbury Tales*, (in *The Riverside Chaucer*, edited by Larry D. Benson), Boston: Houghton Mifflin.
Tolkien, John Ronald Reuel, 1975, *Sir Gawain and the Green Knight, Pearl, and Sir Orfeo*, (translated by J.R.R. Tolkien), Boston: Houghton Mifflin.
---, 1983, *The Monsters and the Critics and Other Essays*, (edited by Christopher Tolkien), London: George Allen & Unwin.
---, 2005, *Smith of Wootton Major*, (extended version; edited by Verlyn Flieger), London: HarperCollins.
--- and Eric Valentine Gordon (eds.), 1925, *Sir Gawain and the Green Knight*, Oxford: At the Clarendon Press.

Myth, Fact and Incarnation

Colin Duriez

> Poetry I take to be the continual effort to bring language back to the actual.
> Letter to R. Bodle in 1949
> (Lewis 2004:947)

> I [...] had incautiously said, 'Of course I realise it's all rather too vague for you to put into words,' when he took me up rather sharply, for such a patient man, by saying, 'On the contrary, it is words that are vague. The reason why the thing can't be expressed is that it's too *definite* for language.'
> C.S. Lewis, *Perelandra*, 1943

Abstract

C. S. Lewis's attempts to capture the real in literature and thought is explored, mainly through how he sees the imagination as the organ of meaning. He has a poetic sensibility that expresses itself best in mythopoeia, the making of myth. For him great stories and myth have, like poetry, the ability to capture universals and qualities in the particular, and as such appeal to an ideal human consciousness that, though lost, we all remember. In fact such stories, he felt, can give us sensations never before experienced; effectively, giving us changes in consciousness. This ability to explore the cosmic and universal through the concrete, he believed, can also be found in historical narrative; that is, through actual rather than fictional events. The epitome of such a marriage of myth and fact is, for Lewis, the Word made flesh – the incarnation of God himself as a human being in the first century. That incarnation, for Lewis, is like the moments when stories and other products of the imagination hold together "the general with the concrete" (Coleridge). The views of Tolkien, Charles Williams and Owen Barfield shed light on Lewis's quest, especially when seen in the wider context of Romanticism, especially Coleridge and George MacDonald. Reference is made, in particular, to Barfield's *Poetic Diction*, Tolkien's 'On Fairy Stories', Lewis's *Miracles*, and especially relevant essays of Lewis's including 'Myth and Fact', and 'Transposition'.

The quest for the concrete, definite thing or the real as opposed to the abstraction is one of the central themes of C.S. Lewis's life and writings. As we know from the Narnian stories, Lewis was capable of expressing profound ideas in a way that a child could grasp. In 1956 Lewis wrote memorably of the importance and elusiveness of the definite thing to a child, Joan Lancaster, when encouraging her writing skills:

> You describe your Wonderful Night v. well. That is, you describe the place & the people and the night and the feeling of it all, very well – but not the *thing* itself – the setting but not the jewel. And no wonder! Wordsworth often does just the same. His *Prelude* (you're bound to read it about ten years' hence. Don't try it now, or you'll only spoil it for later reading) is full of moments in which everything except the *thing* itself is described. If you become a writer you'll be trying to describe the *thing* all your life: and lucky if, out of dozens of books, one or two sentences, just for a moment, come near to getting it across. (Lewis 1988:456)

Not only did Lewis find the thing elusive to capture in writing, but also elusive when we think about it in order to capture it in a theory:

> Human intellect is incurably abstract. Pure mathematics is the type of successful thought. Yet the only realities we experience are concrete – this pain, this pleasure, this dog, this man. While we are loving the man, bearing the pain, enjoying the pleasure, we are not intellectually apprehending Pleasure, Pain or Personality. When we begin to do so, on the other hand, the concrete realities sink to the level of mere instances or examples: we are no longer dealing with them, but with that which they exemplify. This is our dilemma – either to taste and not to know or to know and not to taste – or, more strictly, to lack one kind of knowledge because we are in an experience or to lack another kind because we are outside it. As thinkers we are cut off from

> what we think about; as tasting, touching, willing, loving, hating, we do not clearly understand. The more lucidly we think, the more we are cut off: the more deeply we enter into reality, the less we can think. You cannot study Pleasure in the moment of the nuptial embrace, nor repentance while repenting, nor analyse the nature of humour while roaring with laughter. But when else can you really know these things? 'If only my toothache would stop, I could write another chapter about Pain.' But once it stops, what do I know about pain?
> (Lewis 2000a:140)

Lewis is pointing out that there is more than one kind of truthful knowledge, and that theoretical thought excludes knowledge by experience – existential knowledge.

As he struggled with this dilemma over many years, Lewis found the key to its solution in a necessary contrast between reason and imagination. In experiential knowledge, he came to believe, the imagination plays as important a role as the intellect in theoretical knowledge. In the literary arts, Lewis found the imagination most profoundly at work in the creation of myth:

> Of this tragic dilemma [the divorce of the abstract and the tangible] myth is the partial solution. In the enjoyment of a great myth we come nearest to experiencing as a concrete what can otherwise be understood only as an abstraction. At this moment, for example, I am trying to understand something very abstract indeed – the fading, vanishing of tasted reality as we try to grasp it with the discursive reason. Probably I have made heavy weather of it. But if I remind you, instead, of Orpheus and Eurydice, how he was suffered to lead her by the hand but, when he turned round to look at her, she disappeared, what was merely a principle becomes imaginable. (Lewis 2000a:140-141)

The work of the imagination, Lewis implies, is larger than its role in the visual or literary or other arts, or in the sciences, and it is the imagination, more than any other of our mental faculties, that is most successful in perceiving and capturing the thing. This is because the imagination, in his words, is the organ of meaning not of truth. The thing captured by the imagination is an object of thought, like any real thing, rather than an abstract truth. It belongs to the world of experience, sensation, and contingency and yet embodies general qualities of meaning by the very nature of imaginative perception, just as a theoretical truth embodies a methodological reduction by the nature of abstract reasoning. Lewis and his friends thought it folly to confuse a theoretical truth with a real thing. As Lewis argued: "Truth is always *about* something, but reality is that *about which* truth is." (Lewis 2000a:141)

The role of the imagination in truth-seeking and knowledge-gaining was much discussed by Lewis and his close friends, such as Owen Barfield and J.R.R. Tolkien. There were many differences as well as affinities between them, as they discussed a theme whose pedigree belongs to the Romantic Movement, in poets and thinkers such as Wordsworth and Coleridge, with as its background the issue of what is called the Enlightenment project and the positivist's claim that the natural sciences and rationalism are the only models for truth and knowledge.

In this chapter I will concentrate mainly on Lewis's developed views of imagination, myth, and incarnation as a quest to capture and understand the thing and the real, while acknowledging that his thinking was shaped in the context of his friends and literary forbears. According to Owen Barfield – and I think he was right – the imagination was the integrating factor in Lewis's thought and writings, even when he was arguing with great power philosophically.

To give a taste of the issues involved, we have Owen Barfield's own picture of what he saw as limitations in Lewis's makeup:

> He had a pretty sharp line between his intellectual self and imaginative self; he accepted the conventionally scientific basis of knowledge and that all real knowledge depended on scientific evidence drawn from sense experience. Lewis would not admit that the kind of experience that came through imagination had anything to do with knowledge of reality; it just enabled you to have more reality to talk about as experience or subject matter. But when it came to converting that imaginative subject matter into actual knowledge you had to go back to the ordinary scientific method, to put it on the laboratory table, so to speak.
> (Barfield 1989:135)

This picture, we shall see, is a little over-simplistic. Lewis in fact made it clear in a number of his writings at different periods that there were, in his view, different kinds of truthful knowledge, as when we recognize for example that a beautiful waterfall is sublime – an example given in his philosophical essay, *The Abolition of Man*.[1]

---

[1] There is not space in this chapter to discuss the question of the development of Lewis's thought. Barfield regards Lewis as static in his thinking. However there is development and seeming contradiction (a mark of development) in Lewis's various reflections on imagination (see Schakel 1984, chapter XIV). This is because, I think, Lewis is reaching towards multiform knowledge (and imagination's place in it) and acknowledges the richness of knowledge even when he characterizes the imagination as a vehicle of meaning, not of truth, a position he held consistently. For Lewis, that is, truthfulness is greater than theoretical truth; e.g. he speaks of the objectivity of qualities like the sublime in his philosophical essay, *The Abolition of Man*. As a faculty, imagination, and aesthetic perception related to it, is meant to conform to an objective state of affairs, just as proper moral judgement does. It does not seek the precision of abstract truth, even though he acknowledged a 'rightness' or 'truth' or goodness to imagination ('Blusphels and Flalanaferes', in Lewis 1969:265).

Art and Life, Imagination and Truth
In *An Experiment in Criticism* Lewis (1961:74) wrote:

> We have to consider a fault in reading which cuts across our distinction between the literary and the unliterary [person]. [...] Essentially, it involves a confusion between life and art, even a failure to allow for the existence of art at all. [...] On a higher level it appears as the belief that all good books are good primarily because they give us knowledge, teach us 'truths' about 'life'. Dramatists and novelists are praised as if they were doing, essentially, what used to be expected of theologians and philosophers, and the qualities which belong to their works as inventions and as designs are neglected. They are reverenced as teachers and insufficiently appreciated as artists.

This attitude, according to Lewis, lacks a view of the goodness proper to literature.

At the heart of the concern of Lewis and his friends such as Tolkien and Barfield with the making of imaginative literature is their view of the interrelated nature of language and literature. They held that elements of fantasy, fiction and poetry are embedded, by necessity, in all human language and thinking. Furthermore, wherever they are found, these elements must operate according to strict inherent laws, if they are not to impair the quality of thought and language.

Lewis himself distinguished reason and imagination, and truth and meaning. The poetic elements of language, for instance, are used in a different way in the process of theoretical thinking than they are within the world of a fictional literary work. A concern Lewis had in common with his friends was an attempt to embody the qualitative, or the abstract, in literary form while retaining the freshness and integrity of these extra-literary qualities. Tolkien for instance embodied the perilous journey and the quest in his *The Lord of the Rings*. Lewis made the quality of joy or *sehnsucht* incarnate in his fictions, particularly *The Pilgrim's Regress, Till We Have Faces* and *The Chronicles of Narnia*. Such universal, archetypal or symbolic elements in a successful narrative are rooted in the concrete and particular nature of the story or account. At times, a principle that appears contradictory and paradoxical as an abstraction (such as the relation of divine providence to free human agency) can work satisfactorily, organically and integrally in a narrative. In this, there was for Lewis and the Inklings a fascinating parallel with history (the most successful marriage of the general and the particular, they believed, being the incarnation of Christ – myth become fact, as Lewis put it). Charles Williams saw myth as a narrative "that has acquired significance beyond its own immediacy – that is, a myth is a story functioning as an image" (Shideler 1962:45). In the light of this view he observed: "In a sense, of course, history is itself a myth; to the imaginative, engaged in considering these things, all is equally myth. We may issue from it into other judgements – doctrinal, moral, historic. But so doing we enter into another kind of thought and judge by other tests – more important perhaps, but not the same. In the myth we need ask for nothing but interior consistence. [...]" (Charles Williams, 'The Figure of Arthur,' quoted in Shideler 1962:80). William's reference to 'interior consistence' is parallel to Tolkien's concept of 'inner consistency' in subcreation, the making of secondary worlds (which for him included invented history). Perhaps Williams had in mind the fact that history is made by human beings (and of course by the hand of God), and is not the result of impersonal forces. This is why myth could become fact.

The ability of myth, narrative and human history to capture the general in the particular is addressed, I think, by a principle outlined by Charles Williams. This was his principle of the 'exclusive-inclusive' thing, most fully realized in God's bi-polar relation to the created world and its objects, in Williams's frequent saying, "This also is Thou; neither is this Thou." By the paradoxical phrase, 'inclusive-exclusive' Williams tried to convey a two-way movement that is important to the life of an abstraction or quality embedded or incarnate in a literary work. A thing, by remaining itself, becomes more potently identifiable with something else. It is more truly a metaphor. This contrasts with allegory, as understood and explored by Tolkien and Lewis. In allegory, a symbol tends merely to be about something else and is not of a great deal of interest in itself. It is quite literal. In a more deeply imaginative, less discursive, making of literary meaning, the particular can be itself vividly and can also embody, point to, and even participate in a higher reality; that is, it can even become one with a quality that cannot be received fully and satisfactorily in any other way. Lewis tried to work out this principle, expressed by Williams as exclusivity-inclusivity, in his sermon, 'Transposition,' as we shall see. The difference between an abstraction of thought and the kind of reality Williams had in mind might be put like this. The word 'tree' and even a very detailed and thorough botanic and scientific description – a literal description – of a tree does not capture the reality and meaning of a tree in the way that an actual tree does. Even a particular tree, when it is perceived concretely by a human being in ordinary experience, embodies more of the general and universal nature of trees than the name and the scientific description. Furthermore, a poetic account or a painting of a tree has the potential to capture more of its reality and actuality than an abstract, quantitative description. The qualitative and quantitative descriptions differ rather as a map of an area does to the actual area, even though a map might be both beautiful and indispensable.

Terms like 'qualities' and concrete 'meaning' – and related terms like 'abstract' and 'literal' – are notoriously elusive, but there does seem to be a pattern to Lewis's concerns with the capture of qualities or generalizations in literature. Even as an undergraduate at Oxford he was preoccupied with such a capture. In a paper on narrative poetry given to a student group, The Martlets, on 3 November, 1928, he quoted from Spenser to show (according to the minutes of that meeting) "to what advantage a great artist could use external surroundings as a background to develop a mood" (Lewis 1969:viii). On another occasion he spoke of *The Faerie Queene* to a discussion class, and Nevill Coghill recorded in the minute book:

> Grandeur and thunder, magic and the bliss
> Of Heavenly Music, and the inner shine
> Of γάνος, [*ganos*] or the gleaming of divine
> Moist, quiet woodland things; all these he found
> Distilled old myths and thoughts into new wine,
> But not new thoughts [...] (Lewis 1969:xi)

Coghill (in Gibb 1965:52) years later commented: "I went home wondering what there was in γάνος which could not be expressed by 'sheen'. I looked it up and found *'Brightness, sheen, gladness, joy, pride'*."

There are numerous other examples of Lewis's concern with qualities and abstractions, and their capture in imaginative literature, in his writings through the years. In his essay on Shakespeare's *Hamlet*, he isolated the *state of being dead* as an overriding quality embodied in the play. He remarked: "It is this which gives to the whole play its quality of darkness and of misgiving. [...] The world of *Hamlet* is a world where one has lost one's way." In another paper, on Sir Walter Scott, he spoke of the "sweetness and light" of Scott's mind, and remarked that it was he who taught us feeling for a period (Lewis 1969:209). In an essay on William Morris, he discussed a balance and yet tension between two moods in his writings; a "positive and violent passion for immortality" and a "feeling [...] that the world of mortality is more than enough for our allegiance" (Lewis 1969:224-26). Finally (many more examples could be cited) I give a favourite of mine: Lewis isolated 'undeception' (the process of becoming undeceived) as the pivot or watershed of four of Jane Austen's novels: "In *Northanger Abbey*, and *Emma*, it precipitates the happy ending. In *Sense and Sensibility* it renders it possible. In *Pride and Prejudice* it initiates that revaluation of Darcy, both in Elizabeth's mind and in our minds, which is completed by the visit to Pemberley." (Lewis 1969:178)

Imagination
In Lewis imagination is an integrating concept, affecting his thought and fiction, as it was for his friend Tolkien. Barfield described him as being in love with the imagination (Barfield 1989:137). The same integration is true of the

nineteenth-century author, George MacDonald, whose ideas on the imagination anticipated those of Lewis and Tolkien. Laying the foundation for many of their ideas was the romantic poet and thinker Samuel Taylor Coleridge (1772-1834). Owen Barfield fairly late on in the development of his thinking, recognized his own very deep affinity with Coleridge.

Central to S. T. Coleridge's radical view of the imagination was the importance of metaphor, and "the perception of similitude in dissimilitude."

The mind, believed Coleridge, is active in making sense of the world. The mind imposes itself on reality, having a central role in knowledge, shaping and adapting it.[2] The poet is the epitome of this process, using a "synthetic and magical power" which Coleridge calls imagination. He was reacting against a growing domination of scientific rationalism, driven by the Enlightenment, which reckoned both the human mind and imagination was passive in knowledge, finding truth as it submitted to material causes. "[Coleridge's] face," Barfield wrote, "was turned [...] in the opposite direction to the one which natural science was taking in his time and, in spite of his efforts and those of a few others like him, has continued to take since his death. For it was his firm conviction that, if knowledge was to advance, there must be a science of qualities as well as quantities." (*Encyclopedia Barfieldiana*, accessed 8 June 2006)

For Coleridge the imagination is 'esemplastic', unifying and shaping. He sets out its pattern, sharply revealed in poetry. Notice his observation that the imagination unites the general and the concrete, an idea that was so central to Lewis, and also the various polarities that are reconciled.

> This power, first put into action by the will and understanding, and retained under their irremissive, though gentle and unnoticed control [...], reveals itself in the balance or reconcilement of opposite or discordant qualities: of sameness, with difference; of the general with the concrete; the idea with the

---

[2] The German philosopher Immanuel Kant (1724-1804) had deeply influenced the intellectual world that Coleridge inhabited, setting the problem of how the mind was active in knowledge rather than passive in it.

> image; the individual with the representative; the sense of novelty and freshness with old and familiar objects; a more than usual state of emotion with more than usual order; judgement ever awake and steady self-possession with enthusiasm and feeling profound or vehement; and while it blends and harmonizes the natural and the artificial, still subordinates art to nature; the manner to the matter; and our admiration of the poet to our sympathy with the poetry. (Coleridge 1949, chapter XIV)

As Tolkien did in his seminal essay 'On Fairy-Stories,' Coleridge tries to distinguish a primary and secondary imagination in his *Biographia Literaria*.

> The Imagination then I consider either as primary, or secondary. The primary Imagination I hold to be the living power and prime agent of all human perception, and as a repetition in the finite mind of the eternal act of creation in the infinite I AM. The secondary Imagination I consider as an echo of the former, co-existing with the conscious will, yet still as identical with the primary in the *kind* of its agency, and differing only in *degree*, and in the *mode* of its operation. It dissolves, diffuses, dissipates, in order to recreate: or where this process is rendered impossible, yet still at all events it struggles to idealize and to unify. It is essentially *vital*, even as all objects (*as* objects) are essentially fixed and dead. (Coleridge 1949, chapter XIII)

The primary imagination is concerned with, and operates in, the primary world. The secondary imagination, employing language and metaphor, reworks and reshapes this primary world. It is notable that Tolkien, thinking on rather similar lines to Coleridge, saw the most exalted function of imagination as sub-creation in linguistic form, creating, if successful, a secondary world.

Coleridge captures the significance of imagination in his poem, *The Rime of the Ancient Mariner*. Killing the albatross alienates the Mariner from God; it closes him in the natural man, the passive state of the ungodly. He consequently sees without feeling:

> The very deep did rot: O Christ!
> That ever this should be!
> Yea, slimy things did crawl with legs
> Upon the slimy sea.

Later, he begins to see with feeling, that is, with imagination, and is able to wonder and then to pray. This change redeems him from the curse upon him. This is how he consequently sees the ocean deep and its creatures:

> Beyond the shadow of the ship,
> I watched the water-snakes:
> They moved in tracks of shining white,
> And when they reared, the elfish light
> Fell off in hoary flakes.
>
> Within the shadow of the ship
> I watched their rich attire:
> Blue, glossy green, and velvet black,
> They coiled and swam; and every track
> Was a flash of golden fire.
>
> O happy living things! No tongue
> Their beauty might declare:
> A spring of love gushed from my heart,
> And I blessed them unaware:
> Sure my kind saint took pity on me,
> And I blessed them unaware.
>
> The selfsame moment I could pray;
> And from my neck so free
> The Albatross fell off, and sank
> Like lead into the sea.

He begins to live a full human life again. Coleridge's seeing-with-feeling is perception that participates in the world that is perceived by way of the human imaginative faculty.

George MacDonald also explored the concept of the imagination in great depths, particularly in his essays, 'The Imagination: Its Functions and Its Culture' (1867) and 'The Fantastic Imagination' (1882) (both in MacDonald 1893). Like Coleridge he locates the image of God in human beings as imagination – as participation in God's creativity which brought the worlds into being. This participation is found in the sciences as well as the arts. In striking contrast, the traditional attribute of the image of God in human beings was reason, not imagination, which by MacDonald's time was perceived widely to be mechanistic rather than organic in operation. His views in these essays remarkably foreshadow those of Tolkien and Lewis, and are worked out creatively in his fantasies.

Like Coleridge, MacDonald sees the foundation for understanding imagination in the relationship between God and his creation. Though he does not use the word, MacDonald sees the product of human imagination as a kind of 'sub-creation'. "The imagination of man," he (MacDonald 1893b, chapter I) writes, "is made in the image of the imagination of God. Everything of man must have been of God first." MacDonald sees the human imagination as living and moving and having its being in the imagination of God.

It follows that the human being is not creative in a primary sense. "Indeed, a man is rather being *thought* than thinking, when a new thought arises in his mind [...] He did not create it." (MacDonald 1893b, chapter I) Even the forms by which a person reveals his thoughts are not created by him in a primary sense; they belong to nature.

MacDonald had a scientific training, and is remarkably modern in pointing out the importance of imagination in science. He (MacDonald 1893b, chapter I) also, like Lewis, Barfield and Tolkien later, and of course Coleridge earlier, valued metaphor highly: "All words [...], belonging to the inner world of the mind, are of the imagination, are originally poetic." He (MacDonald 1893b, chapter I) claims that in both the arts and sciences, imagination is central to knowledge: "We dare to claim for the true, childlike, humble imagination, such an inward oneness with the laws of the universe that it possesses in itself an insight into the very nature of things."

A central function of the imagination (an idea developed by Lewis) is the making of meaning, adding, as it were, to the real world. This making is strictly subordinate to the primary meanings put into his created reality by God. However, in "the new arrangement of thought and figure [...] the new meaning contained is presented as it never was before." He (MacDonald 1893b, chapter I) writes:

> Every new embodiment of a known truth must be a new and wider revelation. No man is capable of seeing for himself the whole of any truth: he needs it echoed back to him from every soul in the universe; and still its centre is hid in the Father of Lights.

He sees the operation of the imagination as choosing, gathering, and vitally combining the material of a new revelation.[3]

> Such embodiments are not the result of the man's intention, or of the operation of his conscious nature. His feeling is that they are given to him; that from the vast unknown, where time and space are not, they suddenly appear in luminous writing upon the wall of his consciousness.
> (MacDonald 1893b, chapter I)

That there is always more to a work of art than the producer himself perceived while producing it, seemed to MacDonald (1893b, chapter I) a strong reason for "attributing to it a larger origin than the man alone – for saying at the last, that the inspiration of the Almighty shaped its ends."

---

[3] In theological terms, what MacDonald means by revelation is *general revelation* (insights into God that are found in the worlds of nature and humanity) rather than *special revelation* (specific verbal communication from God written down in holy Scripture).

MacDonald's view of the imagination is squarely based on the view that all meanings are put into reality by their primary creator, God. All meaning refers to him, and thus is objective rather than subjective. He expresses this view eloquently in the following passage, anticipating Lewis in particular:

> One difference between God's work and man's is, that, while God's work cannot mean more than he meant, man's must mean more than he meant. For in everything that God has made, there is layer upon layer of ascending significance; also he expresses the same thought in higher and higher kinds of that thought: it is God's things, his embodied thoughts, which alone a man has to use, modified and adapted to his own purposes, for the expression of his thoughts; therefore he cannot help his words and figures falling into such combinations in the mind of another as he had himself not foreseen, so many are the thoughts allied to every other thought, so many are the relations involved in every figure, so many the facts hinted in every symbol. A man may well himself discover truth in what he wrote; for he was dealing all the time with things that came from thoughts beyond his own.
> (MacDonald 1893c, chapter XIV)

MacDonald dwells upon the importance of meaning. The question of meaning (both of reality itself and of language) was central to the thought-world of the twentieth century. It is a seminal theme running throughout the writings of Lewis, who was influenced by the ideas of Tolkien, and saw MacDonald as his 'master', and had much in common with both. Tolkien and Lewis were influenced by Owen Barfield, for whom the question of meaning was a life-long preoccupation. Barfield and Lewis, indeed, engaged in what they called a long war about the imagination and meaning. After it was over Barfield concluded, many years after Lewis's death:

> The use of imagination is one thing; a theory of imagination is another. A theory of imagination must concern itself, whether positively or negatively, with its relation to truth. Is it, for instance, or can it be, a vehicle of revelation? [...] Is it objective or subjective? That is certainly not a question to which it can be said that Lewis never addressed his mind. Indeed, he and I had a special, and rather protracted, tussle over it, when we were both young. It *is* a question in which he lost interest at the time of his conversion, or perhaps a little before it. If he no longer denied, as he had done at the time of the tussle, that imagination had a positive relation to truth, he was disinclined to give any attention to it. (Barfield 1989:97)

The 'Great War' with Barfield

The 'Great War' began in 1922 between Lewis and Barfield, his closest friend in this period, then a fellow Oxford undergraduate. The 'war' was, for Barfield, "an intense interchange of philosophical opinions" and, for Lewis, "an almost incessant disputation, sometimes by letter and sometimes face to face, which lasted for years." The dialogue ensued soon after Barfield's acceptance of anthroposophism, a 'spiritual science' based on a synthesis of eastern and Christian thought and developed by Rudolf Steiner (1861-1925). It trailed off by the time of Lewis's conversion to Christian faith in 1931. The dispute centred on the nature of the imagination and the status of poetic insights. It cured Lewis of his 'chronological snobbery,' making him hostile to the modern period, and provided a rich background of sharpened thought for Barfield's important study, *Poetic Diction* (1928). In this Barfield argued that there is a poetic element in all meaningful language. He was refuting the increasingly popular view that scientific discourse was the only means of true knowledge.

The 'war' with Barfield also convinced Lewis that his materialism, if true, in fact made knowledge impossible! It was self-refuting. Barfield jokingly said to his friend after their 'war' was over that while Lewis had taught him *how* to think, he had taught Lewis *what* to think.

Barfield believed that there has been an evolution of human consciousness, in which the imagination has played an integral role. This development of consciousness is reflected precisely in historical changes in language and perception. There was originally a unity of consciousness, now fragmented. Barfield believed, however, that in the future humans would achieve a greater and richer consciousness, in which spirit and nature will be reconciled. The polarity that now exists, and has existed in various forms throughout history, has the seeds of its ultimate and enriched unity.

At the end of the 'war', the differences between the two friends were clear:

- Lewis didn't accept an evolution of consciousness, only significant historical changes in human consciousness (a major one of which is portrayed in his *The Discarded Image*).
- Lewis didn't accept that the imagination could be the organ of truth, but believed rather that it was the organ of meaning (involving contact with reality and real things, even supernatural things). This however did involve truthful knowledge of things.

There was however a significant and substantial agreement:

- Lewis conceded to Barfield that imagination is a necessary condition for the framing of truths in language – without imagination, human knowledge would not be possible. There is a metaphorical element in all our framing of truths.

Just as it was for MacDonald and Coleridge, for Lewis meaning (to use a term not employed by Coleridge) was intimately tied up both with the role of the imagination, and with the fact that the entire universe is a dependent creation of God. Lewis saw reason as the organ of truth, and imagination as the organ of meaning:

> It must not be supposed that I am in any sense putting forward the imagination as the organ of truth. We are not talking of truth, but of meaning: meaning which is the antecedent condition both of truth and falsehood, whose antithesis is not error but nonsense.[4] [...] For me, reason is the natural organ of truth; but imagination is the organ of meaning. Imagination, producing new metaphors or revivifying old, is not the cause of truth, but its condition. [...] All our truth, or all but a few fragments, is won by metaphor.
> ('Bluspels and Flalansferes' in Lewis 1969:265)

Reason and imagination each have their own integrity. Lewis particularly stressed the dependence of even the most abstract of thinking upon imagination. Imagination has a profound role in holding together the general and the concrete.

Lewis, like Barfield and also Tolkien, believed that in some tangible sense the products of imagination in the arts could be truthful, even though they are not abstract truths.[5] As he had with Barfield, Lewis differed however with Tolkien over the role of imagination in knowledge, though only moderately. His friendship with Tolkien was not marked by dialectical opposition, unlike his friendship with Barfield.

It was Tolkien rather than Barfield who persuaded him that myth could become fact, even though this notion, Barfield believed, was to be found in

---

[4] Thus it follows from what Lewis is saying that the nonsense writings of Edward Lear and Lewis Carroll are not erroneous (misleading us about the existence of the Quangle Wangle or the Cheshire Cat) but explorations of meaning.

[5] The kind of truthful knowledge that can be captured in literature and other arts is related to the objectivity of aesthetic responses, as expounded in Lewis's *The Abolition of Man*. If I understand Lewis correctly, such responses are rather like performances, as they involve training in being attentive (as a musician learns to listen, or an artist to see). A violinist, for instance, might practise many hours a day for a public performance to an audience which can appreciate the performance as excellent or good (or poor).

Steiner's anthroposophy.[6] Tolkien felt particularly strongly that in writing a carefully crafted fantasy like *The Lord of the Rings* or the earlier tales of Middle-earth he was discovering inevitable realities that were not the product of theories of the conscious mind (even though rational control is not relinquished in the making of good fantasy). It was this attitude to the making of meaning and myth which prompted Lewis to follow Tolkien in creating consistent secondary worlds, or sub-creations, like Malacandra, Perelandra and Narnia.

Tolkien's view of the imagination very much centres around his idea of sub-creation. This is most clearly set out in his famous essay 'On Fairy-Stories' and reveals his affinity with the ideas of Coleridge and MacDonald. There he speaks of creating secondary worlds with an 'inner consistency of reality', and of the relationship between works of imagination and truth. He also stresses the central importance of human language. It was typical of him to write rather cryptically elsewhere: "Language has both strengthened imagination and been freed by it." ('A Secret Vice', Tolkien 1983:219)

Myth and Fact

The concept of myth was integral to Lewis's understanding of the power of the imagination to embody the abstract and the concrete, the literal and the poetic. He implies that the making of myth is the greatest achievement of the imagination. Myth has the ability to make concrete what would otherwise remain abstract. In fact, without the shaping of our perception by myth, and other imaginative creations (such as metaphors and models), we would not know real things, only abstractions. There is therefore an intimate connection between myth and thought. If Lewis is right about myth, narrative and thought are profoundly linked. He believed that the separation of myth and fact arose from the fall of humanity at the beginning of history (see Kilby 1965:82). In the early days of their friendship, as part of trying to persuade him of the truth of supernaturalism and Christianity, Tolkien wrote a poem to Lewis about the

---

[6] For an account of Rudolf Steiner's view of Christianity see his *Anthroposophy and Christianity* (Steiner 1985). This publication reproduces a public lecture Steiner gave in 1914.

making of myth ('mythopoeia') in which he argued that while speech is invention about objects and ideas, myth is invention about truth, transcending but not annulling thought and transforming the objective into qualities rather than a quantities.

Myth can be defined in terms of the embodiment of a worldview of a people or culture, thus having an important believed element. Myth can also be defined as untrue, fictional, non-literal, and merely imaginative. The existence of myth writes large the dilemma that the 'lies' of the poet and the fiction writer capture profound realities, realities impossible to capture in any other way. Fiction, poetry, and metaphor, though they are 'lies', by necessity have a representational element, making contact with reality.

The dissonance between myth and reason, myth and history, and myth and knowledge, goes back to ancient times. Lewis, following Tolkien, had a tangible confidence that the polarity between myth and fact has been reconciled at a particular point in history, which reflected a more ancient confidence. For Lewis, heaven has come down to earth at a definite point in time, and our humanity has been taken up to God. He was convinced of this by Tolkien, helped by a mutual friend 'Hugo' Dyson (Henry 'Hugo' Victor Dyson Dyson, 1896-1975).

In the grounds of his College, Magdalen, Lewis had had a long conversation with Tolkien, and Dyson, in 1931 which had shaken him to the roots. Tolkien drew on the long night conversation on Addison's Walk, and many previous exchanges with Lewis, in his poem, 'Mythopoeia' (the 'making of myth'). Tolkien had argued for the Christian Gospels on the basis of the universal love of story which, for him, was sacramental. His poem 'Mythopoeia' gives us a good idea of the flow of the conversation. Tolkien wrote of the human heart not being composed of falsehood, but having nourishment of knowledge from the Wise One, and still remembering him. Though the estrangement is ancient, human beings are neither completely abandoned by God nor totally corrupted. Though we are disgraced we still retain vestiges of our mandate to rule. We continue to create according to the "law in which we're made."[7]

Lewis later wrote a powerful essay on the harmony of story and fact in the Gospels, when God became a definite human being at a particular time in history, remembering that life-changing conversation with Tolkien and Dyson: "This is the marriage of heaven and earth, perfect Myth and Perfect Fact: claiming not only our love and Obedience, but also our wonder and delight, addressed to the savage, the child, and the poet in each one of us no less than to the moralist, the scholar, and the philosopher." (Lewis 2000a:142) He realized that the claims and stories of Christ demand an imaginative as much as an intellectual response from us.[8] Tolkien in turn expounded his view more fully in his essay 'On Fairy-Stories' (Tolkien 1992). He argued that the very historical events of the Gospel narratives are shaped by God, the master story maker, having a structure of the sudden turn from catastrophe to the most satisfying of all happy endings – a structure shared with the best human stories. The Gospels, in their divine source, thus penetrate the seamless 'web' of human storytelling, clarifying and perfecting the insights that God in his grace has allowed to the human imagination. In the Gospels, Tolkien concluded, "art has been verified." The integration of myth and fact, the abstract and the concrete, is most fully expressed in the incarnation and resurrection of Christ.

Transposition, Imagination and Myth
In exploring how myth and imagination makes possible an integration of the abstract and concrete Lewis turned to the principle of hierarchy which he believed existed in both nature and supernature. In knowledge-gaining, the principle of hierarchy is the movement from concrete to abstract (lower to higher), and vice versa – for instance, we indwell our bodily facilities in order to

---

[7] Like Coleridge and MacDonald, Tolkien saw the divine image in human beings as reflected primarily in the imagination.

[8] Lewis treated the theme more fully in his book *Miracles* (first published 1947; see Lewis 1960).

perceive higher levels. In thought and the formation of truth claims, the material, causal conditions (such as those of our brains) are transcended – in thinking we actively participate in a higher level. The focus is on something beyond the material; there is intentionality when we think. Thoughts are about something other than themselves. A similar thing happens with metaphor and story. The specific, concrete matrix of the image or story allows the general and universal but is not identical with it. The universal and general is on a richer level, as it retains all that is concrete and particular in its immediate origin, but also has something more. The richer is embodied in a poorer and more humble level. The great king is also an ungrudging servant. Lewis explains all this beautifully in his essay, originally a sermon, called 'Transposition'.

This was Lewis's name for a concept he explained in one of the most important addresses he gave, published in *Transposition and other Addresses* (1949). The talk was preached originally as a sermon on Whit-Sunday (Pentecost) in Mansfield College, Oxford, 28th May, 1944. Owen Barfield believes that this was a rare disclosure of the "the movement [...] of his mind" (Barfield 1989:101) on the subject of imagination. Barfield (1989:102-103) slowly came to realize that, in his view, the essay "amounts in [...] to a theory of imagination, in which imagination is not mentioned." He adds: "Read it carefully and you will find all the proper ingredients – metamorphosis, interpenetration of meanings, interpenetration of mind and body, of spirit and soul."

Lewis's theory of transposition has affinities with the ideas of another Oxford thinker, Michael Polanyi (1891-1976, author of *Personal Knowledge*, 1958), who on at least one occasion spoke at the Oxford Socratic Club and so may have therefore become acquainted with Lewis. Transposition, says Lewis, is an "adaptation of a richer to a poorer medium." No denigration of the poorer medium is implied, only an assessment of its necessary limits. In a Christian universe, as understood by Lewis, all parts have value in themselves.

To explain the idea of transposition, Lewis begins his address considering the phenomenon of speaking in tongues at Pentecost, in first century Jerusalem. Looking from below, in a purely materialist way, one would say that the phenomenon was 'merely' or 'nothing but' an affair of the nerves and sensations, resulting in gibberish. Seen from above, however, both the fact and the meaning are clear – this event is a supernatural act of the Holy Spirit. The spiritual is transposed into physical language.

In a similar way, in our emotional life, we can reduce emotion to mere sensation if we refuse to see its meaning on a higher level. This would be a mistake, as an identical sensation can stand for a variety of emotions, as the emotions are a richer medium translating into a poorer one.

This point about the danger of reduction came home vividly to Lewis during his conversion to Christianity. In his quest for what he called 'joy', or inconsolable longing, he suddenly realized that he had made the basic mistake of identifying the quality of joy with the sensation that it aroused. When his attention focussed on the sensation, joy itself vanished, leaving only its traces (as Eurydice disappeared when Orpheus turned his head to look at her). Lewis had to focus outside of himself on the object of the joy. This dramatically changed the nature of his quest, which helped to lead him eventually to God himself. His sensations were the vehicle, not the reality, of joy.

Lewis illustrated the principle of transposition in language and music. He (Lewis 2000b:271) pointed out, "If you are to translate from a language which has a large vocabulary into a language which has a small vocabulary, then you must be allowed to use several words in more than one sense. If you are to write a language with twenty-two vowel sounds in an alphabet with only five vowel characters then you must be allowed to give each of those five characters more than one value. If you are making a piano version of a piece originally scored for an orchestra, then the same piano notes which represent flutes in one passage must also represent violins in another."

Lewis found the concept of transposition very helpful in understanding the incarnation of Christ. The insight of one of the creeds, he said, is that the incarnation worked "not by conversion of the Godhead into flesh, but by taking of the Manhood into God." The idea of humanity being veritably drawn into and participating in Deity seemed to Lewis a kind of transposition. It was like what happened, for example, "when a sensation (not in itself a pleasure) is drawn into the joy it accompanies." (Lewis 2000b:277)

The idea of transposition also helped him understand the bodily resurrection. It underpins his discussion of nature and supernature in *Miracles*. He did not conceive of the natural and spiritual, or think of the mind and the body, in a kind of Platonic hierarchy, where the natural and the bodily is less real than the spiritual and the mental. Rather, he saw the relationship as transpositional and participative, with the spiritual and natural worlds as equally parts of God's creation. In a fine passage, Lewis speculates that there may be many natures in a transpositional relationship with each other.

> There cannot, from the nature of the case, be evidence that God never created and never will create, more than one system. Each of them would be at least extra-natural in relation to all the others: and if any one of them is more concrete, more permanent, more excellent, and richer than another it will be to that other super-natural. Nor will a partial contact between any two obliterate their distinctiveness. In that way there might be Natures piled upon Natures to any height God pleased, each Supernatural to that below it and Sub-natural to that which surpassed it. But the tenor of Christian teaching is that we are actually living in a situation even more complex than that. A new Nature is being not merely made out of an old one. We live amid all the anomalies, inconveniences, hopes, and excitements of a house that is being rebuilt. Something is being pulled down and something going up in its place.
> (Lewis 1960, chapter XVI)

Michael Polanyi develops ideas rather similar to Lewis's transposition into a theory of how we know and what we know. His theory has the value of avoiding subjectivism (as in existentialist and post-modernist thinking) and objectivism (as in positivism). We grow in knowledge by participating in and being committed to what we already know, not by artificially trying to stand outside our knowledge and neutrally to observe it. It is from a particular vantage point that we see truth. If our attention becomes focussed on our vantage point, we are no longer attending to the truth. For Polanyi, the meaning of the particulars of a lower level resides in a higher level, and is lost if the direction of our attention is wrong. We could say that the higher level has been transposed into the lower level. If we take the genetic code, the meaning of biological life cannot be reduced to the physics and chemistry of that code. It would be like saying that the meaning of a tape recording of Beethoven's Fifth Symphony could be reduced to a description of the magnetic patterns on the tape.

Lewis's notion of transposition is in effect sacramental. Lewis (2000b:272) writes: "The word *symbolism* is not adequate in all cases to cover the relation between the higher medium and its transposition in a lower [...] If I had to name the relation I should call it not symbolical but sacramental." The lower medium might be transubstantiated by contact with a higher. Lewis (2000a:141) regarded the real presence involved in transposition as most like incarnation, writing, "As myth transcends thought, Incarnation transcends myth." His hierarchical theory of transposition has important consequences for theories of knowledge.

That Lewis was aware of the consequences of his view of transposition for knowledge is clear from his ideas on meaning and imagination. Like Barfield, he believed that mankind has moved away from a unitary consciousness into a divorce of subject and object. Theoretical reasoning abstracts from real things, real emotions, real events. In his theory of transposition Lewis is revealing his tangible vision of how all things – especially the natural and the supernatural – cohere. He saw this desirable unity, for example, in the Gospel narrative, dominated by incarnation and resurrection, where the quality of myth is not lost in the historical facticity of the events. There is no separation of story and history, myth and fact.

> There is [...] in the history of thought, as elsewhere, a pattern of death and rebirth. The old, richly imaginative thought which still survives in Plato has to submit to the deathlike, but indispensable, process of logical analysis: nature and spirit, matter and mind, fact and myth, the literal and metaphorical, have to be more and more sharply separated, till at last a purely mathematical universe and a purely subjective mind confront one another across an unbridgeable chasm. But from this descent, also, if thought itself is to survive, there must be re-ascent and the Christian conception provides for this. Those who attain the glorious resurrection will see the dry bones clothed again with flesh, the fact and the myth remarried, the literal and the metaphorical rushing together.
> (Lewis 1960, chapter XVI)

He sees the incarnation of the divine in the human, and the bodily resurrection of the human being, as the complete reconciliation of the abstract-concrete division, rather than Barfield's evolutionary development of consciousness.

The historical moment of the incarnation of Christ and the linked event of his resurrection – when, supremely, myth became fact, and the elusive capturing of the general and the abstract in the tangible happened – marked the vindication of the work of the imagination. This is why Tolkien (1992:66) commented, "Art has been verified." As Coleridge and MacDonald claimed, the human imagination reveals the presence of the image of God in human beings. We have eternity within our hearts (Ecclesiastes 3:11). Through the matrix of our own physical bodies, and while dependent upon our sensations, we are able to look into, and actually participate in, a world far larger than our senses.

Biographical note
Colin Duriez is a writer and editor based in Cumbria, England, who has written a number of books on C. S. Lewis, Tolkien and the Inklings, including *J. R. R. Tolkien and C. S. Lewis: The Story of Their Friendship*, *The C. S. Lewis Chronicles* and *The Inklings Handbook* (with the late David Porter). Colin has also lectured on the same in a number of countries.

Bibliography

Barfield, Owen, 1989, *Owen Barfield on C.S. Lewis*, (edited by G. B. Tennyson), Middletown, Connecticut: Wesleyan University Press.
Coleridge, Samuel Taylor, 1949, *Biographia Literaria*, London: Dent Everyman.
Encyclopedia Barfieldiana. www.owenbarfield.com/Encyclopedia_Barfieldiana/People/Coleridge.html
Gibb, Jocelyn (ed.), 1965, *Light on C.S. Lewis*, London: Geoffrey Bles.
Kilby, Clyde S., 1965, *The Christian World of C.S. Lewis*, Grand Rapids, Michigan: W. B. Eerdmans.
Lewis, Clive Staples, 1943, *The Abolition of Man: Reflections on Education with Special Reference to the Teaching of English in the Upper Forms of Schools*, (Riddell Memorial Lectures, fifteenth series), London: Oxford University Press.
---, 1960, *Miracles*, (revised edition, first edition 1947), London: Collins Fontana.
---, 1961, *An Experiment in Criticism*, Cambridge: Cambridge University Press.
---, 1969, *Selected Literary Essays*, (edited by Walter Hooper), Cambridge: Cambridge University Press.
---, 1988, *Letters of C.S. Lewis*, (edited by Walter Hooper), London: Collins Fount.
---, 2000a, 'Myth Became Fact', in *Essay Collection and Other Short Pieces*, (edited by Lesley Walmsley), London: HarperCollins, 138-142.
---, 2000b, 'Transposition,' in *Essay Collection and Other Short Pieces*, (edited by Lesley Walmsley), London: HarperCollins, 267-278.
---, 2004. *Collected Letters, Volume II*, (edited by Walter Hooper), London: HarperCollins.
MacDonald, George, 1893a, *A Dish of Orts*, (enlarged edition), London: Sampson Low.
---, 1893b, 'The Imagination: Its Functions and Culture', in MacDonald 1893a.
---, 1893c, 'The Fantastic Imagination', in MacDonald 1893a.
Polanyi, Michael, 1958, *Personal Knowledge: Towards a Post-Critical Philosophy*, London: Routledge & Kegan Paul, 1962.
Schakel, Peter J., 1984, *Reason and Imagination in C.S. Lewis: A Study of 'Till We Have Faces'*, Grand Rapids, Michigan: W. B. Eerdmans.
Shideler, Mary McDermott, 1962, *The Theology of Romantic Love: A Study in the Writings of Charles Williams*, Grand Rapids, Michigan: W. B. Eerdmans.

Steiner, Rudolf, 1985, *Anthroposophy and Christianity*, Spring Valley, New York: Anthroposophic Press.
Tolkien, J.R.R., 1983, *The Monsters and the Critics and Other Essays*, (edited by Christopher Tolkien), London: George Allen & Unwin.
---, 1992, *Tree and Leaf Including the Poem 'Mythopoeia'*, London: HarperCollins.
Williams, Charles, 1948, 'The Figure of Arthur', in C.S. Lewis (ed.), 1948, *Arthurian Torso*, London: Oxford University Press.

Iron Crown, Iron Cage: Tolkien and Weber on Modernity and Enchantment

PATRICK CURRY

Abstract

This paper uses both a conceptual and a symbolic-mythological hermeneutic analysis of their very different work to compare the attitudes and understandings of J.R.R. Tolkien and Max Weber towards modernity. It points to fundamental commonalities and suggests that both men also counterposed modernity with enchantment. It therefore includes a closer consideration of the nature of such enchantment and the meta-politics of its relationship with modernist magic.

J.R.R. Tolkien (1892-1973) almost certainly never read the social philosopher Max Weber (1864-1920), yet their diagnoses of modernity, as well as its opposite and perhaps its remedy, were tantalizingly similar. Combining their insights results in a powerful and, in some respects, new perspective which I would like to introduce here. And my starting-point is their strangely shared choice of symbolism which my title encapsulates.[1]

I am aware, of course, that Tolkien's fiction cannot be reduced to his views. Nonetheless it is idle to pretend that those views are not in his fiction and cannot be inferred from it, together with his letters and essays. With that in mind, let us recall that the most powerful evil figure in the entire history of Middle-earth is Morgoth, the fallen Vala, of whom even Sauron the Great was originally only a servant. I further take it as significant that the ultimate token of the legitimacy and authority of Morgoth's rule was his iron crown, containing the three stolen Silmarills. (And note that the iron holds the Silmarills, not

---

[1] An earlier version of this paper was given at the "Tolkien 2005" conference at Aston University in August 2005.

the other way around.) Finally, respecting this part of the story, and leaving aside Morgoth's eventual defeat by the remaining Valar, the only occasion when that crown ever slipped was when Lúthien Tinúviel danced its wearer into a trance and then sleep: in short – and the word is both unavoidable and, as we shall see, important – when she enchanted him.

Next we must turn to Tolkien's essay 'On Fairy-Stories', where he introduces a seminal distinction between magic and enchantment.[2] Pointed out the confusing uses of the first term, he suggested that 'magic' should be reserved for the exercise of power and domination, using the will, in order to bring about changes in the 'Primary World'. Whether the means employed are material or spiritual is ultimately a secondary consideration. Sauron is "the Lord of magic *and* machines" (*Letters* 146; my emphasis). The ultimate symbol of magic within Tolkien's literary world is, of course, the One Ring; again, as we shall see, the 'one' is important.

Enchantment, in contrast, "produces a Secondary World into which both designer and spectator can enter." It is "artistic in desire and purpose," and its purpose is "the realisation, independent of the conceiving mind, of imagined wonder" (OFS 49-50, 18). I take "realisation" here to be doubly meaningful: both to make wonder real and, I suggest, its ultimate meaning: to realise that whatever is experienced as wonderful *is* really so. So, oversimplifying but not egregiously so, the hallmark of magic is *will*, whereas that of enchantment is *wonder*.

Let us turn to Weber. In the world of social and political philosophy, Weber is perhaps best-known for his statement that "The fate of our times is characterised by rationalisation and intellectualisation and, above all, by the 'disenchantment [*Entzauberung*] of the world.'" And what brings about such disenchantment? Is it knowledge of the truth about ourselves and the world?

---

[2] In *Tree and Leaf* (Tolkien 1988); the original essay was first delivered as a lecture in 1939, and first published, somewhat enlarged, in 1947. See also my 'Magic vs. Enchantment' (Curry 1999). See also Verlyn Flieger's important explorations of *faërie* in Tolkien's work in *Splintered Light: Logos and Language in Tolkien's World* (Flieger 2002) and *A Question of Time: J.R.R. Tolkien's Road to Faërie* (Flieger 1997).

No, it is the "belief" – note, the belief suffices – "that if one but wished one *could* learn it at any time. Hence, it means that principally there are no mysterious incalculable forces that come into play, but rather that one can, in principle, master all things by calculation. This means that the world is disenchanted. One need no longer have recourse to magical means to master or implore the spirits, as did the savage, for whom such mysterious powers existed. Technical means and calculations perform the service." (Gerth and Mills 1991:155, 139; Weber's use of the word 'magic' here is loose and therefore ambiguous.)

Here it is important to note that to master all things by calculation requires a master calculus, or more generally principle, truth and/or value from which to derive and by which to legitimate such a calculus. If there is more than one then the possibility of incommensurability between different phenomena arises – this one amenable to this calculus but that one only to that other – and thence ultimate incalculability. In other words, in the exercise of power-knowledge, or what Tolkien called "Magic", there can only be *one* Ring of Power, and only one hand (as Gandalf reminds Saruman) can wear it.

When sufficiently institutionalised and thence pervasive, the result of rationalisation – and this is as close as Weber ever actually got to defining enchantment positively – is that "The unity of the primitive image of the world, in which everything was *concrete magic*, has tended to split into rational cognition and mastery of nature, on the one hand, and into 'mystic' experiences, on the other. The inexpressible contents of such experiences remain the only possible 'beyond,' added to the mechanism of a world robbed of gods." (Gerth and Mills 1991:282)

Now although Tolkien's analysis of enchantment is richer than Weber's, we can use the latter's point about wonder as both concrete and magic (that is, enchanting) to refine Tolkien's point about its 'realisation': enchantment is making it possible (by art) to realise that the world we experience, and/or some part thereof, is *already* wonderous. Wonder is not something we do, create or add to the world; that would be magic. And it is not a wholly ineffable or otherworldly 'mystic' experience; whatever that may be, it is not enchantment.

This means, for example, that the way (whether 'back' or not) to enchantment cannot proceed through a return, collective or individual, to theism; not, that is, as long as its practice conforms to the theological exigencies of a one true God. Indeed, according to Weber, the imperative to calculate, organise and rationalise was originally a religious impulse with its roots in monotheism and especially, in the modern Western world, Protestantism. Whereas the Puritan wanted to work in such a calling, however, "we are forced to do so. For when asceticism was carried out of monastic cells into everyday life, and began to dominate worldly morality, it did its part in building the tremendous cosmos of the modern economic order. This order is now bound to the technical and economic conditions of machine production which to-day determine the lives of all the individuals who are born into this mechanism, not only those directly concerned with economic acquisition, with irresistible force. Perhaps it will so determine them until the last ton of fossilized coal is burnt" (Weber 2001:182). Here again, the resonance with Tolkien's romantic antimodernism, with its hatred (the word is not too strong) of industrialism and fear for the future of the natural world, is entirely apt (see Curry 2004).

In the view of the Puritan divine, Weber (2001:182) continued, "care for external goods should only lie on the shoulders of the 'saint like a light cloak, which can be thrown aside at any moment'. But fate decreed that the cloak should become an iron cage." This has become the dominant metaphor for Weber's analysis of modernity.[3]

He concluded, "No-one knows who will live in this cage in the future, or whether at the end of this tremendous development, entirely new prophets will arise, or there will be a great rebirth of old ideas and ideals, or, if neither, mechanized petrification, embellished with a sort of convulsive self-

---

[3] Although it may well be that a better translation is "iron shell" [*stahlhartes Gehäuse*]; see Pels (2003:26-27).

importance. For of the last stage of this cultural development, it might well be truly said: 'Specialists without spirit, sensualists without heart; this nullity imagines that it has attained a level of civilization never before achieved.'" (Weber 2001:182; we can almost hear Tolkien cheering in the background.)

Without going into any detail, I should add that Weber's account proved very influential on subsequent social theory. It was taken up the founders of Critical Theory, Max Horkheimer, Theodor Adorno and Herbert Marcuse of the Frankfort School, and in particular by the first two in their book *The Dialectic of Enlightenment* (1944): a brilliant and unsettling account of modernity – "the fully enlightened earth radiates disaster" – whose chief weakness is that if everything is really so hopeless then what did its authors hope to accomplish?

More recently, the spirit of Critical Theory passed into the work of Michel Foucault.[4] It has also surfaced in more orthodox branches of the academy such as World System Theory, whose proponents give substantial empirical as well as theoretical flesh to the bones of Weber's suggestion that although modern science has powerfully accelerated the pace of rationalisation, it is only "the most important fraction, of the process of intellectualisation which we have been undergoing for thousands of years [...]" (Gerth and Mills 1991:138). Frank and Gills (1993) find the origins of this process in 1500 BCE.

Now at this point I propose to do something guaranteed to make even the most hardened postmodernist blanch, and turn to the symbolism of iron.[5] Of course most of them haven't ever tried to come to grips with Tolkien's "perfectly sincere, perfectly impossible narrative" (Attebery 1992:46), so I have the edge there. And why would I do so? Because it is just possible that Weber's and Tolkien's choice of metaphors may not be entirely random but rather meaningful in a way that a few thousand years of cultural reflection

---

[4] And not its putative heir, the neo-rationalist Jürgen Habermas.

[5] I gratefully acknowledge key suggestions for this section by Liz Greene.

might throw some light on. Also, of course, subaltern discourses marginalised by modernity can by their alterity reveal the *aporias* of a dominant ideology. (There, that should hold them.)

Hesiod suggested that the ages of humanity have descended in quality from Golden to Silver to Bronze and finally Iron, an unpleasant and brutish period in which we are obviously still living. Persian religious literature apparently concurs. The Bible describes God's instrument of punishment as a "rod of iron" (Psalms 2:9 and Revelation 2:27). And the nails in Christ's cross were, of course, made of iron. (They were purportedly used in the early medieval crown of Lombardy, but note the difference between Charlemagne's and Morgoth's crowns: the latter made of iron but the Emperor's of gold containing, in a narrow band, the iron.)

Another characteristic of iron is more positive; it has long been held to protect against the hostile magical powers of witches, necromancers and vampires. (Hence an iron horseshoe over the threshold.) This not only points to the importance of context, to which I shall return in a moment. It also serves as a reminder to be wary of accepting the claims of our iron age secularism at face value, for the same reason that we should beware the claims of scientism (a closely related phenomenon) to be without prejudices, assumptions or untested and untestable ultimate values. That is, modernity is indeed programmatically disenchanted and disenchanting, but it is nonetheless, as Horkheimer and Adorno perceived, thoroughly magical: "In the enlightened world, mythology has entered into the profane. In its blank purity, the reality which has been cleansed of demons and their conceptual descendents assumes the numinous character which the ancient world attributed to demons." (Horkheimer and Adorno 1994:28).

Probably the fundamental mythic association with iron, underlying these attributes, is Mars, long held to be a 'malefic' planet which is co-extensive in cultural astronomy with the Graeco-Roman god of war and all that that entails: will-power and its correlates the martial virtues: courage, personal power, the ability and willingness to push something through by main force.

The shadow-side of these attributes are not far away, of course: savagery, brutality, callousness.[6]

The centrality of the will here, in either case, emphasises the appropriateness of the choice of iron to invoke the modern empire. The contextual nature of Martian virtues/vices, however, warns us not to see iron as essentially or necessarily negative. Following up this hint suggests that the modernist monism of the iron cage/iron crown is a result of its attempt to usurp the authority of the other deities and replace their messy agonistic plurality with a single, well-ordered – or rather, 'properly managed' – empire: 'Knowledge, Order, Rule,' to quote Sauron's stooge Saruman, but actually ruled, of course, by One Ring.

This point is susceptible to more precise elaboration: Mars-Ares takes much of his nature (in the best fashion of discursive definition through mutually defining terms of opposition) from the planetary deity he forms a pair with: Venus-Aphrodite. Here surely is mythopoetic confirmation of the wisdom of both Tolkien's and Weber's decision to counterpose the iron 'Magic' of modernity with enchantment. For where do the roots of the latter lie if not with the ancient (pre-Olympian) goddess of love and beauty, whose power to enchant was respected and feared by even the most powerful of the other gods?[7] Is not her power precisely that of enchantment, and is not her love 'concrete magic', in which the most precise and tiny physical details of the beloved acquire the most mysterious moment? And note that the Graces, patronesses of the arts, were Aphrodite's attendants (see Friedrich 1978). How appropriate, then, that Morgoth's crown only slipped, and he thereby lost a Silmaril, under the spell of Lúthien Tinúviel as she danced. (In this considerable sense, if in no other, Tolkien was arguably a feminist.)

---

[6] Reflecting differing cultural values, Mars was more positively portrayed and highly valued by the Romans than was Ares by classical Greeks, for whom the latter god's blind fury could inspire contempt as well as fear.

[7] Only Athena, Artemis and Hestia were immune to Aphrodite's spells.

In conclusion, then, we can say that the contemporary triumph of modernist magic – the world system, driven by will and ruled by iron – cannot be doubted, but it is not unqualified. In the interstices of the grid, among places and people (especially 'small' people) overlooked by power, and even, I daresay, in the hearts of many of its servants, enchantment still lives. It is a precarious existence, of course, and cannot (as I have said) compete directly with Magic using the latter's weapons without thereby becoming the Enemy itself. As Weber too pointed out, an intellectually driven pursuit of romantic irrationalism, being programmatically willed, simply extends the bounds of disenchantment.[8]

All that can effectively be done is to protect enchantment where it already exists; to make it possible to perceive it, and encourage people to do so, where it exists but has not yet been noticed, which is the duty and privilege of art, but also education;[9] and to refuse and expose the great modern lie in which Enchantment is tacitly replaced with its power-driven simulacrum, Glamour.[10]

Beyond that, the only hope we have is that "evil will oft evil mars." We are now fast approaching the day when the last ton of fossilised coal is burnt and nature – the *fons et origo*, deified/personified as Venus-Aphrodite, of autonomous enchantment – will reassert herself against Nature plc, an insensible set of external manageable resources to be manipulated by power-knowledge.[11] The former nature is the one we directly experience: a sensuous, "wild and multiplicitous otherness" in which we find ourselves and which we find within ourselves.[12]

---

[8] See Nicholas Gane's excellent *Max Weber and Postmodern Theory*.

[9] Brian Rosebury (2003:177-178) finds my account of enchantment too directly involved with the Primary World. But a successful, i.e. enchanted Secondary World results in seeing the Primary World in a fresh and different way, which is just what Tolkien called "recovery" (OFS 53).

[10] See Curry (1999).

[11] See Curry (2004).

[12] See David Abram's superb *The Spell of the Sensuous*.

Despite other more obvious Earth deities such as Gaia, I am emphasizing the importance of Venus-Aphrodite here on the grounds of the integral connection between erotic love and nature, as well as between aesthetics and nature.[13] It is also worth recalling that Tolkien defined the principal goal of enchantment, as practised by its exemplars the Elves, as "the adornment of [E]arth, and the healing of its hurts" (*Letters* 151-152). Adornment is, of course, precisely the *métier* of Aphrodite.

The more we cling to the latter 'nature', however, the more terrible that re-assertion will prove. But one may hope that before then, there might be a more general disillusionment with modernist magic and the power of iron, thus opening the door, at least, to a more widespread rediscovery of what is useless but makes life worth living – and perhaps even, in the end, possible.

Biographical Note

Patrick Curry is a lecturer in Religious Studies at the University of Kent and the author of several books, including *Defending Middle-Earth: Tolkien, Myth and Modernity* (1997, 2004), *Astrology, Science and Culture: Pulling Down the Moon* (with Roy Willis, 2004) and *Ecological Ethics: An Introduction* (2006).

---

[13] On which see Hepburn (1984).

Bibliography

Abbreviations

Letters: see Carpenter 1981
OFS: 'On Fairy-Stories' in Tolkien (1988:9-73)

Abram, David, 1996, *The Spell of the Sensuous: Perception and Language in a More-Than-Human World*, New York: Vintage Books.
Attebery, Brian, 1992, *Strategies of Fantasy*, Bloomington, Indiana: Indiana University Press.
Carpenter, Humphrey (ed., with the assistance of Christopher Tolkien), 1981, *The Letters of J.R.R. Tolkien*, London: Allen & Unwin.
Curry, Patrick, 1999, 'Magic vs. Enchantment', *Journal of Contemporary Religion* 14.3:401-412.
---, 2004, *Defending Middle-earth*, (second edition; first edition 1997), Boston: Houghton Mifflin.
Flieger, Verlyn, 1997, *A Question of Time: J.R.R. Tolkien's Road to Faërie*, Kent: Kent State University Press.
---, 2002, *Splintered Light: Logos and Language in Tolkien's World*, (revised edition), Kent: Kent State University Press.
Frank, Andre Gunder and Barry K. Gills, 1993, *The World System: Five Hundred Years or Five Thousand?* London: Routledge.
Friedrich, Paul, 1978, *The Meaning of Aphrodite*, Chicago: University of Chicago Press.
Gane, Nicholas, 2004, *Max Weber and Postmodern Theory*, Basingstoke: Palgrave Macmillan.
Gerth, H. H. and C. Wright Mills (eds.), 1991, *From Max Weber: Essays in Sociology*, London: Routledge.
Hepburn, Ronald, 1984, *'Wonder' and Other Essays*, Edinburgh: Edinburgh University Press.
Horkheimer, Max and Theodor W. Adorno, 1994, *The Dialectic of Enlightenment*, (first edition 1944), New York: Continuum.
Pels, Peter, 2003, 'Introduction: Magic and Modernity', in Birgit and Peter Pels (eds.), 2003, *Magic and Modernity: Interfaces of Revelation and Concealment*, Stanford: Stanford University Press, 1-38.
Rosebury, Brian, 2003, *Tolkien: A Cultural Phenomenon*, Basingstoke: Palgrave Macmillan.
Tolkien, J.R.R., 1988, *Tree and Leaf*, edited by Christopher Tolkien, London: HarperCollins.
Weber, Max, 2001, *The Protestant Ethic and the Spirit of Capitalism*, London: Routledge.

A Mythology for England?
Looking a Gift Horse in the Mouth[1]

THOMAS HONEGGER

Abstract

This paper explores the chequered history of the meta-fictional elements Tolkien employed to create a connection between the (largely Elvish) legends and tales and his 'Mannish' (originally English) readership. The early concepts presuppose a direct connection between 'England' and the Elvish homelands and make use of elements already central to the 'national identity' forming processes in Middle English literature after the Norman conquest. These concepts are, as the work on the Legendarium progressed, superseded by more involved and less explicitly 'national' meta-fictional frameworks.

Introduction

Tolkien, in his notes to a letter (dated 1967) answering a reader's inquiry into the nomenclature of *The Lord of the Rings*, writes:

> The most important name in this connexion is *Eärendil*. [...] When first studying A[nglo]-S[axon] professionally (1913-) [...] I was struck by the great beauty of this word (or name), [...]. Before 1914 I wrote a 'poem' upon Earendel who launched his ship like a bright spark from the havens of the Sun. (*Letters* 385)

Eärendil, or 'earendel', occurs in the Old English *Blickling Homilies* and the poem *Christ*, where the context suggests an allegorical interpretation of its literal meaning 'dawn' and 'morning star' as a reference to St John the Baptist or, in the latter poem, even to Christ Himself. The mystery of the word's

---

[1] An earlier version of this paper was published in 2006 in *Hither Shore* 3:13-26.

origins fired young Tolkien's inspiration and the enigmatic 'morning star' became the 'fay-star' that gave Tolkien access to the realm of Faëry. As a traveller in the Perilous Realm, Tolkien proved to be an astute and prolific chronicler of its history, tales and legends – in contrast to Smith of Wootton Major, whose understanding of Faëry seems more intuitive than intellectual. The 'fay-star' and, intimately linked to it, the project of chronicling the history and legends of the realm of Faëry accompanied Tolkien until the last years of his life – it was a gift that would influence his life and work to an unforeseen degree. A gift, moreover, that he could and would not pass on easily.

In the following, I am going to investigate Tolkien's numerous attempts of placing his mythopoeic writings within a framework that would allow him to dedicate it to England, his country.

Absent Mythologies

Tolkiens mythopoeic talent came in useful soon after his encounter with enigmatic Eärendil – namely in connection with his desire to provide England with a mythology of its own and thus share his gift with his fellow countrymen. In his often quoted letter to Milton Waldman (*Letters* 143-161, no. 131), written in 1951 in order to convince the publisher Collins that *The Lord of the Rings* and *The Silmarillion* were intimately linked as part of a greater mythology and should therefore be published together, he bemoans the fact that his country lacks a genuinely English mythology. Tolkien echoes, with his statement, a truth that had already been voiced at about the time when he started working on his Legendarium by the author Edward M. Forster in his novel *Howard's End* (1910)[2] and some eight hundred years before by Jean Bodel in

---

[2] E.M. Forster (1978:262) in *Howards End* (originally published 1910): "Why has not England a great mythology? Our folklore has never advanced beyond daintiness, and the greater melodies about our countryside have all issued through the pipes of Greece. Deep and true as the native imagination can be, it seems to have failed here. It has stopped with the witches and the fairies. It cannot vivify one fraction of a summer field, or give names to half a dozen stars. England still waits for the supreme moment of her literature – for the great poet who shall voice her, or, better still, for the thousand little poets whose voices shall pass into our common talk."

his *Chanson des Saisnes* (late 12 cent.). Bodel, in his famous overview of 'narrative matters', writes:

> Ne sont que trois matieres a nul home antandant;
> De France et de Bretaigne et de Rome la grant;
> Et de ces trois matieres n'i a mile semblant.
> Li conte de Bretaigne sont si vain et plaisant;
> Cil de Rome sont sage et de san aprenant,
> Cil de France sont voir chascun jor apparant.
> (*Chanson des Saisnes*, l. 6-11)

> There are but three narrative matters for any understanding man; / Of France and of Brittany and of great Rome; / And of these three matters there are a thousand appearances. / The tales of Brittany are so tender and pleasing; / Those of Rome are wise and of informed sense, / Those of France are truly each day evident.

The crucial point about this early categorization of narrative matters is the non-mention of a 'Matter of England'. It must be added, however, that this is not really astonishing if one takes into account the cultural predominance of France during much of the Middle Ages. England in particular may well be considered part of the French cultural domain for the first two centuries after the Norman Conquest in 1066. French (or, depending on the context, Anglo-Norman) dominated literature, the royal court, administration, law, and even the church for centuries. English survived largely as a spoken language and was obviously not considered suitable for literary and poetic composition. The works produced in England during that time bear witness to this bias. Neighbouring cultures, like the Celtic (Wales) or the Scandinavian (Iceland), preserved at least some of their mythologies and traditional tales in manuscripts written in the thirteenth and fourteenth centuries – e.g. *The White Book of Rhydderch* and *The Red Book of Hergest*, which were edited and translated by Lady Charlotte Guest as *The Mabinogion*, and the manuscripts of the *Poetic Edda* and *Snorri Sturluson's Edda* respectively. There are no comparable texts for England

and a specifically 'Anglo-Saxon mythology' has not survived – most likely because no one bothered to collect and write down the tales and myths of a conquered and seemingly inferior people. The Norman and French writers and historiographers would try and link the history of the British Isles rather with the 'international' foundation myth that traces the origins of European civilisations (Rome, France, but also the Normans)[3] back to the Trojans. Geoffrey of Monmouth, in his *Historia Regum Britanniae* (c. 1136), gives the 'classic' account of how Britain (< Bruttenes land), formerly called Albion and inhabited by giants, was settled and civilised by Trojans under the leadership of Felix Brutus, Aeneas' great-grandson.

The Matters of Brittany, France, and Rome

Geoffrey of Monmouth is also the 'father' of the Arthurian legend and, as a consequence, of the 'Matter of Brittany' that attached itself to the figure of the legendary king. Arthur makes his first prominent (clearly datable) appearance in written literature in Geoffrey's *Historia* and later historians and authors, such as Wace, Layamon, or Chrétien de Troyes, would further elaborate and add to the story on the basis of his account. The Arthur encountered in the *Historia* is, however, not a very suitable starting point for an 'English' mythology. Apart from his Romano-Celtic roots and the fact that his enemies are Saxons (i.e. the ancestors of the 'English'), he is also too much of an internationally oriented emperor figure as to serve specific nationalistic needs. Geoffrey's Arthur, after having defeated the Saxons in Britain and after conquering large parts of Europe, is on the brink of marching onto Rome and receiving the imperial crown when news of Mordred's betrayal cause him to hurry back home. This Arthur is better suited towards providing 'historical' justification for the Normans' (and later the Plantagenet kings') international aspirations than to become the focus of a new national identity. Some later writers would try and remove at least some of the major obstacles and thus co-opt Arthur for the

---

[3] See Southern (1970:189-195), Eley (1991), and Albu (2001:13-15).

English. The author of *Of Arthour and Merlin*,[4] for example, makes Arthur English by simply equating the Britons with the English: "the Bretouns that beth Inglisse nov" ('the Britons that are English now'; Macrae-Gibson (1973:11), line 119) – and thus prevents any further problems. Also, the Saxons are omitted completely and the Saracens take over their place as Arthur's enemies. The historian Robert Manning (c. 1338) applies a slightly different strategy and claims Arthur for the English by pointing out that he is 'of this land', i.e. England. However, most attempts to 'English' Arthur did not have a lasting impact and the development was in the direction of international chivalric ideal rather than national hero.

Tolkien was most likely aware of the problematic and multi-faceted nature of Arthur in medieval literature, historiography, and politics. Furthermore, he rejected the 'Arthurian matter' because it was, in his opinion, "imperfectly naturalized, associated with the soil of Britain but not with English; [...] For another and more important thing; it is involved in, and explicitly contains the Christian religion" (*Letters* 144). Yet this did not stop him from starting to write an alliterative epic poem on the Arthurian theme (*The Fall of Arthur*) that he, in 1955, still hoped to complete (*Letters* 219). The poem did not appear in print during his lifetime and the Tolkien Estate's policy at present is not to permit the viewing of hitherto unpublished texts. Christopher Tolkien informed me that the poem is unfinished, and not presented in any basically readable form, and also that his own transcription of the poem is itself not, in his opinion, suitable for use, as it would need extensive reworking before he would be ready to stand by its quality. I therefore cannot make any comments on how Tolkien's Arthur would have been linked to the 'Matter of England' – if he were to be seen in such a context at all.

The 'Matter of France' is even less suited to provide the material for an 'English' mythology. The stories of Charlemagne and his douzepeers are closely associated with the territories of France, the idea of the *renovatio imperii*

---

[4] Auchinleck manuscript, c. 1340, edited by Macrae-Gibson (1973/1979).

and with the wars against the Saracens – and thus with the Christian religion. Tolkien may have incorporated some elements from this narrative tradition into his work (e.g. Boromir's horn and last stand; Aragorn as the renewer of the Gondorian empire), yet these are either minor or 'universal' motifs rather than culture-specific ones.

The relationship between England and the 'Matter of Rome' requires closer scrutiny. As mentioned above, the European foundation myth makes, strictly speaking, all other matters into derivatives of this 'original matter'. England, via Britain and Felix Brutus, is likewise linked with the Trojan 'hypermyth' that provides Britain/England with a venerable 'history' of its own. Yet the focus is, in this context, on the common descent of the cultural elite and it is only from this shared foundation that the European nations are going to develop their specific identities. The 'prologue' to the late fourteenth-century poem *Sir Gawain and the Green Knight*, which Tolkien edited together with E.V. Gordon in 1925, illustrates this beautifully. Lines 1 to 24 summarise the events from the fall of Troy and Aeneas' flight to the foundation of Rome and the conquest and colonialisation of most of Europe by Aeneas' descendants. Lines 25 to 26 introduce Arthur as the most famous of the British kings and thus present him as direct heir to the Trojan founding fathers. It would be, of course, a mistake to categorize *Sir Gawain and the Green Knight* as belonging to the 'Matter of Rome', but the poet clearly aims at highlighting the interdependency of the matters of Brittany and Rome.

The Matter of England

Modern scholars have supplemented Jean Bodel's three categories by the 'Matter of England'. This new category comprises Middle English romances like *Boeves of Hamtoun* or *Guy of Warwick* – works that are often translations/adaptations of Anglo-Norman originals and aim at providing the Anglo-Norman noble families with native English ancestral figures. These tales of adventure remained popular into the modern period and it is very likely that they constitute, together with the tales of Robin Hood, the "impoverished chap-book stuff" (*Letters* 144) Tolkien mentioned in his letter to M. Waldman. The greater part of the action of these romances may take place in England and the protagonists are presented as English knights, yet theirs is a constructed, artificial 'Englishness'.[5] Tolkien seemed to consider the descendants of the Angles, Saxons, Jutes and other Germanic tribes that conquered Britain and made it into 'Angle-lond' to be the true representatives of 'Englishness'. The Norman Conquest was, in his view, a deplorable historical mishap that cut short and, after the re-establishment of English as the national language, influenced negatively the natural development of a genuinely 'English' culture and language. Tolkien would therefore seek for 'Englishness' in those parts that were not or only marginally touched by the effects of the Norman invasion and hoped to retrieve some of the original culture by 'bypassing' the Norman additions. The Middle English romances, by contrast, would try and link the Anglo-Norman present with a mythical Anglo-Saxon past in order to construct a new 'national' identity by combining the different elements. Sir Walter Scott's 'historical' novel *Ivanhoe* may be seen as a modern representative of this approach. As a consequence of this peculiar historical situation, 'Englishness' has always been a somewhat vague category and the question of what constitutes 'Englishness' (in contrast to 'Scottishness', 'Welshness' or even 'Britishness') is treated in one way or another in much of post-Conquest medieval literature.[6] Most recently, the matter of national identity has received renewed and greater prominence due to the devolution process within the United Kingdom.[7] The modern struggle to come to terms with 'Englishness' is, as Shippey (2000) argues, mainly due the fact that the English, as the dominant cultural, political and economic force within the British Empire and the United Kingdom, consciously kept a low profile in order to stress the common 'British' elements rather than promoting a specifically English identity.

---

[5] See Rouse (2005) for a discussion of the construction of 'Englishness' in Middle English romances.

[6] See Speed (1994) and Turville-Petre (1996).

[7] See Colls (2002) and Fox (2004:15).

There exists no English national anthem, the Union Jack is a British flag, and most typically 'English' characteristics are, upon closer scrutiny, as much or predominantly British.[8] And those traits that are often perceived as 'typically English', such as the idea of the cultivated rural landscape, common sense, or fair play, do not lend themselves that easily towards the creation of a national identity.

This brief and necessarily incomplete outline gives us a clearer idea under which constraints Tolkien had to work and what his options were when he envisaged writing an 'English' mythology. With much of British and English history already 'occupied' by the Trojan 'hypermyth', he seemed to think it better to place his tales even further in prehistoric times. This does not exclude the possibility that he used – unconsciously or not – the medieval accounts of the Trojan war as the blueprint for his 'The Fall of Gondolin',[9] and thus link his Legendarium, at least indirectly, via structural parallels to the European foundation myth. This and the original Eriol/Aelfwine framestory was, in the late 1930s and early 1940s, superseded by linking the Legendarium – via 'The Fall of Númenor' – to another, more ancient 'foundation and civilisation myth', namely that of Atlantis – which, in turn, was abandoned in favour of the 'narratological' solution found in the preface to *The Lord of the Rings*.

I would like, in the following paragraphs, briefly present and comment on these different and sometimes mutually exclusive stages of the narrative frames. The great importance of the framestories has become clear with the publication of *The History of Middle-earth* and Christopher Tolkien, in the first volume of *The Book of Lost Tales* (*Lost Tales 1* 5), concedes that it was an error to publish *The Silmarillion* without any framework. This literary device is of special import for our task because the linking of Tolkien's Legendarium with England is achieved predominantly, though not exclusively, by means of the

---

[8] See, however, Fox (2004) whose highly readable book tries to reach a definiton of Englishness by means of discussing the hidden rules of English behaviour.

[9] See Lewis and Currie (2005).

frame narratives. Tolkien, in order to make his collection of stories a gift for England, to dedicate it to his country, developed this device in various forms.

Tol Eressëa as England: Eriol aka Ottor Waefre aka Angol (*Lost Tales 1 & 2*)

The first of these frame narratives centres around the figure of Eriol (1916-), who is also known as Ottor Waefre or, according to his homeland, by his by-name Angol.[10] He is of the line of Woden and, through his marriage with Cwén in Heligoland in the North Sea (*Lost Tales 1* 23), the father of Hengest and Horsa – who are known as the semi-historical leaders of the Germanic invaders of Britain. The genealogies of the Anglo-Saxon royal houses do not list an 'Eriol', nor do they feature any of his other names.[11] Yet this non-mention does not rule out the existence of such a figure – the manuscripts of the *Anglo-Saxon Chronicle* as well as those of other important historical records (e.g. Bede's *Historia ecclesiastica gentis Anglorum*) are often at odds with each other. Eriol is thus a late fourth, early fifth century character who fits in with what little is known about this time and though we cannot call him an 'Englishman' – simply because there were no 'Englishmen' in existence at that time – he may be seen as a 'proto-Englishman'. It is this proto-Englishman who, upon the death of his wife, sails west and lands on the Lonely Isle where he not only learns much of the Elvish lore but also marries an elfwoman and witnesses the ruin of Elvish Tol Eressëa. Eriol – and his (half-elvish) son Heorrenda, a name taken from the Old English poem *Deor* – thus become the preservers and transmitters of Elvish legends and lore. This body of tales is 'English' in several ways. First, Tol Eressëa is to become the British Isles when Ulmo uproots it and drags it near the Western Shores of the Great Lands – with the effect that its subsequent history is identical with the history of England. The identi-

---

[10] Angol, of course, refers to Angul or Angeln in southern Denmark, that is the Continental homeland of the Germanic tribe of the Angles who, together with the Saxons and the Jutes, invaded Britain in the fifth century AD.

[11] The Kentish genealogy, for example, names one Wihtgils as the father – or at least predecessor – of Hengest (cf. *Finn and Hengest* 176).

fication of Elvish places with English towns, such as Kortirion with Warwick, or Tavrobel with Great Haywood, stresses this point, as does the fact that poems like 'Why the Mann in the Moon Came Down Too Soon' (March 1915) are, in their earliest stages, clearly rooted in the geography of our modern world,[12] whereas later versions would replace these names with references to Middle-earth places. The important fact is that the stories have thus been told, collected and written down in what is going to be England, i.e. they are linked to, though not necessarily about, the soil of England. Secondly, the preservers of the tales are, on the one hand, intimately connected with the Elves who live in Tol Eressëa. On the other hand, they are also related to one of the races of men that will invade and settle England in the not too distant future. The Elvish legends may thus be considered part of their cultural and – via the half-elven Heorrenda – even racial heritage indeed. Tolkien thus bypasses the 'Celtic' tradition of faery, which he considered "too lavish, and fantastical, incoherent and repetitive" (*Letters* 144).

The choice of an 'Anglian' transmission of the same matter leaves its marks on the form of the tales and poems, too. Many carry Old English titles[13] or are rendered in alliterative metre (e.g. 'The Children of Húrin' 1920-25) – a poetic form associated typically with Germanic and thus also Old English literature (in opposition to Middle English literature that is heavily indebted to Romance models). The formal contrast between the 'Germanic' stress-based alliterative line and the isosyllabic end-rhyming couplets of Romance origin was probably the reason why numerous poets and authors 'revived' the alliterative line during the growth of a national (English) consciousness in the

---

[12] Cf. line 48 'In the Ocean of Almain' = the North Sea; line 51 'Yarmouth' and line 58 'Norwich' in the version printed in *Lost Tales 1* 204-206.

[13] E.g. 'Goblin Feet' (1915) is alternatively called 'Cumaþ þa Nihtielfas' (There come the night-elves), and 'Kortirion' (Nov. 1915) is 'Cor Tirion þǽra beama on middes' (Kortirion in the middle of the trees); cf. *Lost Tales 1* 32; see also the titles of the first finished text of 'Why the Mann in the Moon Came Down Too Soon', which were 'A Faërie: Why the Man in the Moon came down too soon', together with one in Old English: 'Se Móncyning'; cf. *Lost Tales 1* 204.

fourteenth century.[14] Alliteration was obviously recognised as an 'English' form whereas end-rhyme was considered a French import. Yet Tolkien, though experimenting with and exploiting the identificatory potential of alliteration, did not allow his poetic creativity to be limited to a single form only. He could and would, for example, write in rhyming couplets when he thought it appropriate. The content and spirit of 'The Lay of Leithian' (1925-31) for one, harmonises better with rhyming octosyllabic couplets than with alliterative long lines. One effect of this selection of form according to aesthetic or genre-specific principles is a 'chronological' layering of the poems. Alliterative poems – often of heroic or epic nature – are felt to be more ancient than those written in rhyming couplets or other 'more recent' forms. The treatment of similar or identical narrative matter in different forms and according to different aesthetic principles mirrors, to some extent, the structure of the surviving English medieval literature and imitates the slow historical evolutionary process *in vitro*, so that the Legendarium looks and feels as if it had grown organically over the centuries.

Yet Tolkien did not only use typical poetic forms to link his tales to a pre-Conquest era. Many of the narrative elements of his early poems and tales are derived from the Northern tradition. The tale of Túrin Turambar (1919; *Lost Tales 2*), for example, contains echoes of Germanic legends as well as strong Finnish elements derived from Tolkien's reading of *The Kalevala*.[15]

Our discussion of the matter of identity in the earliest stages of the development of the Legendarium has shown that Tolkien relied mainly on the concept of a common territory (Tol Eressëa = Britain/England) and, to a lesser extent, on racial connections between the original representatives of the narrative matter (elves) and its preservers (Eriol and his half-elven son Heorrenda). He thus comes close to the medieval concept of nation as being

---

[14] See Turville-Petre (1977).

[15] This aspect has been studied in detail by several scholars, most prominently Shippey (2003) and Burns (2005), but see also Flieger (2004a) and West (2004), to whom I would like to refer the interested reader.

defined in terms of its territory, its people, and its language (Turville-Petre 1996:vi). The question of language is going to occupy us in the next chapter and also later on in connection with Tolkien's concept of 'native tongue'.

Luthany = England: Ælfwine

The original concept that saw Tol Eressëa as the precursor of the British Isles was superseded by – or received competition from – an alternative idea sometime in the 1920s when Tolkien introduced the eleventh-century Englishman Ælfwine as the link between the tales of the Legendarium and the Elves. England, called Luthany, is no longer identical with Tol Eressëa, although it does have a strong 'elvish' connection in so far as it has been the only land where Elves and Men had dwelt together in peace. The Anglo-Saxons are identified with the Ingwaiar, i.e. the people of Ing(wë), who came to Britain from their homelands in northern Europe. Ing(wë) recalls, of course, one of the mythic founding figures of the Germanic peoples – still to be recognised in the name of the Inguaeones. Tolkien links Ing(wë) further with (Northwest-)Germanic legends by presenting him as a Sheaf-like figure who comes to the people in time of need. Ælfwine, then, is a descendant of the Ingwaiar ("of the kin of Ing, King of Luthany"; *Lost Tales 2* 305) who have been the only of the invading peoples that established, under the influence of Ing(wë)'s teachings, a friendly relationship with those Elves who still remained in Luthany/England. Due to this, Old English is the only mannish language the Elves speak willingly. Ælfwine himself, in a voyage that is merely sketched by Tolkien, reaches Elvenhome where he learns the tales from the mouths of Elves themselves – who, to his astonishment, speak his own language (Old English) fluently. Ælfwine writes down what he learns in *The Book of Lost Tales/The Golden Book of Tavrobel* (*Lost Tales 2* 310) and preserves thus the Elvish legends in late Old English (wheras Eriol and Heorrenda's language would have been a much more archaic and hardly understandable form of proto-Anglian Old English).

This change of focus has several consequences. Tol Eressëa is no longer identical with Britain. Places like Kortirion or Tavrobel on the Lonely Isle are no longer to be identified directly with Warwick or Great Haywood, but named after the older settlements bearing the same names in Luthany/England which the Elves had to leave behind. The elvish legends are thus still 'of England', though once removed. The same is true for the people that are the recorders of the elvish tales. The Ingwaiar possess a rather elusive 'elvish connection' that, ultimately, goes back to Ing(wë), but they are not directly related to the Elves, as were Heorrenda and his descendants. In the end, the transmission of the Legendarium has been moved forward into better documented historical times and the mythic elements have been relegated to the background. Yet the advantage of having the transmission anchored more clearly in a factual historical context and in a well-known linguistic environment (late Old English) is bought with the loss of the narrator's direct involvement. Ælfwine is merely a 'recorder' of tales whereas Eriol and Heorrenda had still actively participated in the events that brought about the departure of the Elves from Tol Eressëa/Britain.

Luthany = England: Ælfwine = Eriol
When, in c. 1930, Tolkien was working on his 'Sketch of the Mythology', the entire narrative framework had disappeared (cf. *Shaping* 42). However, this must not be seen as proof that he had rejected it. The title page of the 'Qenta' states that its contents are drawn from *The Book of Lost Tales* which Eriol of Leithian had written after reading *The Golden Book* (*Shaping* 78). Furthermore, the fragments of the 'Quenta' in (late) Old English (*Shaping* 205-208) as well as the Old English versions of 'The Annals of Valinor' (*Shaping* 281-293) and 'The Annals of Beleriand' (*Shaping* 337-341) respectively are said to be the work of Ælfwine, called Eriol by the Elves. The 'Annals' contain much mythological and (pre-)historical information vital for establishing the place of Valinor and Beleriand within the larger framework of the history of Middle-earth. The 'Annals' also link events and persons from the Legendarium to Anglo-Saxon England. This happens, on the one hand, by means of the annalistic form, which echoes that of the *Anglo-Saxon Chronicle*. On the other

hand, their contents supplement and complement the *Anglo-Saxon Chronicle* and the 'Annals' Old English versions could be easily incorporated into the *Anglo-Saxon Chronicle* just as biblical information has been used to fill the gaps in the historical knowledge of the Anglo-Saxons. 'English history', i.e. the history of the Germanic tribes of the Angles, Saxons, and Jutes, is, in this context, part of a greater (Christian) picture of the history of our world. The 'elvish' pre-history of Middle-earth in general and of what is to become England in particular occupies thus a place that is structurally similar to that of the biblical narrative(s).

Ælfwine and Eriol are now two names for one and the same person, i.e. the eleventh-century Englishman who sailed from England to Tol Eressëa. However, Tolkien did not revise his earlier writings and Eriol would continue to appear, from time to time, as a separate person.

Alwin – Ælfwine – Alboin – Elendil, and the Drowning of Númenor
Tolkien's concept of the Legendarium's transmission has been, up to this date, rather traditional. People (Eriol, Ælfwine) travel by boat or on foot to places where they meet other people (Elves) who tell them tales, which are then written down, copied and read by their descendants and thus reach Tolkien's own time. The factors that render these tales important for the construction of a national 'English' mythology are their links with the soil and, to a lesser extent, with the people (i.e. the Anglo-Saxons). 'The Lost Road' (c. 1937) marks a radical departure from this pattern. Ælfwine makes an appearance in this story, too, but this time as an Englishman of the time of king Edward the Elder (c. AD 918). He is no longer the central transmitter figure but merely part of a series of father-son pairs (although, in one of Tolkien's sketches, he reaches Tol Eressëa and listens to the tales of the Elves). The transmission of the central event – the drowning of Númenor – is no longer by writing or oral transmission, but by 'racial memory'. The memories of this cataclystic event reappear in the dreams and visions of those who are descended from Elendil in direct line.

This idea of 'racial memory' reappears in 'The Notion Club Papers' (c. 1945), which comprise the minutes of the club's meetings between 1980 to 1990. Alwin Arundel (< Ælfwine Earendel) Lowdham, a member of the Notion Club, remembers Old English verses and he and his companion Wilfried Trewin (< Tréowine) Jeremy both regress back in time during their search for the origin of these visions. Ælfwine, here introduced as the linear ancestor of Alwin, appears and, together with Tréowine (a linear ancestor of Wilfried Trewin Jeremy), sails westwards where he "gets view of the Book of Stories; and writes down what he can remember" (*Sauron* 279). This sketched link, which connects 'The Notion Club Papers' to the earlier frame narratives, has not been developed any further. Lowdham and Jeremy regress even farther back in time until they witness, as Elendil (> Alwin) and Voronwë, the drowning of Númenor (*Sauron* 279).

The notion of the genetic transmission of formative experiences links the Legendarium to the people to a much greater extent than the concepts before. With them it has been the soil that functioned, to some extent, as the carrier of identity and the Legendarium was considered 'English' mostly because of its connections to the land that, one day, would become England. The transmission of the matter via inherited memory may be supplemented by written accounts (cf. Ælfwine's rendering of what he remembers of *The Book of Stories*), but the anchoring of the matter itself with the English is by means of the bloodline. The Legendarium is a mythology for England because the English, whether they are aware of this or not, retain the key elements in their 'racial memory'. Verlyn Flieger (2004b:53) puts it like this: "It would make English history and myth, as well as his own pre-English mythology, the property of inborn, genetically transmitted rememberance, possessed by the English whether they know it or not." Tolkien, by connecting the elvish tales with the fall of Númenor, also provided an alternative 'foundation mythology' for European civilisation. It is not the Trojan 'civilisation heroes' that are the founding fathers of Europe, but the descendants of those people who survived the drowning of Númenor/Atlantis. Tolkien's heroes sail out of the west, not out of the east.

The idea of transmission via racial memory is a much more idiosyncratic and personal approach,[16] while the book-based concepts of transmission could be seen as inspired by Tolkien's work as medievalist. We know that Tolkien suffered from "the terrible recurrent dream (beginning with memory) of the Great Wave, towering up, and coming ineluctably over the trees and green fields" (*Letters* 213) and that his son Michael had inherited this very same dream. Furthermore, Tolkien believed in the existence of a 'native language' – which is not identical with one's cradle or mother tongue.[17] This native tongue is an inherited linguistic disposition and is transmitted genetically, whereas the mother/cradle tongue is an acquired language and need not stand in any connection with the racial/genetic origins of the speaker. In Tolkien's case, it was the medieval dialect of the West-Midlands, as preserved in the Middle English work *Ancrene Wisse*, that struck him as familiar on first sight: "I am a West-midlander by blood (and took so early west-midland Middle English as a known tongue as soon as I set eyes on it), [...]" (*Letters* 213). He credited his maternal bloodline, the Suffields of Evesham in Worcestershire (*Letters* 54 and 218), for this and considered himself to be of true English stock with deep pre-Conquest West-Midland roots: "For barring the Tolkien (which must long ago have become a pretty thin strand) you [i.e. Christopher Tolkien] are a Mercian or Hwiccian (of Wychwood) on both sides" (*Letters* 108). The West-Midland dialect evidenced in the *Ancrene Wisse* is, according to Tolkien, one of the few surviving 'native' English tongues that had escaped – for some time at least – the deteriorating effects of the Norman Conquest. As such it goes back in direct line to Mercian Old English and the

---

[16] Similar ideas are to be found e.g. in John Buchan's short story 'The Far Islands' of 1899, (reprinted in Anderson 2003:195-212).

[17] See 'English and Welsh' (Tolkien 1997:190); *Letters* 213; and Bachmann and Honegger (2006) for an in-depth discussion of Tolkien's ideas on blood, language, and race. See also Smith (2007) for a general discussion of Tolkien's attitude towards language.

two must have been, for centuries, the mother tongues and, most likely, 'native' languages of the Suffields' direct ancestors.

Tolkien never explicitly states how the 'linguistic Fall' that caused the (modern) separation of mother tongue and native language came about. I strongly suspect that, for the English, this 'Fall' was the Norman Conquest and the subsequent domination of Romance languages that radically changed the development of English (see *Biography* 48). Without the Normans, the English would speak a language that would still be much closer to their Old English dialects and thus closer to their 'native language'.

What, then, is the relevance of Tolkien's (linguistically heretical) concept of 'native language' for the question of how to connect the Legendarium with England and the English? One possible answer lies in the connection between the language of the Dark-elves and Old English.[18] The language of the Anglo-Saxons, as well as some other 'mannish' languages, are said to derive from the tongue of the Dark-elves. In this context, the elvish matter is additionally linked to the English by means of their shared linguistic heritage. Old English is not only the 'native' language of the Anglo-Saxons, but it also connects them with the true tradition of faery – connections that have been all but severed by the linguistic and cultural impact of the Norman Conquest.

England = The Shire: Bilbo Baggins, Elf-friend
Tolkien continued to work on the frame narrative (with Ælfwine as the transmitter) at least into the 1950s, i.e. a time when *The Lord of the Rings* had been completed and published independently of the Legendarium and, in the first edition, even without the Appendices. The minimal frame narrative provided for the epic tale of the War of the Rings is again one of 'bookish' transmission. The prologue presents the text as a translation of a copy of *The Red Book of Westermarch*, which, ultimately, goes back to Bilbo's diary as the oldest layer, Frodo's account of the subsequent events and Sam's additions. *The Silmarillion*,

---

[18] See Hostetter and Smith (1996:287-88), who base their argument on the information found in *Lost Road* 179.

and much of the Legendarium, could be accomodated in this new context as material collected and translated by Bilbo during his stay at Rivendell. The 'mannish' (proto-) Old English transmitter figures have thus been replaced by hobbits – who had been conceived, similarly to Eärendil, in a moment of philological inspiration and revelation. Although this change severs the Legendarium's ties to semi-mythical Germanic history and to English history in particular, it makes it more English than ever. This is achieved mainly by presenting the hobbits and the Shire as the epitome of (modern) Englishness.[19] Thus, they speak the clearly recognisable English dialect of the Oxford/Warwickshire area (see Johannesson 2004). Also, their cultural and technological know-how is similar to that of an idealised rural Victorian England – stressing the elements of civilisatory comfort such as pipeleaf, tea, potatoes, waistcoats, and clocks, while at the same time avoiding the less savoury aspects of technological progress and industrial development. The hobbits thus function as mediators between the (modern) reader and the heroic-epic world of Middle-earth[20] and the elf-friends Bilbo and Frodo Baggins in particular provide the connection to the larger world of the Legendarium.

Conclusion

Tolkien's Legendarium has remained a work in progress throughout his long life. We have thus no single unified textual corpus, and the English, in spite of Tolkien's astonishing creativity, are still without a 'mythology for England' proper. What they have, however, is, with *The Lord of the Rings*, an epic which captures some of the best elements of 'Englishness' in its (especially hobbit) protagonists, and, with *The Silmarillion, Unfinished Tales* and *The History of Middle-earth* series, a vast and somewhat ramshackle collection of tales and legends that have sprung from the depths of a genuinely 'English' creativity. Its 'Northern spirit' links it to England and to the north-west of Europe, but it

---

[19] See Speed (1994:139): "Tolkien, whose imaginary peoples encode a certain Englishness."
[20] See Shippey (2003:55-93) and also Hopkins (1996).

appeals at the same time to all of mankind. Tolkien's work is thus, on the one hand, a grandiose failure if one were looking for a nationalistically English mythology. On the other hand, his predominantly narrative works (*The Lord of the Rings*, *The Hobbit*) provide a literary appropriation of the mythic matter by means of the 'English' transmitter figures of the hobbits. It is ironic that Tolkien achieved his aim of a 'mythology for England' not so much by linking it with (semi-)mythic and historical English history, but by placing his main work (*The Lord of the Rings*) outside history and by making the anachronistic hobbits the transmitters of the matter. As such, his 'mythology of England' has become a mythopoeic gift to readers all over the world rather than to a limited national audience.

Biographical Note

Thomas Honegger holds a Ph.D. from the University of Zurich and is the author of *From Phoenix to Chauntecleer: Medieval English Animal Poetry* (1996). He edited several volumes on Tolkien, medieval language and literature, and published papers on Chaucer, Shakespeare, and mediaeval romance. He is currently involved in a large-scale project for a web-based interdisciplinary encyclopaedia of animals in medieval literature and teaches, since 2002, as Professor for Mediaeval Studies at the Friedrich-Schiller-University Jena (Germany). Homepage: www2.uni-jena.de/fsu/anglistik/homepage/Honegger3.htm

Bibliography

Abbreviations
Biography: see Carpenter 1995
Finn and Hengest: see Tolkien 1998
Letters: see Carpenter 2000
Lost Road: see Tolkien 1992b
Lost Tales 1: see Tolkien 1994
Lost Tales 2: see Tolkien 1992a
Sauron: see Tolkien 1993b
Shaping: see Tolkien 1993a

Albu, Emily, 2001, *The Normans in Their Histories: Propaganda, Myth and Subversion*, Woodbridge: The Boydell Press.
Anderson, Douglas A. (ed.), 2003, *Tales Before Tolkien. The Roots of Modern Fantasy*, New York: DelRey.
Bachmann, Dieter and Thomas Honegger, 2006, 'Ein Mythos für das 20. Jahrhundert: Blut, Rasse und Erbgedächtnis bei Tolkien', *Hither Shore* 2:13-39.
Beaune, Colette, 1991, *The Birth of an Ideology. Myths and Symbols of Nation in Late-Medieval France*, (translated by Susan Ross Huston, edited by Fredrich L. Cheyette. French original *Naissance de la nation France*, published 1985), Berkeley, Los Angeles, Oxford: University of California Press.
Burns, Marjorie, 2005, *Perilous Realms. Celtic and Norse in Tolkien's Middle-earth*, Toronto: University of Toronto Press.
Carpenter, Humphrey, 1995, *J.R.R. Tolkien. A Biography*, (paperback edition; first edition 1977), London: HarperCollins.
--- (ed., with the assistance of Christopher Tolkien), 2000, *The Letters of J.R.R. Tolkien*, (first published 1981), Boston: Houghton Mifflin.
Colls, Robert, 2002, *Identity of England*, Oxford: Oxford University Press.
Eley, Penny, 1991, 'The Myth of the Trojan Descent', *Nottingham Medieval Studies* 35:27-40.
Flieger, Verlyn, 2000, 'The Footsteps of Aelfwine', in Verlyn Flieger and Carl F. Hostetter (eds.), 2000, *Tolkien's Legendarium. Essays on The History of Middle-earth*, Westport, Connecticut and London: Greenwood Press, 183-198.
---, 2004a, 'A Mythology for Finland: Tolkien and Lönnrot as Mythmakers', in Jane Chance (ed.), 2004, *Tolkien and the Invention of Myth. A Reader*, Lexington, Kentucky: The University Press of Kentucky, 277-283.
---, 2004b, "'Do the Atlantis story and abandon Eriol-Saga'", *Tolkien Studies* 1:43-68.
Forster, Edward M., 1978, *Howards End*, (first published 1910), Harmondsworth: Penguin.
Fox, Kate, 2004, *Watching the English. The Hidden Rules of English Behaviour*, London: Hodder.

Hopkins, Chris, 1996, 'Tolkien and Englishness', in Patricia Reynolds and Glen H. GoodKnight (eds.), 1996, *Proceedings of the J.R.R. Centenary Conference. Keble College, Oxford, 1992*, (*Mythlore* 80/*Mallorn* 30), Milton Keynes and Altadena: The Tolkien Society and The Mythopoetic Press, 278-280.

Hostetter, Carl F. and Arden R. Smith, 1996, 'A Mythology for England', in Patricia Reynolds and Glen H. GoodKnight (eds.), 1996, *Proceedings of the J.R.R. Centenary Conference. Keble College, Oxford, 1992*, (*Mythlore* 80/*Mallorn* 30), Milton Keynes and Altadena: The Tolkien Society and The Mythopoetic Press, 281-290.

Johannesson, Nils-Lennart, 2004, 'The Speech of the Individual and of the Community in *The Lord of the Rings*', in Peter Buchs and Thomas Honegger (eds.), 2004, *News from the Shire and Beyond – Studies on Tolkien*, (Cormarë Series 1, second edition. First edition 1997), Zurich and Berne: Walking Tree Publishers, 13-57.

Lewis, Alex and Elizabeth Currie, 2005, *The Forsaken Realm of Tolkien. J.R.R. Tolkien and the Medieval Tradition*, Oswestry: Medea Publishing.

Macrae-Gibson, Osgar D. (ed.), 1973/1979, *Of Arthour and Merlin*, (two volumes; volume 1 Text (1973), volume 2 Introduction, Notes and Glossary (1979). Early English Text Society Original Series 268 & 279), London: Oxford University Press.

Priestman, Judith, 1994, *A List of the Papers of J.R.R. Tolkien at the Bodleian Library Oxford*, Oxford: Bodleian Library.

Rosenberg, Alfred, 1939, *Der Mythus des 20. Jahrhunderts. Eine Wertung der seelisch-geistigen Gestaltenkämpfe unserer Zeit*, (first edition 1930), Munich: Hoheneichen Verlag.

Rouse, Robert Allen, 2005, *The Idea of Anglo-Saxon England in Middle English Romance*, (Studies in Medieval Romance 3), Cambridge: D.S. Brewer.

Shippey, Tom A., 2000, 'The Undeveloped Image: Anglo-Saxon in Popular Consciousness from Turner to Tolkien', in Donald Scragg and Carole Weinberg (eds.), 2000, *Literary Appropriations of the Anglo-Saxons from the Thirteenth to the Twentieth Century*, Cambridge: Cambridge University Press, 215-236.

---, 2003, *The Road to Middle-earth*, (third edition, first edition 1982), Boston: Houghton Mifflin.

Smith, Ross, 2007, *Inside Language: Linguistic and Aesthetic Theory in Tolkien*, (Cormarë Series 11), Zurich and Berne: Walking Tree Publishers.

Southern, R.W., 1970, 'Aspects of the European Tradition of Historical Writing. 1. The Classical Tradition from Einhard to Geoffrey of Monmouth', *Transactions of the Royal Historical Society* 20:173-196.

Speed, Diane, 1994, 'The Construction of the Nation in Medieval English Romance', in Carol M. Meale (ed.), 1994, *Readings in Medieval English Romance*, Cambridge: D.S. Brewer, 135-157.

Tolkien, John Ronald Reuel, 1992a, *The Book of Lost Tales 2*, (edited by Christopher Tolkien; History of Middle-earth 2; first published 1984), London: HarperCollins.

---, 1992b, *The Lost Road*, (edited by Christopher Tolkien; History of Middle-earth 5; first published 1987), London: HarperCollins.

---, 1993a, *The Shaping of Middle-earth*, (edited by Christopher Tolkien; History of Middle-earth 4; first published 1988), London: HarperCollins.

---, 1993b, *Sauron Defeated*, (edited by Christopher Tolkien; History of Middle-earth 9; first published 1992), London: HarperCollins.
---, 1994, *The Book of Lost Tales 1*, (edited by Christopher Tolkien; History of Middle-earth 1; first published 1983), London: HarperCollins.
---, 1997, 'English and Welsh', (original lecture delivered 21 October 1955, published 1963), republished in *The Monsters and the Critics*, (edited by Christopher Tolkien), London: HarperCollins, 162-197.
---, 1998, *Finn and Hengest: The Fragment and the Episode*, (edited by Alan J. Bliss, first edition 1982), London: HarperCollins.
Turville-Petre, Thorlac, 1977, *The Alliterative Revival*, Cambridge: D.S. Brewer.
---, 1996, *England the Nation: Language, Literature, and National Identity, 1290-1340*, Oxford: Clarendon Press.
West, Richard C., 2004, 'Setting the Rocket Off in Story: *The Kalevala* as the Germ of Tolkien's Legendarium', in Jane Chance (ed.), 2004,*Tolkien and the Invention of Myth. A Reader*, Lexington, Kentucky: The University Press of Kentucky, 285-294.

Lewis's View of Myth as a Conveyer of Deepest Truth

DEVIN BROWN

Abstract

An examination of C. S. Lewis's writing and of what he had to say about writing suggests that Lewis saw a necessity for a creative, mythic platform rather than an expository one in order to fully address life's most important issues. His fiction is an attempt to cast what he considered to be fundamental truths into an imaginary world, for it is only in this manner, he maintained, can they "appear in their real potency."

Near the end of *Out of the Silent Planet*, the first volume in his Space Trilogy, C.S. Lewis steps in and tells us, somewhat in the fashion of Dr. Watson, that it has been he who has provided this record of Ransom's adventures. He writes:

> It was Dr. Ransom who first saw that our only chance was to publish in the form of *fiction* what would certainly not be listened to as fact. He even thought – greatly overrating my literary powers – that this might have the incidental advantage of reaching a wider public, and that, certainly, it would reach a great many people sooner than 'Weston.' (Lewis 1996b:153)

In the second act of Shakespeare's *As You Like It*, Rosalind tells Touchstone, "Thou speakest wiser than thou art ware of" (2.4.54). In the same way perhaps Lewis's short comment about the format of his writing contains a deeper truth than it delivers within the context of the story. While Lewis continued to publish both fiction and non-fiction all of his life, there are indications that he often found a *creative* format to be more powerful than an *expository* one. This distinction between fictional and non-fictional writing and the relative value

Lewis placed on the two forms of expression may also be reflected somewhat in his early shift away from studying philosophy to studying literature. In a letter written to his father shortly after being awarded a fellowship in English at Magdalen, a posting that would cement his professional move from the one field to the other, Lewis wrote that:

> As to the other change – from Philosophy to English […] I am rather glad of the change […] A continued search among the abstract roots of things, a perpetual questioning of all things that plain men take for granted, a chewing the cud for fifty years over inevitable ignorance and a constant frontier watch on the little tidy lighted conventional world of science and daily life – is this the best life for temperaments such as ours?
> (*Letters*, Lewis 1993:212)

The difficulty in achieving worldwide recognition in even a single genre makes all the more remarkable Lewis's ability to switch back and forth from the apologetic, non-fictional writing found in many of his works such as *The Problem of Pain* (1940) and *Miracles* (1947) to the mythic style seen first in the space trilogy and later in the seven Narnia books. It is clear that Lewis both consciously and sub-consciously understood the need for a creative, mythic platform rather than an expository one in order to most fully address life's most fundamental questions. Speaking of himself he said that "there may be an author who at a particular moment finds not only fantasy but fantasy-for-children the exactly right form for what he wants to say" (*On Stories*, Lewis 1982:36). He echoed this point in title of the essay "Sometimes Fairy Stories May Say Best What's to Be Said," where he repeated, "I wrote fairy tales because Fairy Tale seemed the ideal form for the stuff I had to say" (*On Stories*, Lewis 1982:47). Lewis held that only by conveying spiritual truths through a story format, by "casting all these things into an imaginary world, stripping them of their stained-glass and Sunday school associations," could one for the first time make them appear "in their real potency" (*On Stories*, Lewis 1982:47).

By using imaginative writing to convey truth, Lewis felt that he was able to steal past "the watchful dragons" (*On Stories*, Lewis 1982:47). There is a suggestion that Lewis, who was always quite humble about his accomplishments, may have recognized that his greatest gift was his ability to express truth through a mythic format. In a letter written in 1955, Lewis offered this evaluation of his talents: "If I am now good for anything it is for catching the reader unawares – thro' fiction and symbol" (Glover 1981:131).

Lewis saw myth not as "misunderstood history, [...] nor diabolical illusion, [...] nor priestly lying, [...] but, at its best, *a real though unfocused gleam of divine truth falling on human imagination*" (*Miracles*, Lewis 1996a:134, italics added), as a form which, unlike his apologetic works, enabled man "to express the inexpressible" (Kilby 1964:81). In his preface to *George MacDonald: An Anthology*, Lewis wrote that the storymaking found in myth "gets under our skin" and "hits us at a level deeper than our thoughts" (Lewis 1946b:xxviii). In *Surprised by Joy*, Lewis describes how he finally "learned what writing means" – not merely to "state" but to "suggest" (Lewis 1955:74). I would argue that it is in his mythic works, his Narnia stories and his space trilogy, that Lewis most fully achieves this goal of not merely stating but suggesting.

As Leanne Payne – and others – have pointed out, Lewis is recognized as having "one of the most logical minds of this century" (Payne 1988:160); yet in spite of the significance that logic played in his life and work, Lewis saw in himself that imagination, not reason, played the central role. In a letter addressed to the Milton Society of America written in 1954, Lewis was asked to "make a statement" about himself and his books. He wrote:

> The list of my books which I send in answer to Mr. Hunter's request will, I fear, strike you as a very mixed bag. Since he encourages me to "make a statement" about them, I may point out that there is a guiding thread. The *imaginative man in me is older, more continuously operative, and in that sense more basic than either the religious writer or the critic.* It was he who made me attempt (with little success) to be a poet. It was he who, in response to the poetry of others,

> made me a critic. [...] It was he, who, after my conversion led me to embody my religious belief in symbolical or mythopoeic forms, ranging from *Screwtape* to a kind of theologized science-fiction. And it was, of course, he who has brought me, in the last few years to write the series of Narnian stories for children.
> (*Letters*, Lewis 1993:444, italics added)

This fact – that the "imaginative man" was more primary in Lewis – is also revealed in the break-through moments which are recorded in *Surprised by Joy*, the chronicle of the influences of his early years. Over and over again we find that the works that affect and transform his character are myths not philosophy. In Lewis's autobiography, we read about the influence of *Squirrel Nutkin* by Beatrice Potter, of Tegner's lines about the death of Balder, of the tales of Siegfried, and most importantly of the effect that *Phantastes*, the mythic tale by George MacDonald, had on him and his thinking.

Certainly Lewis's tutelage under William Kirkpatrick, the teacher Lewis claimed was near to being a "purely logical entity" (*Joy*, Lewis 1955:135), was a huge factor in his development. Still, Lewis came to recognize the limits of logical argument, and so the character of MacPhee in *That Hideous Strength*, who was modeled after Kirkpatrick, is never fully able to grasp the reality of what is happening within the house at St. Anne's. In the essay 'Myth Became Fact' Lewis describes the limits to reason:

> Human intellect is incurably abstract. [...] Yet the only realities we experience are concrete – this pain, this pleasure, this dog, this man. While we are loving the man, bearing the pain, enjoying the pleasure, we are not intellectually apprehending Pleasure, Pain, or Personality. [...] This is our dilemma – either to taste and not to know or to know and not to taste [...] As thinkers we are cut off from what we are thinking about. [...] The more lucidly we think the more we are cut off: the more deeply we enter into reality, the less we can think.
> (*Joy*, Lewis 1955:65)

The solution which Lewis proposes for this dilemma is the creative act of mythmaking, the type of writing he attempted to do in his own fiction. According to Lewis, it is when we read this type of writing that "we come nearest to experiencing as a concrete what can otherwise be understood only as an abstraction" (*Dock*, Lewis 1970c:66). Lewis scholar Donald Glover suggests that in his fictional writing Lewis found the power to cast a magical spell over us. In his book, appropriately titled *C.S. Lewis The Art of Enchantment*, Glover (1981:51) notes that Lewis was well aware of the power which story has to "present in understandable form concepts which could be approached in no other direct fashion." Glover (1981:2) explores the reasons why he finds Lewis's fiction so "compellingly readable," one reason being that it offers "more meaning than that found in the explicit content." In describing Lewis's decision to write in fiction rather than in the expository prose of his other apologetic pieces, Glover (1981:3) states that Lewis did so because he believed that this "indirect" approach could "bring the reader closer to the truth."

Perhaps the best way to illustrate the power that myth has, as Lewis said, to get under our skin and hit us at a deeper level than our thoughts, might be to look at three issues which Lewis dealt with in both a creative and an expository format, to hold the two versions side by side, and see whether the mythic or the non-fictional expression is the more compelling.

As a first example, we might turn to the section in *The Problem of Pain* where Lewis describes our desire for God to leave us alone and the subsequent resentment we feel when he intrudes into our lives. Lewis writes:

> [...] when men attempt to be Christians without this preliminary consciousness of sin, the result is almost bound to be a certain resentment against God as to one who is always making impossible demands and always inexplicably angry. Most of us have at times felt a secret sympathy with the dying farmer who replied to the Vicar's dissertation on repentance by asking "What harm have I ever done *Him?*" There is the real rub. The worst we have

done to God is to leave Him alone – why can't He return the compliment? (Lewis 1996c:51)

Lewis portrays this same sentiment in *That Hideous Strength* through the character of Jane Studdock; and in this fictional portrayal, I would propose, Lewis's vision is communicated in its full power:

> It came over her with sickening clarity that the affair of her dreams, far from being ended, was only beginning. The bright, narrow little life which she had proposed to live was being irremediably broken into. Windows into huge, dark landscapes were opening on every side, and she was powerless to shut them. It would drive her mad, she thought, to face it alone. The other alternative was to go back to Miss Ironwood. But that seemed to be only a way of going deeper into all this darkness. This Manor at St. Anne's – this kind of company – was 'mixed up in it.' She didn't want to get drawn in. It was unfair. It wasn't as if she had asked much of life. All she wanted was to be left alone.
> (Lewis 1946a:83)

For a second comparison of the two formats, we can turn to *Mere Christianity* where Lewis discusses the repentance which man must undergo on the way to salvation. We read:

> Now what was the sort of 'hole' man got himself into? He had tried to set up on his own, to behave as if he belonged to himself. In other words, fallen man is not simply an imperfect creature who needs improvement: he is a rebel who must lay down his arms. Laying down your arms, surrendering, saying you are sorry, realizing that you have been on the wrong track and getting ready to start life over again from the ground floor – that is the only way out of a 'hole.' This process of surrender – this movement full speed astern – is what Christians call repentance. Now repentance is no fun at all. It is

> something much harder than merely eating humble pie. It means unlearning all the self-conceit and self-will that we have been training ourselves into for thousands of years. It means killing part of yourself, undergoing a kind of death.
> (Lewis 1952:59-60)

Lewis included several portrayals of repentance in his mythic fiction; perhaps the most moving occurs in *The Voyage of the 'Dawn Treader'* when Eustace, as a dragon, has a life-changing meeting with Aslan. In the following lengthy excerpt, Eustace meets Edmund at night on the beach and tells the story of his meeting with Aslan:

> "So at last we came to the top of a mountain I'd never seen before and on the top of the mountain there was a garden – trees and fruit and everything. In the middle of it there was a well.
>
> I knew it was a well because you could see the water bubbling up from the bottom of it: but it was a lot bigger than most wells – like a very big, round bath with marble steps going down into it. The water was as clear as anything and I thought if I could get in there and bathe it would ease the pain in my leg. But the lion told me I must undress first. […]
>
> I was just going to say that I couldn't undress because I hadn't any clothes on when I suddenly thought that dragons are snaky sort of things and snakes can cast their skins. Oh, of course, thought I, that's what the lion means. So I started scratching myself and my scales began coming off all over the place. And then I scratched a little deeper and, instead of just scales coming off here and there, my whole skin started peeling off beautifully, like it does after an illness, or as if I was a banana. In a minute or two I just stepped out of it. I could see it lying there beside me, looking rather nasty. It was a most lovely feeling. So I started to go down into the well for my bath.
>
> Well, exactly the same thing happened again.

> And I thought to myself, oh dear, how ever many skins have I got to take off? For I was longing to bathe my leg. So I scratched away for the third time and got off a third skin, just like the two others, and stepped out of it. But as soon as I looked at myself in the water I knew it had been no good.
> Then the lion said – but I don't know if it spoke – "You will have to let me undress you." I was afraid of his claws, I can tell you, but I was pretty nearly desperate now. So I just lay flat down on my back to let him do it.
> The very first tear he made was so deep that I thought it had gone right into my heart. And when he began pulling the skin off it hurt worse than anything I've ever felt." (Lewis 1970b:88-90)

A final illustration pairs up a passage on healing from *Miracles* with one from the *Chronicles of Narnia*. In *Miracles*, Lewis *tells* us about healing:

> All who are cured are cured by Him, not merely in the sense that His providence provides them with medical assistance and wholesome environments, but also in the sense that their very tissues are repaired by the far-descended energy which, flowing from Him, energizes the whole system of nature. But once He did it visibly to the sick in Palestine, a Man meeting with men. What in its general operation we refer to laws of Nature or once referred to Apollo or Aesculapius thus reveals itself. The Power that always was behind all healings puts on a face and hands. (Lewis 1996a:184)

Towards the end of *The Lion, the Witch and the Wardrobe*, Lewis *shows* us miraculous healing rather than *telling* us about it, and in doing so, is able to fully capture the inexpressible power and joy. Lucy and Susan have come with Aslan to the Witch's castle and suddenly find themselves in the middle of a wide stone courtyard full of statues:

> "What an extraordinary place!" cried Lucy. "All those stone animals – and people too! It's – it's like a museum."
>
> "Hush," said Susan, "Aslan's doing something."
>
> He was indeed. He had bounded up to the stone lion and breathed on him. [...]
>
> I expect you've seen someone put a lighted match to a bit of newspaper which is propped up in a grate against an unlit fire. And for a second nothing seems to have happened; and then you notice a tiny streak of flame creeping along the edge of the newspaper. It was like that now. For a second after Aslan had breathed upon him the stone lion looked the same. Then a tiny streak of gold began to run along his white marble back – then it spread – then the colour seemed to lick all over him as the flame licks all over a bit of paper – then, while his hindquarters were still obviously stone the lion shook his mane and all the heavy, stony folds rippled into living hair. [...]
> (Lewis 1970a:164-65)

In his book *The Healing Power of Stories*, Daniel Taylor (1996:4) has written that it is story, and not philosophy, which can best tell us "who we are, why we are here, and what we are to do," that it is story which gives us "our best answers to all of life's big questions, and to most of the small ones as well." According to Taylor (1996:155), story has the power to "receive us at birth, accompany us through the stages of life, and prepare us for death," giving pattern "to otherwise chaotic experience, making it memorable and meaningful."

In her recent book *Story as Truth: The Rock that is Higher*, Madeleine L'Engle explores the interconnection between story and truth. She writes:

> People have always told stories as they searched for truth. As our ancient ancestors sat around the campfire in front of their caves, they told the stories of their day in order to try to understand what their day had meant, what the truth of the mammoth hunt was, or the roar of the cave lion, or the falling

> in love of two young people. Bards and troubadours throughout the centuries have sung stories in order to give meaning to the events of human life. [...] As a child I read avidly and in stories I found truths which were not available in history or geography or social studies. (L'Engle 1993:90)

L'Engle (1993:103) asks, "How do we come to meaning and truth except through story?" concluding that the "storyteller is a storyteller" because he or she cares about truth, about searching for truth, about expressing truth, and about sharing truth.

In choosing to use myth as an indirect vehicle for truth, Lewis was following the lead of his model and spiritual mentor – George MacDonald. In MacDonald's fiction, Lewis said, he could feel the winds of Joy blowing out into the real world, transforming all things (*Joy*, Lewis 1955:180-81). In choosing to convey truth through myth, Lewis chose a format that was full of power to reach into the human heart. In this he was also following the lead of Jesus – who when he was asked the question "Who is my neighbor?" did not answer with an exposition on the numerous forms of brotherly love, but instead answered by saying: "There was a man who was going down from Jerusalem to Jericho, and fell among robbers, who stripped him and beat him, and left him for dead. Now by chance a priest was going down that road [...]." (Luke 10:30).

And so the story goes.

Biographical Note

Devin Brown is a Lilly Scholar and a Professor of English at Asbury College in Lexington, Kentucky. In addition to a number of articles about Lewis and Tolkien, he has also published three books: *Inside Narnia*, *Inside Prince Caspian*, and *Not Exactly Normal*. He is currently serving as Visiting Writer-in-Residence at Transylvania University.

Bibliography

Glover, Donald, 1981, *C.S. Lewis: the Art of Enchantment*, Athens, Ohio University Press.
Kilby, Clyde, 1964, *The Christian World of C.S. Lewis*, Grand Rapids: William B. Eerdmans.
L'Engle, Madeleine, 1993, *Story as Truth: The Rock that is Higher*, Wheaton, Illinois: Harold Shaw.
Lewis, Clive Staples, 1946a, *That Hideous Strength*, (first published 1945), New York: Macmillan.
--- (ed.), 1946b, *George MacDonald: An Anthology*, London: Bles.
---, 1952, *Mere Christianity*, New York: Simon & Schuster.
---, 1955, *Surprised by Joy*, New York: Harcourt Brace.
---, 1970a, *The Lion, the Witch and the Wardrobe*, (first published 1950), New York: Macmillan
---, 1970b, *The Voyage of the 'Dawn Treader'*, (first published 1952), New York: Macmillan.
---, 1970c *God in the Dock: Essays on Theology and Ethics*. Grand Rapids: William B. Eerdmans.
---, 1970d, 'Myth Became Fact', in *God in the Dock: Essays on Theology and Ethics*, Grand Rapids: William B. Eerdmans, 63-7.
---, 1982, *On Stories*, New York: Harcourt Brace.
---, 1993, *Letters of C.S. Lewis*, New York: Harcourt Brace.
---, 1996a, *Miracles*, (first published 1947; revised edition 1960), New York: Simon & Schuster.
---, 1996b, *Out of the Silent Planet*, (first published 1938), New York: Scribner Paperback Fiction.
---, 1996c, *The Problem of Pain*, (first published 1940), New York: Simon & Schuster.
Payne, Leanne, 1988, *Real Presence: The Christian Worldview of C.S. Lewis as Incarnational Reality*, Wheaton, Illinois: Crossway Books.
Taylor, Daniel, 1996, *The Healing Power of Stories*, New York: Doubleday.

'A Kind of Orpheus-Legend in Reverse':
Two Classical Myths in the Story of Beren and Lúthien[1]

Miryam Librán-Moreno

Abstract

The following essay is an inquiry into the influence of two Greek myths in the shaping of the matter of Beren and Lúthien: the myths of Orpheus and Eurydice (Orpheus-legend) and Protesilaus and Laodameia (Protesilaodameia romance).

Among the stories and elements that formed Tolkien's legendarium, the matter of Beren and Lúthien was central to his whole mythology, and arguably closest to his heart for deeply personal and intimate reasons. As is well known, the tale of Beren and Lúthien Tinúviel, the kernel of Tolkien's mythology, arose, in Tolkien's own words, "at a small woodland glade filled with hemlocks at Roos in Yorkshire [...]" (*Letters* 420), a place where the Professor and his wife Edith Bratt used to walk hand in hand, and where Edith sang and danced for her husband during the year of 1917. Even as late as 1972, Tolkien still considered his wife, then recently dead, "my Lúthien", and he made provisions to have the words 'Lúthien' engraved on her tomb as her sole epitaph (*Letters* 420.)

A measure of the importance attached by Tolkien to the matter of Beren and Lúthien is the fact that he wrote, rewrote, revised, altered, and modified it untiringly and unceasingly during all his creative life. The earliest version now extant is 'The Tale of Tinúviel', published in *The Book of Lost Tales, Part Two*, dated to ca. 1918. Afterwards, Tolkien returned to the story in

---

[1] This chapter is a part of a research project (HUM 2005-04375) financed by the M.E.C of Spain.

'The Lay of Leithian' ('Release from Bondage', published in *The Lays of Beleriand*) a long, unfinished poem in rhyming couplets written mostly between 1925 and 1931, and subjected to a thorough revision after he had completed *The Lord of the Rings*. A few elements of the matter of Beren and Lúthien reappeared again in 'The Earliest Silmarillion' (§ 10) and in 'The Quenta Silmarillion' (§ 10), both published in *The Shaping of Middle-earth*.[2] The tale was told also in the poem 'Light as Leaf on Lindentree' (originally published in 1925), adapted and subsequently incorporated into both 'The Lay of the Children of Húrin' (ll. 403-74) and the discussion of the fates of Beren and Lúthien found in *The Fellowship of the Ring* (FR I.11, 187-90).[3] The fullest version, characterised as an abbreviated and condensed prosification of 'The Lay of Leithian', is the chapter entitled 'Of Beren and Lúthien', in *The Silmarillion* (ch. 19.) The textual history of the tale of Beren and Lúthien presents us with a small labyrinth of versions and modifications that, however, do not substantially alter the kernel of the original story, as told in the first attested version ('The Tale of Tinúviel'): a semi-divine creature who excels in song, enchantments, and dance, must overcome many hindrances and adverse circumstances to be reunited with her true love. The last and greatest of those obstacles is death itself which she vanquishes with the aid of her love, her ability to sing, and her grief.

Despite Tolkien's avowal that the tale had been originated in a real life event, and that the character of Lúthien was an idealised portrayal of the youthful Edith (*Letters* 420-421), the fact remains that the eventful story of Beren and Lúthien has attracted critical attention in search for possible mythological sources. This quest for mythological parallels might find an unlikely ally in Tolkien himself, who intimated that it was his practice to present the intimate and personal kernel of real life enshrined in the heart of the tale

---

[2] See an overview of its complex textual history in Shippey (2003²:258) and, in more detail, in *Lost Tales 2* 50-60; *Lays* 183-189; *Shaping* 213-216; *Lost Road* 292-296.

[3] The apparition of the story of Beren and Lúthien in this precise passage is very significant, given that the choice of Lúthien serves to make explicit the metaphysical undercurrent running through *The Lord of the Rings* that makes itself present in the union of Aragorn and Arwen (cf. *Letters* 193; *RK* App. I <1>, 1010.)

through the veil of a mythical superstructure. This procedure fits well with Tolkien's reserve and his habit of expressing his most deeply felt emotions and feelings through the distance afforded by the assumption of a mythological garb.[4]

Be that as it may, it is generally conceded that a great many traditional elements taken from previously existing literary sources ('bones', as Tolkien used to call them)[5] were put together to form the entirely original and idiosyncratic story of Beren and Lúthien.[6] Tolkien himself hinted as much, when he confessed that his tales were 'new' in that "they are not directly derived from the myths and legends," although, he pointed out, "they must inevitably contain a large measure of ancient wide-spread motives or elements" (*Letters* 147).[7] The present chapter will attempt to trace the influence of two Greek myths in the shaping of the matter of Beren and Lúthien: the myths of Orpheus and Eurydice (Orpheus-legend) and Protesilaus and Laodameia (Protesilaodameia romance) will be particularly analysed in that regard.[8] Needless to say, the objective of the present work is not to posit the existence of Classic roots for the whole or even the major part of the tale to the exclusion of other mythologies or literatures. Rather, its aim is to examine a few of its episodes through the lens of the two classical myths mentioned above.

---

[4] "My nature [...] expresses itself about things deepest felt in tales and myths" (*Letters* 420-421.)

[5] 'On Fairy-Stories' (OFS 120), "By 'the soup' I mean the story as it is served up by its author or teller, and by 'desire to see the bones', its source or material." See further Shippey (2003²:289-290) and Librán-Moreno (2005a:28).

[6] See some of these sources in West (2003), Shippey (2003²:258-259) and Stevens (2004).

[7] An example of Tolkien's modus operandi is the final battle between the Valar and Morgoth: although it "owes [...] more to the Norse vision of Ragnarök than to anything else," still "it is not much like it." (*Letters* 149.) What we have here is an acknowledgement of direct inspiration in a pre-existing myth and an example of what Tolkien conceived of as reelaboration.

[8] It is to be hoped that the influence of classical mythology on the formation of Tolkien's legendarium will no longer be contested: see e.g. Stevens (2004:120-121) and Librán-Moreno (2005a:28-30).

I. THE ORPHEUS-LEGEND[9]

I.1 Lúthien as Orpheus

Let us start with the matter of Orpheus, an influence Tolkien himself acknowledged in print ("a kind of Orpheus-legend in reverse, but one of Pity not of Inexorability", *Letters* 193). The characters and stories of Orpheus and Lúthien share a few common elements: both are the only offspring born from the union of a goddess and a lesser father.[10] Both came into being in the Northern edge of the world.[11] Their divine lineage on their mother's side accounts for the enchanting power of their song. When Lúthien and Orpheus sing, the inanimate world stands still and listens, everyone and everything falling under the spell of their music.[12] However, the closest parallels between Orpheus and Lúthien belong to the best-known part of the Thracian singer's legend: Orpheus' descent into the Underground in order to recover his beloved dead wife is an element that was present since the beginning of the matter of Beren and Lúthien. Despite the manifold versions and revisions undergone by the tale, this part of the story was never altered in any significant form. Morover, it was important enough to call forth the most moving and loving remembraces in Tolkien's latest letters (see *Letters* 193).

---

[9] English translations of classical texts are by A.S. Kline unless where indicated.

[10] Lúthien is, of course, the daughter of a Maia, Melian, and an Elf, Elu Thingol (see e.g. *Silmarillion* ch. 4, 58), while Orpheus is the only son born of the union of one of the Muses and Oeagrus, a Macedonian or Thracian man (see e.g. Sch. Pi. *P.* 4.313a, Apollod. *ApB* 1.3.2).

[11] Lúthien was born in Doriath, one of the Lands to the North (see e.g. *The Silmarillion* ch. 4, 58); Orpheus, on his part, was born near mount Rhodope, in Thrace, the extreme North for Greeks and Romans (Verg. *ecl.* 6.30, Ov. *Ars* 3.321). Orpheus' Thracian ancestry is highlighted by King Alfred's translation of Boeth. *Cons. Phil.* 3.m 12 ("an hearpere wæs on ðære ðiode ðe Ðracia hatte", XXXV 1.).

[12] See e.g. Aesch. *Ag.* 1629-1632, Eur. *I.A.* 1211-1214, *Ba.* 560-564. A further point of comparison may be adduced: Tinúviel's comparison with the nightingale may have been inspired, at least partially, by an extremely beautiful and tirelessly imitated Virgilian simile, which compared Orpheus' song of grief with the cry of the nightingale (*georg.* 4.511 *qualis populea maerens philomela sub umbra*, 'as the nightingale grieving in the poplar's shadows').

§ 1 Gaining physical entrance into the Underworld while still alive

One of the elements that tells Orpheus' katabasis apart from that of other heroes and heroines that come back from death (such as Protesilaus or Alcestis), is that all sources stress the fact that, unlike others, Orpheus was bold enough to enter the world of the dead *while still alive*. Orpheus availed himself of one of the Ploutonia or 'mouths of the Underground', caves that served as entry gates into Hades. The Thracian singer's Ploutonion was located at Cape Tainaron, in Southern Laconia:

> Vergil (=Verg.), *georg.* 4.467-469
> <u>Taenarias etiam fauces</u>, alta ostia Ditis
> Et caligantem nigra formidine lucum
> <u>Ingressus</u> Manesque adiit regemque tremendum
> (<u>He even entered the jaws of Taenarus</u>, the high gates of Dis, and the grove dim with dark fear, and came to the spirits, and their dread king.)

> Ovid (=Ov.), *met.* 10.13
> <u>Ad Styga Taenaria est ausus descendere porta</u>
> (he dared to go down to Styx, through the gate of Taenarus)

> Seneca (=Sen.), *H.Oet.* 1061-1062
> <u>Quin per Taenarias fores</u>
> manes cum tacitos adit
> (When he approached the silent ghosts / <u>through the gates of Taenarus</u>, my tr.)

Similarly, earlier versions of the tale of Beren and Lúthien had Lúthien accomplish the feat of crossing, while still alive,[13] the pass of Helcaraxë, the awful and impassable ice stretch that separated Valinor from Middle-earth, in order to reach the Halls of Mandos to plead her suit:

---

[13] The fact that she was still alive when she reached the Halls of Mandos (*Shaping* 65 "there is no suggestion here that Lúthien herself died at the time of Beren's death") seems significant enough, given that the earliest version of the tale has her die of grief and follow Beren ('The Tale of Tinúviel', *Lost Tales 2* 39) – a version much more in keeping with the story of Laodameia and Protesilaus than with that of Orpheus. See below II § 2.

Some say that Lúthien went even over the Grinding Ice [...] to Mandos' halls and won him (sc. Beren) back. ('Sketch of Mythology' § 10 = *Shaping* 28.)

§ 2   Crossing a body of water trusting in their mothers' powers.

Greek sources stress that Orpheus dared to sail the shuddering sea of the dead trusting solely on the power of his lyre

> Hermesianax fr. 7.1-8 Powell (s. III B.C.E.)
> οἵην μὲν φίλος υἱὸς ἀνήγαγεν Οἰάγροιο
> Ἀργιόπην Θρῆσσαν στειλάμενος κιθάρην Ἀϊδόθεν·
> ἔπλευσεν δὲ κακὸν καὶ ἀπειθέα χῶρον
> ἔνθα Χάρων κοινὴν ἕλκεται εἰς ἄκατον
> ψυχὰς οἰχομένων, λίμνη δ' ἐπὶ μακρὸν ἀϋτεῖ
> ῥεῦμα διὲκ μεγάλων ῥυομένη δονάκων.
> ἀλλ' ἔτλη παρὰ κῦμα μονόζωστος κιθαρίζων
> Ὀρφεύς.
> (Such was she whom the dear son of Oeagrus, armed only with the lyre, brought back from Hades, even the Thracian Agriope. Ay, he sailed to that evil and inexorable bourne where Charon drags into the common barque the souls of the departed; and over the lake he shouts afar, as it pours its flood from out the tall reeds. Yet Orpheus, though girded for the journey all alone, dared to sound his lyre beside the wave, tr. Charles Burton Gulick.)

Orpheus accomplished his mission of entering the Underwold while still alive because of his divine ancestry: specifically, he was aided in his endeavour by the songs his divine mother the Muse Calliope had taught him:

> Boethius (=Boeth.), *Cons. Phil.* 3 m. 12.20-23[14]
> *Illic blanda sonantibus*
> *Chordis carmina temperans*

---

[14] Cf. Hor. *carm.* 1.12.7-12 *Vnde uocalem temere insecutae / Orphea siluae / arte materna rapidos morantem / fluminum lapsus celerisque uentos, / blandum et auritas fidibus canoris / ducere quercus*; Augsburg; MS., Bischöfliches Ordinariat 5, fol. 1ʳ (s. XII), ll. 56-57 *Quos vocalis / Temperas, Calliope.*

> *Quicquid praecipuis deae*
> *Matris fontibus hauserat.*
> (There he tuned his songs to soothing tones, and sang the lays he had drawn <u>from his mother's fount of excellence</u>, W.V. Cooper tr.)
>
> Cf. also Horace (=Hor.), *carm.* 1.12.9-10
> *<u>arte materna</u> rapidos morantem*
> *fluminum lapsus celerisque uentos*
> (that held back the swift-running streams and the rush / of the breeze, <u>by his mother the Muse's art.</u>)[15]

We now turn to Lúthien. Just like Orpheus did the Stygian lake, Lúthien, while still alive, was able to cross the Sundering Seas that divide the land of the living from the dwelling places of the dead:

> The <u>Sundering Seas</u> between them lay,
> and yet at last they met once more.
> (*FR* I, 11, 189)
>
> Bidding him await her <u>beyond the Western Sea</u> [...] until Lúthien came to say her last farewell upon <u>the dim shores of the Outer Sea.</u>
> (*Silmarillion*, ch. 19, 226)

Furthermore, Lúthien was permitted to cross the Grinding Ice and reach Valinor alive precisely for the same reason Orpheus was, that is, the mediating power of her divine mother:

> Lúthien went even over the Grinding Ice, <u>aided by the power of her divine mother</u>, Melian, to Mandos' halls and won him back.
> ('Sketch of Mythology' § 10 = *Shaping* 28)

---

[15] Contrast with "thence Lúthien won him, / the Elf-maiden, <u>and the arts of Melian</u>" ('The Lay of the Children of Húrin' ll. 392-393.)

> Some songs say that <u>Melian summoned Thorndor</u>, and he bore her living into Valinor. And she came to the Halls of Mandos [...]
> ('The Quenta Silmarillion' § 10 = *Shaping* 138-139)

> Some have said that <u>Melian summoned Thorondor</u> and bade him bear Lúthien living to Valinor, claiming that <u>she had a part in the divine race of the gods</u>. ('The Quenta Silmarillion', text C, footnote eliminated from the final version)[16]

§ 3   Undying love as the cause of the katabasis

A further point of contact between the katabases of Orpheus and Lúthien is the reason that prompted their attempt: undying and desperate love for the dead spouse:

> Diodorus of Sicily (=D.S.) 4.25.4 (s. I B.C.E.)
> διὰ τὸν ἔρωτα τὸν πρὸς τὴν γυναῖκα καταρῆναι μὲν εἰς ᾅδου παραδόξως ἐτόλμησε
> (<u>For love of his wife</u> he dared to descend into Hades, contrary to all expectations, my tr.)

> Ov. *met.* 10.23-6
> *causa viae est coniunx [...]*
> */ [...] /*
> *[...] vicit Amor.*
> (My wife is the cause of my journey [...] Love won.)

§ 4   The magic spell of music, together with the spectacle of love and grief, move the gods of the Underworld to pity

Once in the presence of the King and Queen of the Dead, Orpheus pleads with them to allow his wife to return with him to the surface and to life (cf. Ov. *met.* 10.15-17.) Greek and Latin authors remarked insistently on the fact that the enchanting power of Orpheus' music and song was strong enough to bewitch even Hades himself:

---

[16] See Christopher Tolkien's remarks on the elimination of this footnote in *Lost Road* 303.

Euripides *Alc.* 357-362
εἰ δ' Ὀρφέως μοι γλῶσσα καὶ μέλος παρῆν,
ὥστ' ἢ κόρην Δήμητρος ἢ κείνης πόσιν
<u>ὕμνοισι κηλήσαντά σ'</u> ἐξ Ἅιδου λαβεῖν
κατῆλθον ἄν,
(If I had the voice and music of Orpheus so that I could <u>charm Demeter's daughter or her husband with song</u> and fetch you from Hades, I would have gone down to the Underworld, tr. D. Kovacs)

Scholium in Euripides *Alc.* 357
τῇ <u>μουσικῇ θέλξας</u> τὸν Πλούτωνα καὶ τὴν Κόρην
(putting a spell on Hades and Kore with his music)

D.S. 4.25.4
διὰ τῆς εὐμελείας ψυχαγωγήσας
(ensorcelling them through the beauty of his music)

Tzetzes (=Tz.) *Chil.* 849 (s. XII C.E.)
Ὀρφέως Ἅιδην <u>θέλξαντος</u> καὶ Κόρην <u>μουσουργίαις</u>
(putting a spell on Hades and Kore through his music)

Together with the charm poured down in his music, Orpheus' inconsolable grief moved Hades, who had never known pity before, to pity:

Verg. *georg.* 4.469-470
regemque tremendum
<u>nesciaque humanis precibus mansuere corda.</u>[17]
(and came to the spirits, and their dread king, and <u>hearts that do not know how to soften at human prayer</u>)

Ov. *met.* 10.45-46
tunc primum lacrimis victarum carmine fama est
Eumenidum maduisse genas

---

[17] Cf. Augsburg MS., Bischöfliches Ordinariat 5, fol. 1ʳ (s. XII), ll. 31-2, 35-7 *Tandem mitis carmine vatis / Superum terror, inferum rector / [...] / Proserpine / Dire manent lacrime / Prius incontigue.*

(Then they say, for the first time, the faces of the Furies were wet with tears, won over by his song.)

Sen. *H.Oet.* 1063-1067
manes cum tacitos adit
maerentem feriens chelyn,
cantu Tartara flebili,
et tristes Erebi deos
vicit
(when he approached the silent ghosts / striking his mourning lyre, / with his tearful song Hell / he conquered, and the stern gods Below, my tr.)

Sen. *H.F.* 567-569
Immites potuit flectere cantibus
umbrarum dominos et prece supplici
Orpheus, Eurydicen dum repetit suam.
(Orpheus was courageous enough to prevail with his song / on the lords of shadows, and with a suppliant's prayer, / while he sought for his Eurydice)

Boeth. *Cons. Phil.* 3 m. 12.20-22, 40-41
quod luctus dabat impotens,
quod luctum geminans amor,
deflet Taenara commovens [...]
tandem 'vincimur' arbiter
umbrarum miserans ait
(His unrestrained grief did give him power, his love redoubled his grief's power: his mourning moved the depths of hell. [...] At last the lord of the shades in pity cried: 'We are conquered', W.V. Cooper tr.)

Won over by the conjunction of Orpheus' love and his music, the Lord and Lady of the Underworld consented to the unprecedented measure of sending one of their subjects back to life:

Plato (=Pl.) *Smp.* 179d2
οὕτω καὶ θεοὶ τὴν περὶ τὸν ἔρωτα σπουδήν τε καὶ ἀρετὴν μάλιστα τιμῶσιν

(In this manner even the gods give special honor to zeal and courage in concerns of love)

Plutarch (=Plu.) *Am.* 761E11
δηλοῖ τὰ περὶ [...] Εὐρυδίκην τὴν Ὀρφέως, ὅτι μόνῳ θεῶν ὁ Ἀιδης Ἔρωτι ποιεῖ τὸ προσταττόμενον.
(The story of Eurydice Orpheus' wife shows that Hades bows only to Love among all gods, my tr.)

Manilius *Astronomia* 5.326-328
Qua quondam somnumque feris Oeagrius Orpheus
Et sensus scopulis et silvis addidit aures
Et Diti lacrimas et morti denique finem.
(The lyre of Orpheus, son of Oeagrus, caused animals to sleep, / rocks to feel, / trees to listen, / Hades to have tears, and death, finally, to come to an ending, my tr.)

Boeth. *Cons. Phil.* 3.m. 12.40-43
tandem 'uincimur' arbiter
umbrarum miserans ait.
'donamus comitem uiro
emptam carmine coniugem';
(At last the lord of the shades in pity cried: 'We are conquered; take your bride with you, bought by your song', W.V. Cooper tr.)

As far as Lúthien is concerned, the same constellation of motives that granted Orpheus' initial success with the Gods of the Underworld, that is, (1) grief, (2) enchanting song, and (3) devotion to one's dead spouse, moved Mandos (as it did Hades), who had never known mercy before, to pity and persuaded him to permit Beren to return to life:

> Now the beauty and tender loveliness <u>touched even the cold heart of Mandos</u>, so that he suffered her to lead Beren forth once more into the world [...] and many songs and stories are there of <u>the prayer of Tinúviel</u> before the throne of Mandos.
> ('The Tale of Tinúvuiel', *Lost Tales 2* 39)

> And she came to the halls of Mandos, and she <u>sang</u> to him a tale of moving <u>love</u> so fair that he was <u>moved to pity, as never has befallen since</u>.
> ('Quenta Silmarillion' § 10, *Shaping* 138)

> Lúthien came to the halls of Mandos, but her beauty was more than their beauty, and her <u>sorrow</u> deeper than their sorrows, and she knelt before Mandos and <u>sang</u> to him [...] the song most fair that was in words was woven, and the song most sorrowful that ever the world shall hear [...] and as she knelt before him <u>her tears fell upon his feet</u> [...] <u>and Mandos was moved to pity, who never before was so moved, or has been since.</u>
> (*Silmarillion* ch. 19, 'Of Beren and Lúthien', 227)

> The <u>grief</u> of Lúthien was so great that according to the Eldar it <u>moved the pity of even Mandos the unmoved</u>
> ('Athrabeth Finrod ah Andreth', *Morgoth* 340 n.3)

§ 5   Conditions

Both Orpheus' and Lúthien's story include the common detail that the Powers that rule the lands below agree to give their spouses back only conditionally. In the case of Orpheus, Hades and Persephone establish as an unnegotiable law (*lex*) that Orpheus may not look back at Eurydice during their ascension to the land of the living:

> Verg. *georg.* 4.487
> *namque hanc dederat Proserpina <u>legem</u>*
> (since Proserpine had set this condition.)

> Ov. *met.* 10.50
> *hanc et <u>legem</u> Rhodopeius accipit heros*
> (The poet of Rhodope received her, and, at the same time, accepted this condition.)

Sen. *H.F.* 581
lege tamen data
(with this condition)

Boeth. *Consol. Philos.* 3.m.12.44
sed *lex* dona coerceat[18]
(but one condition binds our gift, W.V. Cooper tr.)

Fulgentius *Myth.* 3.10
post quam maritus ad inferos descendit et legem accepit
(her husband went down into Hell looking for her, and accepted the following condition)

Lúthien, on her part, must give up her elven immortality and share Beren's mortal nature to fulfill the conditions set by the doom of Mandos:

> When Mandos let Beren return with Lúthien, it was only at the price that Lúthien should become as shortlived as Beren the mortal.
> ('Sketch of Mythology' § 14, *Shaping* 37)

> Mandos suffered them to depart, but he said that Lúthien should become mortal even as her lover.
> ('The Quenta Silmarillion' § 10, *Shaping* 138)

> Upon Beren and Tinúviel fell swiftly that doom of mortality that Mandos had spoken when he sped them from his halls.
> ('The Nauglafring', *Lost Tales 2* 241)

> For Lúthien had won this doom from Manwë, that Beren might return to live again, and she with him, but only so that she too hereafter should be as mortal as he […] This doom she chose.
> ('Grey Annals' § 214, *War of the Jewels* 70)

---

[18] Cf. Augsburg MS., Bischöfliches Ordinariat 5, fol. 1ʳ (s. XII), ll. 40-2 *Tollat, inquid, Orpheus / Meritam melodibus / Lege certa.*

Lúthien's readiness to exchange her immortal lifespan for a mortal's death might also hint at the speech made by Ovid's Orpheus before the throne of Hades, declaring his willingness to die with Eurydice if his wife is not given back to him (*met.* 10.38-39):

> *Quod si fata negant veniam pro coiniuge, certum est*
> *Nolle redire mihi; leto gaudere duorum*
> (but, if the fates refuse my wife this kindness, <u>I am determined not to return</u>: you can delight in both our deaths.)

§ 6   Final reunion after death

Ovid is the only classical author who describes the reunion of Orpheus and Eurydice after the singer's violent and traumatic death. The lovers, secure in their knowledge that no force can tear them apart now, walk the same path together in the Elysian plain (*met.* 11.61-66):

> *umbra subit terras et quae loca viderat ante*
> *cuncta recognoscit .quaerensque per arva piorum*
> *<u>invenit Eurydicen</u> cupidisque amplectitur ulnis.*
> *<u>Hic modo coniunctis spatiantur passibus ambo</u>*
> *Nunc praecedentem sequitur, nunc praevius anteit,*
> *<u>Eurydicenque suam iam tuto respicit Orpheus.</u>*
> (The ghost of Orpheus sank under the earth, and recognised all those places it had seen before; and, searching the fields of the Blessed, <u>he found his wife again</u> and held her eagerly in his arms. <u>There they walk together side by side</u>; now she goes in front, and he follows her; now he leads, <u>and looks back as he can do, in safety now, at his Eurydice</u>.)

This famous Ovidian passage may account for some traces of a different version that had Beren and Lúthien meet again in the lands of the dead, in some sort of earthly paradise (see also below II § 3, III § 2). There they walk together once more, only this time there is no fear of their being parted again:

> And thus they met again, Beren and Lúthien, beyond the Great Sea; and their paths led together, and passed long ago beyond the confines of the world. (*The Return of the Shadow* 184)

> The Sundering Seas between them lay,
> and yet at last they met once more,
> and long ago they passed away,
> in the forest singing sorrowless.[19]
> (*FR* I.11, 189)

> That they dwell for ever [...] in days ageless
> and the grass greys not in the green forest
> where East or West they ever wander.
> ('The Lay of the Children of Húrin' ll. 395-397, *Lost Road*)

As Aragorn mentioned, after their return Beren and Lúthien lived together in happiness only for a brief time, before passing out of knowledge together. The notion that their regained life will be brief ("Lúthien obtains a brief respite in which both return to Middle-earth 'alive'," *Letters* 193) and that they must return sooner or later to Mandos ("and know when ye fare hither again it will be for ever," 'The Tale of Tinúviel', *Lost Tales 2* 39, cf. 'Athrabeth Finrod ah Andreth' n.3, *Morgoth* 340) might find an inspiration in the same Ovidian lines. Although the motif of the simultaneous death of the lovers is a cliché present in all European literatures, it may be worthwhile to point out that there is a close thematic parallel in one of Tolkien's favourite Latin authors, Ovid. Ovid's Orpheus is well aware of the sad fact that in a little while, even if he succeeds in his task, both he and Eurydice must return to the dead. He ends his plea by offering to share his wife's deceased status and remain in Hades if Eurydice is denied to him (*met.* 31-36, 38-39):

---

[19] Tolkien harmonized this version with the final and more common one by having Aragorn explain the verse as "after a brief time walking alive once more in the green woods, together they passed, long ago, beyond the confines of the world." (*FR* I.11, 189)

> *omnia debemur vobis, <u>paulumque morati</u>*
> <u>*serius aut citius sedem properamus ad unam.*</u>
> *tendimus huc omnes, haec est domus ultima, vosque*
> *humani generis longissima regna tenetis.*
> *haec quoque, cum iustos matura peregerit annos, iuris erit*
> *vestri:*
> */ […] /*
> *quodsi fata negant veniam pro coniuge, certum est*
> *nolle redire mihi: leto gaudete duorum.*
> (<u>All things are destined to be yours, and though we delay a while, sooner or later we hasten home</u>. Here we are all bound, this is our final abode, and you hold the longest reign over the human race. Eurydice, too, will be yours to command, when she has lived out her fair span of years, to maturity. […] but, if the fates refuse my wife this kindness, I am determined not to return: you can delight in both our deaths.)

§ 7 Success of the desperate endeavour

Finally, the fact that Lúthien suceeds in bringing Beren back from the dead may seem to point away from a close influence from the Orpheus-legend, in that Orpheus notoriously failed in his task. However, there are reasons to believe that the oldest strata of the Orpheus-legend, attested in a scattered fashion mainly in Greek literature,[20] ended on a triumphant and joyful note, with Orpheus' successfully leading his wife away from the Underworld and up into the world above.[21] Latin poets, on the other hand, made it a point to stress the failure of Orpheus's attempt.[22] Strange as it may sound, in the Latin Middle Ages the legend went full-circle and ended up right where it had begun, that is, with Orpheus' successful rescue of Eurydice.[23] The reason for this

---

[20] E. *Alc.* 357-362, Heraclitus *De incred.* 21.2, Isocr. *Bus.* 8.1-3, Mosch. 3.123-124, D.S. 4.25.4, Luc. *D. Mort.* 28.2, Sch. E. *Alc.* 357.

[21] Dronke (1962:200-205) and Sansone (1985:53).

[22] Lee (1965:404-405).

[23] Dronke (1962:206).

volte-face is as follows: the legend of Orpheus underwent a process of Christianization, and thus the Thracian singer's katabasis in search of his wife became blended with Christ's descent into Hell to save mankind. Of course, it soon became obvious that Christ/Orpheus simply could not conceivably fail in his object of rescuing Eurydice.[24] Thus, a few Latin versions written between 1075 and 1085 dealt with the subject in an appropriately optimistic and positive manner, with Orpheus finally redeeming Eurydice from death and leading her back to the light.[25] Tolkien could not possibly fail to be aware of the mediaeval depelopment of the Orpheus-legend and of its roots in ancient Greek literature: for starters, the Professor himself translated and studied a late thirteenth-century Middle English poem, *Sir Orfeo*, based on some of the Christianised Latin versions mentioned above, in which Sir Orfeo finally managed to recover his wife Heurodis from the custody of the Fairy King.[26] Furthermore, Tolkien would know by heart the Anglo-Saxon glosses and commentaries written on Boethius' *Consolatio philosophiae* that dealt with the character of Orpheus, particularly King Alfred's prose translation of the Boethian version found at *Cons. Phil.* 3. m. 12 (XXXV = Otho A.vi). It would be safe to posit also that Tolkien would not be unaware of the Middle English poem by Robert Henryson on the same subject.[27]

---

[24] Dronke (1962:209-10), Gil (1974:144-5,) Tabaglio (1999:65-82). Cf. e.g. John of Salisbury, *Polycraticus* (Pat. Lat. 199 col. 565C) *non modo leones et tigrides, eloquentiae beneficio lenisse dictus est Orpheus, sed apud ipsum Ditem vox dulcior peroravit, canemque tricipitem exoravit causa favorabilior, ut admissam semel Eurydicen contra morem inferorum liceret educere.*

[25] Dronke (1962:198, 206-210). Cf. Augsburg MS., Bischöfliches Ordinariat 5, fol. 1ʳ (s. XII), ll. 63-64 *atque solam fidicen / rettulit Euridicen.*

[26] Dronke (1962:215) and Gil (1974:145-154) shows that there are a great many parallels between classic mythology and this intriguing Middle English poem. It must be mentioned, however, that there are significant differences of detail between the account in *Sir Orfeo* and the tale of Beren and Lúthien that point away from a direct influence by *Sir Orfeo* and lead back to the classical material: the bewitching nature of Lúthien's song, which she shares with Orpheus', is wholly absent from the corresponding passage in *Sir Orfeo* (435-452), as is the the condition set on both Lúthien and Orpheus to permit their spouse's return (inexistent in *Sir Orfeo*), or the fact that Sir Orfeo never mentions to the King of Faeries that the reason for his visit is love of his wife.

[27] Gros Louis (1966:643, 645) and Friedman (1966:22).

I.2 Dairon/Daeron as Orpheus

The importance attached by Tolkien to the Orpheus-legend in the constitution of his tale of Beren and Lúthien may be proven also by the fact that some aspects from the figure of Orpheus may be discerned in two of the other main characters from the tale, the minstrel Daeron and Beren himself.

§ 1   The singer's power over the inanimate world.

Let us start with Daeron. In its initial incarnation, as seen in 'The Tale of Tinúviel', Dairon (older spelling of Daeron), here Tinúviel's brother, delighted to play the pipes whereas his sister's taste was more for dancing. Dairon was named among the three 'most magic' players of the Elves ('The Tale of Tinúviel', *Lost Tales 2* 8.) Thus, Lúthien's later character as a magical singer was initially the province of her 'brother' Dairon: Tinúviel's greatest magical charm lay in her dancing, not her singing. The magically enthralling nature of Dairon's music is shown clearly in 'The Lay of Leithian', where it is said that Dairon "played with bewildering wizard's art / music for breaking of the heart" (ll. 499-500.) The magical effect of Dairon's music is also traditionally associated with Orpheus' art; in fact, the Thracian singer's temporary recovery of his wife is commonly explained as the result of bewitching the Lord of the Dead himself with the aid of his music and song. Just as it happened with Orpheus, the whole natural realm stands still to listen to Dairon's mourning songs:

> Yet his pipe took
> and sadly trembling the music shook;
> <u>and all things stayed while that piping went</u>
> wailing in the hollows, <u>and there intent</u>
> <u>they listened</u>, their business and mirth,
> their hearts' gladness and the light of earth
> forgotten; and bird-voices faded
> while Dairon's flute in Doriath wailed.
> ('The Lay of Leithian' ll. 1270-1277, *Lost Road*)

Orpheus' grieving song receives similarly rapt attention on the part of animals, stones, and trees in Ovid (*met.* 11.1-2):[28]

> *Carmine dum tali silvas animosque ferarum*
> *Threicius vates et saxa sequentia ducit*
> (While the poet of Thrace, with songs like these, drew to himself the trees, the souls of wild beasts, and the stones that followed him)
>
> Boeth. *Cons. Phil.* 3.m.12.5-13
> *quondam funera coniugis*
> *uates Threicius gemens*
> *postquam flebilibus modis*
> *siluas currere mobiles,*
> *amnes stare coegerat*
> *iunxitque intrepidum latus*
> *saeuis cerua leonibus*
> *nec uisum timuit lepus*
> *iam cantu placidum canem*
> (The singer of Thrace in olden time lamented his dead wife: by his tearful strains he made the trees to follow him, and bound the flowing streams to stay: for him the hind would fearlessly go side by side with fiercest lions, and the hare would look upon the hound, nor be afraid, for he was gentle under the song's sway, W.V. Cooper tr.)
>
> Cf. also Hor. *carm.* 1.12.7-12
> *Unde uocalem temere insecutae*
> *Orphea siluae*
> *arte materna rapidos morantem*
> *fluminum lapsus celerisque uentos,*
> *blandum et auritas fidibus canoris*
> *ducere quercus.*

---

[28] Tolkien might have taken this detail either directly from Ovid and Boethius or indirectly, through the reelaboration found in *Sir Orfeo* (272-280) and King Alfred's translation of Boeth. *Cons. Phil.* 3.m.12 (XXXV 6-11).

(where the trees followed thoughtlessly after / Orpheus's call, / that held back the swift-running streams and the rush / of the breeze, by his mother the Muse's art, / and seductively drew the listening oaks / with enchaining song.)

§ 2   Distracted behaviour after their bereavement

When Daeron learned that Tinúviel was lost to him forever, he strayed away from Doriath, full of the incurable grief caused by the disappearance of Lúthien, who was his inspiration to sing:

> Daeron the minstrel of Thingol <u>strayed from the land</u>, and was seen no more. He it was that made music for the dance and song of Lúthien [...] and he had loved her, and set all his thought of her in his music. He became the greatest of all the minstrels of the Elves east of the sea [...] but <u>seeking for Lúthien in despair he wandered upon strange paths,</u> and <u>passing over the mountains he came into the East of Middle-earth,</u> where for many ages <u>he made lament beside dark waters for Lúthien.</u>
> (*Silmarillion* ch. 19, 222-223)[29]

Orpheus' behaviour in similar circumstances parallels closely that of Daeron. After the loss of Eurydice, Orpheus wandered alone to the desolate Northern reaches of the world. Once there, he tried to assuage his grief singing of his wife night and day by the bank of the river Strymon.[30]

---

[29] References to Daeron's disappearance searching for Lúthien appear also in 'The Grey Annals' § 209, Synopsis I of Canto V and Canto XIV from 'The Lay of Leithian'.

[30] This might be taken directly from Virgil, or indirectly through the reelaboration of the Virgilian lines found in *Sir Orfeo* (239-280) and in King Alfred's translation of Boeth. *Cons. Phil.* 3.m.12 (XXXV 6-11).

Verg. *georg.* 4.464-465
ipse, cava solans aegrum testudine amorem
<u>*te dulcis coniunx, te solo in litore secum,*</u>
<u>*te veniente die, te decedente canebat*</u>
(Orpheus, consoling love's anguish, with his hollow lyre, <u>sang of you, sweet wife, you, alone on the empty shore, of you as day neared, of you as day departed</u>)

Verg. *georg.* 4.507-509
septem illum totos perhibent ordine menses
<u>*rupe sub aeria deserti ad Strymonis undam*</u>
<u>*flevisse, et gelidis haec evolvisse sub antris*</u>
(They say he <u>wept</u> for seven whole months, <u>beneath an airy cliff, by the waters of desolate Strymon, and told his tale, in the icy caves</u>)

Verg. *georg.* 4.517-520
<u>*solus Hyperboreas glacies Tanaimque nivalem*</u>
Arvaque Rhipaeis numquam viduata pruinis
<u>*Lustrabat, raptam Eurydicen*</u> *atque inrita Ditis*
Dona <u>querens</u>
(<u>He wandered the Northern ice,</u> and snowy Tanais, and the fields that are never free of Rhipaean frost, <u>mourning his lost Eurydice</u>, and Dis's vain gift.)

From the point of view of a sustained comparison with the Virgilian Orpheus, a few details in the narrative of Daeron's reaction after losing Lúthien are noteworthy. It is the love of Lúthien that inspired him to sing and play, as was the case with Orpheus. He lamented Lúthien's eternal loss by a water course, near the sea. Looking for the lost Lúthien he himself became lost.[31]

Thus it may be reasonably conjectured that Tolkien might have thought it expedient to divide between the female protagonist and her male 'double' the traits originally joined together in a single character (Orpheus.)

***

But why choose the Orpheus-legend to form the background of the tale of Beren and Lúthien at all? In addition to the most obvious explanation, that is, the powerful resonance of the Orpheus-legend in all Western art and literature, there might be an answer to such a question that is specifically suited to Tolkien's legendarium. An allegorical explanation by the fifth-century C.E. mythographer Fulgentius (*Myth.* 3.10), extraordinarily influential during the Carolingian age,[32] declared that the legend of Orpheus symbolized the deeper, metaphysical nature of music and art:[33]

---

[31] Curiously enough, in earlier stages of the narrative it was Beren's, not Dairon's, part ceaselessly to search all the Earth for Tinúviel after her fading, straying himself in the process and becoming an example of utter destitution and despairing loneliness ('The Nauglafring', *Lost Tales 2* 241, 'Sketch of Mythology' § 14, *Shaping* 37). The clearest verbal echo from Virgil's account is put precisely on Beren's lips: "she dreamed that she / heard Beren's voice over hill and fell / 'Tinúviel' call, 'Tinúviel.'" ('The Lay of Leithian' ll. 1415-1417.) Contrast with Verg. *georg.* 4.525-527: *Eurydicen vox ipsa et frigida lingua, / ah miseram Eurydicen! Anima fugiente vocabat; / Eurydicen toto referabant flumine ripae* (the voice alone, the ice-cold tongue, with ebbing breath, cried out: 'Eurydice, ah poor Eurydice!' 'Eurydice' the riverbanks echoed, all along the stream.) There is at least another clear verbal echo from Virgil in the sentences that describe Lúthien's death-like swoon: "and her body lay like a flower that is suddenly cut off and lies for a while unwithered on the grass." (*The Silmarillion*, ch. 19, 227) Compare with Verg. *Aen.* 11.68-71 *qualem virgine demessum pollice florem / seu mollis violae, seu languentis hyacinthi, / cui neque fulgor adhuc, nec dum sua forma recessit; / non iam mater alit tellus, virisque ministrat* (like a flower plucked by a young girl's fingers, / a sweet violet or a drooping hyacinth, whose brightness / and beauty have not yet faded, but whose native earth / no longer nourishes it, or gives it strength). See also above n. 11 for further Virgilian echoes.

[32] See e.g. Friedman (1970:86-145).

[33] Ostheimer (1998:19-35). There was a separate allegorical and theological tradition, taking as its departing point Boethius' moralization of the myth, that equated Eurydice with earthly delights, but this interpretation is of no relevance here. On this Boethian, theological tradition see e.g. Gros Louis (1966:643-655).

> *Orpheus Euridicem ninfam amavit; [...] illa [...] mortua est. Post quam maritus ad inferos descendit et legem accepit, ne eam conversus aspiceret; quam conversus et aspiciens iterum perdidit. <u>Haec igitur fabula artis est musicae designatio</u>. Orpheus dicitur oreàfone, id est optima vox, Euridice vero profunda diiudicatio.*
>
> (Orpheus was in love with the nymph Euridice [...] but she died. Her husband went down into the Underworld and accepted as a condition that he may not turn to look at her. But he did, and while looking at her he lost her again. <u>This fabula is a figure of the art of music</u>. Orpheus is called oreàfone, that is, 'excellent voice', while Euridice is called 'deep perception', my tr.)

In this interpretation, Orpheus embodied the practice of music, whereas Eurydice stood for the secret theory of musical art.[34] Medieval authors and commentarists such as Hrabanus Maurus, Alcuin, Johannes Scottus Eriugena, Remigius of Auxerre, Regino of Prüm, and the anonymous author of the Carolingian *Musica enchiriadis* followed Fulgentius' interpretation of the Orpheus-legend as an allegory for the art of music and poetry.[35] The notion that the Orpheus-legend was the mythical symbol of the secret and mystic nature of the art of music became thus highly influential with Carolingian music theorists, to such an extent that the characters of Orpheus and Eurydice, as interpreted through the lens of Fulgentius, became associated with treatises on the deeper sense of the art of music:[36]

> Johannes Scottus, *De Harmonia* 9
> *Eurydice dicitur profunda intentio. <u>Ipsa ars musica in suis profundissimis rationibus Eurydice dicitur</u>, cuius quasi maritus Orpheus dicitur, hoc est ωριος (sic) φωνη, is est pulchra vox.*

---

[34] Tabaglio (1999:73).

[35] Tabaglio (1999:73-74), Ostheimer (1998:19-20), and Boynton 1999.

[36] Tabaglio (1999:77) and Ostheimer (1998:19-35).

(Eurydice is named 'deep perception.' The very same art of music is called 'Eurydice' in its most arcane aspect, and her husband, as it were, is called 'Orpheus', that is, 'excellent voice', my tr.)

It is conceivable that Tolkien may hint at this Carolingian allegoric tradition when he explains that the value of the Silmarils lies in the Light of Valinor trapped inside, in so far as

> the Light of Valinor [...] is the light of art undivorced from reason, that sees things both scientifically (or philosophically) and imaginatively (or subcreatively) and says that they are 'good' [...] as beautiful. (*Letters* 148)[37]

It must be remembered that Tolkien laid much emphasis on the fact that Lúthien took to wearing one Silmaril, and that the light of the deathless jewel shining on Lúthien's breast meant that, however briefly, a mirror-like reflection of the Gods' creative powers became unveiled in the sublunar world, from which they are usually hidden:[38]

> It is said and sung that Lúthien wearing that necklace and the immortal jewel on her white breast was the vision of greatest beauty and glory that has ever been seen outside of Valinor, and that for a while the Land of the Dead that Live became like a vision of the land of the Gods, and no places have been since so fair, so fruitful, and so filled with light. ('Quenta Silmarillion' § 14, *Shaping* 160-161)

---

[37] See the illuminating words of Lee (1965:410): "The unifying element in all the myths connected with Orpheus is the all-compelling power of his song, which holds sway over all nature, harmonizing and transforming it when he overcomes death, not by force [...] or by magic [...] but by art." Cf. also Thierry de Saint-Trond, *Liber quid suum virtutis: sic ars naturam vicit, studio mediante, / virtuti dominae cedere cuncta probans*.

[38] See further on this topic Flieger (2003²).

Thus the association between Orpheus, Lúthien, the Silmarils, and the secret nature and mystic value of music and poetry, derived from Fulgentius' *Mythologiae* and elaborated on by Carolingian commentarists, come together intimately through the adoption of the Orpheus-legend.

When did the Orpheus-hypotext enter the frame of the story of Beren and Lúthien? It is impossible to know with certainty, although some conjectures may be made. Initially, Dairon, as a magical minstrel and brother of Tinúviel in 'The Tale of Tinúviel' (ca. 1918), is not particularly close to Orpheus: he might as well be as much a derivative of Väinämönen, the wizard-singer in *The Kalevala* (XLIV 232-305), as of Orpheus.[39] However, as Lúthien's visit to the halls of Mandos to retrieve Beren remains a constant and substantially unchanged feature in the tale from its earliest attestation (cf. 'The Tale of Tinúviel', *Lost Tales 2* 39), it may be that originally this was the sole aspect of the legend Tolkien felt was relevant to the tale as it stood at the time. On successive re-writings, probably prompted by association with the Orpheus-material that was already present in Lúthien, he may have decided to introduce further resonances and points of contact between Orpheus and his own minstrel, Daeron, that were not present in the figure of Väinämönen, such as his unconsolable grief, his wandering, and his lament by the waters. These points of contact seem to have been first introduced in the 'Sketch of Mythology' (ca. 1931) and in 'The Lay of Leithian' (1925-1931.)

II. THE PROTESILAODAMEIA ROMANCE

As indicated above, the tale of Beren and Lúthien underwent a fair number of re-writings and modifications that produced many differences of detail with the final, definitive version that was published posthumously as chapter 19 of *The Silmarillion*. Some of the variants that were discarded in the final shape of

---

[39] As is well known, Tolkien always acknowledged that *The Silmarillion* had been inspired, in part, by his readings of *The Kalevala* (e.g. *Letters* 87).

the tale might have been inspired by another Classical myth that addressed the subject of love stronger than death and resurrection for love:[40] this is the story of Laodameia and Protesilaus, which, although not as influential in later times as the Orpheus-legend, was made to complement it by Greek and Latin writers.[41] Briefly told, the Protesilaodameia romance narrates how Laodameia lost her husband, Protesilaus, in the Trojan War. They had been married for only a few weeks. Protesilaus, still ardently in love with Laodameia even though already dead, begged Hades for permission to return to Earth for a very brief period of time in order to see his wife one last final time.[42]

§ 1   The dead husband begs to return to life

The dead Protesilaus pleaded in person with the King and Queen of the dead to allow him to go back to Earth briefly, because his love for Laodameia was much too strong to be withstood, even in cold Hades:

> Propertius 1.19.7-8
> *illic Phylacides iucundae coniugis heros*
> *Non potuit caecis immemor esse locis*
> (The hero, Protesilaus, could not forget his sweet wife even in the dark region.)
>
> Eustathius *Il.* 1.507 (s. XII C.E.)
> Πρωτεσίλαος καὶ μετὰ θάνατον ἐρῶν τῆς γυναικὸς […] ᾐτήσατο τοὺς κάτω σθένοντας ἀνελθεῖν
> (Protesilaus continued to love his wife even after death […] and he begged the powers below to be allowed to return to earth)
>
> Sch. Aristides 3 pp. 671-2
> τοὺς κάτω δαίμονας ᾐτήσατο καὶ ἀφείθη μίαν ἡμέραν καὶ συνεγένετο τῇ γυναικὶ αὐτοῦ.

---

[40] Cat. 68.117 *sed tuus altus amor barathro fuit altior illo.*

[41] See on these subjects Berenson and Aitken (2001:liii-lv).

[42] All classical sources may be consulted in Mantero (1966:200-205).

(He begged the gods below to be granted leave for a single day, during which he conversed with his wife)

Lucian (=Luc.) *D. mort.* 28
Ὦ δέσποτα καὶ βασιλεῦ καὶ ἡμετέρε Ζεῦ καὶ σὺ Δήμητρος θύγατερ, μὴ ὑπερίδητε δέησιν ἐρωτικήν [...] οὐ τοῦ ζῆν, Ἀϊδωνεῦ, ἐρῶ, τῆς γυναικὸς δέ [...] ὁ οὖν ἔρως τῆς γυναικὸς οὐ μετρίως ἀποκναίει με, ὦ δέσποτα, καὶ βούλομαι κἂν πρὸς ὀλίγον ὀφθεὶς αὐτῇ καταβῆναι πάλιν.
(PROTESILAUS: Lord, King, our Zeus! and thou, daughter of Demeter! Grant a lover's boon! ay, dread lord, 'tis not life I love, but the bride that I left --- My lord, that yearning gives me no peace. I return content, if she might look on me but for an hour, tr. H. W. Fowler - F. G. Fowler.)

Tz. *Chil.* 2.766-9
οἱ μυθογράφοι δὲ φασίν, ὡραῖον ὄντα τοῦτον
ἡ Κόρη κατῳκτείρησεν ἰδοῦσα Περσεφόνη
στέρησιν ὀδυρόμενον τὴν τῆς Λαοδαμείας.
καὶ δέεται τοῦ Πλούτωνος ζωοῖ τε τοῦτον πάλιν.
(Storytellers say that Persephone took pity on him, / seeing him so young and so heart-broken after being deprived of Laodameia /, and she asked Hades to allow him to live again, my tr.)

The gods took pity on Protesilaus' love and bereavement (Eutecnius, *Paraphrasis in Oppiani cynegetica* 27.3), as they had done before with Orpheus. An inspiration in Protesilaus' petition[43] may account for an aberrant and isolated detail found solely in the 'Sketch of Mythology' § 10 (*The Shaping of Middle-earth* 28) that has Beren himself, not Lúthien, plead with Mandos for a brief return to life:

---

[43] Other versions, probably stemming from Euripides' treatment of the material in his lost play *Protesilaus*, have Laodameia beg herself for her husband's return to life (Apoll. *Ep.* 3.29.9-10, Hyg. *Fab.* 103.2). There is a good parallel with Lúthien's situation here, in that both Lúthien and Laodameia are married females asking for the temporary return of their husbands from death, although Tolkien preferred solely to acknowledge the influence of the Orpheus-legend in this part of the tale.

> some songs say that Lúthien went [...] to Mandos' halls and won him back; others that <u>Mandos hearing his tale released him</u>. Certain it is that he alone of mortals came back from Mandos.

§ 2 The grieving wife chooses to follow her husband in death

In some instances of the tale, Lúthien did not visit Mandos' halls in spirit, that is, while she was still alive (see above, I.1 § 1.) Rather, she died physically and truly of grief and followed Beren to the world of the dead, that she may not be parted from him:

> For Beren died there [...] and <u>Tinúviel</u> crushed with sorrow and finding no comfort or light in all the world <u>followed him swiftly down</u> those dark ways that all must tread alone.
> ('The Tale of Tinúviel', *Lost Tales 2* 39)[44]

> Beren was slain <u>soon after their marriage</u>, and <u>Lúthien died of grief</u>.
> ('Athrabeth Finrod ah Andreth', *Morgoth* 340 n.3)

Similarly, Laodameia, sick with the love she still bore for her dead husband, and unwilling to be separated from him so soon after their wedding, resolved to take her own life in order to accompany Protesilaus in death, as she always had done in life.[45] It will not be surprising to find that one of the motifs most commonly associated with Laodameia in Latin elegiac poetry is the fact that she always followed her husband as his companion (*comes*), even till death itself:[46]

---

[44] Cf. W. Wordsworth, *Laodamia*, "Swift, toward the realms that know not earthly day, / He through the portal takes his silent way, / And on the palace floor a lifeless corpse / She lay."

[45] Mantero (1966:204). See Apoll. *Ep.* 3.29.18, Eust. *Il.* 1.507, Hyg. *fab.* 103.2, Serv. *Aen.* 6.447, Tz. *Chil.* 2.781-783.

[46] Mantero (1966:203 n.14), Brescia (1996:31). Cf. W. Wordsworth, *Laodameia*, "But if thou goest, I follow –"

Ov. *Ars* 3.17-18
respice Phylaciden et quae comes isse marito
Fertur et ante annos occubuisse suos
(Think of Protesilaus, and Laodameia who they say followed her marriage partner, died before her time.

Ov. *am.* 2.18.38
et comes extincto Laodameia viro
(and Laodamia faithful companion to the end)

Ov. *Her.* 13.161-162
me tibi venturam comitem, quocumque vocaris,
Sive – quod heu! Timeo, sive superstes eris.
(Wherever you call from to me, I will come to accompany you, whether what – alas! – I fear might be, or whether you survive.)

Ov. *Pont.* 3.1.104-105
si comes extincti manes sequerere mariti
Esse dux facti Laodameia tui
(if you followed your dead husband to the shadows, Laodamia would be your guide in the act.)

Claudian *carm.* 30.148-150
nobiliora tenent animos exempla pudicos
Laodameia sequens remeantem rursus ad umbras
Phylaciden
(Nobler examples hold the hearts of chaste women: Laodameia following her husband after his return to the shadows, my tr.)

As a cursory reading of chapter 19 of *The Silmarillion* would attest, Tolkien portrayed Lúthien along very similar lines, that is, as the eternal companion of Beren, taking an equal share in all his adventures and labours, following wherever his path may lead him, even to the Halls of Mandos and death itself.

But she chose mortality, and to die from the world,
so that she might follow him. (*FR* I.11, 189)

Notice also how much emphasis is put on the detail that both Protesilaus and Beren died very soon after their wedding, and that this caused their brides to die of sorrow (see e.g. *Silmarillion* ch. 19, 224-226 for Beren and Lúthien with *Il.* 2.699-702 for Protesilaus and his wife).

It has been occasionally claimed that Lúthien's relinquishment of her immortality and her acceptance of a mortal fate could answer to an influence by the so-called Alcestis-motif:[47]

> Beren and Lúthien returned to the world, for a while. For Lúthien had won this doom from Manwë, that Beren might return to live again, and she with him, but only so that she too hereafter should be mortal as he […] this doom she chose. ('The Grey Annals' § 214, *War of the Jewels*)

> And this doom [sc. a second and permanent death] they chose, that thus, whatever sorrow might lie before them, their fate might be joined, and their paths lead together beyond the confines of the world. (*Lost Road* 304)

This observation is, in a sense, true, insofar as Alcestis consented to die *instead of* her husband, and was later brought back to life, according to an isolated version, out of the gods' pity for the strength of her love.[48] However, the parallels between Lúthien and Laodameia are closer than they are between Lúthien and Alcestis, in that Laodameia chose to die *with* her husband, not *in his place*.[49] Just like Lúthien, Laodameia, faced with the temporal return of Protesilaus, was presented with a choice: she might either continue to live after the loss of her husband, or share his fate and join him in death. Both

---

[47] Shippey (2003²:316).

[48] Agatharchides, *De mari erythraeo* 7.68, Zen. 1.18.

[49] Cf. Ch. Tolkien's commentary ad loc. (*Lost Road* 304): "The union of Beren and Lúthien 'beyond the world' could only be achieved by acceptance of the second choice, whereby Lúthien herself should be permitted to change her 'kind' and 'die indeed'."

Laodameia and Lúthien chose the latter option, with Lúthien forfeiting her immortality, and Laodameia relinquishing her own life and the prospect of a new husband. Another detail that points Tolkien's account away from the Alcestis-motif and closer to the Protesilaodameia romance is the fact that in the most common versions of the tale Alcestis was brought back to life by violently forcing the gods of the Underworld to release her,[50] while in the Protesilaodameia romance, the gods of the dead let go of Protesilaus out of pity for his grief. However, as will be demonstrated in III, it is probable that the stories of Alcestis, Laodameia, and Orpheus may have occurred to Tolkien simultaneously.

§ 3   The couple's life together after death

As a last point of comparison, an isolated and early version of the tale told how Beren and Lúthien, after their second death, were transported to Valinor, and narrated how they spent their days while in their earthly paradise:

> Tinúviel slowly fade(d) [...] and she vanished in the woods, and none have seen her dancing ever again. But Beren searched all the lands of Hithlum and Artanor ranging after her [...] or ever he too faded from life. Mayhaps what all Elves say is true, that <u>those twain hunt now in the forest of Oromë in Valinor and Tinúviel dances on the green gardens</u> of Nissa and Vána daughter of the Gods for ever more.
> ('The Nauglafring', *Lost Tales 2* 241)

Beren's and Lúthien's joyful post-mortem existence in an earthly paradise brings to mind Philostratus the Elder's remarkable account of the ghostly Protesilaus' activities after his death in front of the walls of Troy, alternatively hunting and taking his rest in a secluded, paradisean spot (*Her.* 11.7-8):

---

[50]   See e.g. Librán-Moreno (2005b:117).

Α. πότε μὲν ἐν Ἅιδου [...] ποτὲ δὲ ἐν Φθίᾳ, ποτὲ δ' αὖ ἐν Τροίᾳ, οὗ οἱ ἑταῖροι, <u>καὶ πρὸς θήρᾳ συῶν τε καὶ ἐλάφων γινόμενος, ἀφικνεῖται κατὰ μεσημβρίαν καὶ καθεύδει</u> [...]
Β. <u>ποῦ δὲ τῇ Λαοδαμείᾳ ξύνεστιν;</u>
Α. <u>ἐν Ἅιδου</u>, ξένε, καὶ λέγει αὐτὴν εὐδοκιμώτατα γυναικῶν πράττειν.
(A: Protesilaus says sometimes he lives in Hades, [...] other times in Phthia, and even sometimes in Troy, where his companions are. <u>When he hunts wild boar and deer he arrives here at midday and falls asleep.</u>
B: <u>And where does he spend time with Laodameia?</u>
A: <u>In Hades</u>, my guest. He says that she fares most favourably among women. (tr. J.K. Berenson and E.B. Aitken)

§ 4   Mystery and vagueness in the couple's return to life

Another point in common between the Tale of Beren and Lúthien and Philostratus' description of the resurrection of Protesilaus is the aura of vagueness, mystery, silence, and metaphysical secrecy, that surrounds Protesilaus' return to life (*Her.* 2.9-11):[51]

Α. <u>ἀναβεβιωκὼς ἢ τί;</u>
Β. <u>οὐδὲ αὐτὸς λέγει</u> [...] <u>τὰ ἑαυτοῦ πάθη</u>, πλήν γε δὴ ὅτι ἀποθάνοι μὲν δι' Ἑλένην ἐν Τροίᾳ, <u>ἀναβιῴη δὲ ἐν Φθίᾳ Λαοδαμείας ἐρῶν</u>.
Α. καὶ μὴν <u>ἀποθανεῖν γε μετὰ τὸ ἀναβιῶναι λέγεται καὶ ἀναπεῖσαι τὴν γυναῖκα ἐπισπέσθαι οἷ</u>
Β. λέγει καὶ αὐτὸς ταῦτα, ἀλλ' ὅπως καὶ μετὰ τοῦτο ἀνῆλθε πάλαι μοι βουλομένῳ μαθεῖν οὐ λέγει, <u>Μοιρῶν τι ἀπόρρητον</u> [...] <u>κρύπτων</u>.
(A: Has Protesilaus come back to life, or what has happened?

---

[51] Cf. W. Wordsworth, *Laodamìa*, "He spake of love, such love as Spirits feel / In worlds whose course is equable and pure; / No fears to beat away – no strife to heal – / The past unsighed for, and the future sure; / Spake of heroic arts in graver mood / Revived, with finer harmony pursued."

> B: <u>He himself does not speak about his own experiences</u>, stranger, except, of course, that he died at Troy because of Helen, but <u>came back to life again in Phthia because he loved Laodameia</u>.
> A: And yet <u>he is said to have died after he came to life again and to have persuaded his wife to follow him</u>.
> B: He himself also says these things. <u>But how he returned afterwards too, he does not tell me</u> even though I've wanted to find out for a long time. <u>He is hiding, he says, some secret of the Fates</u>.
> (tr. J.K. Berenson and E.B. Aitken)

Notice that these lines from Philostratus neatly bring together the main points of contact betweem Beren and Protesilaus on the one hand, and Lúthien and Laodameia on the other: Beren and Protesilaus died an unexpected and sudden death in battle very soon after their wedding. While both heroes came back to life for love, the reason for this unexpected grace from the powers below remained absolutely exceptional and a secret. Their wives, Laodameia and Lúthien, preferred to die that they may be allowed to be with their husbands for ever, rather than continuing to live parted from them.

Lúthien's choice was presented by Tolkien as a metaphysical and mysterious exception, granted to Lúthien alone ("Lúthien is allowed as an absolute exception to divest herself of 'immortality' and become 'mortal'", *Letters* 193). Notice that Tolkien remarked very insistently on the strange fact that, after their return to life, neither Lúthien nor Beren exchanged a single word with a mortal creature ever again:

> He alone of mortals came back from Mandos and dwelt with Lúthien and <u>never spoke to Men again</u>, living in the woods of Doriath [...].
> ('Sketch of Mythology' § 10, *Shaping* 28)

> In recompense Mandos gave to Beren and to Lúthien thereafter a long span of life and joy, and they wandered [...] in the fair land of Broseliand, and <u>no mortal Men thereafter spoke to Beren or his spouse</u>.
> ('The Quenta Silmarillion' § 10, *Shaping* 139)
>
> <u>No mortal man spoke ever again with Beren</u> son of Barahir, and none saw Beren or Lúthien leave the world or marked where at last their bodies lay.
> (*Silmarillion*, ch. 20, 229.)

This reticence reminds the reader of Protesilaus' unwillingness to disclose the precise nature of the operation of Fate and the Gods in his case, and declare his exact metaphysical status after his death.

III. ORPHEUS, LAODAMEIA, ALCESTIS: TOLKIEN AND THE RHETORICAL MOTIF OF THE CATALOGUE OF HEROINES

§ 1   Rhetorical encomia: the catalogue of exemplary women

It might be objected that, whereas Tolkien acknowledged the influence the Orpheus legend had on the formation of the tale of Beren and Lúthien, he failed to do so with the Laodameia and Protesilaus story. It must be pointed out, however, that drawing a conclusion based on an argument ex silentio is a very risky procedure where Tolkien is concerned, in as much as the Professor had strong objections against revealing the sources he had adopted and then transformed to form his own unique and original creations. At times he went so far as consciously to deny the actual relevance of a literary source whose influence on his writings could be demonstrated easily.[52] This attitude could not be further removed from intellectual or scholarly dishonesty on Tolkien's part; rather, it is but a corollary of Tolkien's preoccupation and concern with

---

[52]   See further Librán-Moreno (2005a:27-28).

the rearrangement of the 'bones' of traditional stories that a new meaning may be created.

Protesilaus' resurrection was famous enough in late ancient times to merit some concern in the eyes of Christian apologists, who worried about the threat Protesilaus' return from the dead could pose to the uniqueness of Jesus' resurrection. Similarly, the story of Protesilaus and Laodameia was a very common iconographic theme on Roman sarcophagi, and its validity as the paradigm of love stronger than death did not abate during the Middle Ages.[53] The relevance of the Protesilaodameia romance may have occurred to Tolkien simultaneously with his consideration of the Orpheus legend, in so far as both legends, together with the myth of Alcestis, unfailingly tended to be brought together in Greek and Latin texts as paradigms and mythical exempla whenever the subject matter dealt closely with love stronger than death. Two examples of this practice will suffice:[54]

> Luc. *D. mort.* 28.2
> ἀναμνήσω σε, ὦ Πλούτων· Ὀρφεῖ γὰρ δι' αὐτὴν ταύτην τὴν αἰτίαν τὴν Εὐριδίκην παρέδοτε καὶ τὴν ὁμογενή μου Ἄλκηστις παρεπέμψατε Ἡρακλεῖ χαριζόμενοι.
>
> (PROTESILAUS: Bethink thee, Pluto. 'Twas for this same cause [sc. love] that you gave Orpheus his Eurydice; and Heracles had interest enough to be granted Alcestis)

---

[53] See on these subjects Berenson and Aitken (2001:liii-lv).

[54] The following is a partial list of passages where Orpheus, Protesilaus and Laodameia, and Alcestis are brought together: E. *Alc.* 357-362 (Alcestis and Orpheus), Pl. *Smp.* 179c5-d7 (Alcestis and Orpheus), Agatarchides *De mari Erythraeo* 7.68 (Alcestis and Protesilaus), Verg. *Aen.* 6.447 (Alcestis and Laodameia), Ov. *Pont.* 3.1.1-5 (Alcestis and Laodameia), *Tr.* 5.14.37-40 (Alcestis and Laodameia), Eutecnius, *Paraphrasis in Oppiani Cynegetica* 27.3 (Alcestis and Protesilaus), Ael. *V.H.* 14.45.2 (Alcestis and Laodameia), Philostr. *Her.* 11.7-8 (Alcestis and Laodameia.) Tzetzes treated all three myths in strict succession in his influential *Chiliades* (2.52-4).

> Plu. *Am.* 761E 11
> δηλοῖ τὰ περὶ <u>Ἄλκηστιν καὶ Πρωτεσίλεων καὶ Εὐριδίκην</u> τὴν Ὀρφέως, ὅτι μόνῳ θεῶν ὁ Ἅιδης Ἔρωτι ποιεῖ τὸ προσταττόμενον.
> (The stories of <u>Alcestis, Protesilaus, and Eurydice</u> the wife of Orpheus, show that Hades bows only to Love among all the gods, my tr.)

Alcestis and Laodameia were all but fixed items in the stereotyped, rhetorical catalogue of good, faithful wives that appears so frequently in Greek literature and Latin elegy.[55] Thus, the name of one of them frequently triggered the apparition of the other in the same text.[56] Tolkien might have been inspired either directly by an actual reading of some of these catalogues in Ovid, Philostratus, or Claudian, or indirectly by the occurrence of Laodameia's name in the catalogue of virtuous Greek and Roman women that appears in Chaucer's *The Franklin's Tale* (*Canterbury Tales* 5.5).

§ 2   Rhetorical encomia of marriage: marriage as a divinizing factor

Positing an inspiration in the rhetorical topos of the catalogue of virtuous heroines, with its fixed roll-call of famous mythical names, may throw some light on the extraordinary fate of Beren and Lúthien after their mysterious return from the Halls of Mandos, as well. Beren and Lúthien inhabited an island, called the 'land of the dead that live', in a liminal state between life and death. There is something awful, exceptional, and forbidding about their new status, insofar as no mortal Man is allowed, or able, to converse with either of them. Beren's and Lúthien's mysterious unavailability is present in all versions of the tale:

> Certain it is that he alone of mortals came back from Mandos and dwelt with Lúthien and <u>never spoke to Men again</u>, living in the woods of Doriath

---

[55] See further on the subject of examplary catalogues of women Hinds (1999).
[56] See Beschorner (1999:170) and Brescia (1996:31-32).

and in the Hunters' Wold, west of Nargothrond.
('Sketch of Mythology' § 10, *Shaping* 28)

For those twain it is that stories name i·Cuilwarthon, which is to say <u>the dead that live again</u>, and they <u>became mighty fairies</u>[57] in the lands about the North of Sirion.
('The Tale of Tinúviel', *Lost Tales 2* 39)

But Lúthien and Beren passed then out of the knowledge of Elves and Men, and <u>dwelt a while alone</u> by the green waters of Ossiriand in that land which Elves named therefore Gwerth-i-Guinar, <u>the Land of the Dead that Live</u>. Thereafter <u>Beren [...] spoke not again with any mortal Man</u>.
('Grey Annals' § 214, *War of the Jewels* 71)

And they passed beyond the River Gelion in Ossiriand, and <u>dwelt there on Tol Galen</u> the green isle, in the midst of Adurant, and all tidings of them ceased. The Eldar afterwards called the country Dor Firn-i-Guinar, the <u>Land of the Dead that Live</u>.
(*Silmarillion*, ch. 20, 229)

Beren and Lúthien returned from the dead as different, superior creatures: while not quite dead, they were nontheless not fully alive ('Dead that Live'). The earliest version of the tale declared that they returned in the guise of powerful fairies ("they became mighty fairies", 'The Tale of Tinúviel', *Lost Tales 2* 39), and it is implied that their converse may not be suitable for mere Men (cf. "those that saw them were both glad and fearful", "no mortal man spoke ever again with Beren", *Silmarillion* ch. 20, 229). They dwelt, as a married couple, on Tol Galen, a lonely and paradisean island set in the middle of a river, in a largely deserted spot. Their fate is remarkably reminiscent of the exceptional post-mortem existence of a few Greek heroes who had family ties with gods and goddess, such as Achilles, Peleus, and Menelaus. After his death

---

[57] This might be also a reflection on the medieval notion that Eurydice became a *fata* (faery, fée) after her return (Dronke 1968²:349).

for love, Achilles came back to life on the strength of his semi-divine nature. He became a demi-god and settled to live with Medea or Helen in Leuke, the White Island, neither living nor dead, apart from all living men[58]. His father Peleus, on his part, obtained the grace of immortality after his convivence with the sea nymph Thetis.[59] Menelaus achieved deathlessness and was granted a permanent residence in the isles of the Blessed because of his marriage to Helen, daughter of Zeus.[60] All ingredients of the post-mortem existence of Beren and Lúthien are present in the cases of Achilles, Peleus, and Menelaus: a liminal status between life and death, enhanced metaphysical status, and residence in an isolated, paradisiacal island (the isles of the Blessed and the Elysian plains) are the outcome of their marriage with a semidivine or divine woman.[61]

---

[58] On the fate of Achilles after his death, his liminal status between death and life, his posthumous marriage to Helen (Medea or Iphigenia in other sources), and his residence in the White Island, see e.g. Ibyc. 291 PMG, Pi. *Nem.* 4.49-50, Pl. *Smp.* 179E, E. *I.T.* 435-437, Paus. 3.19.13, Sch. A.R. 4.814, Sch. Pl. *Phaedr.* 243a. See further Beschorner (1999:206).

[59] E. *Andr.* 1253-1258.

[60] *Od.* 4.561-9.

[61] See Rohde (1898², I:84-90). In the description of Beren and Lúthien's paradisian dwelling and carefree living there are a few verbal echoes and thematic parallels from Greek depictions of the Isles of the Blessed or the Elysian Plain: Beren and Lúthien do not fear "thirst nor hunger" (*Silmarillion*, ch. 20, 229 ~ Hes. *Op.* 171-173, Pi. *Ol.* 2.63-65). Their existence is joyful and "sorrowless" (*FR* I.11, 189 ~ Hes. *Op.* 168 ἀκηδέα [sorrowless], Pi. *Ol.* 2.66 ἄδακρυον [tearless]). Their abode is an island full of luxuriant groves ("Tol Galen, the green island", *Silmarillion*, ch. 20, 229 ~ Hes. *Op.* 171, Pi. *Ol.* 2.131, fr. 129.3-5 Sn.) where they take up residence apart from all mortal Men (*Silmarillion*, ch. 20, 229 ~ Hes. *Op.* 167) with God's special dispensation (*Silmarillion*, ch. 19, 227-228 ~ Hes. *Op.* 167-168). In their new abode they entertain themselves hunting, roaming the woods, and dancing (*The Book of Lost Tales 2* 241 ~ Pi. fr. 129.6-8 Sn.). Most of the details present in Tolkien's fragmentary picture of life in Tol Galen are attested in a single classical passage, Virgil's famous description of the Elysian plains (*Aen.* 6.638-644): *devenere locos laetos et amoena virecta, / fortunatorum nemorum sedesque beatas. / [...] / pars in gramineis exercent membra palestris, / contendunt ludo et fulva luctantur harena; / pars pedibus plaudunt choreas et carmina dicunt* (they came to the pleasant places, the delightful grassy turf / of the Fortunate Groves, and the homes of the blessed. / [...] / Some exercise their bodies in a grassy gymnasium, / compete in sports and wrestle on the yellow sand: / others tread out the steps of a dance, and sing songs.)

This is not to say, of course, that Tolkien must have copied all such myths slavishly when he delineated the later fate of Beren and Lúthien. However, it is interesting to note that rhetorical encomia of love and marriage present Achilles and Medea's wedding, together with that of Alcestis and Admetus and Protesilaus and Laodameia, as evidence that love and marriage may elevate mortal men to immortality:

> Pl. *Smp.* 180B
> θειότερον γὰρ ἐραστὴς παιδικῶν· ἔνθεος γάρ ἐστι. διὰ ταῦτα καὶ τὸν Ἀχιλλέα τῆς Ἀλκήστιδος μᾶλλον ἐτίμησαν, εἰς μακάρων νήσους ἀποπέμψαντες.
> (since a lover, filled as he is with a god, surpasses his favorite in divinity. This is the reason why they honored Achilles above Alcestis, giving him his abode in the Isles of the Blest, tr.Fowler/Lamb)

> Dionysius of Halicarnassus, *Ars Rhetorica* 2.5
> (s. I B.C.E.)
> καὶ ὅσα ἀπὸ τούτων (sc. γάμων) ἀγαθὰ ἐγένετο τοῖς ἀνθρώποις [...] οἷον ὅτι Μενέλεως ἀθάνατος ἐγένετο διὰ τὸ τὸν γάμον τῆς Ἑλένης καὶ ὁ Πηλεὺς διὰ τὸν τῆς Θέτιδος, καὶ ὁ Ἄδμητος διὰ τὴν Ἄλκηστιν τὸν ἐκ τῆς εἱμαρμένης θάνατον διέφυγεν.
> (A great many benefits are given to men because of marriage [...] as an example of that, consider Menelaus, who became immortal because of his wedding to Helen, or Peleus, thanks to his union with Thetis, or Admetus, who escaped his fated death thanks to Alcestis; my tr.)

> Eutecnius, *Paraphrasis in Oppiani cynegetica* 27.3
> (s. III/V C.E.)
> οἶδας γὰρ καὶ νεκροῖς ἐπιτοξάζεσθαι καὶ ψυχὰς ἐξ ᾅδου τοῖς ἐρασταῖς ἀναπομπίμους χαρίζεσθαι καὶ πείθεις γαμήλια ἐνιέναι καὶ θνῄσκουσι καὶ τῶν λεγομένων μάρτυρες <u>Ἀχιλλεὺς καὶ Μήδεια, Ἄδμητος καὶ Ἄλκηστις, Λαοδάμεια καὶ Πρωτεσίλαος.</u>

> (You are aware that love shoots his arrows even at the dead. The souls of the dead who are sent back from Hades find favour with their lovers still, and wedding-offerings are prepared for those about to die. Let <u>Achilles and Medea, Admetus and Alcestis, Laodameia and Protesilaus</u> bear witness to what I just said; my tr.)

Considering Tolkien's preoccupation with the sacred and elevating character of the institution of marriage (see e.g. *Letters* 51-52), his command of Greek sources, and his interest in the legends of Orpheus and Alcestis, it may not be too far fetched to suggest that such texts as the encomia of love and marriage quoted above may have both suggested to the Professor the use of the Protesilaodameia romance as a complementary hypotext, and served as partial inspiration for Beren and Lúthien's life together after their first death, among other materials.

One last consideration remains to be made, which in view of the materials presently at our disposal cannot be but a more or less plausible hypothesis: perhaps the contrast between the remarkably stable core of the 'Tale of Beren and Lúthien', unchanged ever since the first attestation of the 'legend',[62] and the bewildering differences of detail among the several versions and developments that exist[63] may be explained partially by positing an influence on Tolkien's own idiosicratic material by two concurring hypotexts, the Orpheus-legend and the Protesilaodameia romance, that dealt with essentially the same subject-matter (love after death and death conquered by love) in an entirely different and perhaps irreconcilable manner.

---

[62] Shippey (2003²:316).

[63] Discussed above in I.1 § 2, § 6; II § 1, § 2, § 3. See also Shippey (2003²:313-14).

Biographical Note

Miryam Librán-Moreno is an assistant professor at the Universidad de Extremadura (Spain). She holds a doctorate in Ancient Greek Language and Literature and degrees in Arabic and English. She is a member of the Research Group *Nicolaus Heinsius*, specialized in textual criticism of Greek and Latin authors, and one of the editors of *Exemplaria Classica. Journal of Classical Philology*.

Bibliography

Abbreviations

Lays: see Tolkien 1994a
Letters: see Carpenter 1995
Lost Road: see Tolkien 2002a
Lost Tales 2: see Tolkien 1992
LotR: see Tolkien 2001
Morgoth: see Tolkien 1993
OFS: 'On Fairy-Stories' in Tolkien (1990:109-161)
Shadow: see Tolkien 2002b
Shaping: see Tolkien 1995
Silmarillion: see Tolkien 1979
War of the Jewels: see Tolkien 1994b

Berenson, Jennifer K. and Ellen B. Aitken, 2001, *Flavius Philostratus' Heroikos*, Atlanta: Society of Biblical Literature.
Beschorner, Andreas, 1999, *Helden und Heroen, Homer und Caracalla*, (Übersetzung, Kommentar und Interpretationen zum *Heroikos* des Flavios Philostratos), Bari: Levante.
Boynton, Susan, 1999, 'The Sources and Significance of the Orpheus Myth in *Musica Enchiriadis* and Regino of Prum's *Epistola de harmonica institutione*', *Early Music History* 18:47-74.
Brescia, Graziana, 1996, 'Laodameia ammaestra Protesilao (Ov. Her. 13)', *Aufidus* 10:27-70.
Carpenter, Humphrey (ed. with the assistance of Christopher Tolkien), 1995, *The Letters of J.R.R. Tolkien*, London: HarperCollins.
Dronke, Peter, 1962, 'The Return of Eurydice', *Classica et Mediaevalia* 23:198-215.
---, 1968[2], *Medieval Latin and the Rise of European Love Poetry*, Oxford: Oxford University Press.
Flieger, Verlyn, 2002[2], *Splintered Light. Logos and Language in Tolkien's World*, Kent, OH: The Kent State University Press.

Friedman, John B., 1970, *Orpheus in the Middle Ages*. Cambridge MA.: Harvard University Press.
Gil, Luis, 1974, 'Orfeo y Eurídice (versiones antiguas y modernas de una vieja leyenda)', *CFC* <*elat*> 6:135-193.
Gros Louis, Kenneth R.R., 1966, 'Robert Henryson's Orpheus and Eurydice and the Orpheus Tradition of the Middle Ages', *Speculum* 41:643-655.
Hinds, Stephen, 1999, 'First among Women: Ovid, Tristia 1.6 and the Tradition of 'Exemplary' Catalogues', In Susanna Morton Braund and Roldand Mayer (eds.), *Amor, Roma. Love and Latin Literature*, Cambridge: Cambridge Philological Society, 123-141.
Lee, M. Owen, 1965, 'Orpheus and Eurydice. Myth, Legend, Folklore', *Classica et Mediaevalia* 26:402-412.
Librán-Moreno, Miryam, 2005a, 'Parallel Lives. The Sons of Denethor and the Sons of Telamon', *Tolkien Studies* 2:15-52.
---, 2005b, 'ΟΣΑ ΕΝ ΑΙΔΟΥ. Tragedias y dramas satíricos ambientados en el Inframundo', *Lexis*, 23:105-123.
Mantero, Teresa, 1966, *Ricerche sull' Heroikos di Filostrato*, (Pubblicazioni dell'Istituto di Filologia Classica dell'Università di Genova. no. 21.), Genova: Istituto di Filologia Classica.
Ostheimer, Andreas, 1998, 'Orpheus und die Entstehung einer Musiktheorie im 9. Jahrhundert', *Mittellateinisches Jahrbuch* 33.1:19-35.
Rohde, Erwin, 1898, *Psyche: Seelenkult und Unsterblichkeitglaube der Griechen*, Freiburg i.Br.: Mohr.
Sansone, David, 1985, 'Orpheus and Eurydice in the Fifth Century', *Classica et Mediaevalia* 36:53-64.
Shippey, Tom, 2003^2, *The Road to Middle-earth*, Boston and New York: Houghton Mifflin.
Stevens, Jen, 2004, 'From Catastrophe to Eucatastrophe. J.R.R. Tolkien's Transformation of Ovid's Mythic Pyramus and Thisbe into Beren and Lúthien', In Jane Chance (ed.), 2004, *Tolkien and the Invention of Myth: A Reader*, Lexington: The University Press of Kentucky, 119-132
Tabaglio, M., 1999, 'La cristianizzazione del mito di Orfeo', In Anna Maria Babbi (ed.), 1999, *Le metamorfosi di Orfeo* (Convegno internazionale Verona, 28-30 maggio 1998), Verona: Fiorini, 65-82.
Tolkien, John Ronald Reuel, 1979, *The Silmarillion*, edited by Christopher Tolkien, New York: Ballantine Books.
---, 1990, *The Monsters and the Critics and Other Essays*, edited by Christopher Tolkien, London: HarperCollins.
---, 1992, *The Book of Lost Tales 2*, edited by Christopher Tolkien, New York: Ballantine Books.
---, 1993, *Morgoth's Ring*, edited by Christopher Tolkien, Boston and New York: Houghton Mifflin.
---, 1994a, *The Lays of Beleriand*, edited by Christopher Tolkien, New York: Ballantine Books.

---, 1994b, *The War of the Jewels*, edited by Christopher Tolkien, Boston and New York: Houghton Mifflin.

---, 1995, *The Shaping of Middle-earth*, edited by Christopher Tolkien, New York: Ballantine Books.

---, 2001, *The Lord of the Rings*, London: HarperCollins.

---, 2002a, *The Lost Road and Other Writings*, edited by Christopher Tolkien, London: HarperCollins.

---, 2002b, *The Return of the Shadow*, edited by Christopher Tolkien, London: HarperCollins.

West, Richard C., 2003, 'Real World Myth in a Secondary World: Mythological Aspects in the Story of Beren and Lúthien', In Jane Chance (ed.), 2003, *Tolkien the Medievalist*, London and New York: Routledge, 259-267.

A Monster that Matters: Tolkien's Grendel Revisited[1]

EUGENIO M. OLIVARES-MERINO

Abstract

The present paper is an attempt to provide a systematic description of how Tolkien conceived Grendel, the hero's first foe in the Anglo-Saxon poem *Beowulf*. Although one gets scattered glimpses of Tolkien's view on Grendel from his letters and, perhaps, from characters in his works of fiction, my analysis will focus mainly on Tolkien's lecture '*Beowulf*: The Monsters and the Critics' (November 25, 1936). I will make reference to its definite version, as well as to the previous drafts.

Tolkien's essay '*Beowulf*: The Monsters and the Critics'[2] (abbreviated as MC), first delivered as the Sir Israel Gollancz Memorial Lecture (November 25, 1936), has shaped most of 20th century *Beowulfiana*. Perhaps no other single academic article has been so instrumental in granting canonical status to a medieval piece of literature. The influence that this article has exercised is widely attested. As Lewis E. Nicholson (1963:x) noted in the preface to his *Anthology of Beowulf Criticism*, "[It is] widely recognized as a turning point in Beowulfian criticism." Even at the very threshold of the third millennium, his conclusions were still considered a must for *Beowulf* scholars.[3]

In general terms, Tolkien's main contribution to criticism on the poem is that it is a unified work of art. Burton Raffel's words in the introduction to

---

[1] I would like to thank Prof. Fred C. Robinson for his suggestions and comments in the writing of this paper. I am also indebted to him for his constant support.

[2] The lecture was originally published as pamphlet on 1 July 1937. Then it appeared in the *Proceedings of the British Academy* on 30 December 1937 (Drout 2002:5, n. 6). There have been several reprints, *inter alia*: Nicholson (1963:51-103); Ch. Tolkien (1983:5-48). All references to the article in this paper are taken from the *Proceedings*.

[3] Mitchell and Robinson (1998:235) include Tolkien's paper in their bibliography as "*One Essential Essay*", claiming it is the "most influential literary criticism of the poem ever published" (Mitchell and Robinson 1998:236).

his own translation of the poem are a clear instance of post-Tolkien *Beowulf* criticism:

> not only is it [*Beowulf*] unique, the sole survivor of what might have been a thriving epic tradition, but it is great poetry. Approached as an archaeological relic, it is fascinating. Taken as a linguistic document, it is a marvel [...] But *Beowulf*'s position as a great poem must remain primary; the other purposes it serves are important but peripheral to this central fact of sheer literary merit. (Raffel 1963:x)

This influence, of course, is old news for scholars and specialized readers,[4] even if they do not follow Tolkien's conclusions. Therefore I will not discuss in this paper the widely accepted weight of the Professor's stances about such issues as the unity of the poem, its poetic status, what *Beowulf* is and what it is not, nor even any of the topics tangentially touched by Tolkien and prior to his landmark lecture (Christian vs. pagan dimension of the poem, its form or the historical references it contains). Rather, my design here is less ambitious for I aim at exploring a more limited aspect: the way in which Tolkien conceived Grendel. This author's conclusions on the hero's first foe are still the starting point to build up any interpretation of this creature. Philip Cardew (2005), to mention one of the latest discussions of Grendel, has Tolkien's views as a background at the beginning of his article 'Grendel: Bordering the Human'.[5]

On November 25 (2006), exactly 70 years had passed since the Professor read '*Beowulf*: The Monsters and the Critics' (November 25, 1936). Although one gets scattered glimpses of Tolkien's view on Grendel from his letters and, perhaps, from characters in his works of fiction, my analysis will

---

[4] For more opinions on the prominence of the article, see Drout (2002:1-2).

[5] I want to express my gratitude to Prof. Shippey for having sent me this paper before it was published in his anthology of essays *The Shadow-Walkers: Jacob Grimm's Mythology of the Monstrous*. Email on 8 December 2005.

focus mainly on Tolkien's lecture. In order to provide a systematised description of his conception of Beowulf's foe, I had originally planned to compare the references he made to the fiend in the three now published versions of his well-known essay. Thanks to Michael Drout's study and edition of the two previous drafts of MC ('*Beowulf* and the Critics' [A] & [B]),[6] a much more detailed idea of how Tolkien thought of this monster can be attained.[7] However, I soon came to understand that this would be a tedious task, not only for me but also for readers. And a useless one too, since Tolkien himself already provides a rather organised exposition of his conception of the hero's first enemy in his appendix (a) 'Grendel's Titles', the first to be included in the printed version of his lecture. There he developed some of the issues touched upon in his earlier drafts (but which were finally omitted), as well as some other relevant aspects that were not originally dealt with (for example, the monster's humanity or a complementary description of the dam). Tolkien had too many things to say about Grendel, but as a meticulous writer he decided to lighten the references to this man-eater so as not to wander away from his line of argumentation (and yet, at times he is difficult to follow). Needless to say, besides, that he had to compress the text, both for the lecture and for the later publication. Thus 'Grendel's Titles' offers a clear-cut and ordered view of his conclusions about this creature.

My approach to the present topic will initially focus on Tolkien's increasing familiarity and intimacy with *Beowulf*, both as the result of his

---

[6] Tolkien also made a translation of *Beowulf*, which the Tolkien Society has recently decided to publish; Drout is to be the editor. According to Drout himself it will be a two volume work to appear in 2008 [personal communication by the author].

[7] Since a whole new theory on monsters has been developed in the past years, especially after the works of J.J. Cohen, the so-called 'Monsters theory', I deem it necessary to clarify that I am using this term in its most conventional meaning, a semi human creature hostile to men. This corresponds in general terms with one of the definitions provided by the *Oxford English Dictionary*: **3. a.** An imaginary animal (such as the centaur, sphinx, minotaur, or the heraldic griffin, wyvern, etc.) having a form either partly brute and partly human, or compounded of elements from two or more animal forms. Except in heraldic use, the word usually suggests the additional notion of great size and ferocity, being specifically associated with the 'monsters' victoriously encountered by various mythical heroes.

academic career and his life experiences (section 1). I shall proceed afterwards (section 2) with an exposition of the way in which Tolkien conceived Grendel at the time when he wrote MC, with the assumption that this was the image of the creature that he held all his life, as confirmed by the scarce later evidence. This necessarily implies a brief revision of the critical views which he contested (2.1.), before making explicit Tolkien's thoughts about Grendel, as shown mainly in the appendix mentioned (2.2.). Obviously, my elucidation of Tolkien's image of Grendel is not an end in itself, and it will necessarily have a bearing on the foe's role in the poem. In the third section, I will go back to the main body of the lecture (the drafts included) to illustrate how Tolkien understood the creature's relevance in *Beowulf*; 'monsters' is, after all, what MC is about.[8]

These stages in my approach to Grendel (how Tolkien conceived him and his relevance) conform with Tolkien's original design of his lecture, as shown in the two drafts; these, as Drout (2002:3) claims, "present the argument of '*Beowulf*: The Monsters and the Critics' in a simplified form more easily apprehended and examined than the published essay." I would like to make just one more consideration, which is rather an apology. Since this paper is about Tolkien's views on a precise topic, his words are to be the most relevant part of my essay. Although I have tried to reduce them as much as possible, quotations must necessarily be abundant.

1.   Tolkien, Beowulf and war

When Tolkien gave the Sir Israel Gollancz Memorial Lecture at the British Academy, he had been Rawlinson and Bosworth Professor of Anglo-Saxon at Oxford University for more than ten years. It seems that since 1933, he had been lecturing on *Beowulf*.[9] There was always good attendance at his general

---

[8] Interestingly enough, as Drout has shown, the essay was first named '*Beowulf* with Critics' and then 'Beowulf *and the Critics*' (Drout 2002:4). The final title substitutes 'Beowulf' for 'The Monsters', as Tolkien became gradually aware of the centrality of the hero's three adversaries.

[9] See Drout (2002:4, n. 3).

sessions on this poem for undergraduates. His series on *Beowulf* were well remembered by everyone. Tolkien was tutor of the young W.H. Auden,[10] a student in Oxford from 1925 to 1928. The family name, spelled *Audun*, appears in the Icelandic sagas, and Auden had inherited from his father a fascination with Iceland.[11] In a letter to his former tutor, the poet wrote: "I don't think I have ever told you what an unforgettable experience it was for me as an undergraduate, hearing you recite *Beowulf*" (*Letters* 133). Tolkien used to open his lectures reciting the poem aloud and this habit was extremely effective. Elsewhere Auden further adds: "I remember [a lecture] I attended, delivered by Professor Tolkien. I do not remember a single word he said but at a certain point he recited, and magnificently, a long passage of *Beowulf*. I was spellbound" (Duriez 2003:32).[12]

Tolkien had developed a very special bond with the poem. In a letter to the editor of the *Observer* published on 20 February 1938, he openly admitted that *Beowulf* was among his "most valued sources" (*Letters* 31).[13] Tolkien's familiarity with the Old English poem came from his days at King Edward's School, shortly after Master George Brewerton lent him an Anglo-Saxon primer.[14] This text took him smoothly to *Beowulf*, which he first read in translation and then in Old English. It was "one of the most extraordinary poems of all time" (*Biography* 35). Right before he went to university, the TCBS (Tea Club Barrowian Society) was formed and *Beowulf* was part of young Tolkien's fixed repertoire at their meetings.[15] However, when he started the first term in Oxford (1911), he read Classics at Exeter College. By 1913,

---

[10] See *Biography* 132-133.

[11] Shippey (2005:390) claims that the "best translation of the whole of the *Poetic Edda* remains *Norse Poems*, by Paul B. Taylor and W.H. Auden (London: Athlone Press, 1981)."

[12] At several points, Duriez provides more glimpses of the relation between both authors (Duriez 2003:31, 40, 74, 89, 142, 205 & 207).

[13] See also Shippey (2005:388).

[14] See *Biography* 34-35.

[15] See *Biography* 46.

however, following the advice of Dr. Farnell, Rector of Exeter, he began to read English at the Honour School of English Language and Literature. His specialization would be 'Language', in other words Philology, Old and Middle English, and his tutor was none other than Kenneth Sisam. Tolkien, again and again, would read *Beowulf*.

In the late summer of 1914, England declared war on Germany, but Tolkien did not rush in exultation to pick up a rifle in response to Lord Kitchener's appeal for soldiers. After considering things carefully, he decided to defer his call-up until he had finished his degree, which he obtained in the summer of 1915. Then he was commissioned in the Lancashire Fusiliers. A year later he embarked for France and was taken to the Somme. *Beowulf* stayed in England. When he returned, he was different in many ways, as was the poem.

Necessarily, powerful events in our lives exert an influence on how and what we read. In the case of authors, it is the stuff of their creations,[16] as much as their readings. Roughly speaking, Tolkien's life runs parallel to the 20th century, the most violent period in human history as far back as we can go. Until his death in 1973, the world suffered two world wars, the Russian Revolution, the Spanish Civil War, the Cold War, plus innumerable conflicts in Vietnam, Korea, Angola, Algeria, Cuba, …[17] Even the earliest years of his life had a warlike background, a detail that is often overlooked by biographers. Bloemfontein, the city where Tolkien was born, became the seat of the British-administered Orange River Sovereignty (1848-54) and of the Orange Free

---

[16] I do not see a contradiction here with the opinion expressed by Tolkien in the 'Preface' to *The Lord of the Rings*, where he writes: "It is also false, though naturally attractive, when the lives of an author and critic have overlapped, to suppose that the movements of thought or the events of times common to both were necessarily the most powerful influences" (*LotR* 12). I am not claiming that *the events of times* are *the most powerful influences*, but, as Tolkien himself admits, "an author cannot of course remain wholly unaffected by his experience" (*LotR* 12). To put it very simply, we might talk about degrees of influence, and in a passage where the author was trying to reject any link with WW II, the influence of personal experience would be said consequently to fall too short.

[17] Shippey (2005:369-370) mentions some further calamities.

State (an independent Boer republic formed in 1854). This city is closely connected with the Boer War (October 11, 1899 to May 31, 1902). Three-year old Tolkien, his little brother and his mother left for England early in April 1895. Carpenter talks about *a visit*, since several circumstances made Tolkien's mother terribly homesick.[18] I tend to think that among these circumstances, rumors of war might have presented a temporal stay in England as a more than reasonable perspective. The father, though, never left Bloemfontein.

The failure of the conference held in that city (May to June 1899) resulted in the outbreak of the Boer War in 1899, a conflict that lasted until May 31, 1902. Tolkien was ten years old and would surely hear about the victory of the British troops in South Africa, under the command of Lord Kitchener. A strange feeling the boy might have felt, that sense of loss that all wars produce. For him it would be an intimate loss, a reminder perhaps of the death of his father, whose body rested in Bloemfontein.

Later on Tolkien would have a direct war experience. On 14 July 1916, he faced for the first time the German trenches to take part in what war historians call the First Battle of the Somme (July 1 to November 13, 1916). A week-long artillery bombardment preceded the British infantry's assault. Lord Kitchener – Tolkien knew the name from the Boer War – had asked his soldiers to behave with "discipline and steadiness under fire";[19] the men of the 'B' company of the 11th Lancashire Fusiliers were mown down by machine-gun fire as they marched towards the virtually impregnable German positions. The British sustained nearly 60,000 casualties (20,000 dead) on the first day of the attack. Everywhere Tolkien could see the dead and decaying bodies, pierced by the bullets or torn by the shells. He felt the "animal horror" of trench war,[20] the wet comfort of sleeping in a dug-out, the fear of waiting for a counterattack. The Somme offensive gradually deteriorated into a battle of attrition.

---

[18] See *Biography* 14-15.

[19] Quoted in Shippey (2005:94).

[20] See *Biography* 84.

Before he was struck by 'trench fever' – as soldiers called pyrexia –, Tolkien had taken part in the most ancient of all human rituals of violence, war, and he experienced that mixture of courage, brutality and fear that leads men into butchery and annihilation: "One has indeed personally to come under the shadow of war to feel fully its oppression" – Tolkien wrote, years later (*LotR* 12). Thousands of men may volunteer on the battlefield, but they leave it in a complete void, both the living and the dead: war is an achievement of emptiness, food for instincts, but madness for the mind, a bitter taste of brutality and blood. Some will say that the First Battle of the Somme relieved the German pressure on Verdun …

Back to England and to his academic life – in 1920 Tolkien was appointed Reader in English Language at Leeds University –, the texts would be read under a different light. He himself had seen the darkest side of human condition ("The horror! The horror!", as Conrad would put it in *The Heart of Darkness*). One of the pleasures of literature is that it enables men to live vicariously different situations, from the comfort of an armchair by the fireplace. The case for Tolkien was different in as much as, when reading especially Anglo-Saxon epic and war poems, he would most probably remember situations he had been through. In this sense, *The Battle of Maldon*, *The Battle of Brunanburh* or the most violent episodes in *Beowulf* (so much blood in the poem …) would be dramatically colourful.[21] Tolkien's works of fiction are also permeated with the horror of war. As Shippey (2005:374) puts it, "*The Lord of the Rings* in particular is a war-book, also a post-war book, framed by and responding to the crisis of Western Civilisation, 1914-1945 (and beyond)." When trying to write a mythology for England, he built stories not with the intention of making others believe that these things happened, but that there was some degree of truth behind them, a truth that could not be explained in

---

[21] I am convinced that most readers nowadays have what I call a 'filmic' approach to literature. When we read and imagine the scenarios and characters depicted in books, we tend to do so by recreating the images that we have seen in the different movies we have watched. This is obviously the case when we read a book after having watched the movie inspired by it.

any other way; this was the power of myth: "a sudden glimpse of the underlying reality of truth" (*Biography* 92). And one of its most vigorous manifestations was the permanence of violence, "the exact / and tribal, intimate revenge" (Seamus Heaney, 'Punishment', ll. 43-44).

If the greatest of Old English poems had been, for the young Tolkien, as Carpenter (*Biography* 35) puts it, "the tale of the warrior Beowulf, his fight with two monsters, and his death after battle with a dragon," this was the case no longer. Only the great works of literature grow with us and, as Harold Bloom (1995:xx) states, we do not read them but *they* "read us definitively."[22] After life-long intimacy with the poem and its anonymous author, *Beowulf* was above all concerned with the fatality of human existence, despite all man's efforts. Although the figures have been much disputed, the casualties from the First Battle of the Somme perhaps amounted to roughly 650,000 German, 195,000 French, and 420,000 British. The allied's catastrophic assault on the German positions becomes, therefore, a metaphor of the futility of human existence upon earth. Curiously, at the time when Tolkien was lecturing on *Beowulf* at the British Academy, war had already broken out in Spain; Cain would kill Abel hundreds of times again.[23] The central theme of *Beowulf* for Tolkien was not the simple account of the deeds and heroic death of a warrior (not even "the glorification of the ideal hero and king" [Lawrence 1967:229]), but a much more sombre conviction, which crystallized in such forceful statements as: "the wages of heroism is death" (MC 269) or, becoming more universalistic, "*He* [Beowulf] *is a man, and that for him and many is sufficient tragedy*" (MC 260; Tolkien's italics). As Drout (2002:25) rightly points out, for Tolkien the case is "not that the poem participated in a social structure that inevitably leads to violence and death"; this would heavily tie the poem down to a specific historical situation and ideology. But rather, "that the social structures

---

[22] See also Bloom (2000:28).

[23] The triad Tolkien, *Beowulf* and war can also be seen in the former's introduction to the revised edition of Clark-Hall's translation of the poem, published in 1940. Although the German bombers never flew over Oxford, the threat of a German invasion was particularly felt by the British that year.

inherent in the literature are responses to a human fate that inevitably ends in violence and death." As a devout Roman Catholic Tolkien believed in man's flawed nature after the Fall and, therefore, in his inherent inclination to evil (rather than being completely evil). The existence of pain, sorrow and death accompanied man's life in a fallen world. Tolkien, the *Beowulf*-poet and their heathen ancestors (the latter for different reasons) felt the acute poignancy of this conviction. However, for the first two this was not the whole story. Far from being himself a militant pessimist, Tolkien's moral convictions presented him with a much more comforting consolation: the redeeming dimension of human suffering, the immortality of the human soul and, above all, God's merciful love for man and the promise of everlasting happiness in eternity.

2.   Tolkien and Grendel

The dominating authorities in *Beowulf* criticism during the 1930s were Friedrich Klaeber, Raymond W. Chambers and William W. Lawrence ("the reigning triarchy",[24] as Tolkien ([B], Drout 2002:105) called them) and, to a lesser degree, Archibald Strong and Ritchie Girvan. Further back in time, we should include William P. Ker and James Earl. They are all mentioned in [A], [B] and MC. Those of their opinions which are included in Tolkien's work(s) might not be directly addressed to Grendel, but are indeed concerned with the relevance of the monsters in the poem, or are judgments about the validity of the theme chosen by the *Beowulf*-poet – an issue that is directly linked with the Grendels and the dragon. These opinions are symptomatic of the type of evaluations that were being produced about the poem right before Tolkien presented his lecture. Stanley (1994:37) states that Tolkien reacts "to the adverse criticism by critics whom he otherwise respects, in their comments on texts he likes." I will make a passing survey of all these scholars' views on the questions mentioned, in order to see how MC breaks with long standing stances.

---

[24]   He also calls them "undivided trinity" ([B], Drout 2002:105).

2.1. ... and the Critics

All the scholars mentioned above agreed that *Beowulf* was, in any case, worth reading. Many of them appreciated especially the historical information it contained, but they concluded that the text was, in an ultimate sense, a failure. Why so? Because of the monsters and the disproportionate attention that the author had paid to them. This view had originated in Ker's reference to *Beowulf* in *The Dark Ages* (1904). He claimed, basically, that the poem's excellence of style did not fit with the simplicity of the story. Ker's words have been often quoted (by Tolkien also). His two premises and final conclusion might be rephrased as follows:

1. The fault of *Beowulf* is that there is nothing much in the story. [...], a disproportion that puts the irrelevances in the centre and the serious things on the outer edges;

2. But the great beauty, the real value, of *Beowulf* is in its dignity of style; [and]

3. The thing itself is cheap; the moral and the spirit of it can only be matched among the noblest authors.
(Ker 1958:163-166, quoted in MC 251)

The hunt for the monsters had begun.

R.W. Chambers, a former student of Ker, followed this same strain of thought, quoting from his tutor, but overstating matters. In his edition of *Widsith* (1912), he sentences the monsters to death:

> Nothing could better show the disproportion of *Beowulf* which 'puts the irrelevances in the centre and the serious things on the outer edges', than this passing allusion to the story of Ingeld. For in this conflict between plighted troth and the duty of revenge we have a situation which the old heroic poets loved, and would not have sold for a wilderness of dragons.
> (quoted in MC 252)

Similarly, in *'Beowulf* and the Heroic Age' – a most praised prologue to A. Strong's verse translation of *Beowulf* (1925) – there is a passage where Chambers plays the very same tune:

> The inferiority of *Beowulf* is manifest first of all in the plot. The main story of *Beowulf* is a wild folk-tale. [...] The folk-tale is a good servant, but a bad master: it has been allowed in *Beowulf* to usurp the place of honour, and to drive into episodes and digressions the things which should be the main stuff of a well conducted-epic. (Chambers 1925:xxvi.)

According to Drout (2002:6), "Strong's approach to *Beowulf* summed up for Tolkien much that was wrong with *Beowulf* criticism." This would be hard to deduce from MC, since the only reference to this author is just a quotation (MC 247) from his *A Short History of English Literature* (O.U.P., 1921), to illustrate the ubiquitous evaluation of *Beowulf* which priced its historical value above any other consideration. In both [A] and [B], however, Tolkien makes abundant use of Strong's views (quoted in [A], Drout 2002:35): the text is a "historical document", saved from being "a mere recital of the deeds of a giant killer" thanks to the "allusions to legends" in the digressions. Ker's and Chambers' shadows were large enough.

Klaeber (1941:lii, lxviii) also felt inclined to write that the plots of the two parts of the poem were "surprisingly simple," though the overall evaluation of the style "cannot be doubtful." Students of the poem, therefore, needed not any longer "to apologize for *Beowulf* as a piece of literature"! And again, insisting on the same weaknesses Ker and Chambers had already made explicit, Klaeber (1941:liv-lv) writes:

> [...], we have every reason to be thankful for these episodes which not only add fullness and variety to the central plot, but disclose a wealth of authentic heroic song and legend, a magnificent historic background. Still we may very well regret that those subjects of intensely absorbing interest play only a

> minor part in our epic, having to serve as a foil to a
> story which in itself is of decidedly inferior weight.

Demolishing. Klaeber's edition of *Beowulf* soon became the standard for academics, who presumably read the poem in this light.

The last author Tolkien quotes from is Ritchie Girvan, a name that did not appear in either [A] or [B], and was most probably a last minute addition to MC.[25] In 'Folk-tale and History in Beowulf', a lecture given in March 1935 (University College of London), Girvan (1971:84) wondered "why he [the *Beowulf*-poet] chose just this subject, when to our modern judgment there were at hand so many greater, charged with the splendour and tragedy of humanity, and in all respects worthier of a genius as astonishing as it was rare in Anglo-Saxon England."[26]

I have left William W. Lawrence, one of the names in the "international triumvirate" (as Shippey refers to Chambers, Klaeber and the former),[27] for I consider he deserves special attention. He is often mentioned both in [A] and [B], but omitted in MC; even in the two drafts, he is never quoted. It seems that Lawrence was one of the 'monster hunters', but finally Tolkien left him out. I would say that Tolkien agreed with many of Lawrence's views on the poem, as expressed in his *Beowulf and Epic Tradition* (1928). Much might be said about this book's relevance in MC, but for the present moment I will very

---

[25] In MC, Tolkien writes: "In the final peroration of his notable lecture on *Folk-tale and History in Beowulf*, given last year, [...]." Professor Girvan delivered three lectures at University College, London, in March 1935. These lectures were published as *Beowulf and the Seventh Century* (1935).

[26] Cf. MC 254. Drout (2002:xix) writes that "it seems possible to place the composition of much of *Beowulf and the Critics* between August 1933 and 23 October 1935. Unless there is additional information in Tolkien's diaries or in other archival materials that I have not examined, the manuscript cannot be dated with any greater accuracy." Girvan had stated in the preface to the original edition of *Beowulf and the Seventh Century* that "These lectures were printed in the form in which they were delivered." This provides interesting information on the date of composition of MC. I do not know the exact month of publication of Girvan's book, but if it was before 23 October 1935, why did Tolkien not include its bibliographical reference in the endnotes? Maybe he was present at the lecture and took his notes *verbatim* from the speaker.

[27] Shippey and Haarder (1998:62).

briefly gather a few ideas from Lawrence (mainly from his preface) in the light of the following premise: "But the main importance of a great poem must lie in its poetry. As to this, no apologies[28] for *Beowulf* are necessary" (Lawrence 1967:vii). Consequently, as he insists a few lines after, *Beowulf* should be appreciated as "a work of art" (Lawrence 1967:viii). The readers of his book, Lawrence (1967:ix) assumed, would be "those interested in the poem as literature." Certainly, Tolkien did not follow Lawrence (1967:vii) when he said that the historical background in the poem afforded "an unrivalled picture of the early life of our pagan ancestors," but there were other points of encounter between the two scholars. In a softer way than Tolkien, Lawrence (1967:viii) also complained that histories of literature and books of reference had "failed to do the poem justice." Besides, in a previous paper, Lawrence had rejected allegorical readings of *Beowulf*.[29] Though much concerned with the traditions behind them, Lawrence devotes two chapters to the monsters in the poem. In chapter six, 'Grendel and his dam', he makes a few statements that Tolkien would have agreed with (Lawrence 1967:161; 161-162): "Their attributes embody what men most feared in the world about"; or, "They [the 'Grendels'] are pagan in origin, beyond a doubt, but Christian and Hebrew tradition have lent them new terrors, in connecting them with Cain and the devils spawned as his descendants." As for the dragon, though Lawrence was concerned mainly with its Northern precursors, the author emphasizes that the fire-drake (*a type*, he calls it)[30] was not only the worst of foes in Germanic myth, but a most fitting end for the poem: "A great slayer of trolls and a mighty king ought not to die in his bed, tamely, but in glorious combat with a worthy foe, and the dragon was ready to hand, [...]" (Lawrence 1967:206).

---

[28] The "apologies" are, I think, a wink at Klaeber's comment mentioned above.

[29] Reported in Stanley (1994:30, n. 64).

[30] While Lawrence (1967:206) stated that the dragon was "not individualized, but a type," Tolkien used the terms *draco* and *draconitas*.

Nonetheless, Lawrence (1967:21) has to be counted among the 'monster slayers', since, for him, these creatures have very little value for the poem. It is the historical background that dignifies the plot:

> It [the historical material] lends to the rather childish contests with monsters a plausibility not found in folk-tales, and provides an interest which, if secondary, is hardly less absorbing than the main plot. [...] It increases the dignity of the demons and the dragon that so admirable a prince should condescend to slay them.

All in all, I would say that after Lawrence's book, the field was ripe for MC.

We can clearly infer from the previous quotations that it was a consolidated critical stance to claim that the *Beowulf*-poet, a skilled artist demonstrably, had lost his way when preferring Grendel, his dam and the fire-drake, to those more worthy materials he used in the digressions and episodes, as the main subject of his poem. This was the context in which Tolkien wrote his lecture, a solemn tradition (almost undisputed) especially because these scholars were the 'sacred cows' of *Beowulfiana* in the early 20th century. Chambers' presence in particular was impressive, even more when he published his encyclopaedic *Beowulf. An Introduction to the Study of the Poem with a Discussion of the Stories of Offa and Finn*.[31] For Tolkien, he was the greatest living Anglo-Saxonist.

As shown above, the original title Tolkien fashioned for his work was '*Beowulf* with the Critics', soon to be '*Beowulf* and the Critics'; this is the name of drafts [A] and [B].[32] Why then the final modification? Tolkien gradually realized that his defence of *Beowulf* as a piece of literature would not take place on aesthetic grounds; Ker had already granted the *dignity of style* of the poem,

---

[31] Chambers' major contributions to *Beowulfiana* are his 'Foreword' to Strong's translation of *Beowulf* (1925) and his *Beowulf. An Introduction to the Study of the Poem with a Discussion of the stories of Offa and Finn* (originally published 1921). Chambers is also remembered as a great expert on Sir Thomas More.

[32] It seems Tolkien got this name from Chambers, who had entitled the fourth chapter in his edition of *Widsith* '*Widsith* and the Critics' (Drout 2002:6).

and all the others followed in his wake. Rather, the value of *Beowulf* had to be also proved in its theme and structure, and this necessarily conveyed a favourable appreciation of Beowulf's foes. At the beginning of his lecture Tolkien claims:

> I shall confine myself mainly to the *monsters* – Grendel and the Dragon, as they appear in what seems to me the best and most authoritative general criticism in English – and to certain considerations of the structure and conduct of the poem that arise from this theme. (MC 246; Tolkien's italics)

Instead of '*Beowulf* with/and the Critics', '*Beowulf*: The Monsters and the Critics' clearly indicated to the audience (attendants and readers) that the topic to be dealt with would be the monsters and the way they had been *treated* by the critics. In fact, there was another – and possibly more malicious – interpretation of this title. Those critics who had given little or no literary value to the trolls and the fire-drake were the real monsters for *Beowulf*!

2.2. *The Monster[s]* ...

No doubt that Grendel had been prowling around Tolkien's mind ever since he first read *Beowulf*. In July 1910, he wrote a short and descriptive poem entitled 'Wood-sunshine'; Carpenter (*Biography* 47) shows his surprise at the chosen topic: "Fairy spirits dancing on a woodland carpet seem a strange choice of subject for a rugger-playing youth of eighteen who had a strong taste for Grendel and the dragon Fafnir." It is interesting to notice that in MC, while the hero's name is mentioned on 55 occasions, 'Grendel' appears 44 times – excluding the two 'Grendel's mother'. In this same sense, 'dragon' comes 47 times and 'fire-drake' two, but only in thirty-two instances is Tolkien specifically referring to Beowulf's bane. This gradation shows the relevance that Grendel had for Tolkien. Apparently, though, he devoted more lines to the dragon. The winged serpent is indeed a weapon of mass destruction, a beast whose power makes victory over it almost unattainable. Beowulf finds death in the final struggle with the magnificent worm, which would return to life to be fooled by Bilbo in Tolkien's *The Hobbit*.[33] And yet it is against Grendel that Beowulf makes public his heroic status. If the dragon is the right end for the hero, it is because Beowulf made such a brilliant debut against his first foe. For the Danes and Beowulf himself Grendel is the embodiment of their primitive barbarity, a remnant of old uncivilized days.[34] For the Christian audience of the poem and the narrator himself – a Christian also, if not monk –, Grendel is a living caveat about/of their heathen past. For Tolkien, a Roman Catholic, the creature is a being caught in the right moment to scare both heathens and Christians: a character sprung from the trolls and *draugar* of Northern folklore, but explicitly a descendant of Cain. On top of all, Grendel, not the dragon, is the topic of one of the three appendices at the end of MC.

I think that Tolkien saw in Grendel the dark, sombre attraction with which the other great (maybe the greatest) fiend in English literature was endowed: Milton's Satan. Both are *feond mancynnes*, both are cursed, both carry God's anger on their backs. Springing originally from the evil creatures of Northern mythology, Grendel is said to be Cain's descendant and is thus clearly placed on the wrong side of that cosmic confrontation that takes place in the Christian conception of time, up to the Final Judgement when evil will be finally (and forever) defeated. The dragon seems to be outside this dualism, a fact to which Tolkien as a Catholic was not insensitive. As much as Milton's

---

[33] The fight between Beowulf and the fire-drake can also be assumed behind a similar episode in Tolkien's 'The Children of Húrin' (*Biography* 96).

[34] In his otherwise 'politically correct' movie *Beowulf & Grendel* (2005), Sturla Gunnarsson presents the fiend as a kind of Neanderthal, a primitive creature who takes vengeance on the Danes for Hrothgar's killing of his father. The implication is that Grendel is one of the last of his kin, a species that cannot coexist with its more advanced enemies. This is also the case in *The 13th Warrior* (John McTiernan, 1999) based on M. Crichton's *Eaters of the Dead*, a cocktail prepared with *The Travels of Ibn Fadlan* and *Beowulf*. The *wendols*, a tribe of Grendel-like creatures, are also presented as primitive humans in constant warfare with Hrothgar's Danes. In any case, this view is by no means a recent invention. Peter E. Müller, writing in 1815, established a link between Grendel and the *Jotuns*, "hardly just mythological creatures but (as Professor Verlauff has observed [...]) also historical, that is, remnants of an older people that had been pushed back into forests and deserts and led an almost savage existence" (quoted in Shippey and Haarder 1998:106).

Satan is strangely attractive in his wicked pride, for his doomed revelry and his epic majesty, so Grendel, Satan's minion, appeals to our darkest instincts for his brutality, his anti-social independence, his apparent invulnerability and his defiant rejection of all conventions. Evil must be attractive to be tempting. Grendel, a deranged man, is a reminder of the high price we would have to pay if we decided to follow his path. This seems to me also one of the keys to understand Bilbo's ambiguous attitude towards Gollum, formerly one of his kind: he is the hobbit's distorted *alter ego*, illustrating what would happen if Frodo were overwhelmed by the power of the Ring. The relation between Gollum and Grendel, apart from being alliterative, is strikingly interesting in more than one sense. Cain (Grendel's ancestor) killed his brother, Abel; Sméagol (later known as Gollum) also killed his 'brother' Déagol (his cousin, in fact). As a result of this transgression, both Grendel and Gollum are exiles. This could be graphically depicted as follows:

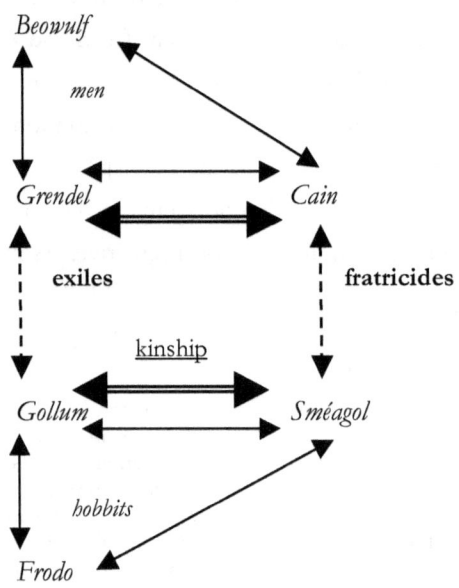

The starting point of Tolkien's argumentation about Grendel is a widely accepted consensus. As result of the gradual conversion of the barbarians to Christianity and monotheism,[35] heathen divinities and, more in particular, monsters were transformed into a wide-ranging and heterogeneous category of beings that we might gather under the label of demons or,[36] as Tolkien (MC 278) writes, "the mediaeval devil." Elsewhere ([A], Drout 2002:66) he says: "So the old monsters became images of the evil spirit or spirits, or rather the evil spirits entered into the monsters and took visible shape in the hideous bodies of the *þyrsas* and *sigel-hearwan* of heathen imagination." However, as Tolkien painstakingly tries to demonstrate, Grendel belongs to a historical moment in which this mutation had not yet been fully accomplished. In the opening sentence of his appendix we read (MC 278): "The changes which produced (before A.D. 1066) the mediaeval devil are not complete in *Beowulf*, but in Grendel change and blending are, of course, already apparent." Almost at the end of his appendix Tolkien returns to his initial statement, ending where he began (MC 280; my italics): "It is thus true to say that Grendel *is not yet* a real mediaeval devil […]."Here, probably, lies the key to an understanding

---

[35] The beginning of the medieval mission was the baptism of Clovis, King of the Franks (A.D. 496) and lasted, roughly speaking, until the conversion of Finland (A.D. 1291). To deny the Christian roots of Europe or to avoid explicit mention of this fact (as in the recent attempts to establish a European *Magna Carta*) is by no means historically justified. The monks that converted the early Europeans instructed them in the faith and in statecraft. Thus, the major result of this 1000-year mission was the creation of European civilization. However, an ideologically biased debate has been artificially provoked. Leading politicians claim that present day European realities (such as multiculturalism or the practice of different religions) demand the convenience of diminishing the undeniable role of Christianity in the consolidation of the medieval states on the Old Continent.

[36] Tolkien makes explicit reference to this issue in note 37 (MC 295): "The Christian theory was that such gods did not exist, and were inventions of the Devil, and that the power of idols was due to the fact that he, or one of his emissaries, often actually inhabited them, and could be seen in their real hideousness if the veil of illusion was removed." Fred C. Robinson (1982:12) shares this view and illustrates it with Aelfric's sermon *De falsis diis*. The *Beowulf* poet himself explicitly identifies pagan deities with demons: "Hwilum hie geheton æt hærgtrafum/wigweorþunga, wordum bædon/þæt him gastbona geoce gefremede/wið þeodþreaum. Swylc wæs þeaw hyra,/hæþenra hyht;" (ll. 175-179). "At times they [the Danes] offered honor to idols/at pagan temples, prayed aloud/that the soul-slayer [the devil] might offer assistance/in the country's distress. Such was their custom,/the hope of the heathens […]" (Liuzza 2000:58-59).

of the (at times contradictory) complexity of this creature, one caught in a moment of transition.

Already in his '*Beowulf* and the Critics' [A], Tolkien had clearly stated that "[i]n spite of the terminology applied to Grendel he is not yet 'medieval'" ([A], Drout 2002:66). The same is to be said about version [B], where he reproduces almost verbatim the previous statement: "In spite of the terminology applied to him (déofol (devil)) Grendel is not yet mediaeval" ([B], Drout 2002:129).[37] These two sentences (especially the second one) are obviously behind the quotation from MC. However, the careful reader will have noticed that, apart from the fact that the author plays with the repetition of sounds by adding *real* and *devil* before and after *mediaeval* in the final wording of the idea,[38] in MC and [B], *mediaeval* is not written in between inverted commas. In [A] it is, as if Tolkien were quoting someone else, or at least, as if he were using the word in a specific sense. I would say both. The relevant passage the author had in mind was by R.W. Chambers – whom Tolkien qualifies as the "[*Beowulf-*]poet's best friend" (MC 252). It is a section taken from '*Beowulf* and the Heroic Age in England', Chamber's 'Foreword' to Strong's prose translation of *Beowulf*,[39] and it is included in the three versions of MC. In [A] (Drout 2002:60-61, 66) Tolkien quotes a long piece of text and proceeds shortly after to its discussion; in [B] (Drout 2002:116-118, 129) and in the definitive version (MC 19-20,

---

[37] I am using Drout's square brackets, small brackets and types.

[38] "[...] Grendel *is not yet* a <u>real mediaeval devil</u> [...]." The pronunciation of the three underlined words is: /ˈriːəl/, /mɛdɪˈiːvəl, miːdɪˈiːvəl/, /ˈdɛv(ə)l, ˈdɛvɪl/. What I mean is that there is a clear assonane between /ˈriːəl/ and /mɛdɪˈiːvəl/. Besides since the /v/ in the second is in a weak position, we could almost talk about feminine rhyme. In /mɛdɪˈiːvəl/ and /ˈdɛv(ə)l/, we have "onomatopoetic associated effect" from the stressed syllable. Apart from this, there is clear consonance between /dɪˈiː/ (often perceived as a single stressed syllable /ˈdiː/) and /ˈdɛ/. All in all, the sounds /əl/ in these three words also appear in *Grendel* /ˈgrɛndəl/, located nearby as the subject of the proposition, *real mediaeval devil* being the subject complement. Prof. Jesus M. Nieto-Garcia (from my Department) kindly helped me to give form to what simply was an intuition.

I wish I had been at the British Academy lecture on November 25 (1936) just to see whether Tolkien was reading these words with some kind of emphasis on the sounds discussed!

[39] See Chambers (1925:xxvii-xxx).

34), Chamber's words are quoted long before Tolkien's evaluation of their meaning, so that the inverted commas make no sense.[40]

Leaving aside this minor detail, Chambers' passage deserves quotation so as to clarify what was meant by "medi[a]eval" and – more relevant for my concern – to proceed with my analysis of Grendel, since Chambers' words on this creature force Tolkien to further illustrate his own conception of the foe. In MC, the passage from '*Beowulf* and the Heroic Age in England' is considerably reduced. I therefore quote from Chambers (1925:xxviii-xxix) himself.

> In the epoch of *Beowulf* a Heroic Age more wild and primitive than that of Greece is brought into touch with Christendom, with the Sermon on the Mount, with Catholic theology and ideas of Heaven and Hell. We see the difference, if we compare the wilder things – the folk-tale element – in *Beowulf* with the wilder things of Homer. Take for example the tale of Odysseus and the Cyclops – the No-man trick. Odysseus is struggling with a monstrous and wicked foe, but he is not exactly thought of as struggling with the powers of darkness. Polyphemus, by devouring his guests, acts in a way which is hateful to Zeus and the other gods: yet the Cyclops is himself god-begotten and under divine protection, and the fact that Odysseus has maimed him is a wrong which Poseidon is slow to forgive. But the gigantic foes whom Beowulf has to meet are identified with the foes of God. Grendel and the dragon are constantly referred to in language which is meant to recall the powers of darkness with which Christian men felt themselves to be encompassed. They are the "inmates of Hell", "adversaries of God", "offspring of Cain", "enemies of mankind". Consequently, the matter of the main story of *Beowulf*, monstrous as it is, is not so far removed from common mediaeval experience as it seems to us to be from our own. It was believed that Alcuin as a

---

[40] It is also noticeable how Tolkien gradually reduces the extent of the quotation.

> boy had been beset by devils because he neglected divine service in order to read Virgil. Grendel hardly differs from the fiends of the pit who were always in ambush to waylay a righteous man. And so Beowulf, for all that he moves in the world of the primitive Heroic Age of the Germans, nevertheless is almost a Christian knight.[41]

I have quoted directly from the foreword in Strong's text, since the anecdote about Alcuin's literary tastes is omitted by Tolkien, and I consider it necessary to grasp what Chambers understood at this particular point by *mediaeval*. This adjective comes in the phrase "common medieval experience" (Chambers 1925:xxviii), to mean a view of human existence in which it was taken for granted that devils from hell were always ready to tempt the righteous man and make him fall. Generally speaking, this is the sense in which the adjective is often (pejoratively) used: men were too concerned (or rather, obsessed) about the salvation of their souls, which were permanently under the devil's threat. Grendel belongs to this historical context, so that he "hardly differs from the fiends of the pit" whose sole purpose was to destroy the human soul. It is precisely at this point that Tolkien disagrees with 'the poet's best friend'. Besides, Tolkien also rejected another affirmation in the previous quotation: that all Beowulf's foes were God's foes too. Taking into account these discrepancies, in what follows I will try to clarify in some detail who Grendel was for Tolkien.

2.2.1. *On Grendel's humanity*

Grendel is a man, or better, he is "nearly human" (MC 276). This statement should by no means be taken for granted or obviated, for it must lie at the basis of any theorization about this creature. The medieval audience of the poem never lost sight of this, 'medieval' as they were.

---

[41] See also MC 261-262.

First of all, Grendel is a man *ab origine*, ever since the moment that he is *Caines cynne* (*Beowulf* l. 107), of Cain's kin. His genealogy thus takes him back to Adam, the first man and so Beowulf's ancestor as well. The term 'monster' is too often applied loosely to Grendel, so that his humanity gets blurred, especially for modern readers overly familiar with heroes fighting against monstrous foes in 20th century fiction and movies. Neither Tolkien nor the *Beowulf*-poet were ignorant of this. Grendel, as Tolkien points out (MC 279), is referred to by terms applicable to ordinary men, such as *wer* (l. 105), *rinc* (l. 720), *guma* (l. 973), *maga* (l. 978); we might also add *heal-ðegnes* (l. 142), *hæþene[s]* (l. 852; l. 986).

Besides, and this is also a definitive attribute of Grendel, he – like any other man – has an immortal soul, a privilege shared by no other earthly creature: "he [Grendel] is conceived as having a spirit, other than his body, that will be punished" (MC 279);[42] later on, the author insists (MC 279): "[Grendel] is doomed when slain to be numbered among the evil spirits."

Yet it would be foolish to claim that Grendel, although essentially human, is a normal man. As I stated before, his body is the outer image of his depraved human nature. Tolkien himself seems to have hesitated when confronted with the issue of Grendel's real status, as can be inferred from the three versions of his lecture. When comparing Northern and Classical mythologies in [A], he states that in the first case gods and men fight together against the monsters, whereas in the second man often struggles against gods and monsters, usually the offspring of the former; and so "[…] the Gods of Asgard do not recognize kinship with the Wolf of Fenrir anymore than men with Grendel" ([A], Drout [2002:66]).[43] We might deduce from this that there is a great chasm between men and this creature, so that Tolkien would be, to a

---

[42] Tolkien goes on: "Thus alegde hæþene sawle: þær him hel onfeng, 852; while Beowulf himself says ðær abidan sceal miclan domes, hu him scir Metod scrifan wille, 978."

[43] The greater gods in Norse mythology (Odin, Thor, Freyja, …) lived in Asgard, their heavenly realm. The wolf of Fenrir or Fenris-wolf is the son of Loki, another god. It is chained up until the final destruction of the gods, when it escapes to devour Odin. The wolf itself is then killed by Vidarr.

certain extent, contradicting himself. Interestingly enough, in the rewriting of this section for [B] (Drout 2002:128), the author makes a subtle but meaningful modification: "[…] the Gods of Ásgarðr do not recognize kinship with Fenris wolf anymore than men with *the Dragon*" (the emphasis is mine). In MC the previous comments are reserved for a note and, this time, Tolkien was skilful enough as to avoid the contradiction mentioned, including both examples in his comparison (MC 292, n. 23): "[…] the gods do not recognize any bond with *Fenris úlfr*, any more than men with Grendel or the serpent."

Leaving aside the dragon, we might not be willing to *recognize* kinship with Grendel, as much as we would not *recognize* kinship with Hitler or Stalin. The verb is carefully chosen, for recognizing means accepting something that is factual, whether we like it or not;[44] we all *know* that, at least technically speaking, the dictators were human beings. I could push this line of thought further into the realm of theological argumentation, to be confronted eventually with necessary (though striking) conclusions: Since Grendel is essentially human, a) in his body and soul, he was created by God; b) he was a free being and so, he might have chosen another path of action; and c) since Christ's Redemption was universal and sufficient, Grendel could have also benefited from it. These speculations would be out of the question and, besides, I am no theologian. Neither was Tolkien, but he had received a solid doctrinal formation which would make him wonder about these issues at some point. In fact, the explicit references to the fiend's soul seem to be the result of his maturing of this idea, for they are absent from both [A] and [B].[45] I am inclined to think

---

[44] *OED:* 4. a. acknowledge by special notice, approval or sanction; to treat as valid, as having existence or as entitled to consideration; to take notice of (a thing or person) in some way.

[45] In [A], there is an enumeration of ideas among which Tolkien includes: "(6) 977: Beowulf says that Grendel shall abide miclan domes (the great judgment) and what scir metod (the glorious Measurer) shall doom for him" (Drout 2002:71). In [B], on the other hand, a similar statement is made when analyzing one of the most outstanding ambiguities in the poem, the concepts of God (*dryhten, metod, Godes* …) and Fate (*wyrd*): "There remain in considering the utterances of Beowulf himself his declaration that Grendel shall abide miclan domes (the great judgment) and the judgment of scír metod (the glorious Measurer)" (Drout 2002:136).

that this complexity provoked further comments about this creature. For Tolkien (as for the anonymous poet) Grendel suffers from an inherited curse (being Cain's descendant). This is dubious ground and a risky theological issue, one which lies at the very core of the Reformation: predestination or, as Luther would put it, *De servo arbitrio*. However, Tolkien (with the poet) takes pains to emphasise that Grendel is willingly sinful (MC 279): "*manscaða, synscaða, synnum beswenced* [sic], he is also *fyrena hyrde*. [...] *hæpen*, 852, 986, and *helle hæfton, feond on helle*."[46] The problem, it goes without saying, is not solved, but for Tolkien (maybe more than for the poet himself) the conviction is that Grendel freely chose the wrong path ..., just as anyone of us might.[47] That is the reason why, independently from moral convictions and beliefs, the fiend reflects – as a distorted mirror – our own evil potentialities, the dark side within:

> [Grendel becomes] more like the inner enemy, the evil possibilities of debased human nature, just as in defining him and his broods as Godes andsaca (the enemy of God) he has become in fact offspring of Cain; that is ultimately of Adam.
> ([A], Drout 2002:76)

> [...] in Grendel we see, [...], also a parody of man misformed by hate (earmsceapen on weras wæstum) (a wretched creature in the shape of a man), who bears hell with him, feond on helle (enemy in hell) even as he walks in Denmark, being rejected by God. The poet has made him spring ultimately from Adam.
> ([B], Drout 2002:145)

---

[46] Interestingly enough, there is a typo in this quotation: instead of *beswenced it should be geswenced. This has been reproduced in all the reprints of the article I have checked.

[47] As expounded in 561 at the Council of Braga, God created the angels (Satan too) free and good by nature (Denzinger 2000:237). Therefore, when the devil and his followers chose evil, they did so freely. See the Fourth Lateran Council (A.D. 1215) (Denzinger 2000:427, 428).

For MC Tolkien extracts this idea from its context in [A] and [B] and uses it to emphasize his argument about Grendel's chosen (not just inherited) malice. The point is thus more potent than in the previous drafts, for the link between moral and physical monstrosity is stressed:

> Their [the monsters'] parody of human form (*earm-sceapen on weres wæstmum*) becomes symbolical, explicitly, of sin, or rather this mythical element, already present implicit and unresolved, is emphasized: this we see already in *Beowulf*, strengthened by the theory of descent from Cain (and so from Adam), and of the curse of God. So Grendel is not only under this inherited curse, but also himself sinful [...] As an image of man estranged from God [...] (MC 279)

Grendel's malice is perceived as more sophisticated than the dragon's ([A], Drout 2002:76). It is much more rational (since human) and much more evil, because freely chosen. Already in the days of his life, he is condemned to eternal punishment in hell. Not only is Grendel "synnum geswenced" (l. 975), but he is unwilling to atone for his sins: "ond no mearn fore" (l. 136). In this sense, there is one essential distinction between Grendel and the Dragon, a detail that Chambers seems to have missed, when he claimed that Beowulf's foes were, with no distinction, "the foes of God" (Chambers 1925:xxviii; in MC 261). The dragon is evil, brutal, but his wickedness is amoral. In other words, it seems to be outside the dichotomy of good and evil in the Christian sense. The poet never states it is demonic or an enemy of God, even when its likeness with the snake in Paradise or the Serpent in the *Book of Revelation* was at hand.[48] So Chambers' equality of both creatures "is not strictly true. The dragon is not referred to in such terms, which are applied to Grendel [...]" (MC 291 n. 14).[49]

---

[48] The association of the dragon with Satan occurs in other Anglo-Saxon poems: *Physiologus* (l. 16), *Elene* (l. 765), *Solomon and Saturn* (ll. 25 ff.), *Christ and Satan* (ll. 97 ff.).

[49] See Chambers' statement: "They[14] are the 'inmates of Hell', [...]."

2.2.2. *Grendel vs. demons*

Chambers had concluded that Grendel hardly differed from the fiends of the pit, a periphrasis softly suggesting that Grendel was a demon. Tolkien, however, stated that Grendel differed from demons in important points (MC 291, n. 15),[50] an issue that has already been emphasized at the beginning of 2.2.

As a man accustomed to intellectual argumentation and a reader of the Classics, Tolkien used for his discussion on Grendel a common rhetorical device: admitting that which is true in the view he is to refute. There are indeed several details in the poem that might lead us to consider Grendel as a demon. Among these, Tolkien (MC 279) emphasises "his ceaseless hostility to men, and hatred of their joy, his super-human size and strength, and his love of the dark, [...], his hideousness and habitation in dark forsaken places." Apart from that, it cannot be denied that the poet refers to Grendel and his dam as *deofla* (l. 1680), while the former is said to flee to *deofla gedræg* (l. 756). We could further add *wergan gastes* (l. 133), "an expression for 'devil' later extremely common, and actually applied in line 1747 to the Devil and tempter himself" (MC 279). However, though the process of transformation of monsters into demons had already begun, Grendel has not become a devil yet. This can be deduced from the fact that real 'devilish qualities' are not present in him; among them, Tolkien singles out two (MC 279): "deception and destruction of the soul."[51] As reported in 2.2., already in [A] the author had exposed this idea: there are no devils in *Beowulf* as hideous as this *þyrs* (Grendel), and as fleshly, whose purpose is to destroy the soul, to tempt ([A], Drout 2002:66). Grendel although a *feond on helle*, is primarily *feond mancynnes*. Both he and his dam are physically in this world, feeding on human flesh ([A],

---

[50] These are words in an end note about Chambers' statement: "Grendel hardly differs[15] from the fiends of the pit who were always in ambush to waylay a righteous man."

[51] Satan is described by St. John with the following words: "Ille homicida erat ab initio et in veritate non stabat, quia non est veritas in eo. Cum loquitur mendacium, ex propriis loquitur, quia mendax est et pater eius." (Jn VIII, 44). "He was a murderer from the beginning and does not stand in truth, because there is no truth in him. When he tells a lie, he speaks in character, because he is a liar and the father of lies"; see: http://www.vatican.va/archive

Drout 2002:66-67). In [B] he proceeds much in the same way ([B], Drout 2002:129): "But Grendel though called <u>feond on helle</u> (enemy in hell) is primarily <u>feond mancynnes</u> (enemy of mankind); he and his kin are in this world, eaters of the flesh of men, they are in the physical world and of it – they are indeed in a sense it itself." Grendel's intentions, his motivations behind his raids on Heorot, are not proselytistic, in other words, he is not a "soul-destroying evil" (MC 280), but rather one concerned with the body of his victims. Just as the Danes are heathens, so Grendel is. In other words, he is not endowed with some kind of demonic wisdom that makes him strive to get the immortal soul of his victims (a precious trophy for a real medieval devil), but simply to kill the body so as to satiate his hunger and his hatred. Very soon, demons would be solely concerned with the soul, rather than with the body, as they gradually became more and more spiritual. But Grendel is not yet one of them. The distinction of the two constituent elements of human nature recalls a well known passage from the New Testament:

> Dico autem vobis amicis meis: Ne terreamini ab his, qui occidunt corpus et post haec non habent amplius, quod faciant. Ostendam autem vobis quem timeatis: Timete eum, qui postquam occiderit, habet potestatem mittere in gehennam. Ita dico vobis: Hunc timete.[52]

> Et nolite timere eos, qui occidunt corpus, animam autem non possunt occidere; sed potius eum timete, qui potest et animam et corpus perdere in gehenna.[53]

---

[52] Lc XII, 4-5. "I tell you, my friends, do not be afraid of those who kill the body but after that can do no more. I shall show you whom to fear. Be afraid of the one who after killing has the power to cast into Gehenna; yes, I tell you, be afraid of that one."

[53] Mt X, 28. "And do not be afraid of those who kill the body but cannot kill the soul; rather, be afraid of the one who can destroy both soul and body in Gehenna."

In any case, these passages did not offer any consolation to the pagan Danes, but were most likely in the mind of the *Beowulf*-poet who certainly knew who the real enemy of mankind was, the devil, *gastbona* (l. 177), 'the soul-slayer'.

Grendel's abode is consistent with the view that he is not a devil, his abode is not hell, but a haunted mere in the fens of Zealand. The poet provides a detailed (though at times contradictory and confusing)[54] description of his dwelling place.[55] The action of *Beowulf* "is incarnate in the world of history and geography" (MC 257). There are several instances in MC (as in the two previous quotations from [A] and [B]) to illustrate this: "Grendel inhabits the visible world [...]"; "[...] Grendel was in Denmark"; "[He] was a fleshly denizen of this world" (MC 265, 267, 279).

In any case, Tolkien is aware of the fact that Grendel's closeness to demons is more than obvious. When reading phrases such as *On helle* and *helle* (as in *helle gast*, l. 1274), he has to appeal to the non-literality of the terms: "[These words] mean 'hellish', and are actually equivalent to the first elements in the compounds *deapscua, sceadugengea, helruna.* [...]; and even *feond on helle* could be so used" (MC 279-280). We must assume that, since not explicitly stated, Tolkien also understood that the poet was using the term *deofla* in a metaphorical sense.[56] The argument is well understood by readers, for every now and then we use similar expressions; when writing about Tolkien's conception of evil in his fiction writings, T.A. Shippey (2005:168-169; my italics) writes: "One of the strange features of the twentieth century has been the

---

[54] Lawrence (1967:183-187).

[55] Niles (1983:16-19), as others before him, has emphasized the hellish overtones of the haunted mere.

[56] Tolkien (MC 279-280) writes about the term *feond* that "it still means 'enemy' in *Beowulf*, and is for instance applicable to Beowulf and Wiglaf in relation to the dragon, [...] even *feond on helle* could be so used [meaning 'hellish']. Wyclif applies *fend on helle* to the friar walking in England as Grendel in Denmark." Other terms (*feond, lað, sceaða, feorhgeniðla, laðgeteona*) are frequently used for Grendel, but these are applicable to enemies of any kind (MC 280). A similar statement is made about some other titles referring to Grendel's condition as an exile (*heorowearh, dædhata, mearcstapa, angengea*), for these are especially fitting to him as a man (both anti-social and a descendant of Cain) or to a devil (MC 280).

curious bloodlessness of its major *demonic* figures, and the repeated origin of disaster in loudly proclaimed good intentions."

When ascribing Grendel to a category in the catalogue of (semi-) human monsters, Tolkien claims that he "remains primarily an ogre" (MC 280),[57] a label under which the critic welcomes terms from the poem such as *fīfelcyn*, *þyrs* or *eoten*.[58] I think it is relevant to point out that in [B] he had also used another word, *troll*.[59] Behind his preference for *ogre* in MC,[60] I see a way to address an audience wider than culturally non-Northern or Anglo-Saxon, but also Tolkien's awareness that *ogre* might be a more fitting term for Grendel, as he is described in the poem, human and monstrous. With this term Tolkien shows that he does not conceive of this creature solely in terms of his Northern literary ancestors or parallels,[61] but also taking much into account those other traditions that merge with them, mainly Judeo-Christian.[62] For as an ogre, Grendel is again related to devils, though not necessarily one of them. In other words, Beowulf's foe is a "devilish ogre […] a monster, devouring the body

---

[57] The term is also used in MC 257, 276 and again three more times in 280. Although the term is anachronistic when applied to Grendel (it was first used by Perrault in his *Contes*, as late as 1697), it seems to fit him well. According to the *O.E.D.* "It has been suggested that Perrault may have formed *ogre* on an It. dial. *ogro* for *orgo* = It. *orco* demon, monster, from L. *Orcus*, Hades, the god of the infernal regions, Pluto. The OSp. reprs. of *Orcus* were *huerco* (Percivall), *huergo*, *uergo* (Diez); Mod.Sp. *ogro* 'ogre' is from Fr. (Conjecture has tried to see in *ogre* the ethnic name *Ugri*, *Ungri*, *Ongri*, applied by early writers to the Hungarians or Magyars: see Ugrian. But this is historically baseless.) In folk-lore and fairy tales: A man-eating monster, usually represented as a hideous giant; hence, a man likened to such a monster in appearance or character."

[58] Interestingly enough, Tolkien omits *orcneas* (l. 112), a term etymologically related to *ogre*. After all, strictly speaking, the poet does not apply it to Grendel but to Cain's descendants (ll. 111-114).

[59] See [B] (Drout 2002:95, 144, 145). *Ogre* is also used both in [A] (Drout 2002:34, 54) and [B] (Drout 2002:82, 91, 124).

[60] In the final version Tolkien consistently avoids using *troll*.

[61] The bibliography of Grendel with Northern supernatural creatures, the *draugar* mainly, is abundant see: Chambers 1963, Garmonsway and Simpson 1968, Chadwick 1946, Ellis 1943 and Ellis 1981, and Hallakarva.

[62] As Nicolas K. Kiessling (1968:192) pointed out: "the demon Grendel is an amalgam of northern and southern traditions, […] he possesses a unique combination of characteristics of Latin, German, Scandinavian, and even Celtic figures."

and bringing temporal death, that is inhabited by an accursed spirit" and not "a devil revealing himself in ogre-form [...] a spirit of evil aiming ultimately at the soul and bringing eternal death (even though he takes a form of visible horror, that may bring and suffer physical pain)" (MC 280).

Before further proceeding, I would like to recapitulate the main aspects dealt with in this section:

1. Grendel is a man, and as such he has an immortal soul and a mortal body. His malice is not only reflected in his wicked actions, but also in his abnormal physical appearance.

2. As evil as he is, he is not yet an incorporeal demon striving for souls, but a creature of flesh and blood, who feeds on his victims' bodies.

For Tolkien these two qualities defined who Grendel was and they were the defining factors for the fiend's relevance in the poem and its overall success as a master piece of Old English literature. Tolkien dealt with this issue profusely in the main body of MC.

3. Grendel's relevance in '*Beowulf*: The Monsters and the Critics'

Tolkien's arguments about the importance of Grendel are obviously within the major topic of the monsters' centrality in the poem. Therefore, most of the considerations that he made about the fire-drake are also applicable to Grendel, and vice versa. And yet, this is not always so, for quite often the critic – as seen in the previous section[63] – focuses solely on the ogre.

At the end of Appendix (a), Tolkien (MC 280) makes one final comment about the creature: "In *Beowulf* the weight is on the physical side: Grendel does not vanish into the pit when grappled. He must be slain by plain prowess, and thus is a real counterpart to the dragon in Beowulf's history."[64] This state-

---

[63] Mainly, that Grendel is sinful and demonic, whereas the dragon is not.

[64] Cf. 'pit' (O.E.D. 4th meaning): "The abode of evil spirits and lost souls; hell, or some part of it, conceived as a sunken place, or as a dungeon or place of confinement."

ment is a concise exposition of Grendel's prominence in the first part of the poem. For the last time in his essay, Tolkien insists on one idea that he has developed in the appendix: Grendel is flesh and blood. The physicality of the ogre is tackled in detail within the body of the article, constituting one of the bases of Tolkien's justification of the monster's value. Similarly, the fact that he considers Grendel *a real counterpart to the dragon in Beowulf's history* also serves to underline the relevance the ogre holds in the overall design of the poem, "essentially a balance, an opposition of ends and beginnings" (MC 271). The explicit link between the monsters (material as they are) and the structure of the poem had been referred to for the first time early in MC, when presenting Tolkien's main purpose in writing his paper: "I shall confine myself mainly to the *monsters* […] and to certain considerations of the structure and conduct of the poem that arise from this theme" (MC 246).

3.1. *Grendel: allegory, the physical side and symbolism*
The historical moment in which the poem was written, one that Tolkien identifies "without argument" as the "Age of Bede" (MC 262),[65] is one of transition. The old pagan mythology is slowly dying and its monsters are gradually turning into wicked demons. The struggle against them is not, ultimately, a defense of the body, but of the soul; that is the prize demons hunger for. And yet, the change is not complete yet in *Beowulf*. This ends up necessarily in a reaffirmation of Grendel's physicality. The reader might very well keep in mind all the titles given to Grendel, any of which (if not all) takes for granted his material existence. Everything in him seems to point at his corporeal nature. There is just one word that might question his bodily existence. The very first time Grendel is referred to in *Beowulf*, the poet calls him *ellengæst* (l. 86), a compound. Leaving aside the reading of *ellor* (alien) instead of

---

[65] This is not any longer an opinion to be accepted *without argumentation*, especially after the publication of Colin Chase's *The Dating of Beowulf*, first in 1981, and reissued with an introduction by Nicholas P. Howe (University of Toronto Press). In any case, the question of Beowulf's date of composition is still open to debate.

ellen (powerful, bold),[66] which is irrelevant for our present concern, *gæst* is also problematic. It is difficult to decide whether the poet meant *gæst/gāst* (ghost, spirit) or *gæst/gīst/gest* (guest, stranger), since both might equally be applied to Grendel: a (let us say) ghostly visitor or a guest (unwelcome and unexpected).[67] I have on purpose omitted Tolkien's reference to this noun in my analysis of his first appendix, in order to deal with it in this section. Of this word Tolkien writes (MC 279):

> [...] little can be made of the use of *gāst, gæst*. For one thing it is under grave suspicion in many places (both applied to Grendel and otherwise) of being a corruption of *gæst, gest* "stranger"; [...] In any case it cannot be translated either by the modern *ghost* or *spirit*. *Creature* is probably the nearest we can now get. Where it is genuine it applies to Grendel probably in virtue of his relationship or similarity to bogies (*scinnum ond scuccum*), physical enough in form and power, but vaguely felt as belonging to a different order of being, one allied to the malevolent "ghosts" of the dead.

As much as his titles, Grendel's diet and his submission to *the laws of matter* tie him down to earth: "Grendel inhabits the visible world and eats the flesh and blood of men; he enters their houses by the doors" (MC 265). With all his might, he is forced to feed on human flesh. His cannibalism not only presents him as an abomination, but also underlines his materiality: flesh for his own flesh, blood for his own blood (ll. 120ff; ll. 445-450; ll. 739ff). Although his body cannot be pierced by conventional weapons (ll. 798-805), it is the break-

---

[66] "or, quite possibly, *ellorgæst*" (Klaeber 1941:131, n. 86; his italics); "Grein's emendation to **ellor-gæst** is very attractive" (Wrenn 1953:187, n. 86; his emphasis).

[67] As far as I know, with the exception of Kemble, who takes *gæst* to mean "hospes", that is, "guest" (Kemble 1833:167), the vast majority of editions and translations of the poem tend to favor the first reading: Klaeber (1941:322) "demon"; Strong (1925:2) "spirit"; Alexander (1995:8) "demon"; Liuzza (2000:55) "demon"; Heaney (1999) "demon". On the other hand, some other scholars follow Tolkien in assuming no ghostly connotations: Bradley (1982:413) "being"; Jack (1995:33) "creature"; Mitchell & Robinson (1998:255) "creature".

ing of it that kills him. No need to wonder at the ultimate cause of his death, for Grendel bleeds to death (as any man would) after his arm is torn off (ll. 815-823). The poet subtly underlines Grendel's kinship with the fiends of the pit when he states that Bewoulf's victory over the foe has purified the Hall of Heorot (ll. 875, 1176). But there are no ritual words to exorcise a demon, no prayers, but hand to hand struggle.

All the descriptions of his killings – especially Hondscioh's brutal death (ll. 739-45; 2076-080) – are consistent with this. The overall result of this emphasis prevents the story of Beowulf and his exploits from becoming an allegorical fable. Grendel is a threat for the body, not for the soul. The danger of his visits is less transcendental (which would have been felt as foreign to the poem), but much more immediate, intimate, and instinctively frightful. The author, Tolkien emphasizes (MC 265), "was still dealing with the great temporal tragedy, and not yet writing an allegorical homily in verse." In the Preface to the first book of *The Lord of the Rings* (*LotR* 12), he had written: "I cordially dislike allegory in all its manifestations, and always have done so since I grew old and wary enough to detect its presence."[68] It seems that the Professor did not detect its presence in *Beowulf*.

However, it is one thing to claim that "neither the dragon nor Grendel have become abstract, or allegorical" ([B], Drout 2002:145), yet another to imply that, for Tolkien, there was little else in them than flesh, bones and blood. This is, I think, one of the subtlest nuances in his conception of Beowulf's foes. Even at the risk of sounding preposterous, let me use a comparison with other monsters as they appear in movies that most readers will be familiar with – at least with some of them, I hope. Despite all its cruelty and wickedness, very few would claim that the white shark in Steven Spielberg's *Jaws* (1975) is anything more than a huge hungry fish; the same could be said about other monsters in less acclaimed films, such as high budget *Godzilla*

---

[68] *Bibliography* 92 also quotes a similar declaration: "I dislike allegory wherever I smell it." In his letter to Sir Stanley Unwin (14 September 1950), he writes: "I dislike Allegory – the conscious and intentional allegory –" (*Letters* 145; see also 174).

(Roland Emmerich, 1998) or the long list of wicked reptiles, insects and fishes in *Anaconda* (Luis Llosa, 1997), *Crocodile* (Tobe Hooper, 2000), *The Thing* (John Carpenter, 1982), *Tentacoli* (O.G. Assonitis, 1977), *Piranha* (Joe Dante, 1978), ... Other creatures are more meaningful, such as *Alien* (Riddley Scott, 1979), *Nosferatu* (F.W. Murnau, 1922), or *Der Golem* (Peter Wegener & Carl Boese, 1920), *Dracula* (Francis Ford Coppola, 1992), the monster of *Frankenstein* (James Whale, 1931), as well as the literary inspired white whale in *Moby Dick* (John Huston, 1956). I say 'meaningful' to mean *symbolic*; this is the key term, as inferred from Tolkien's argumentation, to understand much of the value of the monsters in *Beowulf*.

Before proceeding with my discussion, it would be useful to clarify how Tolkien understood the terms 'symbol' and 'allegory'. One may safely assume that the Professor agreed with the definition of these two concepts – often loosely used as synonyms – given by his colleague and friend C.S. Lewis in *The Allegory of Love*, finished in 1935 and first published in 1936 (coincidentally the date of Tolkien's lecture).[69] In the second chapter, there is a long (at times complex) argument about the different nature of both ways of establishing "this fundamental equivalence between the immaterial and the material" (Lewis 1990:44); Lewis (1990:44-45) writes:

> On the one hand, you can start with an immaterial fact, [...], and can then invent *visibilia* to express them. [...]. This is allegory, [...]. The attempt to read that something else through its sensible imitations, [...], is what I mean by symbolism [...]. The allegorist leaves the given [...] to talk of that which is confessedly less real, which is fiction. The symbolist leaves the given to find that which is more real.[70]

---

[69] Duriez (2003:64). Tolkien is mentioned in the 'Preface' of the book (Lewis 1990:vii).

[70] Lewis (1990:45) also uses the term "sacramentalism" to mean the same as symbolism.

To put it very simply, in allegory we move from *invisibilia* to *visibilia*, and in symbolism, contrariwise, we move from *visibilia* to *invisibilia*.[71]

And so, coming back to Grendel, the *Beowulf*-poet did not start somewhere else, thinking about evil, malice or wickedness to end up with the ogre as an abstract and rigid allegory of these realities in a, consequently, allegorical poem. Rather, the monster is the centre of attention *per se*, and his behavior is – as Lewis (1990:45) would put it – "the flat outline of that which elsewhere veritably is in all the round of its unimaginable dimensions." Not so flat, though, Mr. Lewis, for Grendel is always perceived by the audience "as real a creation as anything in 'realistic' fiction":[72] his massive body, the baleful light in his eyes, his claws, his strength, the weight of his head or the abundant blood that gushes from his severed neck prevents him from becoming a mere 'outline'. We never lose sight of the materiality of the monster, pregnant as he is though with implications and links with the notion of evil:

> [...] the monsters become 'adversaries of God', and so begin to *symbolize* (and ultimately to become identified with) the powers of evil, even while they remain, as they do still remain in *Beowulf*, mortal denizens of the material world, in it and of it.
> (MC 262; the first italics are mine)

---

[71] Though this is not the place to enter into a detailed discussion of the terms in focus, yet for my present concern a further clarification is convenient. The term allegory can be used in a wide sense, to refer to a whole work in which the author willingly conceives each of his characters, relationships and settings to equate spiritual, psychological, or abstract intellectual concepts. When we say, for example, that the *Roman de la Rose* is an allegory (or allegorical poem), we mean that most of the details of the garden have a fixed connotation in terms of courtly love; as Lewis (1990:115) put it: "the 'abstract' places and people in the *Roman de la Rose* are representations of actual life." On the other hand, we may use allegory more specifically to refer precisely to each of those abstract places, peoples, objects or animals which have a concealed meaning. In European medieval morality plays vices and virtues are represented by human-like allegories. If the name of the thing personified is clearly proclaimed (Patience, Good Deeds, Death, Fellowship, Giant Despair or Sloth) then allegory is known as personification.

[72] Tolkien on orcs (*Letters* 82).

At this stage, Grendel reminds us of abstract notions (sin, evil), rather than being himself the abstraction. A similar point could be made about the dragon, though the danger of becoming an allegory seems to be closer this time, so wide was and would be its use as an allegory of sin, evil or Satan.[73] For this reason, Tolkien establishes clearly the boundaries of symbol and allegory when discussing the fire-drake, rather than the ogre. Apparently, though aware of the real material existence of the dragon within the fiction, Tolkien seems to be inclined to admit that, after all, it tends to be a personification:

> this dragon is real worm, with a bestial life and thought of his own, but the conception, none the less, approaches *draconitas* rather than *draco*: a personification of malice, greed, destruction (the evil side of heroic life), and of the undiscriminating cruelty of fortune that distinguishes not good or bad (the evil aspect of all life). (MC 258-259)

In other words, Beowulf's bane, rather than being an individual dragon (*draco*), is a compilation of all those qualities that conform the abstract concept that the audience had of 'dragonness' (*draconitas*) and, at the same time, the personification of the evil side of heroic life.[74] At this point, however, Tolkien abruptly interrupts the progress of his thoughts by avoiding that which readers might be expecting as his logical conclusion. For the first time, both terms in our discussion are put together to emphasize their difference; the passage has been often quoted:[75]

> In this poem the balance is nice, but it is preserved. The large *symbolism* is near the surface, but it does

---

[73] As claimed before, the snake in *Genesis* and the serpent in St. John's *Book of Revelation* were already suggestive parallels. In his introduction to *Beowulf*, Klaeber (1941:l) writes that "the dragon was in ecclesiastical tradition the recognized symbol of the archfiend." Later on, the iconography of St. Michael and St. George, both defeating the devil in the shape of a dragon, would confirm the potentialities of the winged reptile.

[74] Here Tolkien is using the term personification in the sense specified above.

[75] See, for example, Duriez (2003:71) or Shippey (2005:192).

> not break through, nor become *allegory*. Something more significant than a standard hero, a man faced with a foe more evil than any human enemy of house or realm, is before us, and yet incarnate in time, walking in heroic history, and treading the named lands of the North. (MC 259; my italics).

Indeed, as much as the dragon was a for Tolkien "a potent symbol" (Duriez 2003:70), the serpent always remains a material being, scales, bones, poisonous blood and fire; using Shippey's (2005:55) metaphor, the dragon has a claw planted on fact. Thus we feel the burning heat of his flames (ll. 2594-5) almost melting helmets (l. 2605) and shields (ll. 2672-2673); the deadly fumes (l. 2661); the bite of his jaws in Beowulf's neck and the gushing blood (ll. 2691-2693); the toughness of the reptile's scaly skin and the irons finally piercing its softer belly (ll. 2699ff). Let me put it this way: Beowulf's bane is not the dragon in Spenser's *The Faerie Queene*, an allegorical beast par excellence, nor is the Red Cross Knight a brother-in-arms of the Geatish hero.

Tolkien could not see *Beowulf* as an allegory, for the mode of meaning of the poem was quite different. He obviously had a clear-cut notion of this device when he spoke, for example of the "just allegory" (MC 249), a concept that Shippey defines as one in which "all the bits should fit exactly together, compelling assent (and amusement) by their minuteness"; or "everything in this story can be 'equated'" (Shippey 2005:50, 53). Tolkien well knew how to write one, as can be seen in his 'Leaf by Niggle' (published in 1945) or in two instances included in MC, explicitly named as such: a brief sketch of *Beowulfiana* and the so called 'Tower Allegory' (MC 246, 248-248).[76] But this mode of meaning was completely foreign to the *Beowulf*-poet, as much as it was to most authors of the so-called Dark Ages.[77] The poem was not an allegory, neither political, nor mythical or moralizing.[78] I cannot help thinking that behind

---

[76] Shippey (2005:53-54) develops a lucid interpretation of this allegory.
[77] Lewis (1990:83-87).
[78] See MC 248, 249; 248, 249, 256; 265.

Tolkien's rejection of the allegorical readings of *Beowulf* there lies, again, his discomfort with those readings of the *LotR* that assumed an equation between his fiction and World War II, Nazism or Communism. To all attentive readers who had deduced such implications, Tolkien (*LotR* 11, 12) addressed the following comments: "The real war [WW II] does not resemble the legendary war in its process or its conclusion"; later on he explicitly denied "any allegorical significance or contemporary political reference whatsoever." This rigidly specific contextual dependence would have deprived both *Beowulf* and Tolkien's fiction of their symbolic potentialities, which have proved to be as multiple and varied as readers of all times and places. The *Beowulf*-poet and Tolkien had several things in common and, among them, they were both concerned with symbolism rather than allegory.[79] Klaeber's words illustrate precisely the type of reading that Tolkien rejected; the whole passage is worth quoting:

> The poet has raised him [Beowulf] to the rank of a singularly spotless hero, a "defending, protecting, redeeming being," a truly ideal character. We might even feel inclined to recognize features of the Christian Savior in the destroyer of hellish fiends, the warrior brave and gentle, blameless in thought and deed, the king that dies for his people. Though delicately kept in the background, such a Christian interpretation of the main story on the part of the Anglo-Saxon author could not but give added strength and tone to the entire poem. It helps to explain one of the great puzzles of our epic. It would indeed be hard to understand why the poet contented himself with a plot of mere fabulous adventures so much inferior to the splendid heroic setting, unless the narrative derived a superior dignity from suggesting the most exalted hero-life known to Christians. (Klaeber 1941:51)[80]

---

[79] Duriez (2003:71-72).

[80] For other Christian allegorical readings of the poem, see McNamee (1960) and Bloomfield (1949-51).

For Klaeber, writing in 1922, there *had to* be allegory in *Beowulf*. How else could one explain "a plot of mere fabulous adventures so much inferior to the splendid heroic setting, unless the narrative derived a superior dignity from suggesting the most exalted hero-life known to Christians"?[81] It was, once again, the vexed question of the imbalance between the "dignity of style" and "there is nothing much in the story" (Ker 1958:164, 163). For Tolkien, certainly, Beowulf was adorned with all the virtues and excellences that Klaeber had mentioned, and he might gladly 'recognize features of the Christian Savior' in the Geatish hero fighting against 'hellish fiends' (always in the sense described above). No doubt, besides, that this might give 'added strength and tone to the entire poem'. But to claim that *Beowulf* was consequently an allegory was a far-fetched implication. Rather, Tolkien would say that in the Christian context in which the poem was written – and also for himself as a Christian reader – the fight between the magnificent hero and his terrible foes was highly symbolic in the sense discussed. However, the symbolism might be different in a different context. Tolkien's words on this are particularly clarifying: "I think that many confuse 'applicability' with 'allegory', but the one resides on the freedom of the reader, and the other in the purposed domination of the author" (*Biography* 12).[82] I do not mean that an author has no intention, main theme or purpose when writing a text, but the greatness of good literature and its symbolic potentialities render that, simply, another aspect of the text. Inexorably, new readers will endlessly add new meanings to

---

[81] Tolkien was explicitly responding to Chambers, Ker and Girvan, but Klaeber's words might also be behind the following quotation from MC (255): "Where then resides the special virtue of *Beowulf*, if the common element (which belongs largely to the language itself, and to a literary tradition) is deducted? It resides, one might guess, in the theme, and the spirit this has infused into the whole. For, in fact, if there were a real discrepancy between theme and style, that style would not be felt as beautiful but as incongruous or false. And that incongruity is present in some measure in all the long Old English poems, save one – *Beowulf*. The paradoxical contrast that has been drawn between matter and manner in *Beowulf* has thus an inherent *literary* improbability."

[82] In April 1959, Tolkien had also written: "most readers appear to confuse it [allegory] with significance or applicability" (*Letters* 297-298).

good books; in Bloom's (1995:3) words about Shakespeare, these "constitute a perpetual challenge to universal performance and to criticism."

Grendel's symbolic potentialities have opened the way for continuous interpretations of his significance. Before Tolkien, he had merged with the Norse deity Loki, Satan himself or was constrained to a role as the Sea in mythical allegories of nature.[83] After Tolkien's lecture, the ogre has been carrying on his back, not only God's anger (l. 711) but a variety of multiple connotations that range from his nihilism in John Gardner's ecologist *Grendel* (1971), to become recently the embodiment of the "Anglo-Saxon fascination with *extimité*."[84]

3.2. *Grendel: a real counterpart to the dragon*

Grendel is at the very center in the first part of *Beowulf*, as much as the dragon is in the second. But also, he is a vital instrument in the poet's design of the overall structure of the poem. At first sight, *Beowulf* could be summarized just by making reference to its three central episodes: the fights with the monsters. But first sights have never been good friends to literary critics. This, I know, is old news, though many would still talk about texts without having read them; Tolkien's caveat is still valid.[85]

As seen in the previous section, the monsters are, in a sense, the symbols of the evil side of the Anglo-Saxon world. The poet chose them precisely because they were timeless (there have been and there always will be monsters in the mental landscape of man) and for this, more valid than any other historical embodiment of malice and chaos in order to represent the persistence of evil. If there is a monster at the end of the poem, there must be a monster at the beginning and vice versa. The poem itself is a tautology; as Tolkien puts

---

[83] Grendel and Loki (Stanley 1994:18); Grendel as the devil (Klaeber 1941:l); Grendel and the sea (Drout 2002:181, n. 107).

[84] See Cohen (1999:25-28).

[85] See, for example, Cohen's (1999, note 183) summary of *Beowulf*.

(MC 275), "[...] if the hero falls before a dragon, then certainly he should achieve his early glory by vanquishing a foe of similar order."

For Tolkien – this I infer from his words in MC –, there is a *crescendo* in the difficulties the hero has to overcome in order to slay his three enemies: it is surprisingly (even disappointingly) easy to defeat Grendel; the hero finds it unexpectedly[86] harder – almost too hard – to kill the dam; and, finally, Beowulf does not survive his encounter with the dragon.[87] In other words, Grendel is a suitable podium upon which a man becomes a hero. The confirmation of his heroic status is, afterwards, the killing of the ogress and, at the end, his tragic destiny, his *wyrd*, comes with the winged serpent, the worst of foes in Nordic mythology.

> If the dragon is the right end for Beowulf, and I agree with the author that it is, then Grendel is an eminently suitable beginning. They are creatures, *feond mancynnes*, of a similar order and kindred significance. Triumph over the lesser and more nearly human is cancelled by defeat before the older and more elemental. (MC 276)

Far from being blindly passionate about *Beowulf*, Tolkien was aware that the poem suffers from minor deficiencies or, as he calls them, "defects of detail" (MC 274). Dealing with the structure of *Beowulf* he calls our attention to one passage that has been traditionally considered as repetitive or even redundant: the retelling of the fight with Grendel in Hygelac's court (ll. 2000-2151). Leaving aside the Geatish king's curiosity about the details of his champion's fight against the monsters (and new details Beowulf gives in first person),[88] the

---

[86] The audience might very well take for granted, with the characters in the poem, that Grendel's mother is weaker than her son (ll. 1282-1287).

[87] In fact, it is Wiglaf who first pierces the belly of the dragon with his sword (ll. 2698-2701).

[88] Robinson's (1991:146) analysis of the recapitulation puts the emphasis precisely on the new light it casts on Beowulf: "This detailed recapitulation of what we have just been told by the narrator gives us our first insight into the mind and character of the hero, for his way of telling the story we have just witnessed, and the details he omits to tell his king [...] and the details he adds [...] reveal the hero's generosity, his perceptiveness and good judgement."

long recapitulation has for me an explanation in accordance with the logic of the fiction. It is no secret that Beowulf had not a very heroic youth at home (ll. 2183-2188).[89] Whatever he might have been or done, Beowulf's place at Hygelac's court was by no means prominent. Besides, he was the son of Ecgtheow, one of the Waegmundingas, 'only' related to Hygelac as being 'his sister's son'. As Chambers (1963:11) claims: "since that daughter had three brothers, there would have been no prospect of his [Beowulf] becoming king." On top of this, Ecgtheow was an exile in the land of the Danes: because he had killed Heatholaf and the Geats refused to harbor him, he took refuge under Hrothgar, who paid the *wergild* to put an end to the feud with the Wylfings (ll. 459-472). What I am stating is that Beowulf needed to proclaim his heroic achievements back home in order to make up for his past deficiencies, and also to secure himself a place of prominence. Not that he was ambitious, but certainly eager for praise from his people.

Tolkien would say that, however, the recapitulation is not justifiable. And yet, he provides another explanation. The poet did not invent the hero's fights with the three monsters, and so this might not be the ideal vehicle to transmit the main theme of the poem: "it would probably have been better, if we had no journeying" (MC 272). The fact that Don Quixote's adventures take place in a relatively reduced geography (*La Mancha*) does not diminish the universality of his drama. In this sense, if Beowulf had never left the land of the Geats, the stage of his story – that contrast between youth and death – would not have been narrower, "but symbolically wider" (MC 272); Tolkien was anticipating what some now call 'the universality of localism'. In the land of the Geats, in front of his audience, he tells them of his adventures among the Danes. Grendel and his dam were not only Hrothgar's foes, but – in the

---

[89] And yet, Beowulf tells Hrothgar that he has performed many heroic deeds in his youth (l. 409). About, Beowulf's *peccadilloes*, Lawrence (1967:21) points out that folklorists are familiar with this theme, known as "the male Cinderella". Klaeber (1941:207, note on l. 2183ff) states, on the other hand, that this "introduction of the commonplace story of the sluggish youth is not very convincing"; see also a detailed account of the two possible traditions of Beowulf used by the poet in Wrenn (1953:218, note on ll. 2183-2189).

light of their dark symbolism – also the Geats' enemies and, ultimately, those of every man, anytime and everywhere. Beowulf's report of his fights to Hygelac is an attempt to relocate these episodes in the very same soil where he will face the dragon, bringing together all his achievements. Beowulf is not a wandering monster-killer or a mercenary (MC 273). In his report, Beowulf defeats again the ogres before he dies against the dragon, and every time we read the poem, the sequence is reenacted once more: the cycle is complete, there and here, then and now. There lies the strength of the poem.

3.3. *Grendel and* wyrd

Little do we know about the beliefs of the pagan Anglo-Saxons. The assumption is that their pantheon of gods was similar to that in other Germanic cults. Whether or not the heathen Anglo-Saxons believed in life beyond death or if Valhalla was simply a late creation in an attempt to comfort the pagan warriors under the pressure of Christianity with its promise of everlasting joy is still open to debate. The often-quoted passage from Bede's *A History of the English Church and People* might show the uncertainties of the Anglo-Saxons before their conversion:

> "Your Majesty, when we compare the present life of man on earth with that time of which we have no knowledge, it seems to me like the swift flight of a single sparrow through the banqueting-hall where you are sitting at dinner on a winter's day with your thanes and counselors. In the midst there is a comforting fire to warm the hall; outside, the storms of winter rain or snow are raging. This sparrow flies swiftly in through one door of the hall, and out through another. While he is inside, he is safe from the winter storms; but after a few moments of comfort, he vanishes from sight into the wintry world from which he came. Even so man appears on earth for a little while; but of what went before this life or of what follows, we know nothing."
> (Bede 1986:127)

The very last words sound poignant in the mouth of one of King Edwin's heathen counselors, and might very well be a motto to be added after the final lines of *Beowulf*. The comfort and warmth offered by the bonfires, the songs of past achievements and the company of thanes are the only reward (albeit ephemeral) that noble warriors can expect. The joys of the hall are a metaphor for the passing moments of happiness that men experience in life. What comes after no one knows, but it will be somber and obscure. Tolkien had defined *Beowulf* as an elegiac-epic poem, for the lines are permeated with a sense of loss, of incompleteness, that the brief episodes of solace can but emphasize.

For Tolkien, the tragedy of the Danes and the Geats is that they have no ultimate resort, no heaven's doors to knock on when the whole world tumbles down and falls. Their gods pay a high price for their anthropomorphism. They and the men who created them are on the same side. In this "essential hostility of the gods and heroes on the one hand and the monsters on the other, we may suppose that pagan English and Norse imagination agreed" (MC 263). However, the gods are not invulnerable, they are not almighty, for they will also be defeated. It is the potent image of the *Götterdämmerung*, which leaves the warriors without protection, fighting hopelessly, with a courage that is all the more perfect since it expects no reward: "naked heroism", Tolkien calls it.

The gods – and their human allies – are doomed, tragically heading to death in their battle with *wyrd*, the ominous and only absolute truth in the Germanic *weltanschauung*, and the monsters are the materialization of this reality: "but in the final movement of *Beowulf* he [the dragon] lodges himself in the imagination as *wyrd* rather than *wyrm*, more a destiny than a set of reptilian vertebrae" (Heaney 1999:xix). Could monsters be more important, more central? For the poet, and this Tolkien clearly understood, there was no better way to embody the pathos of human existence. He did not need 'a wilderness of dragons', or a host of ruthless invaders to recreate 'the great tragedy' of human existence. It is not true that the theme of defeat could have been more appalling, and appealing too, if the hero had died fighting human foes, with names such as Cadwallon, Penda or Anlaf, more political in their ambitions. Tolkien, maybe anticipating Sauron's equation with Hitler or Stalin, was sympathetic enough with the *Beowulf*-poet to follow a different path. Politics change, enemies become friends, or the other way round: the two dictators signed a non-aggression pact to conquer and divide Poland, or the soldiers shaking hands at the Elba River would soon be watching each other's movements with suspicion over the Iron Curtain. However, the monsters remain always on the same side, their own:

> Grendel is an enemy who has attacked the centre of the realm, and brought into the royal hall the outer darkness, so that only in daylight can the king sit upon the throne. This is something quite different and more horrible than a "political" invasion of equals – men of another similar realm, such as Ingeld's later assault upon Heorot.
> The overthrow of Grendel makes a good wonder-tale, because he is too strong and dangerous to any ordinary man to defeat, but it is a victory in which all men can rejoice because he was a monster, hostile to all men and to all humane fellowship and joy. Compared with him even the long politically hostile Danes and Geats were Friends, on the same side. It is the monstrosity and fairy-tale quality of Grendel that really makes the tale important, surviving still when the politics have become dim and the healing of Danish-Geatish relations in an "entente cordiale" between two ruling houses a minor matter of obscure history. In that political world Grendel looks silly, though he certainly is not silly, however naif may be the poet's imagination and description of him. (*Letters* 242)

Had Grendel been a soul-tempting devil and the dragon the demonic beast, the anonymous author would have never suffered the pitiful remarks of learned men from a distant future, men who considered the poem an incomplete achievement. Probably, critics would have forgiven the *Beowulf*-poet if the monsters had been less material. And yet, the symbolism – not the allegory – is so appealing that the story, set in a precise geography and in a remote time, is able to go beyond its limits and can be enjoyed by readers from other places and other epochs; this, Tolkien claims, is achieved thanks to the monsters. Beowulf is not *Everyman*, but simply *Man*.

As much as Tolkien himself recreated antiquity in his works of fiction to talk about man's life on earth, the *Beowulf*-poet located his work *in geardagum*. He was familiar with a great many instances of human defeat and tragedy, both if the poem was written before or after the Viking invasions of the 9th century. But desolation, faced with cowardice or courage, is recurrent from the very beginnings of humanity: "[*Beowulf*] is a poem by a learned man writing of old times, who looking back on the heroism and sorrow feels in them something permanent and something symbolical" (MC 269). In all their poignancy, the story of Ingeld, the Finnsburgh Fragment, or Hygelac's death on Frisian shores were well known to the audience of the poem. He might have done very well with these materials (or with any other). However, all these episodes were but the manifestations of a universal truth, the senseless logic that has always ruled man's life on earth: defeat, desolation, fate, fatalism. The unknown poet was ambitious enough to leave aside the incidental, since he knew how to deal with the essential.

> Something more significant than a standard hero, a man faced with a foe more evil than any human enemy of house or realm, is before us, and yet incarnate in time, walking in heroic history, and treading the named lands of the North. [...]
>
> [I]t is in *Beowulf* that a poet has devoted a whole poem to the theme, and has drawn the struggle in different proportions, so that we may see man at war with the hostile world, and his inevitable overthrow in Time. (MC 259-260)

The monsters, therefore, are not the weakness of the poem, but its real achievement. Because inhuman, they are timeless, and their symbolism "glimpses the cosmic and moves with the thought of all men concerning the fate of human life and efforts; it stands amid but above the petty wars of princes, and surpasses the dates and limits of historical periods, however important" (MC 277). Besides, the poet was skilled enough to tell us very little about their physical appearance, and this is especially the case with Grendel. Red-eyes, claws, huge size, … the rest is for the audience to complete. And so, different readers from different epochs and cultures will picture him according to their own fears. As Lawrence (1967:206) rightly pointed out: "A monster is more fearful if pictured in the imagination. This is sound art, […]." The etymology of the word monster itself clearly shows its far reaching implications. Filtered through the French *monster*, it derives from Latin *monstrum*, a term eventually derived from the verb *monstrare*. And so monsters show to us, as in a fairground mirror, our social, moral or infantile fears. An anecdotic detail: Edmund Ollier, an English literary *amateur*, writing in 1854 for *Household Words*, refers either to *Beowulf* or a section of the poem as 'The Vampyre of the Fens'. Guess who was the blood-drinker? (Cf. Olivares-Merino 2007).

Grendel is for Tolkien, I presume, the first meeting Beowulf has with his fate. Men of courage are able to postpone their appointment with *wyrd* – "*Wyrd* often spares / an undoomed man, when his courage endures" (ll. 572-573) – but not for long, maybe 50 years: "*Wyrd* always goes as it must!" (l. 455). The hero himself is not at all confident about the outcome of the fight (ll. 685-687), and none of his Geatish thanes "thought that he should thence / ever again seek his own dear homeland" (ll. 691-692); a good band of supporters he brought with him! His boasting at Heorot is but a requirement of the warriors' ethic. He commits himself to success for this is expected of the hero-to-be. If he wins, his victory will be more magnificent, not mere chance. However, if he is defeated (and devoured), he will be shortly remembered as nothing but a bigmouth. As much as Beowulf performs the expected rhetoric (ll. 407ff), he does not go too far. Besides, he is sufficiently mindful as to state his last will about his belongings, should he lose the match since nothing will remain from him to be buried; is this what they call *British phlegm*?

But the audience knows more and they are temporally relieved to read that God will grant victory to the new hero. This does not diminish at all the intensity of the moments previous to Grendel's invasion of the Hall of Heorot, the terrifying description of the creature's approach to the place were all the Geatish warriors, but one, are asleep.[90] If horror, as a genre, began to appear in the eighteenth century,[91] there were traces of it ever since man began to write. No doubt that Grendel's progress towards Heorot is one of them. The poet has not spoilt the effectiveness of the passage by disclosing who is to succeed that night; it is the detailed description of the gradual approach of the creature that counts. We forget about the outcome and enjoy the pathos of the thrilling *momentum*. Similarly, is there any reader who has not enjoyed Stoker's *Dracula* because he or she knew beforehand that the vampire would be killed at the end?

For the audience of the poem, Grendel's attack (though doomed to fail) is in itself dramatic, standing as it does for Beowulf's first encounter with *wyrd*. Beowulf will defeat Grendel, but by the time he hardly escapes alive from the mere, readers may anticipate the tragic ending:

> In the struggle with Grendel one can as a reader dismiss the certainty of literary experience that the hero will not in fact perish, and allow oneself to share the hopes and fears of the Geats upon the shore. In the second part the author has no desire whatever that the issue should remain open, even according to literary convention. There is no need to hasten like the messenger, who rode to bear the lamentable news to the waiting people (2892 ff.). They may have hoped, but we are not supposed to.

---

[90] Grendel's night walk towards the Hall of Heorot has been analyzed in detail in several works; see, for example: Lapidge (1993), Brodeur (1959), and Irving (1969:100ff).

[91] Carroll (1990:4). See my: 'Some Considerations on the Absence of Horror Literature in the Middle Ages' (Olivares-Merino 2000).

> By now we are supposed to have grasped the plan. Disaster is foreboded. Defeat is the theme. Triumph over the foes of man's precarious fortress is over, and we approach slowly and reluctantly the inevitable Victory of death. (MC 274)

At the end of the poem, when the *wyrm* is equated with *wyrd*,[92] the monstrous skeleton of the poem (as if seen through X-Rays) shows all its effectiveness. Grendel, his dam and the dragon constitute a chain of events that marks the progression of the hero's life. The path along which he has trodden leads inevitably to defeat. The exultation of his first victory and the relief of the second amount to nothing, when confronted with the tragedy of Beowulf's defeat. Impersonal and inscrutable, *wyrd* has been playing with the hero and with the audience. Beowulf's death is even more dramatic for it is the culmination of a heroic career, one that had begun against Grendel, the worst of night terrors. At the end of the thirties, Tolkien was already anticipating that theoretical frame that has been named 'Monsters Theory'.[93]

4. Conclusion

I hope to have shown how Tolkien visualized Grendel at the time when he was working on MC. His main line of thought about this creature could be condensed as follows.

---

[92] Wanner (1999:5).

[93] In his *Of Giants*, J.J. Cohen (one of the theorists of this school) pays due homage to MC in its defence of the relevance of the monsters. However, I am sorry to say, Tolkien's paper seems not to have been properly understood by this critic. Cohen claims that the Grendels and the dragon "are beneath their lurid flesh ethical allegories", since "Grendel is an adversary of the soul; the poem is about *pietas*." Besides, what did Tolkien write his paper for, if Cohen writes the following: "Whereas Tolkien believed that *the literary remnants of Anglo-Saxon culture may be studied in spite of its monsters*, more recent critics have asserted that the corpus deserves critical analysis because of its monstrous content" (Cohen 1999:1; my italics)?

1. Grendel is a man alienated from creation, not a demon, with a monstrous body and a wicked immortal soul that is to be condemned.
2. Within the fiction, he is as real as the hero that kills him. His existence is located in place and time. Besides, he has a lineage, a dwelling place and his bodily existence imposes on him the usual limitations: he has to feed and he is mortal.
3. Despite this, he is highly symbolic at several levels: primitivism, anti-social existence, moral evil and *wyrd*.
4. Grendel's role in the structure of the poem is fundamental, both as a minor precursor of the dragon in the first part of the poem and as a mobile piece to provide coherence to the hero's deeds.

I am not a devoted reader of Tolkien's fiction, though I assume that much could be said about the relevance of Grendel behind some of the creatures in *The Hobbit* or *The Lord of the Rings*. Orcs, goblins, trolls and uruk-hais bear ubiquitous similarities with the marauder of the fens. In this sense, it is remarkable that the *Beowulf*-poet uses the word *orc-neas* to describe Grendel's race and, as we have seen before, Tolkien consistently uses the word 'ogre' to refer to Grendel. But there are also some other creations – such as the spectral Nazgûl or the ghosts of the marshes – that seem to be related to Grendel. In this sense, it is relevant to point out that it was at the time when he was working hard preparing his lecture, that Tolkien finished *The Hobbit* and began the composition of *The Lord of the Rings*.

Biographical Note

Eugenio M. Olivares-Merino (BA, Granada 1990; PhD, Granada 1994) teaches Medieval and Renaissance English literature at the University of Jaén (Spain). He is the autor of two books (*Del amor los caballeros y las damas. Hacia una caracterización de la 'cortaysye' en* Sir Gawain and the Green Knight, 1998; *Padre Mío Amado. Margarita Moro Roper. Perfil biográfico y epistolario*, 2007). He has also published articles on Thomas More, J. Luis Vives, Margaret More, Chaucer, Juan Ruiz and *Beowulf* in international journals. He was Visiting Scholar at the Universities of Urbana-Champaigne (1992) and Yale (2003). He is member of several organisations, both Spanish and international, and has recently been appointed member of the administration board of *Moreana*.

Eugenio M. Olivares-Merino is married and is the father of three boys and two girls.

Bibliography

Abbreviations

Biography: see Carpenter 1977.
Letters: see Carpenter 1995.
LotR: see Tolkien 1990.
MC: see Tolkien 1936.

Alexander, Michael (ed.), 1995, *Beowulf*, Harmondsworth: Penguin.
Bede, 1986, *A History of the English Church and People*, translated by Leo Sherley-Price, first edition 1955, Harmondsworth: Penguin.
Bloom, Harold, 1995, *The Western Canon. The Books and School of the Ages*, New York: Riverhead Books.
---, 2000, *How to Read and Why*, London: Fourth Estate.
Bloomfield, Morton W., 1949-51, '*Beowulf* and Christian Allegory: An Interpretation of Unferth', *Traditio* 7:410-415.
Bradley, S.A.J. (trans.), 1982, *Anglo-Saxon Poetry*, London and Melbourne: Everyman's Library.
Brodeur, Arthur, 1959, *The Art of Beowulf*, Berkeley, CA: The University of California Press.
Cardew, Philip, 2005, 'Grendel: Bordering the Human', In Tom Shippey (ed.), 2005, *The Shadow-Walkers: Jacob Grimm's Mythology of the Monstruous*, Tempe, AZ: Ariona Center for Medieval and Renaissance Studies, 189-205.
Carpenter, Humphrey, 1977, *Tolkien. A Biography*, Boston: Houghton Mifflin.
--- (ed.), 1995, *The Letters of J.R.R. Tolkien*, 1st edition 1981, London: HarperCollins.

Carroll, Noel, 1990, *The Philosophy of Horror (or Paradoxes of the Heart)*, New York: Routledge.
Chadwick, Nora, 1946, 'Norse Ghosts (A study in the *Draugr* and the *Haugbúi*)', *Folklore* 57:50-65.
Chambers, Raymond W., 1925, '*Beowulf* and the Heroic Age', In Archibald Strong, 1925, *Beowulf Translated into Modern English Rhyming Verse*, London: Constable and Company, vii-xxxii.
---, 1963, *Beowulf. An Introduction to the Study of the Poem with a Discussion of the Stories of Offa and Finn*, 3rd edition, 1st edition 1921, Cambridge: Cambridge University Press.
Cohen, Jeffrey J., 1999, *Of Giants. Sex, Monsters, and the Middle Ages*, Minneapolis: University of Minnesota Press.
Denzinger, Heinrich, 2000, *Enchiridion symbolorum. El magisterio de la Iglesia. Enchiridion symbolorum definitionum et declarationum de rebus fidei et morum*, 38th edition, actualized by Peter Hünermann, 1st edition 1854, Barcelona: Herder.
Drout, Michael D. C., 2002, *Beowulf and the Critics by J.R.R. Tolkien*, (Medieval and Renaissance Text Studies 248), Tempe, AZ: Arizona Center for Medieval and Renaissance Studies.
Duriez, Colin, 2003, *J.R.R. Tolkien and C.S. Lewis. The Story of Their Friendship*, Gloucestershire: Sutton Publishing.
Ellis, Hilda R. 1943, *The Road to Hel: A Study of the Conception of the Dead in Old Norse Literature*, Cambridge: Cambridge University Press.
---, 1981, 'The Restless Dead: An Icelandic Ghost Story', in H.R.E. Davidson and W.M.S. Russell (eds.), 1981, *The Folklore of Ghosts*, Wellinborough: St Edmundsbury Press, 155-175.
Garmondsway, George N. and Jacqueline Simpson, 1968, *Beowulf and Its Analogues*, London: Dent.
Girvan, Ritchie, 1971, *Beowulf and the Seventh Century. Language and Content*, 1st edition 1935, London: Methuen.
Hallakarva, Gunnora, 'The Walking Dead: *Draugr* and *Aptrgangr* in Old Norse Literature', http://www.vikinganswerlady.com/ghosts.shtml
Heaney, Seamus, 1999, *Beowulf. A New Translation*, London: Faber and Faber.
Irving, Edward, 1969, *Introduction to Beowulf*, Englewood Cliffs, NJ: Prentice-Hall.
Jack, George, 1995, *Beowulf. A Student Edition*, Oxford: Clarendon Press.
Kemble, John M., 1833, *The Anglo-Saxon Poems of Beowulf, The Traveller's Song and the Battle of Finnesburgh*, London.
Ker, William P., 1958, *The Dark Ages*, 1st edition 1904, New York: Mentor.
Kiessling, Nicolas K., 1968, 'Grendel: a New Aspect', *Modern Philology* 65.3:191-201.
Klaeber, Friedrich (ed.), 1941, *Beowulf and the Fight at Finnsburg*, 3rd edition with supplement, 1st edition 1922, New York: D.C. Heath.
Lapidge, Michael, 1993, 'Beowulf and the Psychology of Terror' in Helen Damico and John Leyerle (eds.), 1993, *Heroic Poetry in the Anglo-Saxon Period: Studies in Honor of Jess B. Bessinger*, Jr., Kalamazoo, MI: Medieval Institute Publications, 373-402.
Lawrence, William W., 1967, *Beowulf and Epic Tradition*, 1st edition 1928, New York: Hafner.

Lewis, Clive S., 1990, *The Allegory of Love. A Study in Medieval Tradition*, 1st edition 1936, Oxford: Oxford University Press.
Liuzza, Roy M. (ed. and trans.), 2000, *Beowulf. A New Verse Translation*, Peterborough: Broadview Press.
McNamee, M.B. S.J., 1960, '*Beowulf* – An Allegory of Salvation?', *Journal of English and Germanic Philology* 59:190-207.
Mitchell, Bruce and Fred C. Robinson (eds.), 1998, *Beowulf. An Edition*, Malden, Mass.: Blackwell Publishers.
Nicholson, Lewis E. (ed.), 1963, *An Anthology of Beowulf Criticism*, Notre Dame: University of Notre Dame Press.
Niles, John D., 1983, *Beowulf: The Poem and Its Tradition*, Cambridge, Mass.: Harvard University Press.
Olivares-Merino, Eugenio M., 'Some Considerations on the Absence of Horror Literature in the Middle Ages', in J. López-Peláez *et al.* (eds.), 2000, *Literatura y Estudios Culturales*, Jaén: Servicio de Publicaciones, 149-157.
---, 2005, 'The Old English Poem 'A Vampyre of the Fens': A Bibliographical Ghost', *Miscelánea* 32:87-102.
Raffel, Burton (ed. and trans.), 1963, *Beowulf*, New York: New American Library.
Ramey, Bill, 'The Unity of *Beowulf*: Tolkien & the Critics', at http://ourworld.compuserve.com/homepages/billramey/beowulf.htm
Robinson, Fred C., 1982, *Beowulf and the Appositive Style*, Knoxville: The University of Tennessee Press.
---, 1991, '*Beowulf*', in Malcolm Godden and Michael Lapidge (eds.), 1991, *The Cambridge Companion to Old English Literature*, Cambridge: Cambridge University Press, 142-159.
Shippey, Tom, 2005, *The Road to Middle-Earth*, revised edition, 1st edition 1982, London: HarperCollins.
--- and Andreas Haarder (eds.), 1998, *Beowulf. The Critical Heritage*, London: Routledge.
Stanley, Eric G., 1994, *In the Foreground: Beowulf*, Cambridge: D.S. Brewer.
Strong, Archibald, 1925, *Beowulf Translated into Modern English Rhyming Verse*, London: Constable and Company.
Tolkien, Christopher (ed.), 1983, *The Monsters and the Critics and Other Essays*, London: George Allen and Unwin.
Tolkien, John R.R., 1936, '*Beowulf*: The Monsters and the Critics', *Proceedings of the British Academy* XXI:245-295.
---, 1990, *The Lord of the Rings*, 3 vols, revised edition of 1966, 1st edition 1954-55, London: Unwin Paperbacks.
Wanner, Kevin J., 1999, 'Warriors, *Wyrms*, and *Wyrd*: The Paradoxical Fate of the Germanic Hero/King in *Beowulf*', *Essays in Medieval Studies* 16. http://www.luc.edu/publications/medieval/emsv16.html
Wrenn, Christopher L. (ed.), 1953, *Beowulf with the Finnesburg Fragment*, London: George G. Harrap & Co.

A Tale as Old as Time, Freshly Told Anew: Love and Sacrifice in Tolkien, Lewis and Rowling

Margarita Carretero-González

> To love at all is to be vulnerable.
> C.S. Lewis, *The Four Loves*

Abstract

My paper addresses the issue of the importance J.R.R. Tolkien, C.S. Lewis and J.K. Rowling give to the 'magical' power of sacrifice as an act of love in their writings. The way they deal with this ancient topic has indeed contributed to the popularity Tolkien and Lewis have been enjoying for the past fifty years and the enormous success of the Harry Potter books. In writing about sacrificial deaths as acts of love, these authors have dressed old myths in new clothes, but the result is, as always in good mythopoeia, much more than "lies […] breathed through silver."

Introduction: Rowling and the Inklings

The most successful writer for children in the last ten years is, according to some sources, an Inkling. That, at least, is the thesis put forward by John Granger in *The Hidden Key to Harry Potter* (2002). Granger's book was the first one in a series of many to offer a counter-attack to a crusade started by Christian fundamentalists in the US which later spread to Britain. Books such as those by Richard Abanes and John Houghton – both published in 2001 – echoed the worries of many parents and educators who wanted to have the Harry Potter novels removed from school and public libraries (the most famous case is possibly that of Ms. Laura Mallory, a mother of four who has recently announced she may appeal against the Georgia Board of Education's decision to support the Gwinnet County School Board in their refusal to remove the Harry Potter books from government school libraries in Gwinnet County). Abanes and Houghton summarise this controversy and make their position clear in the subheadings accompanying their books' main titles. While Abanes studies the "dangerous fascination" provided by Harry Potter and points at the "menace behind the magick," Houghton considers the series as one of the constant forces at work "bending and shaping the minds of our children." The argument runs as follows: Rowling's characters are wizards and witches – unless Muggles – and since witchcraft is incompatible with Christian doctrine as shown in the Bible, no Christian should enjoy Harry's adventures. As a response, Granger, an Orthodox Christian, embarked on a detailed search for all the Christian symbols in the series that, according to his study, provide 'hidden keys' to unlock the books' Christian message. For Granger, Rowling turns out to be a Christian fantasist, following the steps of J.R.R. Tolkien and, most importantly, C.S. Lewis.

After the success of his first book and fuelled by the ongoing debates on the Net, Granger published in 2004 *Looking for God in Harry Potter*, and, more recently, *Unlocking Harry Potter: Five Keys for the Serious Reader* (2007). He has also edited *Who Killed Albus Dumbledore? What Really Happened in Harry Potter and the Half-Blood Prince? Six Expert Harry Potter Detectives Examine the Evidence* (2006), becoming, in the meantime, 'Hogwarts Professor'.[1] Many more books on the subject keep appearing[2] together with innumerable articles and public demonstrations defending (or attacking) the Christian (or Wiccan) Rowling. As the titles of Granger's books suggest, some defenders are trying to put forward the idea that the magic key to explain Harry's success may lie in the hidden Christian messages they have apparently uncovered.

---

[1] See Granger's website <www.HogwartsProfessor.com>
[2] See, for example, Bridger (2001), Dalton (2003), Kern (2003), Killinger (2002), Neal (2001 and 2002), or Wohlberg (2005).

The ultimate reason why a book becomes a hit always remains a mystery, and not even the best orchestrated marketing campaign can guarantee its success. Perhaps the most sensible thing to do would be to ask readers what they like about the books; one would certainly become very surprised by the variety of answers.[3] Everyone, however, can have a go at trying to find out where the success of a particular book lies, but those of us who earn our living by teaching and writing about books somehow feel the imperious need to do so. Usually, our conclusions have a lot to do with the type of critical approach we apply or, using the famous Hindu story of the elephant in the dark room, depending on what part of the elephant we touch.

I have looked elsewhere into the reasons for the success of the Harry Potter books in terms of their literary heritage and the way they appeal to the archetypes conforming the collective unconscious (Carretero-González 2002). Apart from her ability to weave intricate plots and surprising twists, Rowling excels at making a very good use of different traditions in children's literature to produce an appealing tale for the young, which adults also enjoy – there are even literary references intended just for them. The books are not only packed with magic, mystery and adventure, but they also give young readers a feeling of empowerment provided by the apparently insignificant wizard apprentice. After all, Harry is another hero undergoing a quest, a recurrent myth in cultures from all over the world.

One can also look at the success in terms of the conditions of the publishing industry in the context of Tony Blair's Britain, as Andrew Blake (2002) has done, and conclude that Harry Potter is a 'retrolutionary' creation, the latest contribution to Britain's rebranding and reglobalising. Alternatively, some have chosen to look at the way J.K. Rowling follows the steps of other

---

[3] In fact, this is precisely what Sharon Moore did in a study published in 1999, after she interviewed 52 children aged 6 to 13 on why and what they loved about the books. The most important conclusion to be extracted after reading all the answers is that the books fuel children's already lively fantasy life.

successful Christian writers such as J.R.R. Tolkien and C.S. Lewis and consider that she is an heir of the Inklings.

In my view, the entire fad about the supposedly anti-Christian or Christian messages 'hidden' in the Harry Potter novels shows that a work of fiction is once more being judged exclusively by external factors. This is a perfect legitimate practice – after all, any work of art is a product of its age, marked by the signs of its times – but, in the same way as forgetting about the context to study the product is just looking at one part of the elephant, so is forgetting about the product and concentrating on the context. In the case of J.K. Rowling, it seems that the debate has been relegated to arguing whether she is a witch or a preacher, consequently reducing her books to the category of mere instruments to achieve some ulterior end – either converting children to witchcraft or Christianity – rather than a work of fiction susceptible of providing an aesthetic experience. Following this line of reasoning, readers would just be passive recipients of those hidden messages, and may turn into witches or saints depending on whoever brandishes the argument.

To make matters worse, so much has been written about this topic that it is now virtually impossible to know where to stand. For example, the argument of Rowling being an Inkling gains credibility for the fact that she is said to admire them greatly and that C.S. Lewis is, in fact, a mentor. Apparently, Rowling has even admitted "to being physically incapable of being in the same room with a Narnia book and not sitting down to read it" (Granger 2004a). If she has really admitted to that, she has also been quoted as saying that she is not "a huge fan of fantasy," as well as not having finished reading *The Lord of the Rings* or all of C.S. Lewis's Narnia stories, or even declaring that there is "something about Lewis's sentimentality about children that gets on her nerves" (Grossman 2005). Moreover, while Lewis obviously intended to make the Christian doctrine more palatable to children – helping them steal past those famous "watchful dragons" – Rowling denies writing with any didactic or moralistic intention, insisting on the fact that, although the books may not be that secular, "Dumbledore is not Jesus" (Grossman 2005).

Can it be possible for anyone to admire so utterly what one has not even finished reading? Is Rowling giving misdirections depending on whether she wants to be ascribed or separated from the tradition of Christian fantasy? Or is it simply that reporters and critics are very good at putting into an author's words their own readings of their books? If the debate around the Harry Potter series proves anything, it is, once more, that one can always read one's own beliefs into a book. And this seems to be particularly true when we are dealing with mythopoeia.

J.R.R. Tolkien was a committed Roman Catholic and yet, it would be extremely simplistic to put the tremendous appeal of *The Lord of the Rings* down to its author's religion, particularly because, even if, as Tolkien admitted, *The Lord of the Rings* is compatible with Christian beliefs, there is no overt creed in Middle-earth. The responses given to a questionnaire I handed out in 1995, when I was studying Tolkien's work from a reader-response perspective, showed that everyone approaches the act of reading with their own particular 'identity theme', described by Norman N. Holland (1975:vi-vii) as "an invariant style running all through a person's chosen behavior, like the theme in a musical theme and variations." Depending on that identity theme, every reader will enjoy some aspects of the book while others will go unnoticed. Among those responding to the questionnaires on *The Lord of the Rings*, there were certainly some readers who linked reading the book to a religious experience, interpreting it from a Christian perspective; on the other hand, the Finnish immediately detected echoes from the *Kalevala*, particularly in *The Silmarillion*, and a Japanese respondent assured me that students in Japan are "fascinated by this story because it teaches how to overcome difficulties" (Carretero-González 1996:700). The success of *The Lord of the Rings* lies undoubtedly in Tolkien's mastery at story-telling and in writing a tale that touches on many 'identity themes'. That is precisely what mythopoeia is about. As Lewis said, "[a] myth points, for each reader, to the realm he lives in most. It is a master key; use it on what door you like" (Lewis 1989:115).

I will be stating the obvious by saying that J.K. Rowling simply cannot be an Inkling, not even a closeted one, and not just because to call her that would be an anachronism, but, most importantly, because saying, as Granger does, that she continues their steps is to ignore the many other genres Rowling draws upon. Although Granger has qualified some of his earlier remarks,[4] he insists on seeing the connection with the Inklings through the allegedly Christian component (see Granger 2004a), forgetting about the many things they do not share at all. As Meredith Veldman has pointed out, like the Inklings themselves, the literary creations of both Tolkien and Lewis were a product of Oxford in the thirties, and "[t]he roads to both Middle-earth and Narnia cut through the quads and common rooms of this elite university," a world that was "male dominated, hierarchical, and communal" (Veldman 1994:45). In contrast, Lev Grossman (2005) argues that Hogwarts is "secular and sexual and multicultural and multiracial and even sort of multimedia [...] If Lewis showed up there, let's face it, he'd probably wind up a Death Eater." Rowling and the Inklings are, quite simply, products of different times.

Having said that, there is something that, from my point of view, brings Rowling closer to the Inklings than any supposedly hidden Christian message, something that has more to do with a conception of literature. J.K. Rowling shares with C.S. Lewis, J.R.R. Tolkien, Charles Williams and the rest of their friends her being "'unabashedly' romantic in an age of realism," an expression Margaret Wright used to describe the Inklings (qtd. in Grotta 1992:97). This is, however, not exclusive to this group of writers, since it is common to many key authors in English literature, especially those writing for children. From

---

[4] In 2005 he admitted that Rowling cannot be an Inkling because "to her (as with all of us) World War I is ancient history from the dawn of time before television. Her concerns, like all of ours, are PostModern [*sic*]. We are different people of a different historical age and different mindset, blindspots, and tastes and sentiments than moderns like Lewis and Tolkien". Moreover, he granted that "there are at least ten genres from the English literary tradition in the Harry Potter books, of which Christian fantasy is an important one but perhaps not the central one. [...] Her usage of magic, though, in a work that is at least in part Christian inasmuch as it is a celebration of a literary tradition that is almost exclusively Christian, points to her being post-modern in her disregard for conventional and traditional boogeys". (*Christian Fandom*)

George MacDonald, Edith Nesbit, Beatrix Potter, A.A. Milne or Kenneth Grahame to Philippa Pearce, Eoin Colfer, Phillip Pullman or Georgia Byng, J.K. Rowling is among the long list of authors who have chosen the fantastic as a vehicle to tell their stories, many of whom also play – like Lewis, like Rowling – with the existence of two parallel worlds. In a time like ours, hungry for myths, the Harry Potter books are a hit because, going beyond the materialistic assumptions of our age, they put us in touch with "the magic and mystery of life, the dimension beyond the ordinary, the sense of wonder that makes even commonplace experiences shine with the brilliance of celestial bodies" (Killinger, qtd. in Chattaway 2003).

John Killinger's words are familiar to anyone who has studied the Inklings. They refer to what Tolkien defined as "Recovery […] regaining of a clear view." While Tolkien suggested that by meeting the centaur and the dragon, we could "perhaps suddenly behold, like the ancient shepherds, sheep, and dogs, and horses – and wolves" (Tolkien 1988:53), his dear friend 'Jack' expressed himself in very similar terms when stating that "[t]he value of the myth is that it takes all the things we know and restores to them the rich significance which has been hidden by 'the veil of familiarity'" (Lewis 1989:120).

What is there, then, hidden by the veil of familiarity that Rowling has 'recovered' and that children so much require? Again, the answers can be almost as varied as the readers; therefore, I will provide mine. In a collection of essays dedicated to myth, magic and art, I will devote the lines that follow to the magic, the art of love and the sacrifices we make for love. For me, the extraordinary appeal of *The Lord of the Rings*, *The Chronicles of Narnia* – particularly *The Lion, the Witch and the Wardrobe* – and the Harry Potter series resides in the centrality of love and sacrifice as structuring element running through these 'inventions of truth'.

I

Ever since human beings began to tell stories, they have recorded the deeds of people who sacrificed themselves for the benefit of a particular community. That, indeed, is a common theme to most epics all over the world. These sacrificial actions are not relegated to the realm of fiction, though, since the stories seem to have evolved from real practices. Scholars such as Sir James Frazer, Jane Harrison and members of the Cambridge Ritual School studied and contributed to the popularisation of all these rites by displaying the similarities found in cultures separated from each other by space and time. In connection with these sacrificial practices and following Nietzsche's views on the birth of tragedy, literary anthropologists describe the tragic mode as "the ritual by which the individual's submission to the social whole strengthens its corporate life" (Eagleton 2003:60).

However, the idea of sacrifice does not seem to enjoy much popularity these days; sacrifice is, to say the least, an uncomfortable notion. For Terry Eagleton, the reasons behind the perception of sacrifice as somewhat insidious may rely on the fact that it combines "a whiff of barbarism with a streak of self abnegation." The word itself "has unpleasant overtones of self-repression and self-laceration, of bogus appeals to tighten one's belt in the general interest. [...] It suggests false asceticism, anthropological exoticism, ruling-class ploys" (Eagleton 2003:275). In truth, Eagleton grants, sacrifice may have all these connotations, but also carries the idea of renovation:

> it also means that there are times when something must be dismembered in order to be renewed. If a situation is dire enough, it must be broken to be repaired. It is just the same for individual lives – not that they should be violently extinguished, since such terror is a parody of sacrifice. [...] It is rather that for political change to take root we must *divest ourselves of our current identities*, staked as they are on a false situation, and this demands *a painful process of self-abandonment*. (Eagleton 2003:275; my emphasis)

We are all used to making sacrifices in our daily lives – sometimes we are not even aware, many we don't even consider sacrifices – for our own benefit or for that of others. The sacrifices we make are more or less demanding depending not only on the difference of what we give up and what we gain in return, but also, when that is the case, on the relationship with the person for whom that sacrifice is made. In other words, it is easier to give up things when we do it for the welfare of those we love.

Yet, sometimes people make willing sacrifices for others they do not even know. In *The Golden Bough*, Frazer gives accounts of men and women who voluntarily played the part of scapegoats by diverting to themselves whatever evil could threaten others; he even records the instance of an old man who reputedly earned his living "by taking on himself the sins of the dead and thenceforth devoting his life to prayer for their souls" (Frazer 1993:542). This is clearly not an instance of sacrifice for love, it is not a response to what Harry G. Frankfurt (2004:29) calls "commands of love", but it obeys a "command of rationality" or, in this case, even of necessity, since that was the old man's source of income. In most cases, the scapegoats were slaves or already miserable outcasts, poor, ugly or deformed, who were offered a year of luxury at the end of which they were sacrificed. It should come as no surprise that they accepted to perform this role, even when, very frequently, it involved a terrible death. Theirs was not truly a free choice; they had nothing to lose and a year of decent life to win. Needless to say, it was not love that moved them to do such sacrifice, but sheer necessity.

Apparently similar actions can spring from different motives; if we remain on the surface, we can hardly see any difference between them. Love and sacrifice have accompanied humankind from its origins, but they do not always go together. There are many instances of sacrifices without love – as the ones above mentioned – or occurrences of sacrifices that are said to be done in the name of something disguised as love. We could cite many examples of sacrifices done in the name of love but, for my purposes here, I will limit myself to the narrative of Jesus' Passion, the one closer to us in the Western world, shared by the three authors dealt with in this essay.

The basic tenet of faith for any Christian is that Jesus of Nazareth was the Son of God who gave his life to atone for people's sins. Despite the insistence on his divinity, one must never lose sight of the fact that Jesus was also a human being. Forgetting that would mean to skip the most important part of the tragedy: that he was subject to human pain, fears, doubts – like any other human being – but that he put all that aside and accepted his fate for something he believed in. The Gethsemane scene, together with the last words Matthew and Mark record just before his death – "My God, My God, Why hast thou forsaken me?" (Matthew 27:46; Mark 15:34) – show us Jesus at his most human, closer to us, who are enabled to sympathise with his suffering. Terry Eagleton precisely uses the Gethsemane scene to argue about the meaning of sacrifice:

> Jesus plainly does not welcome his own impending torture and death, even though he seems impelled by an obscure conviction that such failure will prove the only way in which his mission will succeed. [...] His death is a sacrifice precisely on this account. *Sacrifice is not a matter of relinquishing what you find worthless, but of freely surrendering what you esteem for the benefit of others.* It is this which marks the difference between the suicide and the martyr.
> (Eagleton 2003:35; my emphasis)

And what is it really that would make anyone freely surrender what one loves for the benefit of others if not love itself? The sacrifice is greater the more we love what we are surrendering, and Jesus was surrendering, willingly, his life. This does not mean that he – or anyone in similar circumstances – did not love living; it simply shows that one may love something very much and yet be willing to harm it, in order to protect something – or someone – else for which their love is greater (Frankfurt 2004:46). Jesus could trust on what his sacrifice would help to achieve but, because of his human frame, he most certainly did not welcome the suffering.

II

It should come as no surprise to find many instances of individual acts of sacrifice in the stories by J.R.R. Tolkien, C.S. Lewis and J.K. Rowling, revolving as they do around a sort of cosmic battle between good and evil, where the possibility of death is always round the corner. Every individual has to give up something for the benefit of the community, even when it may entail the loss of their lives.

I would like, once more, to insist on the idea that not all sacrifices are the product of an act of love, generally understood as "a *disinterested* concern for the existence of what is loved, and for what is good for it" (Frankfurt 2004:42). Albeit reluctantly, one could say that, to a certain extent, the Dursleys sacrifice something of their family comfort (granted, almost nothing) to keep Harry at home. But this can hardly be said to be a response to a command of love. They do not *care* about Harry, but this task is imposed upon them and they perform it most unwillingly, reducing him to a Cinderella figure. On the other hand, professor Quirrell puts his whole self to the service of Voldemort, giving up his physical integrity by acting as a host for the dark wizard's non-corporeal self, while Wormtail goes to the extreme of sacrificing his right hand to make his master corporeal again. Their actions, however, are far from being the product of a disinterested concern for Voldemort – who, incidentally, is not really loved, but rather feared, or needed for the benefit he can give to those who follow him. Like the 'voluntary' scapegoats, neither Quirrell nor Wormtail were acting disinterestedly; they simply had something to get in return.

These instances cannot be compared, for example, with the sacrifice made my members of the Fellowship of the Ring to save Middle-earth from falling under Sauron's yoke – Gandalf even gives up his life in Moria –, with Aslan's sacrifice at the Stone Table or, arguably, with Dumbledore's at the end of *The Half-Blood Prince*.⁵ Likewise, Frodo accepted to go on his quest to destroy the Ring "out of love – to save the world he knew from disaster at his own expense" (Carpenter 1990:327). While the quest succeeded, Frodo could not enjoy it, having to leave his beloved Shire. Even Harry makes a big sacrifice at the end of *The Half-Blood Prince*: he sacrifices his love for Ginny precisely out of love. The "stupid, noble reason" that Ginny refers to as the cause for their break-up is, precisely, the love Harry feels for her.

III

From its very beginning, Harry Potter's life is linked to a terrible event which leaves an indelible mark on him: the violent death of his parents. While James Potter died fighting against Lord Voldemort, his wife Lily did so trying to protect Harry, an act which not only prevented Voldemort from killing the baby but also caused his loss of power. Lily's death was the consequence of an act of love, an action that also empowered her son, as Dumbledore explains to the young wizard apprentice towards the end of *The Philosopher's Stone*:

> Your mother died to save you. If there is one thing Voldemort cannot understand, it is love. He didn't realise that love as powerful as your mother's for you leaves its own mark. Not a scar, no visible sign [...] to have been loved so deeply, even though the person who loved us is gone, will give us some protection for ever. It is in your very skin. Quirrell, full of hatred, greed and ambition, sharing his soul with Voldemort, could not touch you for this reason. It was agony to touch a person marked by something so good. (Rowling 1997:216)

---

[5] I will go back to this issue later on. I now say "arguably" because, at the time of writing this essay, the seventh book of the Harry Potter series, *The Deathly Hallows*, has not yet been published and any assertion regarding Dumbledore's death at the hands of Snape remains debatable.

Because of its altruistic and generous nature, maternal love has generally been considered the noblest form of love, the most sacred of all emotional bonds (Fromm 1988:55). However, it is also the most instinctive type of love, responding to a basic, animal drive: any female – as long as she is healthy in body and mind – will do anything to protect her offspring. Of course, this does not mean that it is less valuable – I cannot put it any better than C.S. Lewis did when he wrote that "[n]othing in Man is either worse or better for being shared with the beasts" (Lewis 1977:33) – it means that it is only natural for a mother to care so much for her children that she is willing to sacrifice her life for theirs. Lily's action was not the product of a decision taken after long deliberation; she was not responding to commands of rationality but to commands of love.

Through his own painful experience, Voldemort learnt of the power of love. When trying to attack Harry, his curse was deflected by Lily's sacrifice, rebounding upon the attacker and causing him to lose his corporeity. When he regains it again towards the end of *The Goblet of Fire*, Voldemort is fully conscious of Lily's powerful legacy: "His mother left upon him the traces of her sacrifice [...] this is old magic" (Rowling 2000:566).

This instance of "old magic" does not differ much from the "Deeper Magic from before the Dawn of Time" of C.S. Lewis's *The Lion, the Witch and the Wardrobe*, although Aslan's sacrifice is not an innate reaction, but the product of a conscious decision, of an act of deliberation, therefore a response to both commands of rationality and of love. More importantly, he was acting out of love for someone who had betrayed him. As said above, while it is easier to sacrifice anything for those we love, it requires a higher degree of sophistication to love someone who has harmed us.

After arranging with the White Witch to take Edmund's place at the Stone Table, Aslan has to face his own Gethsemane at the Fords of Beruna. As in the case of Jesus, this scene is particularly poignant because the narrator makes sure that the reader knows of the internal turmoil Aslan is going through. After the interview with the Witch, everyone around the lion can perceive a change in his mood: he seems to be lost in thought, sad, often sighing deeply. When Susan and Lucy see him as he heads for the place of his sacrifice, they notice he walks heavily, "his great, royal head drooped so that his nose nearly touched the grass. Presently he stumbled and gave a low moan" (Lewis 1988:136). Aslan responds to the girls that he is not ill, but "sad and lonely," and willingly accepts their company while asking them to lay their hands on his mane, "so that I can feel you are there" (Lewis 1988:136). He most certainly cannot welcome the torture he is about to endure, even if he embraces it because he knows of the ulterior end it will serve to reach.

The similarities between this scene and Jesus' agony in Gethsemane, as both Matthew and Mark render it to us, are evident. According to Matthew (26:37), Jesus "began to be sorrowful and very heavy," whereas for Mark (14:33), he "began to be sore amazed, and to be very heavy." In both cases, Jesus doesn't want to be alone, and asks his disciples Peter, James and John to keep watch with him, while confessing to them that his soul is "exceedingly sorrowful" (Matthew 26:38; Mark 14:34). While the narrator in *The Lion, the Witch and the Wardrobe* allows readers to see Aslan only from Lucy and Susan's perspective, the two evangelists give us access to Jesus' prayers; even if he accepts God's will, Jesus asks Him, if at all possible, to take away that cup from him (Mark 14:36; Matthew 26:39 and 39-42). That vulnerability is inherent in Jesus' humanity, and makes his sacrifice even more tragic. To see the strong, energetic and powerful Aslan suddenly vulnerable produces the same effect on the reader.

Despite the fears and the possible doubts, sacrifices like these are responses to commands of love fuelled by a hope that the suffering really serves a purpose. Hence, despair is the most terrible weapon to brandish in order to undermine one's will. It proves to be a powerful instrument in the hands of the forces of evil in *The Lord of the Rings*, as Pippin has the opportunity to experience when he hears a cry from a Ringwraith, "piercing the heart with a poisonous despair" (*LotR* 840). It is also the device used by Jadis against Aslan, in order to destroy him both physically and spiritually:

> And now, who has won? Fool, did you think that by all this you would save the human traitor? Now I will kill you instead of him as our pact was and so the Deep Magic will be appeased. But when you are dead what will prevent me from killing him as well? And who will take him out of my hand *then*? Understand that you have given me Narnia forever, you have lost your own life and you have not saved his. In that knowledge, despair and die.
> (Lewis 1988:140-141)

Lewis's "despair and die" is a direct quote from the words the ghosts of all those killed by Richard III in Shakespeare's play whispered to the king the night previous to his defeat at Bosworth Field, uttered immediately before they wish Richmond to "live and flourish," a scene Rowling seems also to be paying homage to towards the end of *The Goblet of Fire* (cf. Carretero-González 2002:55). When the jets of light issuing from Voldemort's and Harry's wands get in contact, a powerful golden beam originates and, as the ghosts of all those killed by Voldemort emerge from that beam, they "whispered words of encouragement to Harry, and hissed words Harry couldn't hear to Voldemort (Rowling 2000:578-579). On these two occasions, the use of the weapon is successful, since despair necessarily affects a guilty conscience. But, over those who trust in higher forces at work, whether God or the "Deeper Magic from before the Dawn of Time," dejection has no permanent power. Even if the pill is bitter to swallow, the cup painful to drink, despair is, Gandalf tells us, "only for those who see the end beyond all doubt," and neither Jesus, nor Aslan, nor Gandalf belong to that group. Against evil, they have the advantage of knowing better.

Jadis, like Voldemort, is ignorant to the power of love, which works to Aslan's advantage:

> [...] though the Witch knew the Deep Magic, there is a magic deeper still which she did not know. Her knowledge goes back only to the dawn of time. But if she could have looked a little further back, into

> the stillness and the darkness before Time dawned, she would have read there a different incantation. She would have known that when a willing victim who had committed no treachery was killed in a traitor's stead, the Table would crack and Death itself would start working backwards.
> (Lewis 1988:148)

In willingly offering himself to be killed in Edmund's place, Aslan was responding to a command of the greatest love: Charity, an action which not only saved Edmund but eventually vanquished the White Witch, bringing new life to Narnia.

IV

Even if the Harry Potter books and *The Chronicles of Narnia* are full of instances of sacrifices every individual has to do for the community, it is in the pages of *The Lord of the Rings* that we find the clearer instance of individuals from all walks of life merging into a Fellowship, bound together by the will to overcome Sauron. On the surface a story of war, suspense and adventure, *The Lord of the Rings* is mostly a story about the power of renunciation and sacrifice in the name of love. Elves, Dwarves, Men and Hobbits form a single body where individuality does not count, because fragmentation is the beginning of the end. Like this "tale that grew in the telling," the external manifestation of love and sacrifice become the central theme as the narrative progresses. Hence, at the beginning, the hobbits are thrilled to go on an expedition to take the Ring to Rivendell, while they are unknowingly embarking upon an adventure to the centres of their own beings, where their loyalty, resilience and the quality of their love will be put to the test.

Galadriel makes it clear that the Fellowship can thrive only if everyone sacrifices their individuality; "hope remains while all the Company is true" (*LotR* 376), she assures them in Lothlórien. Her words become prophetic when Boromir fails, unable to give up his own individual wishes. The Ring finds a way to his heart – his love for Minas Tirith and its people, together with his thirst for fame – and it brings about the breaking of the Fellowship. In a vain attempt to keep the company together and save Merry and Pippin, Boromir faces the orcs courageously, somehow redeeming himself. The rest, however, keep their word and, even if inwardly hoping that it need not come to that, are ready to give up their lives for the goal that binds them.

Of all the members of the Fellowship, Gandalf is the one who actually has to sacrifice his life so that the rest can go on with the quest. The way Aslan's sacrifice mirrors Jesus' agony in Gethsemane is completely absent from Gandalf's. Because of his death as Gandalf the Grey and later return as Gandalf the White, the wizard is traditionally perceived as a Christ figure. The same "descent to the underground" has been used by Granger (2004a) as a clear indicator of Harry's nature as a Christ figure. Although this can be a perfectly plausible interpretation, Granger seems to obviate that the descent to the underground is a stage common to most hero-quests. Tolkien's 'applicability' seems to be a better concept to work with in cases like these.

Gandalf's death in Moria, like Aslan's sacrifice, is the consequence of his acceptance of the part he has to play in the greater picture of the War of the Ring. From the very beginning of the quest, the wizard is not only the guide of the Fellowship, but also the figure the reader most trusts, so that when the Fellowship loses him, we are also somewhat lost. Even if Aragorn, Boromir, Legolas and Gimli, rather than Gandalf, conform to the traditional image of the hero-warrior, when the Fellowship is in Moria he is not only the leader that has been guiding the company all along, but becomes indeed a shield that protects the rest from the orcs' attacks, remaining behind whilst urging the group to advance. Previous to his fall with the Balrog, Gandalf also appears weakened, vulnerable, like Dumbledore before his death in *The Half-Blood Prince*. The narrator is preparing the reader for the events at the bridge of Khazad-dûm:

> I found myself suddenly faced by something that I have not met before. [...] What it was I cannot guess, but I have never felt such a challenge. The

> counter-spell was terrible. It nearly broke me. I had to speak a word of Command. That proved too great a strain. [...] Ah! I have never felt so spent, but it is passing. (*LotR* 345)

Soon enough, Gandalf knows what he was facing. The impressive presence of the Balrog proves too much for the exhausted wizard, who seems to foresee the fate awaiting him: "'Now I understand.' He faltered and leaned heavily on his staff. 'What an evil fortune! And I am already weary'" (*LotR* 348). Nevertheless, despite his physical exhaustion, Gandalf acts as an obstacle between the Balrog and the rest of the company, smiting the bridge, an action that costs him his staff – thence, a loss of power – and his life. The reader has a last glimpse of Gandalf's attempts to save his life, staggering, falling, and grasping at the stone, before falling into the abyss. His descent to the underground and the fight with the Balrog are hidden from the readers' eyes who, like the Fellowship, will know of it only through Gandalf the White's report.

We cannot talk of the Harry Potter series in the same terms as *The Chronicles of Narnia* or *The Lord of the Rings* simply because the last instalment – *Harry Potter and the Deathly Hallows* – has not been published at the time of writing this essay. What happens to Dumbledore at the hands of Severus Snape is a matter of controversy and any interpretation the result of deduction and guesswork. From my point of view, Snape's killing of Albus Dumbledore was a plan arranged by Dumbledore. I have real problems in seeing Severus Snape as a villain in the story because, despite the dislike he evokes in most characters and readers, he has a very special relationship with Dumbledore, similar to that existing between Gandalf and Aragorn. Both know things the rest of the characters are kept ignorant of. When Dumbledore feels his strength disappearing after drinking from the cup, he insistently asks to be taken to Snape and, quite simply, I cannot imagine Dumbledore making such a mistake. For that reason, I will argue that his "Severus, please" is uttered not to ask Snape's mercy, but to urge him to go on with a plan that Snape may feel reluctant to follow. Perhaps so that the Death Eaters could trust Severus and to keep Draco Malfoy, for the time being, innocent of murder, Dumbledore sacrifices his own life. Whether the pattern will repeat and, like Jesus, Aslan or Gandalf, Dumbledore will come back is something many readers expect, but I feel less confident – although willing to be proved wrong – on that issue. Even if they can be read as allegories of Christ – Aslan intentionally is one – the lion and the two wizards are embodiments of mythical archetypes which offer instances in which the sacrifice of individual lives are necessary to strengthen the corporate life of the social whole, thus assuring their final victory over evil.

The figures I have been dealing with up to this point all have in common their heroic stature; they belong to Frye's 'high mimetic mode'. They die tragically but also gloriously in order to save the world they love. Moreover, all of them display the greatest of the four loves that C.S. Lewis deals with: Charity. Jesus, Aslan, Gandalf, and Dumbledore are capable of displaying love even for those who are not lovable, not 'naturally loved'. Judas, Edmund, Gollum, Draco Malfoy are loved "because Love Himself is in those who love them" (Lewis 1977:121).

Tolkien, however, in his intention to give *The Lord of the Rings* a "hobbito-centric" structure, thus exalting the humble, concentrates on developing a relationship based on another type of love, more natural, imperfect, for that same reason, but no less worthy: the *philia* that binds Frodo and Sam together. To this type of love, shared by the Inklings, especially appreciated by Tolkien and Lewis, I will devote the last part of this essay.

V

To talk about Frodo and Sam's relationship as friendship is not as easy a task as it may appear at first sight. Lewis defines friendship as arising "out of mere Companionship when two or more of the companions discover that they have in common some insight or interest or even taste" (Lewis 1977:61-62). It follows, then, that for a relationship like that to develop, the people involved should be in a position that enables them to share those insights. At the beginning of *The Lord of the Rings*, there is nothing that indicates that this is the case with Sam and Frodo. Merry and Pippin are the ones introduced to the reader as Frodo's friends; Sam is the son of the Gaffer, Bilbo's gardener, who follows in his father's footsteps. It is the quest to Mount Doom that brings Frodo and Sam together as friends. What they have in common is the urgent need to destroy the Ring, a task appointed to Frodo, but which Sam makes also his own.

At the beginning of the quest, both Sam and Frodo believe it to end in Rivendell. Frodo volunteers to take the dangerous item away from his beloved community and leave it to the wise in Rivendell to decide what to do with the Ring. After the Council, he takes once more charge of the burden and offers to carry the Ring to Mount Doom while later, when the Fellowship breaks after Boromir's attempt to take the Ring, Frodo decides to go on his quest alone. On these three occasions, Sam partakes in Frodo's quest; first accidentally but willingly – Gandalf 'punishes' him with accompanying Frodo after catching him eavesdropping – later he simply does not consider the possibility of leaving his master. Sam's love for Frodo, together with his 'plain hobbit-sense' is vital for the success of the quest; their relationship moves the reader like no other does and renders Sam one of the best-loved characters.

Yet, this strong love Sam feels for Frodo also renders him blind to other types of love, renders him incapable of Charity – the greatest love, according to Lewis, because of its divine nature – a love which Frodo, in contrast, does indeed display. Possibly for that reason, Sam remains closer to the reader than his master. Whereas Frodo's is, in Lee D. Rossi's (1984:123) words, "the quest of a saint," since it involves a terrible internal struggle to overcome the Ring's power, Sam's remains closer to Everyman's. Like Lucy in *The Lion, the Witch and the Wardrobe*, Sam is appointed as healer, and it is up to him to bring the Shire back to life, renewing also himself by starting his own family, which Frodo cannot do. Yet, it is also necessary that Frodo leaves the Shire, thus moving away from Sam if the latter's quest is to be completed. As I said, his love for his master is both Sam's strongest and weakest aspect of this character's nature. It is crucial for the success of the quest but, under other circumstances, it could have also frustrated it.

In *The Four Loves*, Lewis distinguishes between Affection, Friendship, Eros and Charity, pointing at the way the four merge into another, but insisting on the necessary differences between them. Lewis's thesis, in a nutshell, is that the first three loves can be dangerous if deprived of the grace of Charity, the love of God. To develop his argument, Lewis makes use of Denis de Rougemont's assertion in *Love in the Western World* that "love ceases to be a demon only when he ceases to be a god" and re-states it in the form "begins to be a demon the moment he begins to be a god" (Lewis 1977:11-12). It was their deification of love that led Romeo and Juliet to kill themselves or Othello to kill Desdemona, to mention just two popular instances where love becomes a demon when it is made a god.

In a way – although saving the distances – Sam's love for Frodo partakes of this deification; it leaves room for almost nothing, almost even taking preference over his own family, and reveals the hobbit's less palatable side: his lack of mercy and his cruelty towards Gollum. One can even play with the idea that, if there was any possibility of redemption in the wretched creature, Frodo acted as a catalyst, while Sam contributed to thwart it. I have no doubt that, had Sam been exposed to the power of the Ring for a longer period, the jewel would have managed to use this devoted love as the way to reach his heart, as it would have chosen Gandalf's "pity for weakness and the desire of strength to do good" (*LotR* 330) as the vehicle to bend the wizard to its will.

I have argued elsewhere (Carretero-González 1996:329-330) that, as a matter of fact, we cannot even be sure that the Ring had not already started working on Sam's will when he found Frodo in Cirith Ungol. When the moment came to give it back to Frodo, Sam, according to the narrator, "felt reluctant to give up the Ring and burden his master with it again" (*LotR* 946). A terrible scene follows in which an enraged Frodo accuses Sam of theft, while Sam can only kneel before his master, "his face wrung with pain, as if he had been stabbed in the heart; tears well[ing] from his eyes" (*LotR* 946). The reader, who does not question Sam's good intentions, cannot help suffering for Frodo's unjust behaviour. This may be one of the most moving passages in the book, not only because we feel the pain with Sam, but also because it reveals the terrible effect of the Ring on Frodo. However, it can also be taken to show the beginning of the Ring's attempt to find a way to Sam's heart.[6]

If love is the impulse that moved Frodo to carry the burden of the Ring, it was the same that moved Sam to share his torment, agony and terror. For Aragorn, Sam's has been "the darkest road" (*LotR* 990) and, although he seems to be the only one capable of moving on with life, his quest is incomplete. He has not really travelled the same road as Frodo. Through his suffering, Frodo has learnt to feel pity, mercy and, eventually, to love even that which seemed to be unlovable. To the miserable Gollum that he wished dead at the beginning of his quest, Frodo displays Charity, the divine goal which, for Lewis, must be the sum and goal of the other three. That is the love Sam has yet to give.

VI

I started this essay commenting on the possibility – soon discarded – that J.K. Rowling could be considered an Inkling. I hope to have made clear that this cannot be so, not only because the tradition of (Christian) fantasy is just one of the many different genres detectable in the Harry Potter books, but because there are many ideological and contextual elements that separate Rowling from the Oxford group.

The three writers studied here also share the fact that their books have enjoyed an extraordinary public acclaim while being, as usual, ridiculed in some academic circles. No one who has read the Tolkien's, Lewis's or Rowling's books without prejudice can feel comfortable with the explanation that

---

[6] An opinion also shared by director Peter Jackson according to the way he shot Sam's reaction in the scene at Cirith Ungol. Cinematic constraints prevented him from making it more subtle, but it helped to make clear for the viewers that absolutely no one, not even down-to-earth Sam, is immune to the corrupting power of the Ring.

their success is solely due to good marketing campaigns. We all know that *The Lord of the Rings* became a campus cult before achieving world-wide reputation and that the Narnia stories and the first Harry Potters became popular by word of mouth. Reluctant critics should at least consider the possibility that there is something men, women and children are craving that these books can offer, and avoid using the simplistic argument of the "lifelong appetite for juvenile trash."

I have argued that part of the appeal may reside in the way the three authors deal with the topics of love and sacrifice, retelling a tale as old as time, and providing their own 'inventions of truth' to feed their readers' hunger for myths (not just appetite – and certainly not for trash). As both Tolkien and Lewis argued, by dressing old myths in new clothes we are enabled to contemplate and enjoy from a different perspective what the veil of familiarity usually covers. Pain does not necessarily have to be meaningless, and there are occasions where sacrifice can be willingly, joyously embraced, because "though pain is generally to be avoided as an evil, there are kinds of affliction in which loss and gain go curiously together" (Eagleton 2003:38). And this is what these stories talk about; they are much more than lies "breathed through silver," they are expressions of the firm belief that, after all, it is love that truly makes the world go round.

Biographical Note

Margarita Carretero-González is Senior Lecturer in English Literature at the University of Granada (Spain). She got her Ph.D. with a dissertation on J.R.R. Tolkien's *The Lord of the Rings* (1996) and her current research interests focus on fantasy, Utopia, children's literature, women's literature and ecocriticism. She is at present working on a book on Mabel, Edith and Priscilla Tolkien and is also engaged on a project about the relationship between women and the environment in English fiction written by women.

Bibliography

Abbreviations

*Lot*R: see Tolkien 1992

Abanes, Richard, 2001, *Harry Potter and the Bible. The Menace behind the Magick*, Camp Hill, Penn.: Horizon Books.
Blake, Andrew, 2002, *The Irresistible Rise of Harry Potter*, London: Verso.
Bridger, Francis, 2001, *A Charmed Life. The Spirituality of Potter World*, New York: Doubleday.
Carretero-González, Margarita, 1996, *Fantasía, épica y utopía en The Lord of the Rings: análisis temático y de la recepción*, Granada: Servicio de Publicaciones de la Universidad.
---, 2002, 'A Male Cinderella: Heritage and Reception of the Harry Potter Books', in Margarita Carretero-González, Encarnación Hidalgo-Tenorio, Neil McLaren, and Graeme Porte (eds.), 2002, *A Life in Words. A Miscellany Celebrating Twenty-Five Years of Association between the English Department of Granada University and Mervyn Smale (1977-2002)*, Granada: Editorial Universidad de Granada, 51-58.
Carpenter, Humphrey (ed.), 1990, *The Letters of J.R.R. Tolkien*, London: Unwin Paperbacks.
Chattaway, Peter T., 2003, 'Harry Potter's Christian fans come to his defense', *Canadian Christianity*, <http://www.canadianchristianity.com/cgi-in/na.cgi?nationalupdates/030619harrypotter> Accessed 10th May, 2006.
Christian Fandom, 2005, 'Interview: John Granger', <www.christian-fandom.org/oli-jg.html> Accessed 20th May, 2006.
Eagleton, Terry, 2003, *Sweet Violence. The Idea of the Tragic*, Oxford: Blackwell Publishers.
Dalton, Russell W., 2003, *Faith Journey Through Fantasy Lands. A Christian Dialogue with Harry Potter, Star Wars and The Lord of the Rings*, Minneapolis, MN: Augsburg Books.
Frazer, Sir James G., 1993, *The Golden Bough. A Study in Magic and Religion*, Ware: Wordsworth Editions.
Frankfurt, Harry G., 2004, *The Reasons of Love*, Princeton & Oxford: Princeton University Press.
Fromm, Erich, 1988, *El arte de amar. Una investigación sobre la naturaleza del amor*, (translated by Noemi Rosenblatt), Barcelona, Buenos Aires & México: Paidós.
Granger, John, 2002, *The Hidden Key to Harry Potter: Understanding the Meaning, Genius, and Popularity of Joanne Rowling's Harry Potter Novels*, Hadlock, Washington: Zossima Press.
---, 2004a, 'Harry Potter and the Inklings: The Christian Meaning of the Chamber of Secrets', *The Golden Key*, <http://www.ev90481.dial.pipex.com/harry_potter_granger.htm>, Accessed 25th May, 2006.
---, 2004b, *Looking for God in Harry Potter*, Carol Stream, IL: Tyndale House Publishers.

---, 2006, *Who Killed Albus Dumbledore? What Really Happened in Harry Potter and the Half-Blood Prince? Six Expert Harry Potter Detectives Examine the Evidence*, Hadlock, Washington: Zossima Press.

---, 2007, *Unlocking Harry Potter: Five Keys for the Serious Reader*, Hadlock, Washington: Zossima Press.

Grossman, Lev, 2005, 'J.K. Rowling, Hogwarts and All', *Time* 17th July, 2005, <http://www.time.com/time/magazine/article/0,9171,1083935-4,00.html> Accessed 24th May, 2006.

Grotta, Daniel, 1992, *The Biography of J.R.R. Tolkien, Architect of Middle-earth*, Philadelphia, Penn.: Running Press.

Holland, Norman N., 1975, *The Dynamics of Literary Response*, New York & London: W.W. Norton & Company.

Houghton, John, 2001, *A Closer Look at Harry Potter. Bending and Shaping the Minds of Our Children*, Eastbourne: Kingsway Publications.

Kern, Edmund M., 2003, *The Wisdom of Harry Potter: What Our Favourite Hero Teaches us about Moral Choices*, Amherst, N.Y.: Prometheus Books.

Killinger, John, 2002, *God, the Devil, and Harry Potter: A Christian Minister's Defense of the Beloved Novels*, New York: St. Martin's Press.

Lewis, Clive Staples, 1977, *The Four Loves*, London: Fount Paperbacks.

---, 1988, *The Lion, the Witch and the Wardrobe*, London: Lions.

---, 1989, *Of This and Other Worlds*, (edited with a Preface by Walter Hooper), London: Fount Paperbacks.

Moore, Sharon, 1999, *We Love Harry Potter! We'll Tell You Why*, New York: St. Martin's Griffin.

Neal, Connie, 2001, *What's a Christian to Do with Harry Potter?* Colorado Springs, Colorado: Waterbrook Press.

---, 2002, *The Gospel According to Harry Potter: Spirituality in the Stories of the World's Most Famous Seeker*, Louisville, Kentucky: Westminster John Knox Press.

Rossi, Lee D., 1984, *The Politics of Fantasy. C.S. Lewis and J.R.R. Tolkien*, Michigan: UMI Research Press.

Rowling, Joanne K., 1997, *Harry Potter and the Philosopher's Stone*, London: Bloomsbury.

---, 2000, *Harry Potter and the Goblet of Fire*, London: Bloomsbury.

---, 2005, *Harry Potter and the Half-Blood Prince*, London: Bloomsbury.

Tolkien, John Ronald Reuel, 1988, 'On Fairy-Stories', in *Tree and Leaf*, (edited by Christopher Tolkien), London: Unwin Paperbacks, 75-95.

---, 1992, *The Lord of the Rings*, (first published 1954-55), London: HarperCollins.

Veldman, Meredith, 1994, *Fantasy, the Bomb and the Greening of Britain. Romantic Protest, 1945-1980*, Cambridge: Cambridge University Press.

Wohlberg, Steve, 2005, *Hour of the Witch: Harry Potter, Wicca Witchcraft and the Bible*, Shippensburg, PA: Destiny Image, Inc.

The Hidden Meanings of the Name 'Ransom': Strange Philology and 'Contradiction' in C.S. Lewis's Cosmic Trilogy

FERNANDO J. SOTO AND MARTA GARCÍA DE LA PUERTA

> 'Ransom!' This time he made no reply. Another minute and it uttered his name again; and then, like a minute gun, 'Ransom... Ransom... Ransom,' perhaps a hundred times.
> C.S. Lewis, *Perelandra*

Abstract

This paper will set out to explore a 'philological' aspect of the name 'Ransom' in an attempt to give a derivation for Lewis' literary baptism of the main character in the celebrated *Space Trilogy*. At the same time, as this paper outlines the hidden meanings of this curious name, these meanings will also be used to explain an apparent 'contradiction' between *Perelandra* and *Out of the Silent Planet*: one that concerns Ransom's 'real' as opposed to his 'fictitious' name.

Many scholars and readers of C.S. Lewis's popular 'Ransom Trilogy' – *Out of the Silent Planet, Perelandra,* and *That Hideous Strength* – have probably wondered who the protagonist of all three books, Elwin Ransom, is supposed to represent, allegorically or otherwise. Because Ransom plays such a key role in all three books and a 'philological' C.S. Lewis often hinted throughout the narratives about 'meanings' regarding this central character's name, scholars and readers may have been right to wonder what the name 'Ransom' really means. This paper will set out to explore a 'philological' aspect of the name 'Ransom' in an attempt to give a derivation for Lewis's literary baptism of the main character in the celebrated trilogy. At the same time, as this paper outlines the hidden meanings of this curious name, these meanings will also be used to explain apparent 'contradictions' between *Perelandra* and *Out of the Silent Planet*: one that concerns Ransom's 'real' as opposed to his 'fictitious' name.

I   *Philology and Identity*

There is little doubt that Ransom is an archetypal 'saviour' in Lewis's *Space Trilogy*. Not only does he help 'save' Malacandra (Mars), Venus, and Earth, within the stories in question, but his actions are supplemented by many verbal descriptions of him as a 'saviour'. Particularly in Perelandra – a planet where he plays an instrumental part in saving the Venusian versions of 'Eve' (and indirectly 'Adam') from 'original sin' – he is portrayed and described as a type of 'Christ figure'. One of the many instances of Ransom as a 'Christ figure' is found in chapter eleven of *Perelandra*:

> As the Lady had said, the same wave never came twice. When Eve fell, God was not Man. He had not yet made men members of His body: since then He had, and through them henceforward He would save and suffer. One of the purposes for which He had done all this was to save Perelandra not through Himself but through Himself in Ransom.
> (Lewis 1989:274-275)

Ransom, then, appears to be an 'incarnation of God' – which the above quotation implies is very close to the 'incarnation' of the 'terrestrial' Jesus. This interesting passage, however, is soon followed by a much more informative and puzzling one:

> 'It is not for nothing that you are named Ransom,' said the Voice.
> And he knew that this was no fancy of his own. He knew it for a curious reason – because he had known for many years that his surname was derived not from *ransom* but from Ranolph's son. It would never have occurred to him thus to associate the two words. To connect the name Ransom with

> the act of ransoming would have been for him a mere pun. But even his voluble self did not now dare to suggest that the Voice was making a play upon words. All in a moment of time he perceived that what was, to human philologists, a mere accidental resemblance of two sounds was in truth no accident. (Lewis 1989:277)

The enigmas encountered in the above quotation are many. The Voice implies that the name 'Ransom' holds some hidden meaning which is important for the past, present, and future events in the stories. This, of course, is interesting enough. However, the rest of the passage appears to make very little sense given that 'Ransom' is not supposed to be the real name of the protagonist in any of the stories! In chapter twenty-two of *Out of the Silent Planet*, Lewis, the fictional character who supposedly wrote the novels, clearly states that the name Ransom was supposed to be a fictitious one within the story:

> Dr Ransom – and at this stage it will become obvious that that is not his real name – soon abandoned the idea of his Malacandrian dictionary and indeed all idea of communicating his story to the world. (Lewis 1989:136)

These last two quotations, while sounding extremely contradictory, (for in what sense could the whole idea of a pun on 'ransoming' be possible if the protagonist's name is not after all Ransom?) may nevertheless lead to a deeper understanding of the protagonist. So what did the Voice mean by insinuating that the name 'Ransom' meant something in addition to the idea, referred to by the narrator, that the pun was based on this character's name? In other words, what does the name 'Ransom' mean? And could this meaning allow Lewis to have his linguistic *Out of the Silent Planet* cake and in *Perelandra* eat it too?

A clue to what Lewis probably intended by this 'contradiction' may be found by analysing particular parts of the above quotation from *Perelandra*. (After all, few would think that Lewis was capable of committing such a gross literary error as forgetting this very important theme – the fictitious or 'real' status of Ransom's name). It must be remembered that Ransom provides his own partial explanation for the meaning of his own name. He thinks that the 'Voice' refers to Ransom as a variation of 'Ranolf's son'. For a fictional philologist this is not a bad guess, but for the real philologist, C.S. Lewis, this may be a clue to a much deeper and meaningful linguistic riddle.

One would think that if Ranolf's son had been intended as the 'roots' for Ransom, then some background may have been provided for the reader to begin to understand just who 'Ranolf' was, and how the name had changed to Ransom. However, even if these explanations had been furnished, the 'contradiction' regarding the fictitious name 'Ransom' and the supposed pun on 'ransoming' would remain. Thus, 'Ranolf's son' as an explanation may be partially helpful, but it does not make sense of the 'contradiction' between *Out of the Silent Planet* and *Perelandra*.

In addition, if Lewis did create another historical fictional character – Ranolf – then he might have been more linguistically consistent and called the new character 'Ramolf'. 'Ramolf's son' would still not have solved the puzzle regarding the 'ransoming' pun, but it may have accounted for the shift between the letters 'M' and 'N' needed in order to sidestep the linguistic problem of ending up with 'Ranolf's som'. However, if this is in fact a linguistic puzzle, then 'Ramolf's son' may have presented the careful reader with too easy a clue regarding the 'mystery' involved with the protagonist's name.

If the name provided by Lewis in his story had been 'Ramolf's son', then many might have noticed something quite important: 'Ramolf's son' shortened to ram-son, a descriptive name for a 'lamb'. (It must be noticed that if a ram is a 'male sheep' then by definition a 'ram-son' would have to be 'a lamb'.) A Ram-son, on the other hand, implies that what is at stake here is 'the Lamb', a metaphorical name for Christ. It is in this way that all of the different threads begin to weave themselves into the much more complex meaning implied by the Voice and by the rest of the narratives. The shift to the name 'Ramson' (i.e. 'the Lamb' or 'Christ') could easily have allowed Lewis to consider his character a 'ransom' or 'payment'. In this complex metaphor he would have been supported by many old linguistic and literary sources as outlined in two entries in *The Oxford English Dictionary*:

> Ransom, v. Forms: see the sb (also 4 rauncenen, 5 rampsoun, 6 ramsion, *Sc.* ransson; *pa. t.* 4 rauncede). [a. OF *ransonner, -conner*, etc. f. *ranson*: see prec.]
> 1. *trans.* To redeem (from captivity or punishment) [...]
> b. To redeem, deliver in religious sense.
> *a* 1300 *Cursor M. 9784 If godd had wroght another man For to ransun wit adam* [...].*1667* MILTON *P. L.* III 297 *His Brethren ransomd with his own dear life.* (Simpson & Weiner 1989:182)

Equally important for this paper is another definition of "ransom" found in the same dictionary:

> Ransom, *sb.* Forms: a. 3-4 ransum [...] 4-6 ramson [...] [a. OF *rançon, ran-, raunson, raencon, -son, ra(a)nceun, rampçon*, etc. (see Godef.): **re(d)empçon:*-L. *redemption-em*: see REDEMPTION. For the change of *-on* to *-om*, which appears quite early, cf. *randon*, RANDOM.] [...]
> b. *fig.*, in religious use, of Christ or His blood.
> *a* 1300 *Cursor M.* 21731 *On cros godd boght ur saul liues par-on he gaf him-seluen ranscun* [...] *1667 MILTON P.L.* x 61 *Sending thee...his Mediator...Both Ransom and Redeemer voluntarie.* (Simpson & Weiner 1989:181)

As both words 'ransom' and 'ramson' are variants of each other and both derive from the Latin *'redemption'*, the inconsistencies outlined above begin to disappear. Not only does this information produce more puns on the name 'Ransom' but it also helps to account for the pun directly referred to within the narrative. The word 'ramson' (i.e. 'the Lamb') both figuratively accounts for the reference to a ransom (payment) as well as etymologically accounting for the reference to Edwin Ransom being a 'redeemer'. This is in fact exactly how Ransom views himself when he realised that the 'Voice' belonged to another 'redeemer':

> 'My name also is Ransom,' said the Voice.
> It was some time before the purport of this saying dawned upon him. He whom the other worlds call Maleldil, was the world's ransom, his own ransom, well he knew. But to what purpose was it said now? Before the answer came to him he felt its insufferable approach and held out his arms before him as if could keep it from forcing open the door of his mind. But it came. So *that* was the real issue. If he now failed, this world also would hereafter be redeemed. If he were not the ransom, Another would be. Yet nothing was ever repeated. Not a second crucifixion: perhaps – who knows – not even a second Incarnation [...]
> (Lewis 1989:278)

Thus it appears that in Lewis's mind 'ranson', 'ren-soom', 'ram-son', and 'redeemer' are all interconnected, if not interchangeable. Some of this interconnectedness is again linguistically supported by approaching the problem not from the Ransom-Ramson direction but from Ramson-Ransom. *The Oxford English Dictionary* lists the following under the heading of Ramson:

> Ramson, obs. form of RANSOM
> (Simpson & Weiner 1989:163)

It is with the above types of linguistic 'switcheroos' that Lewis can remain consistent within his two narratives. Ransom is probably not the protagonist's 'real' or literal name within the stories, as outlined in *Out of the Silent Planet*: he is most likely named by the variant Ramson throughout the stories. And, as these two close sounding words are interchangeable, Lewis may consistently go on to imply in *Perelandra* that a pun or several puns exist. After all, both words – 'ransom' and 'ramson' – not only derive from the Latin 'redemption' but both at many levels (linguistic, allegorically, and historically/religiously) mean a particular type of event – a 'ransom'.[1] Thus, if Lewis had a genius for philology and the manipulation of words and meanings, this instance should probably count as one of his most impressive and subtle linguistic successes.[2]

It may be noticed that many other strands offered in the above dictionary definitions and quotations resonate with what is known of C.S. Lewis's linguistic knowledge and literary projects. If he did not encounter the derivation of Ransom from the Latin Redeemer in his youth, then he surely came across the reference in his constant studies of word changes or while working on Milton's *Paradise Lost*. It is well known that Lewis began his work on *Perelandra* soon after writing the 'Preface' to *Paradise Lost*, and that this work on Milton – who was another story teller concerned with cosmic 'good versus evil' narratives – heavily influenced Lewis's fictional narratives. Milton's phrase "Both Ransom and Redeemer voluntary" (Milton, *Book X*, 190) would have probably appealed to Lewis the philologist and twentieth-century writer concerned with 'cosmic battles'. Thus Milton's work may have played a much more important linguistic/symbolic role in Lewis's *Perelandra* than most scholars have thought probable.

When the above arguments are considered, it becomes easier to understand the character of Ransom, in a much deeper and richer form, in other segments of the trilogy. It helps to know that Ransom is also a Ramson or 'the Lamb'. In *Out of the Silent Planet* it is obvious that Weston and Devine view

---

[1] The fictitious name in the stories, Ransom, directly implies a 'ransom'. On the other hand, the name 'Ramson' linguistically (as shown in *The Oxford English Dictionary*), allegorically (as implied by the connection between Ransom and the 'ransom-of Jesus'), and historically/religiously ('the Lamb' has for centuries been a symbol for a sacrifice and a 'ransoming of Humanity') all mean a 'ransom'.

[2] An interesting idea of Lewis's theory of synonymy may be gathered from C.S. Lewis *Surprised by Joy* (Lewis 1977:115). Here Lewis explains that the Greek word 'naus', the Latin word 'navis' do not mean the English word 'ship' but that all these words mean an 'object' (and that they are supposed to conjure up "a Picture of a dark slender mass with sail or oars, climbing the ridges, with no officious English word intruding"). Therefore, in the case of Ransom, Ramson, etc., all these words, for Lewis, may be meant to conjure up a 'god/man who is sacrificed', or perhaps a 'bleeding, willing sufferer redeemer, sacrificed in some cosmic 'good-evil struggle'.'

Ransom as a "sacrifice" or a type of "sacrificial lamb" (Lewis 1989:28). Later on in the story, Ransom himself thinks that he will be a "sacrifice" and a "victim" (Lewis 1989:29). This opinion does not change until he meets Oyarsa who pronounces that Ransom is a "copy of Maleldil" and will not be sacrificed in Malacandra (Lewis 1989:106-108). And, from what has been presented thus far, it may be quite easy to argue that Ransom as Ramson is indeed "a copy of Maleldil."[3]

There are too many examples of Ransom as a Christ figure within all three books to present here, so that only a few more of the 'highlights' will be given. In *Perelandra,* Ransom is continually spoken of as being "in the body of Christ":

> 'Look on him, beloved, and love him,' said the first. 'He is indeed but breathing dust and a careless touch would unmake him. And in his best thoughts there are such things mingled as, if we thought them, our light would perish. But he is in the body of Maleldil and his sins are forgiven. His very name in his own tongue is Elwin, the friend of the eldila.'[4] (Lewis 1989:322)

---

[3] Interestingly by reversing the name Maleldil, one arrives at a curious name 'lidle lam' which may be, among other things, a curious dialect version of 'little lamb' or nothing at all. Given that Ransom is a philologist and that in *That Hideous Strength* the reader is told that he wrote a book titled *Dialect and Semantics* it may prove useful to further pursue the dialectal reading of Maleldil. *The English Dialect Dictionary* lists the word 'lam' (used at least in Scotland) as a variant of 'lamb' (Wright 1970, vol. III, 510). A close variant of 'lidle' (i.e. 'liddle') is also found in the same dictionary for the word 'little' (Wright 1970, vol. III, 626). This or similar readings, while not being very convincing, may allow Lewis to escape the theological problems associated with naming both 'God' and 'Jesus' with the prefix 'mal' – and all of the well known 'bad' or 'evil' connotations associated with this prefix.

[4] There may be further allusion to meaning in Ransom's given name, Elwin, which Lewis may have developed in *That Hideous Strength. The Century Dictionary* lists only one famous Elwin who was "Born probably in 585: died 633. King of Northumbria 617-633, son of King Ella of Deira. He was the fifth Bretwalda, and his overlordship extended over all Teutonic Britain except Kent. He was defeated and slain in the battle of Heathfield in 633 by the rebellious Mercians under Penda in alliance with Cadwall of Wales. During his reign Christianity was introduced into Northumbria." (Smith 1906:353)

The King of Perelandra, whom Ransom met near the end of the book, also appears as another (type of) Christlike figure and this seems once again to allow for the possibility of multiple 'incarnations' or the propagation of 'lambs':

> It was hard even for Ransom to tell me of the King's face. But we dare not withhold the truth. It was that face which no man can say he does not know. You might ask how it was possible to look upon it and not commit idolatry, not to mistake it for that of which it was the likeness. For the resemblance was, in its own fashion, infinite, so that almost you could wonder at finding no sorrows in his brow and no wounds in his hands and feet.
> (Lewis 1989:332)

It is this same King along with his 'wife', who end Ransom's adventures on the planet Perelandra (and the book) with a direct reference to Ransom being their Saviour:

> 'Farewell, Friend and Saviour, farewell,' said both voices. 'Farewell till we three pass out of the dimensions of time. Speak of us always to Maleldil as we speak always of you. The splendour, the love, and the strength be upon you.'
> Then came the great cumbrous noise of the lid being fastened on above him. Then, for a few seconds, noises without, in the world from which he was eternally divided. Then his consciousness was engulfed.
> (Lewis 1989:348)

II New Identity

In *That Hideous Strength* the allusions to the Ransom/Ramson/Saviour/Jesus connection are played down while an attempt is made to refer to Ransom as the 'Director'. Considering all the arguments for the meaning of the name

'Ransom', one would expect that as the name changes so would the characteristics of the man that shed it. In the last book of the trilogy the reader is directly told by MacPhee that the protagonist *was* a philologist and is no longer known as Ransom:

> 'I should premise at the outset, Mrs Studdock,' he said, 'that I have known the Director for a great many years and that for most of his life he was a philologist. I'm not just satisfied myself that philology can be regarded as an exact science, but I mention the fact as a testimony to his general intellectual capacity. And, not to forejudge any issue, I will not say, as I would in ordinary conversation, that he has always been a man of what you might call an imaginative turn. His original name was Ransom.'
> (Lewis 1989:545)

With the change of 'promotion' to the position of 'Director' in *That Hideous Strength*, Ransom takes on an administrative and advisory role while turning his back on the 'hands-on' approach of the first two books. In order to make part of this 'Ransom' to 'Director' transition clear, it may be helpful to see how Lewis may have understood this latter word:

> Director [...] [a. AF. *directour* = F. *directeur*, ad. L. *director, agent-n. from *dirigére* to direct.]
> 1.a. One who or that which directs, rules, or guides; a guide, a conductor; 'one that has authority over others; a superintendent; one that has the general management of a design or work' (J) [...].
> b. *spec.* A member of a board appointed to direct or manage the affairs of a commercial corporation or company [...]
> d. *Eccl.* (chiefly in *R.C.Ch.*) An ecclesiastic holding the position of spiritual adviser to some particular person or society. (Simpson & Weiner 1989:700)

So, once again, at least on a superficial level, the 'meaning' of his name or title appears to dictate the protagonist's character and his actions. While there is an attempt by Lewis to change 'Ransom' into 'The Director' this does not appear to be a demotion in rank. The Director is presented as a type of 'God' who continually suffers and bleeds while leading forces of good against those of evil. And while in the last book there is an attempt to describe Ransom as a type of King Arthur/Kingfisher figure, his 'Saviour/Jesus' qualities are hard to suppress.[5] It must be remembered that upon first meeting Ransom, Jane Studdock had what some might call a 'religious experience' – one probably not warranted by merely meeting a 'terrestrial' King:

> Jane looked; and instantly her world was unmade.
> On a sofa before her, with one foot bandaged as if he had a wound, lay what appeared to be a boy, twenty years old. [...] all the light in the room seemed to run towards the gold hair and the gold beard of the wounded man. [...]
> Pain came and went in his face: sudden jabs of sickening and burning pain. [...] How could she have thought him young? Or old either? It came over her, with a sensation of quick fear, that his face was of no age at all. (Lewis 1989:494-95)

From this moment on in the narrative, the reader is reminded of Ransom's supernatural 'agelessness' or immortal nature and the pain he must suffer throughout the story. Ransom's 'immortal-man' status is discussed in a curious conversation between Camilla and Jane:

---

[5] The idea that Ransom/Ramson is a type of King Arthur figure is neither supported by the first two books of the trilogy nor is this aspect of Ransom very convincing in *That Hideous Strength*. Jane Studdock not only appears to be the only one who directly makes this Ransom/Arthur connection but the only eye-witness, Merlin, who is in a position to identify Ransom as Arthur, fails to do so. Therfore, while there are implied similarities between Ransom and King Arthur, these appear to be a late and undeveloped afterthought in the trilogy.

> 'How does Mr MacPhee explain the Director's age?'
>
> 'You mean his looking – or being- so young – if you call it young? That is what people are like who come back from the stars. Or at least from Perelandra. Paradise is still going on there; make him tell you about it some time. He will never grow a year or a month older again.'
>
> 'Will he die?'
>
> 'He will be taken away, I believe. Back into Deep Heaven. It has happened to one or two people, perhaps about six, since the world began.'
>
> 'Camilla!'
>
> 'Yes.'
>
> 'What – what *is* he?'
>
> 'He's a man, my dear.'
>
> (Lewis 1989:550-51)

It must be noted that these claims of Camilla's imply (by the statement "[...] make him tell you about it some time") that these stories originated with Ransom's own telling of past events. He, himself, appears to claim to be 'god-like', or at least an immortal man. This 'immortal-man' status for Ransom and the power that comes with the title is apparent in many parts of *That Hideous Strength*. Ransom not only tells his followers the story of his adventures in 'Deep Heaven', his cavorting with very powerful supernatural agents, but he is also the self (God?) appointed leader in the supernatural battle in England (the world?) against 'evil'. The Director appears to be very aware of his own importance as he chauvinistically calls the very important 'seer' (Jane Studdock) 'child' and is quite willing to be obeyed in his own right! In a crucial moment in the action of the story the following curious exchange is found between Jane and Ransom:

> 'Do you place yourself in the obedience,' said the Director, 'in obedience to Maleldil?'
>
> 'Sir,' said Jane, 'I know nothing of Maleldil. But I place myself in obedience to you.'
>
> 'It is enough for the present,' said the Director. 'This is the courtesy of Deep Heaven: that when

> you mean well, He always takes you to have meant better than you knew. It will not be enough for always. He is very jealous. He will have you for no one but Himself in the end. But for tonight, it is enough.' (Lewis 1989:588)

Later on, as though going back to the old Ransom/Ramson meaning, the reader learns that the choice to endure pain is his own, as alleviatives were apparently on hand when he patronisingly tells Merlin:

> 'No,' said the director. 'God's glory, do you think you were dug out of the earth to give me a plaster for my heel? We have drugs that could cheat the pain as well as your Earth-magic or better, if it were not my business to bear it to the end.'
> (Lewis 1989:650)

From the above quotations it is clear that the Director is a 'man' who does not age, will not die, and, like a select group of prophets, will be carried directly, body and all, to (Deep) Heaven. It is also clear that the Director can vicariously take on God's authority and sees his pain as a duty. Given all of these 'Christ-like' characteristics near the end of *That Hideous Strength*, it is interesting to note that Lewis still reserved a surprise for his readers. The Director, while explaining the nature of the cosmic war, speaks as though he will finally fulfil his sacrificial role as 'Ransom/Lamb', given that Weston had already fulfilled the role of Judas:

> 'And so the wicked man had brought about, even as I have become a bridge,' said Ransom. 'Sir,' said Merlin, 'what will come of this? If they put forth their power, they will unmake all Middle Earth. Judas brought about the thing he least intended. For now there was one man in the world – even myself – who was known to the Oyeresu and spoke their tongue, [...]. Our enemies had taken away from themselves the protection of the Seventh Law. They had broken by natural philosophy the barrier which

> God of His own power would not break. [...] And that is why Powers of Heaven have come down to this house, and in this chamber where we are now discoursing Malacandra and Perelandra have spoken to me.'
>
> Merlin's face became a little paler. The bear nosed at his hand, unnoticed.
>
> 'Their naked power, yes,' said Ransom. 'That is why they will work only through a man.'
> (Lewis 1989:653)

However much this may sound like the old Ransom is finally going to fulfil his role as a 'Ransom/Redeemer', this is not to be the case. Who the sacrificial victim is to be and the interesting reasons for this choice are explained as the above conversation continues between Merlin and the Director:

> The magician drew one large hand across his forehead.
>
> 'Through a man whose mind is opened to be so invaded,' said Ransom, 'one who by his own will once opened it. I take Our Fair Lord to witness that if it were my task, I would not refuse it. But He will not suffer a mind that still has its virginity to be so violated. And through a black magician's mind their purity neither can nor will operate. One who has dabbled [...] in the days when dabbling had not begun to be evil, or it was just beginning [...] and also a Christian man and a penitent. A tool (I must speak plainly) good enough to be so used and not too good. In all these Western parts of the world there was only one man who had lived in those days and could still be recalled. You –.'
> (Lewis 1989:653-654)

Thus, while Ransom is a Christlike figure, in many respects he appears to have more in common with the angels of Revelation (and in particular perhaps the Archangel Gabriel) than with the New Testament 'God of love', 'the Redeemer', 'the Lamb'. Near the end of *That Hideous Strength*, Ransom/Ramson –

as 'the Director' – appears to have risen in status: he is not only much less humble ('too good' to be sacrificed) but his callousness and perhaps hypocrisy continues when Merlin reacts 'badly' to the 'cosmic plans' – plans that characterize Merlin as merely possessing a mind that is not 'virginal', is ready to be 'violated', and is an 'impure tool' that was recalled only to be forced to perform a suicide mission.

> He stopped, shocked at what was happening. The huge man had risen from his chair, and stood towering over him. From his horribly opened mouth there came a yell that seemed to Ransom utterly bestial, though it was in fact only a yell of primitive Celtic lamentation. It was horrifying to see that withered and bearded face all blubbered with undisguised tears like a child. All the Roman surface in Merlinus had been scraped off. He had become a shameless, archaic monstrosity babbling out entreaties in a mixture of what sounded like Welsh and what sounded like Spanish.
> 'Silence,' shouted Ransom, 'Sit down. You put us both to shame.' (Lewis 1989:654)

It appears that Ransom (and the narrator) is not only willing to sacrifice Merlin but that he also expects the latter to 'keep a stiff upper lip.' And even though Merlin may have just been damned to a horrid death, if not eternal suffering, the Director has little patience or understanding for his plight. Thus, it appears that it was not only Merlin's actions and words that put them "both to shame"!

If a serious inconsistency is present in *The Cosmic Trilogy*, it is found in the development of the main character in *That Hideous Strength* and not in the outright contradiction between *Out of the Silent Planet* and *Perelandra*. By the end, Ransom has ceased to be a sacrificial 'Ram-son' and has almost become a cold, pragmatic 'Director' – a defied 'man' willing to see another sacrificed. Therefore, if there has been a change in Ransom's personality, it appears to have been for the worse. Perhaps by the end Ransom had finally become a victim.

A victim, not as an external sacrifice at the hands of the powerful, but a victim at the hands of power itself. Ransom as the Director may have fallen prey to the 'worm' – that hideous Strength – that gnaws at human souls, a process encapsulated in the maxim 'Power tends to corrupt and absolute power corrupts absolutely.'

III   Conclusion

> [...] It even occurred to him that the distinction between history and mythology might be itself meaningless outside the Earth [...]
> Long since on Mars, and more strongly since he came to Perelandra, Ransom had been perceiving that the triple distinction of truth from myth and of both from fact was purely terrestrial.
> (Lewis 1989:129, 273-274)

This article set out to provide enough examples to support the thesis that the name Ransom, as implied by Lewis, is very meaningful in *The Cosmic Trilogy*. Several interesting, and hopefully helpful, meanings were presented to support this reading of Ransom/Ramson while an attempt was made to solve what appeared to be gross literary inconsistency between *Out of the Silent Planet* and *Perelandra*. These examples and the 'unifying theory' were also supported by the available biographical data on the life, interests, and works of C.S. Lewis. Thus, many streams appear to converge into the name of the philologist, Ransom, giving this character a much more solid role and direct meaning within the trilogy. That Ransom is a Christlike figure few would have disputed. However, just how deep the connection is between Ransom/Ramson and Christ or 'the Lamb' few, we think, would have surmised. And even though it seems Lewis attempted to change Ransom to the Director in the last book of the trilogy, the protagonist could not easily shed the 'Christ-like' redeemer persona buried deeply within the stories and inside his very name. In this 'hiding' of Ransom's 'true name', Lewis may have followed the old superstitious traditions of keeping God's name(s) secret as stated or implied in several parts of the Bible (eg. Exodus 3:13-15) and that a name fully describes an entity's attributes. Either way, Lewis, as it has been argued, hid the meaning of the name Ransom in the trilogy and once this 'Ransom' became 'The Director', his attributes predictably changed with the name. However, whether this change in name and attributes was a success, remains for the reader to decide.

Biographical Notes

Marta García de la Puerta is Senior Lecturer in English Literature at the University of Vigo (Spain). She got her Ph.D. with a dissertation on C.S. Lewis' secondary worlds. She published and contributed several chapters and essays on C.S. Lewis, J.R.R. Tolkien and children's literature. Her current research interests focus on children's fantasy literature and on the relationship between cartography and fantasy in the work of C.S. Lewis, J.R.R. Tolkien and other major fantasy writers.

Fernando J. Soto is trained in Philosophy (B.A. and M.A.) and is currently finishing a Ph.D. in English Literature at the University of Glasgow. He has presented and published extensively on Lewis Carroll, George MacDonald, and C. S. Lewis. He has edited a book on Carroll (*Reflections on Lewis Carroll*). He has also edited *North Wind: A Journal of George MacDonald Studies* and currently co-edits this journal. His work has appeared in *Studies in Scottish Literature*, *Inklings*, *The Carrollian*, while one of his articles was translated into Russian, to serve as an introduction to *Phantastes*. His latest work will appear as a chapter in a book commemorating the centenary of MacDonald's death, *George MacDonald: Literary Heritage and Heirs*.

Bibliography

Lewis, Clive Staples, 1977, *Surprised by Joy*, London: HarperCollins.
---, 1989, *The Cosmic Trilogy: Out of the Silent Planet. Perelandra. That Hideous Strength*, London: Pan Books.
Milton, John, 1985, *Paradise Lost* in *Milton: Poems*, (selected by Laurence D. Lerner), London: Penguin, 99-234.
Simpson, John A. and Edmund S.C. Weiner (eds.), 1989, *The Oxford English Dictionary*, Oxford: Clarendon Press.
Smith, Benjamin (ed.), 1906, *The Century Dictionary*, New York: Century.
Wright, Joseph (ed.), 1970, *The English Dialect Dictionary*, Oxford: Oxford University Press.

'As Under a Green Sea':
Visions of War in the Dead Marshes[1]

JOHN GARTH

Abstract

J.R.R. Tolkien's letters to his son Christopher during the writing of Book Four of *The Lord of the Rings* in 1944 make it possible, as nowhere else, to scrutinise the early stages of its composition in the context of the author's contemporaneous experiences. Such an analysis reveals that, contrary to allegations of escapism, Tolkien's writing reflected or refracted day-to-day concerns in his life and the world around him. Scrutiny of 'The Passage of the Marshes' uncovers the shaping influence of Tolkien's feelings about the Second World War, then raging, and the First, memories of which had been newly stirred by a visit to his Birmingham school. The chapter is revealed as a mature literary product of the trench experience to rival the work of canonical First World War writers such as Siegfried Sassoon and Wilfred Owen.

At the start of April 1944, the sequel to *The Hobbit* had languished untouched for more than a year, with Isengard overthrown but Frodo and Sam still only a page into their journey alone to Mordor. Tolkien had been 'dead stuck'. Then, urged on by his friend C.S. Lewis, he resumed work.[2]

---

[1] This paper is a slight enlargement of one delivered at the *Tolkien 2005* Conference at Aston University, Birmingham, August 2005, to be published in *The Ring Goes Ever On: Proceedings of the 2005 Tolkien Conference*, edited by Sarah Wells (The Tolkien Society, forthcoming). It appears here with the kind permission of the Tolkien Society of Great Britain. Parts have previously appeared in other forms, in Italian in 'Tolkien e la Grande Guerra: "orrore animalesco" nella Terra di Mezzo,' in *Mitopoiesi: Fantasia e storia in Tolkien*, edited by Franco Manni (Brescia: Comune di Brescia/Grafo, 2005), and in English in 'Frodo and the Great War', in *The Lord of the Rings, 1954–2004: Scholarship in Honor of Richard E. Blackwelder*, edited by Wayne G. Hammond and Christina Scull (Milwaukee: Marquette University Press, 2006).

[2] J.R.R. Tolkien to Jane Neave, 8–9 September 1962 (*Letters* 321); J.R.R. Tolkien to Christopher Tolkien, 30 March 1944 (*Letters* 79).

This was typical of their friendship: when from time to time Tolkien lost creative momentum, Lewis provided the push he needed to get going again. Since they first met in 1926, Lewis had helped Tolkien forge ahead with his extended narrative poem, 'The Lay of Leithian'; he had listened to *The Hobbit* as a work in progress; a mutual pact to write science-fiction thrillers had produced Lewis's *Out of the Silent Planet* and Tolkien's abortive 'The Lost Road'; and for the past few years Tolkien had been reading his *Hobbit* sequel to their informal literary club, the Inklings. While Lewis's brisk encouragement could not rescue all of Tolkien's projects from incompletion and obscurity, it is entirely plausible that without him *The Lord of the Rings* would never have reached publication. The evidence from Tolkien's letters of 1944 appears plain: Lewis provided the necessary shove at the end of March, and Book Four then poured out in the space of less than two months. What began with a struggle to overcome writer's block very quickly became a damburst of creativity.[3]

Yet such was the speed, facility and power of Tolkien's writing that even the forceful Lewis cannot be wholly to blame. Focusing closely on a single chapter, 'The Passage of the Marshes', I hope to demonstrate that Tolkien was tapping into a huge reservoir of personal experience, and profound feelings long suppressed. For Book Four contains an unprecedented agglomeration of memories from the Great War, as we shall see. And although Tolkien himself did not perhaps recognise the incident's catalytic effect, I would argue that a disturbing experience that he recorded in a letter at the start of April 1944 brought these memories of the last war flooding back.

Before he forced himself back to the writing desk at Lewis's urging, Tolkien took the train from Oxford to Birmingham, the home town of his childhood, for a reunion of Old Boys from King Edward's School on 1 April. War had been raging across the globe for almost five years, and Tolkien felt that he had been "born in a dark age out of due time" blighted not only by

---

[3] *War of the Ring* 77-78, 183-184.

bombs but by state control, heavy industry, and faceless modernism.[4] He found Birmingham a sad reflection of its former self, as he told his son Christopher in the letter in question, written on 3 April:

> Except for one patch of ghastly wreckage (opp[osite] my old school's site) it does not look much damaged: not by the enemy. The chief damage has been the growth of grey flat featureless modern buildings. The worst of all is the ghastly multiple-store erection on the old site.[5]

A parade of shops had been flattened in an air-raid on 9 October 1941. But the old King Edward's School opposite, an early and pre-eminent example of Victorian Gothic, had been demolished by developers, who had put up a modern shopping complex in its place.[6] "I couldn't stand much of that," Tolkien told Christopher, "or the ghosts that rose from the pavements." He headed swiftly out of the city centre for the new school site in Edgbaston.

It would be quite wrong to assume that by 'ghosts' Tolkien meant simply the memories of old friends whom he had not seen for years because of the usual mundane vagaries of life and shifting circumstance. The loss that Birmingham represented for him was also literally a bereavement, brought on by multiple deaths, brutal and tragic.

As a boy he had thrown himself into school life with great vigour and staked a great deal on his friendships with a remarkable, brilliant and hilarious circle – most notably Rob Gilson, Christopher Wiseman and Geoffrey Bache Smith, core members of a clique calling themselves the T.C.B.S. When Tolkien left what he had once called "giddy old Brum" for Oxford University in 1911 he had felt "like a young sparrow kicked out of a high nest."[7] The T.C.B.S. had

---

[4] J.R.R. Tolkien to Christopher Tolkien, 29 November 1943 (*Letters* 64).

[5] J.R.R. Tolkien to Christopher Tolkien, 3 April 1944 (*Letters* 70).

[6] Trott (1992:55-7).

[7] Christopher Wiseman to J.R.R. Tolkien, 16 November 1916, cited in *Great War*, Garth (2003:206). *Biography* 49.

gone on to provide the first audience for Middle-earth, reading Tolkien's early poetry and prompting him to publish.[8] For Tolkien, the Inklings was heir to the T.C.B.S., and as literary motivator C.S. Lewis wore the mantle first assumed by Wiseman, Smith and Gilson.

Tolkien had last returned to Birmingham for any significant period for a few weeks at the end of 1916, in circumstances he could never have foreseen – as an army officer back from the Battle of the Somme in northern France to be treated for trench fever. By that time, the gentle, sociable and artistic Rob Gilson was dead, killed in No Man's Land on the first day of the Somme. As Tolkien lay in the temporary wartime hospital in December 1916, their intense, witty poet friend G.B. Smith died of gas gangrene after being caught in a shellburst miles from the front line. Of the eight or so who had belonged at various times to the T.C.B.S., two other members died in the Great War, and in all, 243 former King Edward's pupils were killed.[9]

By 1925 Tolkien had drifted apart from Christopher Wiseman – their intense friendship perhaps overshadowed by grief for the deaths of their friends. Priscilla Tolkien remembers being taken in the 1930s to see Smith's mother in Birmingham, by then blind and still mourning the loss of two sons in the war.[10] But the reunion of Old Edwardians – to view the new school buildings – appears to have been an unprecedented event, and therefore a potent one. As Tolkien commented, 1 April 1944 was a "memorable day".[11]

I don't intend to argue that Tolkien saw real ghosts on 1 April 1944, or even that he necessarily thought he did. The vivid image of figures rising from the pavements may be no more than a turn of phrase. Tolkien, perhaps, saw

---

[8] Tolkien's collection of verse, *The Trumpets of Faërie*, was rejected by Sidgwick & Jackson in May 1916; Priestman (1992:30). See also Garth (2003, especially 118-119).

[9] For Gilson and Smith's deaths, see Garth (2003:154-156, 211-212.) The two other T.C.B.S. fatalities were Ralph Stuart Payton (1894-1916) and Thomas Kenneth Barnsley (1891-1917); Garth (2003:182-183, 250).

[10] *Family Album* (John and Priscilla Tolkien 1992:41). Smith's brother Roger was killed in Basra, Mesopotamia, in January 1917; see Garth (2003:233).

[11] J.R.R. Tolkien to Christopher Tolkien, 3 April 1944 (*Letters* 69).

nothing more than 1944 Birmingham, but remembered the city half a lifetime earlier so sharply that it put him in mind of a haunting. Yet the distress was enough to drive him from the city centre, and perhaps the haunting did seem to be present before his eyes, whether we interpret it as a trick played by nostalgia, an after-image imprinted by the trauma of war, or something more.

A few months later Tolkien wrote to his son Christopher about "a sudden vision (or perhaps apperception which at once turned itself into pictorial form in my mind) [...] not long ago when spending half an hour in St Gregory's before the Blessed Sacrament" in which he had seen a human soul suspended as a mote of light in a ray of the Light of God. The ray was his guardian angel, "God's very attention itself, personalized," he said, emphatic that this was to be taken literally:

> I do not mean 'personified', by a mere figure of speech according to the tendencies of human language, but a real (finite) person. The whole thing was very immediate, and not recapturable in clumsy language.[12]

The specificity of the scene he described from the day of the Birmingham reunion suggests that those ghosts rising from the pavements may likewise have been more than a figure of speech. Tolkien's imagination, or his perception, was sometimes indistinguishable from vision. However that may be, it is a striking fact that within three weeks of this incident he had written his account of the passage of the Dead Marshes, in which visions of those long dead haunt the traveller.

Notes, outlines and an abortive opening were all Tolkien had for what became Book Four. Of all the gaps in the writing of his epic, it is at this point that he had been "longest held up – by exterior circumstances as well as interior," he

---

[12] J.R.R. Tolkien to Christopher Tolkien, 7-8 November 1944 (*Letters* 99).

said later.[13] Nothing had been written – except, it seems, his short story, *Leaf by Niggle*, about an unrecognised work of art left unfinished upon the death of its creator. "It arose from my own pre-occupation with *The Lord of the Rings*, the knowledge that it would be finished in great detail or not at all, and the fear (near certainty) that it would be 'not at all'. The war had arisen to darken every horizon."[14]

The Second World War had caught up his sons just as the First had caught Tolkien and his former schoolfriends in their youth. Michael Tolkien had been involved in the defence of aerodromes in the Battle of Britain, and had acted as an anti-aircraft gunner.[15] But by the end of 1943 he had been rendered unfit for service by "severe shock to nervous system due to prolonged exposure to enemy action," as the official papers put it, or shell shock as his father's generation knew it.[16] Meanwhile Christopher Tolkien had also been called up to the Royal Air Force and, in January 1944, had been whisked away to South Africa to train as a fighter pilot.[17] And the war had brought Tolkien *senior* his own official responsibilities, in the firewatching service and as an air-raid warden, entailing regular nights manning a small, damp hut in north Oxford that served as an air-raid station.[18] The war also placed additional domestic and academic burdens on Tolkien. Meanwhile, royalties from *The Hobbit*, published to great success in 1937, had effectively stopped when a

---

[13] J.R.R. Tolkien to Caroline Everett, 24 June 1957 (*Letters* 259).

[14] J.R.R. Tolkien to Stanley Unwin, *c.* March 1945 (*Letters* 113), in which he said *Leaf by Niggle* had been written "more than 2 years ago." In a letter to his aunt Jane Neave, 8–9 September 1962 (*Letters* 321), Tolkien placed it in the hiatus after Book Three of *The Lord of the Rings*; but in the same letter he also claims that the short story was written before the war.

[15] *Family Album* (John and Priscilla Tolkien 1992:65, 71); *Biography* 193.

[16] J.R.R. Tolkien to Stanley Unwin, 29 June 1944 (*Letters* 86, and note, 439). Michael Tolkien became a 2nd lieutenant in the Devonshire Regiment on 2 August 1941 and relinquished his commission on the grounds of ill-health on 31 December 1942, when he was granted the rank of lieutenant (*London Gazette*, 15 August 1941 and 1 January 1943).

[17] Even training for the priesthood had not entirely protected J.R.R. Tolkien's eldest son, John, from the international disaster of 1939, when he had been forced to flee across France from the Vatican.

[18] *Family Album* (John and Priscilla Tolkien 1992:71); *Biography* 193.

bomb destroyed all the remaining unbound stock; Tolkien confessed to his publisher that he was in debt.[19]

Looking back at his creative output since the previous war must have been sobering. Middle-earth had been brewing since 1915, but its sole substantial public expression had been *The Hobbit*, a story for children which barely hinted at his deeper vision. The results of his mid-1930s science-fiction pact with Lewis had underlined his own inability to finish projects: 'The Lost Road' had been shelved, unfinished, but *Out of the Silent Planet* had been published in 1938, and now its sequel, *Perelandra*, had come out in 1943, the year that Lewis also produced *Christian Behaviour*, based on his increasingly popular radio broadcasts. Also in 1943, fellow Inkling Charles Williams published *The Figure of Beatrice*, his book on Dante and Romantic theology, and read to the Inklings chapters from a new gothic thriller he was writing, *All Hallows' Eve*. Williams's star was in the ascendant: in November, all but one member of Tolkien's audience at a lecture on Anglo-Saxon had defected to pack out Williams's lecture on *Hamlet*.[20] Tolkien marked the publication of *The Figure of Beatrice* with a clerihew:

> The sales of Charles Williams
> Leapt up by millions,
> When a reviewer surmised
> He was only Lewis disguised.
> (Carpenter 1978:187)

All this was a great exaggeration of Williams's success, and of Lewis's. Furthermore, it was meant to be light-hearted. Yet Tolkien's chagrin at the productivity of his two closest friends is palpable.

A letter to Christopher in December 1943 gives a flavour of Tolkien's despondency and lack of inspiration among such circumstances: "Life has been such a rush [...] I haven't seen C.S. L[ewis] for weeks or [Charles]

---

[19] Unwin (1998:77). The bombing took place on 7 November 1940.
[20] Duriez and Porter (2001:13).

Williams. [...] The daily round(s) and the common task ++ which furnish so much more than one actually asks. No great fun, no amusements; no bright new idea; not even a thin small joke."[21] As to *The Lord of the Rings*, he recalled later, "Foresight had failed and there was no time for thought." (*LotR* xv)

In the days immediately after the Birmingham visit, however, Tolkien forced himself to tackle Frodo and Sam's journey to Mordor. With a tiny cast and a single linear journey, this was a less daunting task than the tangle of events in Rohan and Gondor. Tolkien wanted, perhaps, to have something to send for Christopher to read, and in the event that is just how Book Four emerged, in instalments despatched to South Africa. At the start of April he was also in the middle of the Easter vacation, freed from many duties. Furthermore, C.S. Lewis was pressing him to resume his task. "I needed some pressure, and shall probably respond," Tolkien said on 30 March, just before the King Edward's reunion.[22]

Tolkien planned to reach the gate of Mordor in a single chapter.[23] "I have begun to nibble at Hobbit again," he wrote on 3 April in the letter to Christopher in which he recounted the Birmingham reunion. "I have started to do some (painful) work on the chapter which picks up the adventures of Frodo and Sam again."[24] He could not overemphasise the effort: "It is a painful sticky business getting into swing again," he wrote two days later. "A few pages for a lot of sweat."[25] But he was able to read the first chapter, 'The Taming of Sméagol', to Lewis and Williams on 12 April.

By that time, he had begun the next, 'The Passage of the Marshes', and had "brought Frodo nearly to the gates of Mordor." In little more than a single week, after initial rough drafting at great speed, he wrote the chapter virtu-

---

[21] J.R.R. Tolkien to Christopher Tolkien, 9 December 1943 (*Letters* 65).

[22] J.R.R. Tolkien to Christopher Tolkien, 30 March 1944 (*Letters* 68).

[23] *War of the Ring* 104.

[24] J.R.R. Tolkien to Christopher Tolkien, 3 April 1944 (*Letters* 70); cf. *War of the Ring* 77-78.

[25] J.R.R. Tolkien to Christopher Tolkien, 5 April 1944 (*Letters* 70).

ally as it stands in the published version, declaring it "practically finished" on 18 April and reading it to Lewis and Williams the next morning.[26]

The marshes, and their dead, existed in outlines and notes long before April 1944. In the original version of the Council of Elrond, written seemingly in late 1939, just after the outbreak of the Second World War, it is said that Gollum had "wandered southwards, through Fangorn Forest, and past the Dead Marshes, until he himself had been caught and imprisoned by the Dark Lord."[27] Notes from a couple of years later, when Tolkien was about to take the Fellowship beyond Balin's tomb for the first time, show he planned to have Gollum guide Frodo and Sam in the marshes: "They make him lead them through the Dead Marshes. (Green faces in the pools.) Lithlad Plain of Ash. The Searching Eye of Barad-dûr."[28] At some point in 1941 or 1942 Tolkien had actually started Chapter One of Book Four, though it "hardly got beyond Sam's opening words," as he later told a correspondent.[29] This scrap of a chapter revealed, however, that the air from the Dead Marshes "seemed heavy with a stench of cold decay and rottenness."[30]

In the complete chapter Tolkien wrote in April 1944, the stench engulfs the hobbits as soon as they enter the Dead Marshes. After they have passed the very heart of the marshes, there is a renewed emphasis: "Often they floundered, stepping or falling hands-first into waters as noisome as a cesspool, till they were slimed and fouled almost up to their necks and stank in one another's nostrils" (*LotR* 614). This 'cesspool' comparison, together with a reference to the 'greasy' surface scurf on the pools, may be the only vestige of an impulse, preserved among notes, to "describe the pools as they get nearer

---

[26] *War of the Ring* 94-5, 104, 107; J.R.R. Tolkien to Christopher Tolkien, 13 April 1944 (*Letters* 71); J.R.R. Tolkien to Christopher Tolkien, 23 April 1944 (*Letters* 73).

[27] *Return* 401.

[28] *Treason* 208.

[29] J.R.R. Tolkien to Caroline Everett, 24 June 1957 (*Letters* 259).

[30] *War of the Ring* 85.

Mordor as like green pools and rivers fouled by modern chemical works."[31] This authorial memo at least proves that Tolkien consciously drew upon the modern world for creative fuel, and was not (as some critics have painted him) some cyclops with his eye fixed only on the past; however, in actual drafts and in the published chapter the industrial parallel is barely communicated, if at all. At the outset, the source of the smell seems obviously natural – a vast exhalation of organic gases from the vegetable decomposition of the stagnant pools and the "dead grasses and rotting reeds" that surround them (*LotR* 612). The mud gurgles as the travellers tread in it; when Sam falls flat on his face, so that his hands sink deep into the mud, there is a hiss as "a noisome smell" goes up (*LotR* 613).

In nature, the decomposition of dead things performs an essential, if frequently malodorous, task in feeding the life that comes after it. But the Dead Marshes are stagnant in a larger sense: all the plant-life is sick or dying where it stands in endless decomposition. "Cold clammy winter" persists into March and, seen through the mist the reeds stand perpetually rotting "like ragged shadows of long-forgotten summers" (*LotR* 612): paradoxical memories of something unremembered. There is only a mockery of regeneration; the seed-plumes are empty. Only primitive forms such as a livid algae eke out a parasitic or vampiric life here, "leprous growths that feed on rottenness." The sole animal inhabitants are creatures habituated to ooze and stagnation: "snakeses, wormses, things in the pools," as Gollum explains (*LotR* 612). Here Lothlórien, where decay is held back by supernatural power, and where the leaves do not fall until their golden litter can enhance the beauty of the springtime, finds its unwholesome counter-image.[32]

The bleared sun, seen through the mists above the Dead Marshes (*LotR* 612), is a rare, portentous visitant in Tolkien's world. The sun appears

---

[31] *War of the Ring* 105.

[32] In Lothlórien, "the autumn their leaves fall not, but turn to gold. Not till the spring comes and the new green opens do they fall, and then the boughs are laden with yellow flowers; and the floor of the wood is golden, and golden is the roof" (*LotR* 326).

"bleared" – dimmed or blurred as if through tears – only one other time in *The Lord of the Rings*, at a single moment seen from two vantage points recounted in separate chapters. About to enter the Chambers of Fire in Mount Doom, Sam sees the sun, "piercing the smokes and haze [...] ominous, a dull bleared disc of red" as Mordor awaits "some dreadful stroke" (*LotR* 924); meanwhile at the "stroke of doom", Faramir and Éowyn, watching from the walls of Minas Tirith, also see the sun 'bleared' while all wind and noise dies away and time seems to stop (*LotR* 941).[33] In Tolkien's mythology of light, even in its full glory the sun is only a memory of the Two Trees which illuminated ageless Valinor. It is a harbinger of mortality and the decline of the Elves. Here in *The Lord of the Rings*, the bleared sun presides over scenes where death hangs heavy yet time seems suspended. Through the pall of fumes in the Dead Marshes, the sun appears either to have sickened, a "faint reminder" of the light of the world, or to have died, becoming just "a passing ghost" (*LotR* 612). Haunted by "some haggard phantom of green spring" (*LotR* 617), the marshes themselves seem a ghost land, a decaying memorial of life. The reeds quiver and rattle as if in a breeze the travellers cannot feel. All the powers of life are reduced to spectral after-images, and so, as the hobbits soon discover, are the remains of the living.

If dwindling Lothlórien dreams of the memory of Valinor, an immortal earthly paradise, the ever-expanding marshes are haunted by war, a nightmare from which the land cannot wake up. The dead faces in the "dark water" at their heart (*LotR* 613) date from the battle between the Last Alliance of Elves and Men at the Black Gate "an age and more ago" (*LotR* 614).[34] Has time been suspended? Or are the faces, as Sam asks, "some devilry hatched in the Dark

---

[33] Otherwise 'blear' appears only twice, to describe eyes: Sam's full of sleep, Wormtongue's full of terror (*LotR* 71, 961).

[34] In *The Lord of the Rings*, three millennia have passed since the Battle before the Gates of Mordor. In the manuscript of 'The Passage of the Marshes', it had already happened when Gollum was a child; in the draft, it happened "long long ago" during his childhood (*War of the Ring* 109, 116 note 9).

Land"?³⁵ The narrator provides no answers to help us assimilate the scene. Gollum only knows that you cannot reach the corpses, which are not simply submerged but mystically remote; the surface of the water appears like "some window, glazed with grimy glass" (*LotR* 613): the threshold of vision but also a barrier to touch.³⁶

We can be certain, at least, that the window looks not only into the remote past of Middle-earth but also into Tolkien's own memory. The real-world provenance of the phantoms in the Dead Marshes would be apparent even if he had not hinted at it, in a roundabout way, by conceding that "in landscape the Dead Marshes and the approaches to the Morannon owe something to Northern France after the Battle of the Somme."³⁷ It is thanks to the Somme, and other First World War battles such as Passchendaele, that dead bodies in the mud have become as universal a symbol of war's waste as poppies. The Battle of the Somme began on 1 July 1916, but from September the battlefield became a mire, and the river Ancre, where the front line had stood, burst its banks. When Gollum says the Dead Marshes have grown and "swallowed up the graves" of the old battle (*LotR* 614), he reports a phenomenon familiar to soldiers of the Somme winter. The entire, vast battlefield was dotted with makeshift cemeteries and littered with unburied dead, numbered in tens of thousands. Ovillers, the German stronghold against which he was first thrown into the assault, was described by one officer as "nothing but shell holes and dead men – horrible."³⁸ That sodden autumn, Tolkien was posted for weeks at a time in trenches seized from the Germans and often

---

[35] (*LotR* 614). Likewise, Faramir suggests the faces in the Dead Marshes may be a vision or illusion produced by Sauron's "foul arts" (*LotR* 652). Sauron, whose name is Quenya for "the Putrid" (*Lost Road* 393), is also known as "the Necromancer".

[36] Final notes for the chapter show uncertainty over whether or not the pools were to show the past: "Gollum says it is said they are memories (?) of those who fell" (*War of the Ring* 105).

[37] J.R.R. Tolkien to Professor L.W. Forster, 31 December 1960 (*Letters* 303).

[38] Carrington (1929:57); the officer was describing the neighbouring few yards of the front on 13 July 1916, the day before Tolkien went into action.

filled with the dead of either side, in various states of decay. Sometimes the earth would reveal older remains, from the previous two years of the war, and they might look as ancient as those that Frodo and Sam see; the memoirist Edmund Blunden described how bones encountered in the trenches might as well date from the defence of Troy.[39] Yet habit could not entirely inure soldiers to the shock of seeing a more recent corpse. One soldier wrote of walking "for over half a mile on half-buried German dead. Every step was on ground that yielded to the foot, as the dead body below the layer of yellow clay gave to our weight. Sometimes a boot, removing a clump of earth, disclosed the nose or hand of the corpse below us. [...] And in a great shell-hole, filled with blood and water, sat a dead Highlander and a dead German, gazing, with sightless yellow eyeballs, into each other's faces."[40] The war poet and memoirist Siegfried Sassoon (1972:435) once saw "floating on the surface of the flooded trench [...] the mask of a human face which had detached itself from the skull." Routinely, soldiers' bodies simply lay swamped by rain in the shellholes where they had died.

The Dead Marshes embody the ineffectual and pitiful waste of war as Tolkien knew it. The moment of starkest realism may be in the odd description of the surface of the pools as 'greasy', if that detail embodies not an image of industrial pollution but a queasy memory of the drowned open graves of the Somme, filled with water and decomposition.[41] But real corpses float, bloated and gassy. Those the hobbits see are ghosts, intangible or out of reach, lit with a terrifying luminescence. The Dead Marshes are a myth-maker's patterning of almost unspeakable reality. Tolkien's use of his memories is highly stylised. The sight of the dead faces is mediated for us through the words of Sam and Frodo while the narrator averts his eyes.

---

[39] Blunden (1982:25-26).

[40] Talbot Kelly (1980:97), describing the entry into Longueval on the Somme around 20 July 1916; Hilary Tolkien's battalion was there at the time.

[41] Alternatively, this may be one of the few details reflecting his plan to describe the pools as if "fouled by modern chemical works" (*War of the Ring* 105).

Composing Frodo's "dreamlike" description (*LotR* 614), Tolkien abandons the credible consistency he worked so hard to achieve elsewhere:

> "I saw them: grim faces and evil, and noble faces and sad. Many faces proud and fair, and weeds in their silver hair. But all foul, all rotting, all dead. A fell light is in them."

The 'evil' and the 'noble' lie side by side, all trace of battle lines hopelessly lost in the chaos of combat. In an echo of Macbeth's witchery, or A.E. Housman's "lovely lads and dead and rotten," even the 'fair' faces are also 'foul'.[42] Thus order is overthrown, qualitative opposites are mixed together or merge completely. As in other sequences of waking nightmare in *The Lord of the Rings*, Tolkien moves here towards surrealism, a technique he had described in 'On Fairy-Stories'. In this 1939 paper, he had gone on to describe the surrealist creative state as characterised by "morbidity or un-ease" and "similar in quality and consciousness of morbidity to the sensations of a high fever, when the mind develops a distressing fecundity and facility in figure-making, seeing forms sinister or grotesque in all visible objects about it" (OFS 159). 'On Fairy-Stories' had defined surrealism in opposition to the healthy inner consistency of fantasy that Tolkien was championing, yet in *The Lord of the Rings* it may fairly be said that he nevertheless approaches the mode not only here in the Dead Marshes but also in Frodo's earlier moments of waking nightmare. Thus, something akin to surrealism emerges during Frodo's encounters with the Barrow-wight and the Ringwraiths – each of them, notably, violating the bounds of life and death – and especially during his illness after being wounded by the Witch-king.[43] Tolkien's comments on surrealism may not give

---

[42] In the draft text, Frodo uses the very words "dead and rotten", and Gollum repeats them. Housman's *A Shropshire Lad* (1896) was extremely popular among Tolkien's generation, not least among those who went to war.

[43] The nightmare scenes in the barrow and during the flight to the ford of Bruinen were composed in the twelve months to September 1938, and thus not long before Tolkien discussed surrealism in his Andrew Lang lecture on 8 March 1939. For discussion of these other quasi-surrealistic episodes in *The Lord of the Rings*, see Garth (2005).

a rounded indication of his own practices as a writer, but they certainly serve to remind us of what we know from his army service record: that in shaping such nightmare-sequences, he had an insider's knowledge of the fevered mind.

The visages in the Mere of Dead Faces, ghostly but putrid, are strikingly reminiscent of hallucinations suffered by Siegfried Sassoon when he was invalided home from the Somme in 1916 with trench fever, as Tolkien was. Sassoon recalled that in hospital, as he lay half-waking, half-sleeping,

> Shapes of mutilated soldiers came crawling across the floor; the floor seemed to be littered with fragments of mangled flesh. Faces glared upwards; hands clutched at neck or belly; a livid grinning face with bristly moustache peered at me above the edge of my bed; his hands clawed at the sheets. Some were like the dummy figures used to deceive snipers; others were alive and looked at me reproachfully as though envying me the warm safety of life [...] (Sassoon 1972:453)

In addition, Sassoon often saw the corpses of soldiers lying about on the pavement when he walked in London, as he told his friend Robert Graves.[44] Now a further parallel must be noted with Tolkien. His own waking nightmare, of ghosts in Birmingham, shares the city-centre setting of Sassoon's London vision and the phantasmal motion of Sassoon's hospital hallucinations. The figures Tolkien imagined rising from the pavements were surely not soldier corpses but boys or young men in the prime of life, walking memories from school. But that recent vision chimes with his comments about the fevered mind in 'On Fairy-Stories'. Even in the mid-1940s he must have been able to remember trench fever as well as Sassoon had when writing his fictionalised war memoir in the mid-1930s.

In the Dead Marshes, Tolkien abandoned a further horror he sketched out for the hobbits in his final preparatory notes and drafting of April 1944.

---

[44] Graves (1960:267).

Some of the pools were to reveal a different image, activated by moonlight as if to suggest lunacy. "The moon came out of its cloud. They looked in," runs an outline. "But they saw no faces out of the vanished past. They saw *their own*. [...] Sam Gollum and Frodo looking up with dead eyes and livid rotting flesh at them" (*War of the Ring* 105, 110). In this conception, the hobbits might reasonably have feared that the pool was a kind of *speculum* revealing the future, like the Mirror of Galadriel and the Palantíri in Books Two and Three. In *The Lord of the Rings* Tolkien was concerned to show how relatively ordinary individuals can carry out an unwelcome duty through extraordinary dangers. He could draw on months of personal experience from the Battle of the Somme, in which demoralisation had posed a greater threat to defensive or offensive action than any amount of enemy firepower. In Denethor, he illustrates how expectancy of certain defeat and death can disfigure and destroy courage. Having planned for Frodo, Sam and Gollum to see images of themselves dead, he must have reflected that if the travellers were to take the thoroughly unambiguous vision as a true forecast of the future, they might as well give up their respective quests; on the other hand, if they were simply to disbelieve the forecast, the episode would lose all its power. Far better, therefore, that the visions in the marshes show only the past, or a semblance of it. In the published version, the idea of the *speculum* is absent, but the faces of the dead from the ancient battle provide as eloquent a *memento mori* as the corpses that soldiers saw around them on the Somme.

A sufficiently metaphysical omen of death persists in the text, in the strange lights that flicker about the Mere of Dead Faces. Gollum refers to them as "candles of corpses" (*LotR* 613), and they herald the appearance of the phantasms. But in English folklore, 'corpse-candles' are the ghostly flames that appear in graveyards to portend imminent death.

In the Dead Marshes they are "tricksy lights" (*LotR* 613), will-o'-the-wisps to lead the unwary astray, a metaphysical phenomenon paralleling the strange allure of the dead faces. Gollum admits he has tried to touch the figures in the meres – so he might eat them, Sam suspects, but morbid fascination seems a more likely reason. Aragorn once caught Gollum lurking there "by a stagnant mere, peering in the water as the dark eve fell [...] covered with green slime" (*LotR* 247). It is even possible that Frodo, whom Sam discovers half in a trance with his hands dripping slime, has not simply tripped over but has gone groping in the depths after the waterlogged forms. The gruesome attempt, if such it is, acts out the general fascination which soldiers on the Western Front felt towards the ubiquitous dead. The war memoirist Charles Carrington, on the way to the front line, was guided like a sightseer to a hole where two bodies lay looking "less human than waxworks. [...] I was neither afraid nor unhappy," he wrote, "but fascinated."[45] Edmund Blunden described the lure of an old Flanders village cemetery which, like the Dead Marshes, had been swallowed up by the battlefield: "Greenish water stood in some of those pits; bones and skulls and decayed cerements there attracted frequent soldiers past the 'No Loitering' noticeboard" (Blunden 1982:56).

Finally, the ghostly lights seem to suggest funeral rites. Church candles, incense and gravecloths: each has its parallel in a variety of marsh light, "some like dimly shining smoke, some like misty flames flickering slowly above unseen candles" and others "twisted like ghostly sheets unfurled by hidden hands" (*LotR* 613). Through his chosen medium of symbolist fantasy, Tolkien creates a counterpart to Wilfred Owen's beautiful but conventional poetic parallelisms in the First World War piece 'Anthem for Doomed Youth':

> What candles may be held to speed them all?
>   Not in the hands of boys, but in their eyes
> Shall shine the holy glimmers of good-byes.
>   The pallor of girls' brows shall be their pall...

---

[45] Carrington (1929:55), describing Charles Carrington's experiences in the same army division as Tolkien, the day before Tolkien himself took the same route on his own maiden journey into the trenches.

In the hands of both writers, the funereal imagery makes the same point: there is no honourable burial for those killed in battle far from home. Owen recruits familial pity and love to take the place of candles and cerements. Tolkien had used a similar image in a 1916 poem, 'The Wanderer's Allegiance', visualising (or seeing as in a vision) the darkened windows of student rooms in Oxford emptied by war but mystically lit "with lamps and candles of departed men." But the picture in 1944's 'Passage of the Marshes' is more bleak. Here the dead of the old battle have only empty mockeries for a memorial. The "candles of corpses" are a triumphant balancing act by Tolkien, finely poised between naturalism and symbolism. Freighted with implication, they may yet also be by-products of the marshes' superabundant methane.

After the Mere of Dead Faces it seems less clear that the marsh-reek is the result of purely vegetable decomposition. Might the stench be a ghost-stench to match the phantom faces: a scent-memory of the ancient battle, or indeed of the Somme? There, Tolkien had lived for weeks with the smell of decaying human bodies. Even three miles from the front line the village where he first arrived stank of them. Meanwhile, there were other odours to contend with in the trenches, where rudimentary sanitation was not helped by the enemy's habit of using latrines as artillery targets. Tolkien characterised the experience of trenchlife as "crouching among the flies and filth" – a word he uses euphemistically in *The Lord of the Rings* when he describes an orc-camp with its "pit of uncovered filth and refuse" (*LotR* 637).[46] It may be such memories, rather than anti-industrial disgust, that underlie the description of marsh-waters "noisome as a cesspool" (*LotR* 614).

A last, more searing memory is suggested by the sight and smell of the marsh-fumes. The Somme air was choked, frequently, by pulverised chalk dust, by smoke released to disguise troop movements, and, worst of all, by gas.

---

[46] Tolkien described trench life to Philip Norman (*The Sunday Times*, 15 January 1967). Ironically, Tolkien owed his survival to the unsanitary conditions, which harboured the bacterium responsible for trench fever.

The horrors of the first German gas attack remained with Tolkien years later.[47] The mouldy-hay smell of phosgene or the nauseating pungency of chlorine sent every soldier fumbling for his mask. Such memories, perhaps, contribute to the "mists [that] curled and smoked from dark and noisome pools" of the Somme-like Dead Marshes. A faint recollection of a gas mask might even be discerned in the view of the dead faces through a "window, glazed with grimy glass," as the gas victim was observed by Wilfred Owen in his poem 'Dulce et decorum est' (Owen 1963:53): "Dim, through the misty panes and thick green light, / As under a green sea. [...]" The same suspicion hovers over the surreal scene of Frodo's spectral encounter in the Barrow – a necromantic foretaste of the Dead Marshes – in which action seems to slow down in a miasma of fear and which is oddly illuminated by a "pale greenish light" (*LotR* 137).

The Dead Marshes have a number of precursors in Tolkien's works. Dying in the mud was a regular feature of troop movements during the worsening Somme autumn, as soldiers slipped off the duckboards and sank while their comrades looked on, powerless to assist.[48] Its mark is apparent earlier in *The Lord of the Rings* when Merry dreams that he is lying in a "soft slimy bog" and fears that he will drown (*LotR* 125). It is clearer still in Tolkien's 1937 poem 'Knocking at the Door', about the anthropophagic Mewlips:

> You sink into the bog, who dare
> To knock upon their door,
> While fireworks flicker in the air
> And shine upon the shore.[49]

---

[47] *Family Album* (John and Priscilla Tolkien 1992:40).

[48] See for example Alfred Bundy, quoted in Brown (1997:225-226).

[49] 'Knocking at the Door', *The Oxford Magazine*, 18 February 1937 403 (signed 'Oxymore'). The creatures live beyond or beside 'the Marsh of Toad', spelt in the later version, 'The Mewlips' (*The Adventures of Tom Bombadil*), 'the Marsh of Tode' – a punning reference, perhaps, to German *Tod*, 'death'. The poem claims to express the anxiety of a supplicant academic knocking on a superior's door, but it is a fantasia on fear rather than a description of university life.

The pyrotechnics seem an odd touch, no doubt, until the connection is made with the Somme. No scene on earth resembles the Mewlips' habitation except the Western Front at night, with its fatal mud and its blaze of artillery fire, star shells and signallers' flares (known as 'fairy lights'). Taken together with those seemingly incongruous fireworks in 'Knocking at the Door', the 'candles of corpses' in the Dead Marshes might also be suspected as ghostly after-images of the Somme illuminations.

The main analogue of the Dead Marshes in *The Silmarillion* is the Hill of Slain, a single monumental heap into which are piled all the dead gathered from the Battle of Unnumbered Tears. Here Tolkien, writing just after the Great War, first produced a grand symbol for the waste, horror and despair of war as he had known it. The Hill of Slain gave death an enduring shape; one that might be imagined towering, sublime and awful, in the background of some particularly gothic piece of landscape art. Somme soldiers knew of vast mounds of corpses, either by sight or rumour. Straight after Tolkien's battalion had helped to seize the village of Ovillers, a reporter described what had become of the German defenders: "From one end to the other the village was strewn with corpses, most of them torn to pieces. In a roadway between two forts defending the approaches to the first houses of the village 800 corpses were heaped one on top of another, making a terrible rampart."[50] Like the Dead Marshes, the Hill of Slain is a grand myth-maker's flourish with an alloy of realism.

By contrast, the metaphysical atmosphere of 'The Passage of the Marshes' is closely related to a visionary and apocalyptic poem Tolkien had written long ago, 'The Last Ark'. This, sadly, is little known, largely because it exists primarily in Qenya, one of Tolkien's invented languages.[51] A ship full of ghosts sails west; the sea and sky are torn in world-rending storm; hills slide; and the ghost-ship founders on the rocks. This short narrative, probably

---

[50] Press Association, Paris, Tuesday 18 July 1916, in *Northern Daily Telegraph*, 19 July 7.

[51] J.R.R. Tolkien, 'A Secret Vice', in *The Monsters and the Critics* (Tolkien 1983c:213-215, 220-223).

written in the 1920s, seems largely unconnected with other aspects of Tolkien's mythographic tapestry, though its vessel is reminiscent of the Black Ship Mornië that ferried the souls of dead men in *The Book of Lost Tales* and the poem anticipates aspects of the downfall of Númenor. But it contains a number of striking congruences with the story of the Mere of Dead Faces. First, of course, there are the phantoms, here wailing like gulls in the bosom of a boat – as if in echo of Tolkien's feverish voyage home from the Western Front in 1916, on a hospital ship packed with wounded and traumatised soldiers. Secondly, the moon appears as a portent of death, as it had in the abandoned story of the travellers seeing their own dead faces in the meres; indeed, the moon is described as "a corpse-candle." Thirdly, in Tolkien's English translation of 'The Last Ark', the sun is *bleared*, but he makes explicit the alternative sense of the word: she weeps as she looks down on the cataclysm. The same alternative sense may thus be implicit in his descriptions of the Dead Marshes and Mount Doom.

After the passage through the marshes, the shifting ground and miasmic air of nightmare give way to firmer ground and unclouded sight. The stagnant, perpetual, unregenerating decay of the marshlands is left behind, the mockery or sickly memory of life finally "dying away into dead peats." These "arid moors," utterly barren, comprise the Noman-lands (or Nomen's-land, as the First Edition has it; in a draft it is called in Elvish *Uvanwaith*). Foreseen from the drafting of 'Farewell to Lórien' in 1941, and with a name from the language of the First World War, this region is passed with little comment.[52] But much of what little detail there is chimes with the Somme. One of the first things that strikes a visitor to the old battlefields in northern France is that this

---

[52] 'Uvanwaith' (*Treason* 283) has been interpreted as a derivation from a negative prefix plus two elements attested in Tolkien's 'Etymologies': *anw* 'a male, man (of Men or Elves), male animal' and *–waith* '-land' (Patrick Wynne, http://groups.yahoo.com/group/lambengolmor/message/847, 12 November 2005). Others, while supporting the view that Uvanwaith is a more-or-less literal rendering of the English, contend that the middle element might be related to *man*, the interrogative pronoun 'who'.

hotly contested downland, where it might take a week and the lives of thousands of soldiers to seize a strategic hilltop, is almost devoid of steep drops and climbs; it is all long, gentle gradients that only the machinegun could turn into a near-impenetrable barrier. In *The Lord of the Rings* the hobbits now find the air "harsh, and filled with a bitter reek that caught their breath and parched their mouths," Tolkien writes; compare the words of fellow officer Charles Carrington (1965:142), "The smell of burnt and poisoned mud [...] was with us for months on end. [...]"

But "the 'bitter reek' in the hobbits' nostrils" now comes on an east wind as a foretaste of the Dagorlad, the old battle plain which the travellers reach next. Here is the apotheosis of ruin:

> The gasping pools were choked with ash and crawling muds, sickly white and grey, as if the mountains had vomited the filth of their entrails upon the lands about. High mounds of crushed and powdered rock, great cones of earth fire-blasted and poison-stained, stood like an obscene graveyard in endless rows. [...] a land defiled, diseased beyond all healing – unless the Great Sea should enter in and wash it with oblivion.
> (*LotR* 617)

The anti-industrial animus seen in Tolkien's notes for the description of the marshes may be discerned more easily on the Dagorlad. But the presiding genius now was the Somme, as he told the *Birmingham Post* (Brace 1968):

> I remember miles and miles of seething tortured earth, perhaps best described in the chapter about the approaches to Mordor. It was a searing experience.

A fresh impetus may have fuelled the description of the Dagorlad: the bomb damage that Tolkien had seen in Birmingham a fortnight or so earlier, possibly (since Oxford itself had never been bombed) the first he had encountered since the Somme.

In marked contrast to the Dead Marshes, the Dagorlad is devoid even of ghosts, let alone 'phantoms of spring'. Yet Frodo, passing the night on watch-duty on the desert of Dagorlad beyond the marshes, is haunted by waking visions and irrepressible memories:

> He looked up at the smoke-streaked sky and saw strange phantoms, dark riding shapes, and faces out of the past. He lost count of time, hovering between sleep and waking, until forgetfulness came over him.
> (*LotR* 618).

The dark riding shapes, in terms of the story, are images of the flying Ringwraiths which Frodo has now glimpsed. But Tolkien described these hallucinatory "faces out of the past" just two weeks or so after his own "memorable day" when "ghosts" had risen from the pavements to drive him out of the heart of Birmingham.[53] In both cases, the memory of people once familiar comes back unbidden, unnerving and uncontrollable. In Tolkien's case, the faces are associated with a real war which comes closer to the surface here in 'The Passage of the Marshes' than anywhere else in *The Lord of the Rings* or his entire opus. But I suspect Frodo's dreams also go back to memories of trench fever. The situation among shadows and sleeping companions, together with Frodo's state of semi-consciousness, are much the same as Sassoon describes in his account of his own hospital hallucinations:

> I wasn't sure whether I was awake or asleep; the ward was half shadow and half sinking firelight, and the beds were quiet with huddled sleepers.
> (Sassoon 1972:453)

---

[53] J.R.R. Tolkien to Christopher Tolkien, 3 April 1944 (*Letters* 69-70).

Tolkien and Sassoon tell the same story about memories appearing as hallucination when the mind moves uneasily between wakefulness and sleep. If the Mere of Dead Faces is a symbolist or mythic representation of death and memory, Frodo's waking hallucination on the Dagorlad is its psychological, realist counterpart.

Within Tolkien's mythology, a similar scene of environmental destruction meets Bilbo at the Desolation of Smaug, a once green land now with "neither bush nor tree, and only broken and blackened stumps to speak of ones long vanished." But the choking wasteland on the doorstep of Mordor, first apparently named not Dagorlad (Battle Plain) but 'Lithlad Plain of Ash', has as its chief *Silmarillion* forerunner Anfauglith: the plain of Gaping Dust on which the Battle of Unnumbered Tears is fought.[54] As originally conceived in the years immediately after the First World War, the Battle of Unnumbered Tears was to have taken place in "the Vale of Fountains", afterwards known as "the Vale of Weeping Waters", on a day of grey rain.[55] The shift from waterlands to ashen desert as the site of the Battle of Unnumbered Tears matches the same shift seen in *The Lord of the Rings* as the hobbits pass from the Dead Marshes to the desert in front of the Black Gate. Tolkien seems to have wanted to find room in his mythology for both faces of the Somme: the blasted, dry wasteland of the summer months when he had first arrived, and the waterlogged wilderness of the ensuing winter.

---

[54] For Lithlad, see *Treason* 208. Christopher Tolkien (*Treason* 213) takes this first mention of Lithlad, in an outline of the story foreseen from Moria probably written late in 1941, as a reference to what the name denoted later, a region inside Mordor itself, east of the Dark Tower; he comments, "there would thus seem no reason for Frodo and Sam ever to have come to it, as seems to be implied in this outline." However, the suitability of the name, and its position in the narrative outline *before* Frodo reaches the pass into Mordor, suggest instead that it was initially conceived by Tollkien for the area between the Nomenlands and the Black Gate. The next outline, the story foreseen from Lórien, passes over the region before the Black Gate without mention (*Treason* 330), but *Lithlad* appears in its now accustomed place within Mordor in the first manuscript of the chapter 'The Black Gate is Closed' (*War of the Ring* 127, note 5) and on section III of Tolkien's 'First Map' (*Treason* 309).

[55] *Lost Tales 1* 239, 240.

The two chief landscapes of this chapter have joined the enduring icons of the Great War, alongside Wilfred Owen's 'Anthem for Doomed Youth' and John Singer Sargent's painting *Gassed*. As proof of this we need only turn to Hugh Cecil's literary survey, *The Flower of Battle: British Fiction Writers of the First World War*. Cecil's book does not actually deal with Tolkien's own fiction, taking a conventional critical view that First World War fiction must be 'realistic'. Yet for his very first, scene-setting quotation, the author calls not on Owen, or Sassoon, or Frederic Manning, but on Tolkien, for his description of the Dagorlad.

By the time Tolkien had finished writing 'The Passage of the Marshes', less than three weeks after his visit to Birmingham and his decision to resume work on *The Lord of the Rings*, his writer's block was well and truly banished. Four or five days later, he had nearly finished a third chapter. "But this story takes me in charge," he told Christopher, "and I have already taken three chapters over what was meant to be one!"[56] This astonishing flood of creativity carried him through Book Four by the end of May.

The flood was not wholly unprecedented. At the very start of his efforts to become a writer, he had declared that the T.C.B.S.'s December 1914 meeting (its first since the outbreak of war that year) was "followed […] by my finding a voice for all kinds of pent up things and a tremendous opening up of everything"; among the results was a sheaf of poems in April 1915 that was, effectively, the prelude to Middle-earth.[57] But Tolkien's sudden rush in April 1944 may be compared most profitably to the one that had produced the first of the 'Lost Tales' that eventually became *The Silmarillion*: the writing, in hospital in late 1916 straight after the Battle of the Somme, of 'The Fall of Gondolin'. That story, depicting a desperate last stand against brute military force – including a phalanx of quasi-mechanical dragons remarkably

---

[56] *War of the Ring* 94-95, 104, 107; J.R.R. Tolkien to Christopher Tolkien, 23 April 1944 (*Letters* 73).

[57] J.R.R. Tolkien to G.B. Smith, 12 August 1916 (*Letters* 10).

reminiscent of tanks – was clearly a product of Tolkien's war experience: partly the artistic consequence of long and deep thought during extraordinary times, partly a catharsis of "pent up" feelings.[58] In the midst of the Second World War, I suggest, Tolkien experienced a similar artistic catharsis.

He had pent-up anxieties a-plenty, telling Michael Tolkien earlier in the war: "I feel like a lame canary in a cage. [...] If only I could do something active!"[59] However, the tribulations of his sons in the armed forces had drawn him back to his own soldiering experience in the First World War, producing long letters in which he reassured them that he had been through similar trials, had hated it all, but had survived and, indeed, had learned from it. Christopher, training in South Africa with the RAF, had been 'grousing' about life in camp. "You are inside a very great story!" his father reminded him on 6 May 1944 (anticipating a conversation he would write in the next few weeks between Frodo and Sam in the Mountains of Shadow).[60] Tolkien went on:

> I think [...] you are suffering from suppressed 'writing'. That may be my fault. You have had rather too much of me and my peculiar mode of thought and reaction. [...] I think if you could begin to *write*, and find your own mode, or even (for a start) imitate mine, you would find it a great relief. I sense among all your pains (some merely physical) the desire to express your *feeling* about good, evil, fair, foul in some way: to rationalize it, and prevent it just festering. In my case it generated Morgoth and the History of the Gnomes.[61]

---

[58] The 'dragons' in *Lost Tales 2* 169-170 are discussed with reference to the Western Front in Garth (2003:220-221).

[59] J.R.R. Tolkien to Michael Tolkien, 9 June 1941 (*Letters* 55). For his son John's experiences during the war, see *Family Album* (John and Priscilla Tolkien 1992:70).

[60] Sam strikes the keynote when he observes that Frodo's star-glass, containing the light of a Silmaril, links them with the ancient heroes Beren and Eärendil, and exclaims: "Why, to think of it, we're in the same tale still! It's going on. Don't the great tales never end?" (*LotR* 696-697).

[61] J.R.R. Tolkien to Christopher Tolkien, 6 May 1944 (*Letters* 78).

Tolkien's 'peculiar mode of reaction', the one that most effectively released his pent-up feelings, that best permitted what he defined as *escape* from oppression of the mind, was fairy-story – a taste not learned as a child but "quickened to full life by war," as he recalled. In 'The Passage of the Marshes', describing how memories of the old Last Alliance intrude into the War of the Ring, we see Tolkien's expressive powers quickened again by memories of the First World War, seen through the prism of the Second. Perhaps even the ghosts of King Edward's School, the memories of friends lost in the trenches, played a part.

Biographical Note

John Garth is the author of *Tolkien and the Great War: The Threshold of Middle-earth* (London: HarperCollins, and New York: Houghton Mifflin Co, 2003), which examines the development of Tolkien's *legendarium* in the context of his experiences during the First World War. For the book, Garth retraced Tolkien's steps on the Somme and examined the military service records of Tolkien and his friends, their private correspondence, the war diaries of their battalions, and many other official and personal archives. *Tolkien and the Great War* was awarded the Mythopoeic Society's Scholarship Award in Inklings Studies in 2004.

Bibliography

Abbreviations

Biography: see Carpenter 1977
Letters: see Carpenter 1981
Lost Road: see Tolkien 1987
Lost Tales 1: see Tolkien 1983a
Lost Tales 2: see Tolkien 1984
LotR: see Tolkien 1995
OFS: 'On Fairy-Stories' see Tolkien 1983b
Return: see Tolkien 1988
Treason: see Tolkien 1989
War of the Ring: see Tolkien 1990

Blunden, Edmund, 1982, *Undertones of War*, London: Penguin.
Brace, Keith, 1968, 'In the Footsteps of the Hobbits', *Birmingham Post*, 25 May 1968.
Brown, Malcolm, 1997, *The Imperial War Museum Book of the Somme*, London: Pan.
Carpenter, Humphrey, 1977, *J.R.R. Tolkien: A Biography*. London: George Allen & Unwin.
---, 1978, *The Inklings*, London: George Allen & Unwin.
--- (ed.), 1981, *The Letters of J.R.R. Tolkien*, London: George Allen & Unwin.
Carrington, Charles (as "Charles Edmonds"), 1929, *A Subaltern's War*, London: Peter Davies.
---, 1965, *Soldier from the Wars Returning*, London: Hutchinson.
Duriez, Colin, and David Porter, 2001, *The Inklings Handbook*, London: Azure.
Garth, John, 2003, *Tolkien and the Great War: The Threshold of Middle-earth*, London: HarperCollins; Boston: Houghton Mifflin.
---, 2005, 'Frodo and the Great War', in Wayne G. Hammond and Christina Scull (eds.), 2005, *The Lord of the Rings, 1954-2004: Scholarship in Honor of Richard E. Blackwelder*, Milwaukee: Marquette University Press, 41-56.
Graves, Robert, 1960, *Good-bye to All That*, Harmondsworth: Penguin.
The London Gazette
Northern Daily Telegraph
Owen, Wilfred, 1963, *The Collected Poems of Wilfred Owen*, (edited by C. Day Lewis), London: Chatto & Windus.
Priestman, Judith, 1992, *J.R.R. Tolkien: Life and Legend*. Oxford: Bodleian Library.
Sassoon, Siegfried, 1972, *The Complete Memoirs of George Sherston.*, (first published 1937), London: Faber and Faber.
Talbot Kelly, R.B., 1980, *A Subaltern's Odyssey*, William Kimber.
Tolkien, John Ronald Reuel, 1937, (as 'Oxymore'), 'Knocking at the Door', *The Oxford Magazine*, 18 February 1937.

---, 1983a, *The Book of Lost Tales, Part One*, (edited by Christopher Tolkien), London: George Allen & Unwin.
---, 1983b, 'On Fairy-Stories', in *The Monsters and the Critics and Other Essays*, (edited by Christopher Tolkien), London: George Allen & Unwin, 109-161.
---, 1983c, 'A Secret Vice', in *The Monsters and the Critics and Other Essays*, (edited by Christopher Tolkien), London: George Allen & Unwin, 198-223.
---, 1984, *The Book of Lost Tales, Part Two*, (edited by Christopher Tolkien), London: George Allen & Unwin.
---, 1987, *The Lost Road*, (edited by Christopher Tolkien), London: HarperCollins.
---, 1988, *The Return of the Shadow*, (edited by Christopher Tolkien), London: HarperCollins.
---, 1989, *The Treason of Isengard*, (edited by Christopher Tolkien), London: HarperCollins.
---, 1990, *The War of the Rings*, (edited by Christopher Tolkien), London: HarperCollins.
---, 1995, *The Lord of the Ring*, (one-volume edition), London: HarperCollins.
Tolkien, John and Priscilla, 1992, *The Tolkien Family Album*, Boston: Houghton Mifflin.
Trott, Anthony, 1992, *No Place for Fop or Idler*, London: James and James.
Unwin, Rayner, 1998, 'An at-last Finished Tale: The Genesis of *The Lord of the Rings*', in *Lembas-extra 1998*, Leiden: Tolkien Genootschap Unquendor, 74-84.

Leaf by Niggle and the Aesthetics of Gift: Towards a Definition of J.R.R. Tolkien's Notion of Art

Eduardo Segura

Abstract

G.K. Chesterton's *Orthodoxy* includes a memorable chapter titled 'The Ethics of Elfland'. The text was initially written as a preface to Andrew Lang's *Violet Fairy Book*. What lies beneath such a suggestive title is the conviction that there is a deep resemblance between Faërie and our world – or, to use Tolkien's terminology, between secondary worlds and the Primary World. More precisely, we should say that Chesterton and Tolkien agreed that the world we call 'real' – for lack of a better word – looks like a mirror where invented, consistent worlds become images of the multiplicity of Truth – as "refracted light" (see Segura 1997). It is my purpose to show what Tolkien thought about his art, the theoretical process of his discovery of a new world through the invention of languages, and the shaping of his personal poetics on the basis of his conversations with the Inklings, and more specifically with Owen Barfield and C.S. Lewis, through a careful reading of *Leaf by Niggle* – the reputedly most allegorical of Tolkien's short stories.

I   Sub-creation according to Tolkien: Art as an echo of Redemption

It is commonly assumed that Tolkien's tales can be easily read as allegories since they are the work of a Roman Catholic. To the supporters of such a hermeneutic approach, his books should – almost only – be understood as a means to reinterpret reality from the point of view of a Christian – no matter the intention of the author. Tolkien's dislike for allegory is well-known, and it won't be stressed here. My target, disguised as it may seem, is this: Did Professor Tolkien *really* try to explain this world through the eyes of a believer? Was that an intentional attempt, part of a designed plan? Or, on the contrary must we trust him as we read those famous lines about *The Lord of the Rings*: "I cordially dislike allegory in all its manifestations, and always have done so since I grew old and wary enough to detect its presence" (*LotR* 11)? In other words, was Tolkien true to himself when he wrote that he 'cordially' disliked allegory? Is it fair to think that he was so deeply in love with "history, true or feigned, with its varied applicability to the thought and experience of the readers" (*LotR* 11) that he simply dismissed 'inner meanings' just because they could easily become some sort of interference in the sovereign task of interpretation that readers are supposed to face up – and so, erasing any shadow of cordiality at all?

Paying closer attention to his words, as well as to the notion of 'myth' Tolkien used in his scholarly writings, and especially all over his published letters, and works – both major and minor –, it becomes clear that Tolkien's preference for what he called 'free applicability' was rooted in his conviction that the relation between myth and truth as depicted in the image of 'splintering light' was to him, as a Catholic, an indisputable truth. This light could be found in legend as well as in history – and, thus, in a multiplicity of stories. The very notion of myth as presenting multiple images of truth provides a better understanding of those explanatory, closing lines to the paragraph quoted from the 'Foreword' to *The Lord of the Rings*. They also clarify his 'Catholic outlook' towards a fuller comprehension of aesthetics and art:

> I think that many confuse 'applicability' with 'allegory'; but the one resides in the freedom of the reader, and the other in the purposed domination of the author.
> (*LotR* 11)[1]

As a Catholic, the notion of art that Tolkien had learnt and put into practice was closer to that of 'gift', and so of *gratia*, of 'grace', than to any kind of

---

[1] Accordingly, it can be deduced that art is a fruit of freedom: the artist is free to create, and also the spectator/reader is free to receive the work of art and 'decode' it according to her or his own aesthetic taste, preferences, experiences, and understanding.

allegorical meaning that could be derived from an intentional, 'designed' architecture of a story, or even from some sort of strategy planned *a priori* by the author in order to 'convince', 'teach', or 'evangelize' the reader.[2] In the epilogue to his essay 'On Fairy Stories' (OFS), Tolkien dealt with redemption as the eucatastrophe of the history of humankind[3] in terms of a totally undeserved present that we all have been granted out of Love. According to this rationale, and provided that the history of Christ's death and resurrection had taken place in the primary world – i.e., it was 'true' in the truest meaning of the word –, *mythopoeia*, the art of making stories, or storytelling, was a unique way to recapture the joy of that key event in the history of humanity. Therefore, the task of any writer was that of a mediator between truth and the readers, since truth was able to shine forth as a light and to become ultimately *evangelium* to any reader, believer or not.[4]

This point of view provides us with a better understanding of the words I quoted earlier: only a full respect for the freedom of the reader can preserve the essence of art, which is a grace, a gift – an undeserved present. Pretending that a story is just an allegory diminishes its true meaning. A story provides an expansion of the meaning of creation, for this is not the only possible world – nor even the best one.[5] Allegorizing always involves minimizing both the meaning and the scope of sub-creative work because it devalues the essence of creation, which was a superabundance of Love. Therefore, a more profound answer to the question on what does it mean for Tolkien to be a Catholic

---

[2] It is revealing that Tolkien used the notion of 'myth' as a synonym for truth when he was asked by his friend Jack Lewis 'What have I to do with Christ?', to paraphrase Shippey's explanation of the stories of Fróda and Frodo as a 'reconstructed myth' (Shippey 2003:chapter 6). To put it another way, Lewis wanted to know what the *real* influence of Christ's death in his actual life and destiny was. What we *do* know according to Carpenter's account is that Tolkien did *not* choose an apologetic approach.

[3] OFS 64-66.

[4] See OFS 64, *passim*. The response to truth is not mainly, or not only, a question of 'religion', or 'beliefs'. It is the automatical answer to a deep anthropological concern.

[5] Suárez and Leibniz asked whether God had created the best of possible worlds or not. The question is of course related to the deeper philosophical problem of God's freedom and omnipotence, but does not ultimately illuminate the way *this* world is.

writer, and from what point of view can his tales be read as those of a Christian, must eventually face up to the following theological questions: Is redemption the *teleology* of art, its main purpose and highest vocation? Is it the task of any artist to recall the echo of that redemption? Tolkien did believe so:

> [...] the 'consolation' of fairy-tales has another aspect than the imaginative satisfaction of ancient desires. Far more important is the Consolation of the Happy Ending. Almost I would venture to assert that all complete fairy-stories must have it [...] – I will call it *Eucatastrophe*. The *eucatastrophic* tale is the true form of fairy-tale, and its highest function.[6] (OFS 62)

If we accept that redemption is a joyful gift, a gift that nobody deserves, and the kind of present no one is obliged to accept – again, it is literally a 'grace' –, then we must expand the notion of God not 'only' as Creator, but more precisely as *the* Sub-creator, so to say, the first and only artist, and thus consider creation and redemption as His masterpieces. In this light, Humphrey Carpenter's account of the conversation between Hugo Dyson, Jack Lewis, and Tolkien concerning myths and their value as real 'wisdom', becomes clearer. Similarly, the explanation Tolkien provided of Christ as *the* myth, the one in which every other story is finally redeemed and finds its truest meaning – the echo of ultimate Truth[7] – is also revealing of his conviction that history, legend, and myth were ultimately one and the same thing.

Yet, how did Tolkien proceed from that notion of allegory to the wider, more adequate dimension of free applicability? First, Tolkien seems to have had in mind a notion of the artist as a kind of 'priest', in the sense of

---

[6] Accordingly, Tolkien presents tragedy as the true form of drama.
[7] See Carpenter (1997:42-44, *passim*).

'mediator', than to the Aristotelian notion of the artist as a craftsman.[8] Every sub-creator, Tolkien says,

> wishes in some measure to be a real maker, or hopes that he is drawing on reality: hopes that the peculiar quality of this secondary world [...] [is] derived from Reality, or [is] flowing into it [...] The peculiar quality of the 'joy' in successful Fantasy can thus be explained as a sudden glimpse of *the underlying reality of truth*. It is not only a 'consolation' for the sorrow of this world, but a satisfaction, and an answer to that question, 'Is it true?'
> (OFS 64, my italics)

Therefore, if we accept that the main question art is supposed to answer deals mainly with truth, with the way things 'really are' – that is, with the world, and ultimately with being[9] –, and not only – or mainly – with meaning, then true artistry becomes a search for the answer to philosophical and theological questions that lie at the heart of our being. These questions are linked to the existential core of our lives: Who am I? Why am I here? Where to am I going? What is the meaning of all these events that excite my spirit? And the more questions there are, the more art becomes a quest for sense. If we accept that life is teleological, then it can be argued that art is the point where the questions about being – metaphysics –, and the questions about the ultimate destiny of every single person – theology – meet. Art provides an explanation to those many loose threads, and it teaches us that this life is never enough, that we are more than mere flesh and blood.

But, would Tolkien have agreed with this view? Would it be possible to find somewhere a complete explanation made by Tolkien himself on what art

---

[8] However, Aristotle and Tolkien agree with regards to the core of the former's *Poetics*, that is, the construction of feasible worlds through the imitation of human actions (*mímesis práxeos*), secondary worlds where the *tékne*, or skill of the author serves the highest purpose of literary art, *kátharsis* – eucatastrophe. See Aristotle, *Poetics*, 49b27-28, 1451b, 1453b.

[9] It is ultimately a metaphysical answer.

is? As usual, we will have to search widely for the answer to those questions, but we will never find it systematically set out. Tolkien developed a true theology of art, a notion of artistic work as a means of redemption, of recovery of initial grace – the grace before the Fall –, and so, of consolation in its deep, truest spiritual sense. It is this that I call his personal aesthetics. According to these notions of art and sub-creation, and from a teleological point of view, storytelling – and also reading and listening to stories, any kind of art worth the name – becomes the exercise of a primordial human right: the right to escape. This escape is not escapism to Tolkien, since escape provides a privileged access to knowledge, to true *epistéme*. From this almost existentialist perspective Tolkien points towards art as the threshold to avoid death, and so art becomes the vehicle for the 'great escape'[10] – the escape from oblivion. In this sense art makes us eternal.

Moreover, Tolkien's theory of sub-creation suggests that imagination is able of re-presenting objects to our rational mind so that the apprehension of universal ideas becomes more an intuition than the fruit of deduction or reasoning.[11] It is a privileged path to wisdom through an almost straight understanding, and with almost no abstraction. 'Mythopoeia', the art of storytelling, is to Tolkien on the one hand an 'art', a skill, a *tékne*. On the other hand, it is a gift, the participation of the creature in God's creative power; and so, an evidence of the narrative condition of human existence:

> [...] in God's kingdom [...] redeemed Man is still man. Story, fantasy, still go on, and should go on. The Evangelium has not abrogated legends; it has hallowed them, especially the 'happy ending'. The Christian has still to work, with mind as well as body, to suffer, hope, and die; but he may now perceive that all his bents and faculties have a purpose,

---

[10] See OFS 61. Niggle escapes death and oblivion by means of his picture. See below.

[11] See Flieger (2002:33, my italics): "Tolkien's response to words, to their shape and sound and meaning, was closer to that of a musician than a grammarian, and *his response to language was instinctive and intuitive as well as intellectual.*"

> which can be redeemed. So great is the bounty with which he has been treated that he may now, perhaps, fairly dare to guess that in Fantasy he may actually assist in the effoliation and multiple enrichment of creation. (OFS 66)

Storytellers are blessed not only because they, as human beings, have been redeemed, but also because they give an echo of the primordial fairy tale every time they build their little, consistent worlds so that eucatastrophe may shine forever. Creation hopes for, it even needs the assistance of sub-creators so that it may be completed, filled with other truths, since God himself commanded man to work and finish His task:[12]

> Blessed are the legend-makers with their rhyme
> of things not found within recorded time.
> [...]
> (and counterfeit at that, machine-produced,
> bogus seduction of the twice seduced).
> (Mythopoeia 99)[13]

Therefore, the right to sub-create derives from the divine *lógos*, or 'primordial design' in which we were created:

> [...] 'twas our right
> (used or misused). The right has not decayed.
> We make still by the law in which we're made.
> (Mythopoeia 99)

Why? Because the 'inner consistency of reality' is that of a saved world, and we (still) are in God's own image. Man finally becomes the animal who tells stories, as Alasdair MacIntyre (1984, esp. chapter 15, *passim*) has pointed out, an animal who is the image of a creator – the narrator – no matter how "dis-

---

[12] See *Genesis* 2, *passim*, and especially verse 15.

[13] In Tolkien's mythology Eru Ilúvatar counts on the Valar, and the Maiar to embellish and complete Arda. The original design is included in the initial music.

graced he may be" because he "yet is not dethroned,/and keeps the rags of lordship one he owned" (Mythopoeia 98). Only by telling stories can we reach a full understanding of ourselves, of who we are, of where we come from, and of where we are going — those metaphysical, anthropological questions I mentioned earlier. The tragedy of an illiterate society sadly underlines the fact that many people will not be able to understand their true nature unless they turn their eyes to what they were and to what they are by reading and writing myths:[14]

> The heart of man is not compound of lies,
> but draws some wisdom from the only Wise,
> *and still recalls him.* Though now long estranged,
> man is not wholly lost nor wholly changed.
> (Mythopoeia 98, my italics)

Sub-creation becomes a process of recalling the human essence. Art provides a way, by means of beauty, to learn and love wisdom. Art becomes some sort of bonus for ordinary life, and for this world, by exceeding them.

II   Tolkien and his Inkling friends: naming the world for the first time

We have focused our attention on what Tolkien thought about 'mythopoeia', the art of story-making. His opinions had been shaped by the early reading of Owen Barfield's *Poetic Diction* (1928), a book which Tolkien admitted to have exterted a great influence on his philological convictions by the time he was simultaneously telling and writing *The Hobbit*.[15] Actually, he wrote on Barfield's book in terms of a new 'linguistic philosophy' — a philosophy that was suggested to him after the reading and which radically changed his views. The notion itself is worth a closer look.

---

[14] The tremendous success and approval New Line movies bear witness to this. Leaving aside the mistakes in Peter Jackson's version, the epic tone of the tale is still there. Many spectators — Tolkien readers, or not — understood the story not simply as 'fantasy' — it is not —, but as a mythical tale, and grasped in it the echo of a redeemed world — the eucatastrophe.

[15] See *Letters* no. 15, *passim*.

Considering that Tolkien was very reluctant to admit 'influences', or even to quote other authorities to support his own opinions, it is revealing that he admitted that his conversations with Lewis, and especially with Barfield, had been a milestone in the formation of his personal ideas on language. What, then, is the central thesis of *Poetic Diction*? To put it in a nutshell, we could say that Barfield held the opinion that "Mythology is the ghost of concrete meaning" (Barfield 1973:92).[16] After reading Rudolf Steiner's writings, Barfield

> came to believe that the universe was the product of design and was suffused with meaning and, moreover, that imagination can be used quite as well as logic and reason to gain a better understanding of that universe and to comprehend the phenomena of the world around us.
> (Flieger 2002:36)

Tolkien came to a similar conclusion. To him this world was the result of a plan, of a lógos –*the* Lógos, the Word made flesh according to the gospel of Saint John. But the original meaning of the word 'lógos' also encloses the notion of 'word'. 'Lógos' includes both the whole design and the word "in which everything was created."[17] Accordingly, naming the world is a privileged means to recover the original meaning of the whole, of the world as design, as "suffused with meaning" by the Lógos. After the Fall, the tool for the writer to accomplish this task is metaphor. And thus poetry becomes not only a chance for delight in beauty, but also true *epistéme*, a way to knowledge and wisdom.[18] The multiplicity of meaning of this world is a testimony to the infinite beauty

---

[16] For a complete and exhaustive explanation of Barfield's influence on Tolkien there is no better reading than the excellent study by Professor Flieger (Flieger 2002).

[17] See the gospel according to Saint John 1, 1-17.

[18] *Poetic Diction* is "not merely a theory of poetic diction, but a theory of poetry: and not merely a theory of poetry, but a theory of knowledge" (Barfield 1973:14). See also Barfield (1973:47), where he uses the chapter-title 'The Effects of Poetry. Pleasure and Knowledge'. See also Segura (2004:13-115).

of truth. It is a chant to the glory of God. Therefore, poets are ultimately prophets, bards of a never-ending re-creation of the world.

This framework provides a better understanding of Tolkien's theory of sub-creation. If we accept Barfield's view that myth, language, and the perception that humankind once had of this world were deeply connected –they were actually inseparable[19] –, then the ultimate purpose of sub-creation is not merely the 'invention' of other worlds and stories, but the re-discovery of the essence of the primary world through the multiple reflections of truth that we can only perceive through mythopoeia, through the making of secondary worlds. In doing so, man recovers

> [...] his world-dominion by creative act:
> not his to worship the great Artefact,
> man, sub-creator, the refracted light
> through whom is splintered from a single White
> to many hues, and endlessly combined
> in living shapes that move from mind to mind.[20]
> (Mythopoeia 98-99)

But to Tolkien the task of sub-creating the world was rooted in linguistic invention, since the power of words to make meaning literal led to the conclusion that words contain a tremendous potential of meaning, that there is an essential connection between words and reality, between perception and concepts. The multiplicity of meaning that we call now 'metaphor' was unknown to humankind before the Fall, but in a redeemed world metaphor becomes a unique way – perhaps the only way – to recover the complete image of the world that once was.[21] In this sense, Middle-earth expands the meaning of the world we call 'real' – again, for lack of a better word –, recovering at the same

---

[19] See Flieger (2002:37, *passim*).

[20] These verses also explain Tolkien's notion of 'free applicability': creative art permits *each* reader a deeper understanding of his own vision of the world, a vision which is somehow confined to the limits of the soul, both infinite and concrete. It is far a wider sense than that of allegory.

[21] See Flieger (2002:38).

time a more complete, quintessential image of it. By knowing a secondary world it is possible to get a better understanding of one's own universe.

Now, what makes Tolkien different from many other writers is precisely his stress on linguistic invention, from Latin *invenire*, 'to find'. Inventing languages became not only a 'secret vice' to Tolkien, but mainly the tool, the magic wand, to make those invented worlds 'real' – in its truest meaning. Tolkien was aware that to induce 'secondary belief', and not only the 'willing suspension of disbelief' Coleridge deemed the highest aim of fantasy, he was obliged to *invent* – to sub-create – a world literally: a literary place and time where words meant exactly what they meant.[22] Thus, when Frodo and Gildor meet, the hobbit feels it fitting to hail the Elf with an Elvish greeting: "I thank you indeed, Gildor Inglorion [...] *'Elen síla lúmenn' omentielvo*, a star shines on the hour of our meeting" (*LotR* 94). To give the scene the 'inner consistency of reality', Tolkien had built a world where the first thing the Elves saw when they opened their eyes to the beauty of the world was the glittering starlight, a light that would stay there forever.[23] As Flieger puts it, what is a metaphor to us, is literal in *The Lord of the Rings*. A star *really* shone on the hour of the meeting in the Old Forest.

Conversations held by the Inklings by the late 1920s and through the 1930s are likely to have been filled with arguments on these notions about language, perception, and the process of wording, or naming reality. Tolkien's writings, both fictional and theoretical, show that, at that time, he was focused on the construction of a body of reflections on the nature of the relation between literature and language, and on the principles of artistic creation. 'On Fairy Stories' is actually an explanation of the finalities of storytelling: escape, recovery, and consolation, and eucatastrophe, all these experiences reproducing the structure of redeemed creation, of man as saved creature. Tolkien was

---

[22] Gandalf's self-identification at his first encounter with Bilbo is another example of this 'concept': "I am Gandalf, and Gandalf means me!" (*Hobbit* 19).

[23] See *The Silmarillion*, 'Quenta Silmarillion', chapter 3, on the arrival of the Elves in Cuiviénen.

deeply aware that *Poetic Diction* had changed his whole outlook, and from that moment on his contribution to the scholarship of words became a search for the answer to the continuity between history, legend, and myth, and of those three steps to wisdom, with truth.

III   *Leaf by Niggle,* allegory, *and* free applicability

It is not my purpose to discuss here the allegorical interpretations of *Leaf by Niggle* in detail. Some brilliant and illuminating explanations have been given already.[24] However, those allegorical readings of the tale normally reduce its meaning to a more or less intentional attempt by Tolkien to talk about himself and his artistry, especially about *The Lord of the Rings,* his scholarship and professional duties, and the interaction between them. Be that as it may, what those explanations ignore is the fact that Tolkien's reluctance to use allegory as 'mythopoeia' was rooted in his conviction that allegory is *not necessary,* since it restricts the infinite potential of meaning art possesses, its creative design, as well as the reader's range of interpretation. Allegory becomes a limitation to the multiplicity of sense we find in being. Autobiographical writing in a form that is open to allegoric interpretation is not the same as writing an allegory proper.[25] Actually, the different ways the tale has been understood show that allegory allows multiple choices.[26]

Other possible, deeper meanings, are more relevant for Tolkien's poetics. They stand even closer to his mind and his aesthetic ideas. A reading of *Leaf by Niggle* as an allegory of Tolkien's art as well as of 'art' sheds some light

---

[24]   See especially *Biography* 199-200, Shippey (2000:266-277), Shippey (2003:40-43), Flieger (1997:256-257), Rateliff (2006:84-86), Baltasar (2004:19-33), and Hammond (2000:20).

[25]   See Lamberton (1986), especially the distinction between 'deliberate allegory' and 'allegorical interpretation'. To me Tolkien was not deliberately writing an allegory, but giving an interpretation of his own poetics mainly *to himself* by means of an allegory.

[26]   Of course, I do not mean those readings are 'false', provided that they are faithful to the text. I simply want to show that, from the point of view of my approach to Tolkien's theory of art, a subtler interpretation could be also illuminating by proposing a far-reaching allegorical reading of *Leaf by Niggle.*

on the understanding of the author as a Catholic writer, and also on what it meant to him to be a Catholic writer.[27] In other words, it can be of interest to explain the roots of his 'cordial dislike' for allegory by means of an explanation of the relation between creation and art, one of Tolkien's main interests.[28]

Leaf by Niggle is a story that grew in Tolkien's mind literally "in the telling", i.e. as he was writing *The Lord of the Rings*. The fact that he wrote it in a rush, as well as the impression of an inherent self-consciousness which is present all over the tale, can be also understood as an attempt of the author to give to himself an explanation of his own artistry, of the way his writings were forming a tapestry, a 'Mythology for England' – and of England. *Leaf by Niggle* may also be read as an allegory of Tolkien the (literal) myth-maker, that is, the sub-creator, the searcher of truth through the linguistic invention of secondary worlds.[29] The tale was written some time between 1938 and 1939, an especially productive period for Tolkien's scholarship and sub-creative fiction, when his ideas on *Beowulf*, fairy stories, mythopoeia, as well as his 'family tales' became all tributaries the one rich and fertile stream.[30]

The plot is too well known to be retold here. After briefly introducing the character and the drama, Tolkien gives a general picture of Niggle's life, his

---

[27] I am conscious that I am just attempting *other* allegorical readings of the tale. However, critical reading involves these limitations: interpretations of a dead writer's mind are worth the effort, but they cannot be checked, or confirmed. I assume the risk of being wrong, but I consider the opinion of the author as the key to the right interpretation of his or her works, and this is especially revealing in Tolkien case.

[28] See *Letters*, especially number 131, to Milton Waldman, where the author explains the relation between his mythology and the Fall, mortality, and the machine, pointing out the relations of art and sub-creation with the primary world as the key to get a deeper understanding of Beleriand and Middle-earth.

[29] See above. *Leaf by Niggle* provides as clear an explanation of Tolkien's concept of art as does 'On Fairy Stories', and 'Mythopoeia'. The reason for including these three works in the edition of *Tree and Leaf* is quite obvious. The volume is the key towards an understanding of Tolkien's poetics from point of view of Aesthetics.

[30] I have studied this period in Segura (2004:56-85). I provide a synchronization of the author's life and work in order to show some interesting and revealing connections between his scholarship, his fiction, his invented languages, and his style, especially in *The Lord of the Rings*. See also Martsch (1995:291-297).

doubts, and his frustration with his art. It is with an increasing feeling of desperation, caused by the thought of his imminent journey that will render impossible the completion of his tree, that one day

> Niggle stood a little way off from his picture and considered it with unusual attention and detachment. He could not make up his mind what he thought about it, and wished he had some friend who would tell him what to think. Actually it seemed to him wholly unsatisfactory, and yet very lovely, the only really beautiful picture in the world.
> (*Leaf* 76)

Now, permanent dissatisfaction is a common feeling to any true artist. Such an impression of a clear, brilliant idea intuitively grasped, as well as the conviction that the work of art lacks the depth, the strength, that rare spiritual quality of eternity in spite of the apparent perfection in the making, leads to the certainty that the work of art is never 'finished'. The very love for the pure idea leads to the unceasing improvement of the work, and in loving the imperfections the artist makes himself able to erase them. Those were Niggle's feelings, and also Tolkien's. However, permanent dissatisfaction is a widespread human condition and not limited to artists. It is because our lives have been modelled by the Artist that we all long for that unattainable perfection. Niggle was first a man, then an artist. And so was Tolkien. In this sense, the tale can be read as a parable of human existence – an allegory with universal applicability.

Niggle's mind seems to be filled with such an impression of failure and exhaustion, when he is suddenly taken away by the Driver to start his journey:

> 'O, dear!' said poor Niggle, beginning to weep. 'And it's not even finished!'
> 'Not finished?' said the Driver. 'Well, it's finished with, *as far as you're concerned*, at any rate. Come along!'
> (*Leaf* 82, my italics)

Tolkien's notion of art as an undeserved gift includes grace as the most important element to judge the work done: as far as the artist is concerned, the work cannot be finished in Time, unless one could cross the borders of Time. In this sense, eternity is the goal and also the last station for artistry. Niggle becomes increasingly conscious of it as the tale goes on. The core of the story, the moment when Niggle comes to discover and recognize his tree, deals with this theological notion of grace, of the undeserved gift:

> Before him stood the Tree, his Tree, finished. If you could say that of a Tree that was alive, its leaves opening, its branches growing and bending in the wind that Niggle had so often felt or guessed, and had so often failed to catch. He gazed at the Tree, and slowly he lifted his arms and opened them wide.
> 'It's a gift!' he said. *He was referring to his art, and also to the result; but he was using the word quite literally.*[31]
> (*Leaf* 88, my italics)

The Tree is not only a granted, free gift – redundant as it seems. His own merits, both as a person and as an artist, were primarily a gift too, and did not necessarily lead to the result, to the completion of the picture. However, the Tree is also the result of Niggle's work, cares, and watchfulness. The Tree that started being just a 'tree' is also *his* Tree by the time of conclusion. And as far as grace counts on human co-operation to bear fruit, art is the way God has redeemed the efforts of people so that they become part of the 'big picture', of the whole design – of the Lógos. Eventually, Niggle's Parish, the secondary world, becomes a place for rest and recovery of those needed, an image of art as a privileged place for escape, recovery, and consolation. And as far as the

---

[31] I think these words represent the core of Tolkien's poetics. According to what was said about Barfield's influence on Tolkien, it seems acceptable that the literal meaning of 'gift' Tolkien is referring to is 'grace', and that Niggle is using it with regard to both his abilities and his picture, both undeserved, both granted for 'free'.

readers can be identified with Parish and his wife at this moment in the plot, we can allegorize that the Tree is Niggle's, but the whole canvas is ours.[32]

As soon as Niggle realizes that the Tree is alive, and also mysteriously finished, he understands that the idea of his tree was just a blurred image of the 'real' Tree.[33] In fact, we are told that he had so often felt or guessed the wind in the branches, "and had so often failed to catch [it]." The infinite distance between the idea and the work of art must be bridged by some sort of miracle, by a superabundance of being.[34] Art provides the miracle. From the moment onwards that Niggle perceives the Tree, he will no longer be worried about getting the work done, since he understands that his work will always be alive – and always was. The echo of his efforts already resounded in eternity as he was working on his canvas. Niggle finally understands that eternity is also a place full of beauty, a place where desires have also been redeemed. This superabundant love that I'm calling 'gift' is also present as Niggle looks at the Tree, and contemplates an unexpected beauty of which he was not conscious as he worked on the picture but only as a glimpse:

> All the leaves he had ever laboured at were there, as he had imagined them rather as he had made them; and there were others that had only budded in his mind, and many that might have budded, if only he had had time. (*Leaf* 88-89)

Grace is that superabundance of God's Art which *freely* leads to creation,[35] fulfilling human desires as Plato points out when he explains the role of 'eros'

---

[32] Tolkien's mythology, all his works, were his. But Beleriand and Middle-earth are ours – as Tolkien's Country, or picture.

[33] The connection between these notions and Plato's theory of Ideas is plainly evident. Some of the Inklings were reputedly Neo-Platonists.

[34] Saint Thomas Aquinas teaches that in being, unity, beauty, truth, and good *convertuntur*, they are all one and the same. In God, however, the transcendentals cannot be identified with His essence.

[35] See Aquinas, *Summa Theologiae*, q. 1.1. Creation was a free act, and not an action derived from some sort of 'necessity'. God did not need creation to be complete, nor to get some kind of perfection He lacked.

and his implication in every artist's work.[36] Human works are fulfilled only beyond the boundaries of this life – beyond death. Niggle's tree becomes a tree in 'heaven'. If grace fulfils desire, and desire is perceived as intuition, as a dream,[37] or as an idea (in the platonic sense), as a glimpse, and ultimately as mystery, then art is also a clue to our immortality. Art becomes fully 'real' only by means of redemption. In fact, Niggle realizes that he is *in* the picture he painted, but the picture also includes some things he did not paint. For example, there is the Forest, and the birds.

Niggle's reaction to the realization of his dream is thankfulness. This is quiet obvious a reaction hoped for from a humble person, as Niggle is indeed. As the tale evolves from the initial insecurity and embarrassment of the character to the increasing consciousness of his selfish attitude towards Parish – no matter Parish's limitations both as neighbour and person, as well as his wife's –, the journey and the stay at the workhouse permit Niggle to think, and especially to be forgiven. His abilities as a painter are put to the test, and the little jobs entrusted to him at the place become more and more part of a plan to turn him into a purified, new man. He is again saved by a grace, since the Second Voice deals with him with deep mercy and sincere affection.

But the main purpose of the Gentle Treatment is to make Niggle conscious of Parish's need for help and understanding. His art was and will be the instrument for that inner redemption. We finally see Parish's perplex astonishment when he recognizes the beautiful landscape as Niggle's. Niggle's Country, the place the painter's art has provided as a set for final recovery and consolation to Parish – and his wife – is the result of redeemed efforts to serve

---

[36] Plato, *Symposium*, 201, *passim*. See also Copleston (1969, chapter XX, esp. pp. 205-209). According to Plato, 'eros' is not only love, but also the desire for happiness and for what is good, and also the desire for immortality. The superior 'eros' leads artists – poets – in the search for virtue, as a testimony of the love that once was between them and beauty.

[37] "[...] and the bicycle was rolling along over a marvellous turf. It was green and close; and yet he could see every blade distinctly. He seemed to remember having seen or dreamed of that sweep of grass somewhere or other. The curves of the land were familiar somehow" (*Leaf* 88).

others through one's own talents. Actually, a part of the place has been granted to Parish – again, as a gift:

> 'Could you tell me the name of this country?'
> 'Don't you know?' said the man. 'It's Niggle's Country. It is Niggle's Picture, or most of it; a little of it is now Parish's Garden.'
> 'Niggle's Picture!' said Parish in astonishment. 'Did *you* think of all this, Niggle? I never knew you were so clever. Why didn't you tell me?'
> 'He tried to tell you long ago,' said the man; 'but you would not look. He had only got canvas and paint in those days, and you wanted to mend your roof with them. This is what you and your wife used to call Niggle's Nonsense, or That Daubing.'
> 'But it did not look like this then, not *real*,' said Parish.
> 'No, it was only a glimpse then,' said the man; 'but you might have caught the glimpse [...].''
> (*Leaf* 92-93)

The place, we are told, is Niggle's Picture "or most of it." What does it mean? It may be understood both as the result of Niggle's effort to paint the tree which eventually becomes his Tree, and also as the landscape Niggle had seen very early on as a backcloth to the whole painting. In both cases Niggle's Picture is not *only* the result of his art, but of art itself – of God's grace. Niggle's original design and lógos also included the opportunity to provide delight to others, though he did not know it by the time he began painting. Art becomes a means for the discovery of one's own soul, for self-knowledge and, ultimately, a path to wisdom.

From this moment on, Niggle will become increasingly conscious that he must surrender his work. He is more and more aware that the Picture is not his, so that he freely decides to give it away, to let it go as soon as he is asked to start on a new journey. Again, gratitude is his main attitude – paradoxical as it may seem:

> He turned and looked back for a moment. The blossom on the Great Tree was shining like flame [...]. Then he smiled and nodded to Parish, and went off with the shepherd. (*Leaf* 93)

This new adventure is metaphorically described as the final stage in Niggle's process of purification, as an image of 'death' and 'heaven', since the shepherd can be understood as an obviously Christian image of Christ himself. The new journey can also be described as an allegory of art and gift, as leading to the threshold of beatific vision, to the completion of desires beyond hopes since human actions and works are fully redeemed only beyond death. Of course, this completion is always a prize that can only be received after death. The text speaks of those "who have climbed them":

> He was going to learn about sheep, and the high pasturages, and look at a wider sky, and walk ever further and further towards the Mountains, always uphill. Beyond that I cannot guess what became of him. Even little Niggle in his old home could glimpse the Mountains far away, and they got into the borders of his picture; but what they are really like, and what lies beyond them only those can say who have climbed them. (*Leaf* 93)

Now, the contradictory attitudes shown in the tale deal, on the one hand with Niggle's initial eagerness and his efforts to achieve a perfect picture of his little tree and its leaves, and, on the other hand, with final oblivion, scorn, and Councillor Tompkins and Atkins' mockery towards Niggle at the end of the story. However, oblivion is also Niggle's ultimate attitude towards his work *itself*, although Niggle does not forget or hold in contempt his picture since he deeply loves his art. He loves the Tree, and Niggle's Country, but he has understood that both are an undeserved gift he received in order to finally surrender. They helped him to render himself worthy of the grace of being redeemed, and also to redeem others. Accordingly, oblivion is not the same to Niggle as to the 'bureaucrats' – the caricatured rationalists –, for whom

Niggle's art is of "no use to Society at all" (*Leaf* 93), and 'art' is itself an empty, useless notion:

> 'Then you don't think painting [art] is worth anything, not worth preserving, or improving, or even making use of?'
> 'Of course, painting has uses,' said Tompkins. 'But [this was ...] private day-dreaming.' (*Leaf* 94)[38]

As is well known, the story ends with Perkins' admission that he never knew Niggle painted, yet he preserved the odd corner of the canvas where a mountain-peak and a spray of leaves could be seen:

> [...] one beautiful leaf remained intact. Atkins had it framed. Later he left it to the Town Museum, and for a long while 'Leaf: by Niggle' hung there in a recess, and was noticed by a few eyes. But eventually the Museum was burnt down, and the leaf, and Niggle, were entirely forgotten in his old country. (*Leaf* 95)

With oblivion as the final destination of Niggle's picture, we could raise the question whether art is to Tolkien just a means to serve a higher, more important end, or whether it has a purpose as an end in itself. The work of art can be forgotten, but art is eternal as Niggle's Country is. Its destiny is to last forever. Tolkien was aware that art had also been redeemed, and so it was a task worth the interest, love, and attention just like any other work in the world. Actually, one of his deepest convictions was that he was serving humankind by writing both his scholarly and sub-creative works. He dedicated his life to (sub)create a world where everyone could find a branch to clutch at,

---

[38] This "private day-dreaming", and the reference to Niggle's picture as "Nonsense, or That Daubing" can also be related to Tolkien's essay 'A Secret Vice' (*MC* 198-223), and to his 'Valedictory Address to the University of Oxford' (*MC* 224-240), where Tolkien makes some depreciating remarks about his invented languages. They can be read as images, allegories of his scholarship and conviction that his main contribution to the 'science of words' was linguistic invention, i.e., sub-creation.

as birds hang on to Niggle's Tree, a country full of beauty, and tears, and joy. The Tree is not only *The Lord of the Rings*, it's rather Tolkien's mythology, and also his scholarship, and his 'secret vice', too. Tolkien's Country is ultimately his interior landscape, that includes his whole life and interests: family, beliefs, friends, work, 'Lit.' and 'Lang.', etc.[39]

But it is also his own art and inspiration, and his notion of art as a means to be redeemed and to redeem others. The conviction his tales would not be finished on earth was also a prayer, a request for time and grace and humility to never forget the many Parishes and wives – the duties of ordinary life, the result of his decisions, and his responsibilities – that appeared to distract him from his goal, from the things he loved most. Then, at the end of the journey to the Mountains, and beyond, we – the readers – will finally meet Tolkien-Niggle again, thankfully joining the First and Second Voices to let them know Tolkien's Country was beautiful, that we found there a place for rest, recovery, and consolation, and the splendour of the refracted light forever splintering in a never-ending eucatastrophe. In doing so, we will surely hear that "they both laughed. Laughed – the Mountains rang with it!" (*Leaf* 95).

---

[39] I think Tolkien seems to have found consolation as he wrote the tale concerning his own worries and perplexities, both as a man and artist. As the tale goes on the conviction of a man deeply aware that his works are not 'necessary' to humankind – no matter how important they are to him – is present all over. Eventually, nothing will happen whether he is able to finish his mythology, or not: eternity is waiting, and he, as Niggle, feels nothing more than a small, mediocre artist. Tolkien knew his work had been already redeemed, in time, and that was a source of hope, recovery, and consolation to him. His mythology – *The Lord of the Rings* was at its very beginning when he wrote *Leaf by Niggle* –, his scholarship, everything he cared for, were God's, and only His, and for all men and women, and not only or primarily for himself.

Biographical Note

Eduardo Segura Fernández (PhD in Philology) teaches at the Instituto de Filosofía Edith Stein, Granada (Spain). He has written two books on Tolkien: a biographical sketch titled *J.R.R. Tolkien, el mago de las palabras* (Casals 2002), and *El viaje del Anillo* (Minotauro 2004), which is based on his doctoral dissertation. He has edited, with Guillermo Peris, *Tolkien o la fuerza del mito: la Tierra Media en perspectiva*, a translation of the Tolkien 1992 Centenary Conference Proceedings. He is also the author of a reader's guide to Narnia (*Guía de lectura de* El león, la bruja y el armario, Pamplona 2007), and is currently working on a volume on Peter Jackson's version of *The Lord of the Rings*.

Bibliography

Abbreviations

Biography: see Carpenter 1977.
Leaf: *Leaf by Niggle* in Tolkien (1982b:75-95)
Letters: see Carpenter 1981.
LotR: see Tolkien 1988.
MC: see Tolkien 1997
Hobbit: see Tolkien 1982a.
Mythopoeia: in Tolkien (1982b:97-101)
OFS: 'On Fairy-Stories' in Tolkien (1982b:9-73)

Baltasar, Michaela, 2004, 'J.R.R. Tolkien. A Rediscovery of Myth', in Jane Chance (ed.), 2004, *Tolkien and the Invention of Myth*, Lexington, KT: The University Press of Kentucky, 19-34.
Barfield, Owen, 1973, *Poetic Diction*, first published 1928, Middletown: Wesleyan University Press.
Carpenter, Humphrey, 1977, *J.R.R. Tolkien: A Biography*, London: Unwin Hyman.
--- (ed.). 1981, *The Letters of J.R.R. Tolkien*, London: Unwin Hyman.
---, 1997, *The Inklings. C.S. Lewis, J.R.R. Tolkien, Charles Williams, and Their Friends*, first published 1978, London: HarperCollins.
Copleston, Frederick, 1969, *A History of Philosophy*, volume 1, London: Burns and Oates.
Flieger, Verlyn, 1997, *A Question of Time: J.R.R. Tolkien's Road to Faërie*, Kent OH: Kent State University Press.
---, 2002, *Splintered Light: Logos and Language in Tolkien's World*, second edition, first edition 1983, Kent OH: Kent State University Press.

Hammond, Wayne G., 2000, "A Continuing and Evolving Creation'. Distractions in the Later History of Middle-earth', in Verlyn Flieger and Carl F. Hostetter (eds.), 2000, *Tolkien's Legendarium. Essays on The History of Middle-earth*, Westport CT: Greenwood Press, 19-29.

Lamberton, R, 1986, *Homer the Theologian. Neoplatonist Allegorical Reading and the Growth of Epic Tradition*, Berkeley: University of California Press.

MacIntyre, Alasdair, 1984, *After Virtue: A Study in Moral Theology*, Indiana: University of Notre Dame Press.

Martsch, Nancy, 1995, 'A Tolkien Chronology', in Patricia Reynolds and Glen H. Goodknight (eds.), 1995, *Proceedings of the J.R.R.Tolkien Centenary Conference*, Milton Keynes and Altadena: The Tolkien Society and Mythopoeic Press, 291-297.

Rateliff, John D., 2006, "And All the Days of Her Life Are Forgotten'. *The Lord of the Rings* as Mythic Prehistory', in Wayne G. Hammond and Christina Scull (eds.), 2006, *The Lord of the Rings 1954-2004. Scholarship in Honor of Richard E. Blackwelder*, Marquette: Marquette University Press, 67-100.

Segura, Eduardo, 1997, 'Tolkien, Chesterton y los cuentos de hadas', *Nueva Revista de Política, Cultura y Arte* 49:110-117.

---, 2004, *El viaje del Anillo*, Barcelona: Minotauro.

Shippey, Tom, 2000, *J.R.R. Tolkien, Author of the Century*, London: HarperCollins.

---, 2003, *The Road to Middle-Earth*, revised edition, 1st edition 1982, New York and Boston: Houghton Mifflin.

Tolkien, John Ronald Reuel, 1982a, *The Hobbit*, revised edition, first edition 1937, New York: Ballantine Books.

---, 1982b, *Tree and Leaf, including the Poem Mythopoeia*, London: Grafton.

---, 1988, *The Lord of the Rings*, 3 vols, revised edition of 1966, 1st edition 1954-55, London: Unwin Hyman.

---, 1997, *The Monsters and the Critics and Other Essays*, edited by Christopher Tolkien, first published 1983, London: HarperCollins.

Walking Tree Publishers was founded in 1997 as a forum for publication of material (books, videos, CDs, etc.) related to Tolkien and Middle-earth studies. Manuscripts and project proposals can be submitted to the board of editors (please include an SAE):

Walking Tree Publishers
CH-3052 Zollikofen
Switzerland
e-mail: info@walking-tree.org
http://www.walking-tree.org

Cormarë Series

The *Cormarë Series* has been the first series of studies dedicated exclusively to the exploration of Tolkien's work. Its focus is on papers and studies from a wide range of scholarly approaches. The series comprises monographs, thematic collections of essays, conference volumes, and reprints of important yet no longer (easily) accessible papers by leading scholars in the field. Manuscripts and project-proposals are evaluated by members of an independent board of advisors who support the series editors in their endeavour to provide the readers with qualitatively superior yet accessible studies on Tolkien and his work.

News from the Shire and Beyond. Studies on Tolkien.
  Edited by Peter Buchs and Thomas Honegger. Zurich & Berne 2004. Reprint. First edition 1997. (Cormarë Series 1)

Root and Branch. Approaches Towards Understanding Tolkien.
  Edited by Thomas Honegger. Zurich & Berne 2005. Reprint. First edition 1999. (Cormarë Series 2)

Richard Sturch. *Four Christian Fantasists. A Study of the Fantastic Writings of George MacDonald, Charles Williams, C. S. Lewis and J.R.R. Tolkien.* Zurich & Berne 2007. Reprint. First edition 2001. (Cormarë Series 3)

Tolkien in Translation.
  Edited by Thomas Honegger. Zurich & Berne 2003. (Cormarë Series 4)

Mark T. Hooker. *Tolkien Through Russian Eyes.* Zurich & Berne 2003. (Cormarë Series 5)

Translating Tolkien: Text and Film.
  Edited by Thomas Honegger. Zurich & Berne 2004. (Cormarë Series 6)

Christopher Garbowski. *Recovery and Transcendence for the Contemporary Mythmaker: The Spiritual Dimension in the Works of J.R.R. Tolkien.* Zurich & Berne 2004. Reprint. First edition by Marie Curie Sklodowska University Press, Lublin 2000. (Cormarë Series 7)

Reconsidering Tolkien.
  Edited by Thomas Honegger. Zurich & Berne 2005. (Cormarë Series 8)

Tolkien and Modernity 1.
  Edited by Frank Weinreich & Thomas Honegger. Zurich & Berne 2006. (Cormarë Series 9)

Tolkien and Modernity 2.
  Edited by Thomas Honegger & Frank Weinreich. Zurich & Berne 2006. (Cormarë Series 10)

Tom Shippey. *Roots and Branches: Selected Papers on Tolkien by Tom Shippey.* Zurich & Berne 2007. (Cormarë Series 11)

Ross Smith. *Inside Language: Linguistic and Aesthetic Theory in Tolkien*.
    Zurich & Berne 2007. (Cormarë Series 12)

How We Became Middle-earth.
    Edited by Adam Lam & Nataliya Oryshchuk. Zurich & Berne 2007. (Cormarë Series 13)

The Silmarillion – Thirty Years On.
    Edited by Allan Turner. Zurich & Berne 2007. (Cormarë Series 15)

forthcoming

Martin Simonson. *The Lord of the Rings and the Western Narrative Tradition*.
    Zurich & Berne.

Beyond Middle-earth: Tolkien's Shorter Works 1.
    Edited by Frank Weinreich & Margaret Hiley. Zurich & Berne.

Beyond Middle-earth: Tolkien's Shorter Works 2.
    Edited by Margaret Hiley & Frank Weinreich. Zurich & Berne.

Constructions of Authorship in and around the Works of J.R.R. Tolkien.
    Edited by Judith Klinger. Zurich & Berne.

Rainer Nagel. *Hobbit Place-names. A Linguistic Excursion through the Shire*.
    Zurich & Berne.

Tales of Yore Series

The *Tales of Yore Series* grew out of the desire to share Kay Woollard's whimsical stories and drawings with a wider audience. The series aims at providing a platform for qualitatively superior fiction with a clear link to Tolkien's world.

Kay Woollard. *The Terror of Tatty Walk. A Frightener*. CD and Booklet.
    Zurich & Berne 2000 (Tales of Yore 1)

Kay Woollard, *Wilmot's Very Strange Stone or What came of building "snobbits"*. CD and booklet.
    Zurich & Berne 2001 (Tales of Yore 2)

www.ingramcontent.com/pod-product-compliance
Lightning Source LLC
Chambersburg PA
CBHW070718160426
43192CB00009B/1238